THE CONVERSO'S RETURN

Stanford Studies in Jewish History and Culture
Edited by David Biale and Sarah Abrevaya Stein

THE CONVERSO'S RETURN

Conversion and Sephardi History in Contemporary Literature and Culture

DALIA KANDIYOTI

STANFORD UNIVERSITY PRESS
Stanford, California

STANFORD UNIVERSITY PRESS
Stanford, California

© 2020 by the Board of Trustees of the Leland Stanford Junior University. All rights reserved.

No part of this book may be reproduced or transmitted in any form or by any means, electronic or mechanical, including photocopying and recording, or in any information storage or retrieval system without the prior written permission of Stanford University Press.

Printed in the United States of America on acid-free, archival-quality paper

Library of Congress Cataloging-in-Publication Data

Names: Kandiyoti, Dalia, author.

Title: The converso's return : conversion and Sephardi history in contemporary literature and culture / Dalia Kandiyoti.

Other titles: Stanford studies in Jewish history and culture.

Description: Stanford, California : Stanford University Press, 2020. | Series: Stanford studies in Jewish history and culture | Includes bibliographical references and index.

Identifiers: LCCN 2019045178 (print) | LCCN 2019045179 (ebook) | ISBN 9781503612297 (cloth) | ISBN 9781503612433 (paperback) | ISBN 9781503612440 (epub)

Subjects: LCSH: Literature, Modern—21st century—History and criticism. | Literature, Modern—20th century—History and criticism. | Marranos in literature. | Sephardim in literature. | Conversion in literature. | Ethnicity in literature.

Classification: LCC PN56.5.M37 K36 2020 (print) | LCC PN56.5.M37 (ebook) | DDC 809/.93382—dc23

LC record available at https://lccn.loc.gov/2019045178

LC ebook record available at https://lccn.loc.gov/2019045179

Cover design by Angela Moody

Typeset by Kevin Barrett Kane in 10.25/15 Adobe Caslon Pro

CONTENTS

Preface vii
Acknowledgments xi

INTRODUCTION
Lost and Found? The Afterlives of Conversion
1

CHAPTER 1
Doubles, Disguises, Splits:
Conversos in Modern Literature and Thought
49

CHAPTER 2
Latinx Sephardism and the Absent Archive:
Crypto-Jews and the Transamerican Latinx Imagination
85

CHAPTER 3
Return to Sepharad:
Blood, Convergences, and Embodied Remnants
124

CHAPTER 4
Sephardis' Converso Pasts:
The Critical Genealogical Imagination
170

CHAPTER 5
Ottoman-Spanish and Jewish-Muslim Entanglements:
Conversos in Contemporary Turkish Fiction
209

CODA
257

Notes 263
Bibliography 271
Index 297

PREFACE

The Converso's Return is a study of recent fiction and memoirs by U.S. Latinx, Spanish, French, and Turkish authors about the current revival of Iberian Jewish history, in particular, the largely forced conversions of Jews to Catholicism in fourteenth- and fifteenth-century Spain and Portugal. This seemingly remote history has been the topic of a substantial library of contemporary literary and popular writing, especially since the 1992 quincentennial commemorations of the 1492 conversions and expulsion of Jews and Muslims from Spain and the conquest of the Americas. The recent claiming of Sephardi converso ancestry by Christian (and to a much lesser extent Muslim) descendants in the Americas, Europe, and Turkey has taken place simultaneously with the fictional and testimonial writing about conversos and their descendants by authors on several continents. What is it about conversos that has sparked their imagination? What do we learn and rethink about conversos' afterlives, including their resurgence in the present, and how does this help us understand how and why we return to and resuscitate the past? The literary writing in English, Spanish, French, and Turkish, the languages of my competence, about the fate of the converts through the centuries that *The Converso's Return* investigates help us to expand on ideas about conversos, contemporary historical consciousness, the role of genealogy in culture, collective memory, missing archives, Sephardi identities, and world literature.

Although I have a long-standing interest in modern Sephardi culture, language, and writing, what spurred me to undertake this project on conversos and their recent reappearance on the literary and social scene did not come from within what is considered normative Jewish culture and literature. Instead, I was inspired by texts in my related field of specialization in U.S. Latinx writing. I became aware after years of the study of Latinx and Chicanx literature that many authors, including those I analyze in *The Converso's Return*, such as Achy Obejas and Kathleen Alcalá, have claimed crypto-Jewish descent and written imaginatively about converso identities and pasts. I had been aware of the media coverage of the "secret Jews of New Mexico" in the 1980s and early 1990s but had not explored these issues further until I realized how much they resonated with some of the Latinx and Chicanx writers I studied and taught. Starting with their works, which are characterized by crossings and convergences of cultures, languages, and histories, defined my choices of other writing: Each chapter is about a different context from the previous but concerns ideas and texts that are similarly compelled by connectivity and overlap of cultures and traumas in breathing new life into what might have been a forgotten, disappeared slice of history.

As the chapters to follow will make evident, I have learned and benefited greatly from many historians' crucial contributions in shaping our knowledge about Iberian converts and their descendants. My overview of contemporary ideas and tropes about conversos in Chapter 1 includes a synthesis of historians' views of crypto-Jewish identities. However, I am not a historian, and this book is not a historical study. *The Converso's Return* does not seek to assert "truths" about crypto-Jewish pasts or assess the claims about its continuity. Rather, it is about how history is viewed and imagined creatively in our times. In relation to descendants of crypto-Jews, who include some of the authors I discuss, I explain the controversial issues surrounding claims to crypto-Jewish ancestries and identities. But my aim is not to evaluate, validate, or invalidate such claims. Instead, I signal their various implications when it is relevant to the literary and cultural analyses I undertake. I do not judge either the historical or the cultural authenticity, a distinction made by Seth Kunin (2009), of surviving crypto-Jewishness in the Americas, which would be inappropriate in any case to the literary, imaginative works I discuss. Even when a memoir is concerned (e.g., in Chapter 3), I explore the meanings and rhetoric of crypto-Jewish testimony and not its "truth." I do not dismiss historians' evaluations in one or the other direction or deny that there are stakes as to whether or not the claims are "real," given also the involvement of organizations and states outside the converso-descendant world and the extensive emotional, social, and spiritual investment of many of those within it. However, my own goal is to investigate what "the converso's return" reveals in literary writing with regard to our contemporary historical and genealogical imaginations. The book parses the consequences, implications, and forms of reviving the past in literary writing and analyzes the ways that narrating converso history opens a path to other, overlapping stories of conquests, exiles, and solidarities.

TERMINOLOGY

The choice of terminology has not been obvious or simple for any of the key terms in this book, which is an indication of their flexible, imperfect, and debated nature. Perhaps most difficult are the terms *converso*, *crypto-Jew*, and *marrano*. I choose *converso* instead of the English *convert*, because this is standard in the scholarship and because it helps to underline the Iberian specificity. Because I refer overwhelmingly to Jewish converts, or Judeoconversos, rather than Muslim ones, I underline here that the term *converso*, unless otherwise specified, pertains to Iberian Jews who have converted and, sometimes, to their descendants. Scholars have come to reject the conflation of the Jew with the crypto-Jew (practicing in hiding) and the converso (e.g., Graizbord and Stuczynski 2011; Kaplan 1997; J. Schorsch 2009). The distinction is meant to avoid a flattening among the terms that essentialize Jewishness, where all conversos must be thought of as secretly practicing Jews, which they were not, or where all converts who have Jewish ancestry are automatically considered Jews.

In the chapters that follow, *converso* refers to Jews who converted to Christianity whether by choice or under duress in the fourteenth and fifteenth centuries, and *crypto-Jew* pertains to those who were *known* to retain secret Jewish practice and/or identity, whether in the historical record or in fiction. However, I also use *converso* as a neutral umbrella term for any kind of Iberian Jewish convert and refer to the two terms interchangeably, when both terms obtain in a particular context. Because of its pejorative connotations (the word's possible origin being a demeaning and provocative reference to a pig) and due to decreasing use in most North American scholarship, I invoke *marrano* only in reference to other writers' and scholars' use. For example, in much French- and Spanish-language scholarship and fiction, *marrano* and *marrane* continue to be the terms of choice to refer to conversos, crypto-Jews, or both (in addition to other sui generis uses), as are *marranisme* and *marranismo*. In relation to the followers of Sabbatai Sevi and their descendants, I use the terms found in English- and Turkish-language scholarship as well as in the community: *dönme*, Sabbatean, or Salonican.

The term *Sephardi* is no less malleable or imperfect than the others. Although most of my own references in this book are to Iberian Jews, because of the particular topic and scope, I recognize, of course, that in many contexts *Sephardi* includes Jews not of Iberian origin.

I have adopted *Latinx* instead of *Latina/o* or *Latino* to refer to cultures and populations of the Caribbean and Latin America in the United States, as the term is currently favored by scholars in the field and community activists aiming for inclusiveness. However, *Hispano* and *Hispanic* are widely used outside academia and in many locations, so I also use this term whenever appropriate.

I have chosen not to adapt *converso* regarding gender, because to my knowledge, there is no call from identifying descendants or from scholars to do so. I treat *converso* as a gender-neutral term for abstract or general use and use *converso* and *conversa* when referring to individuals.

TRANSLATIONS

I have used the available published translations for all works and included original-language passages as well as translations for the primary texts. Translations of works from the Turkish, Spanish, and French originals that are not available in English are mine.

An early version of Chapter 2 was published in *Sephardism: Spanish Jewish History and the Modern Literary Imagination*, ed. Yael Halevi-Wise (Stanford, CA: Stanford University Press, 2012).

ACKNOWLEDGMENTS

Although I spent many solitary hours with this book, I have by no means been alone in the time I have devoted to it. I have leaned on, learned from, and received the support of many. All the book's shortcomings are, of course, my own.

I acknowledge with gratitude the following granting institutions: the Professional Staff Congress of the City University of New York for the several grants that allowed me the time to start and complete this work; the Maurice Amado Chair in Sephardic Studies (UCLA) for research support; the Mellon Foundation fellowship at the Graduate Center of the City University of New York (CUNY) that allowed me to attend a seminar on religion led by Brian Turner and coordinated by Lydia Wilson; and the College of Staten Island (CUNY) Provost Travel Grant. Carleton University, the Sephardi Studies program at the Graduate Center at CUNY, the Association of Jewish Studies, and my own College of Staten Island Department of English helped fund important presentations and panel organizing that served as the basis of chapters.

For precious feedback on various parts of this work, I am deeply grateful to Sarah Casteel (especially), Shari Huhndorf, Robert Latham, and Kerri Sakamoto. For invitations to deliver talks and workshops that furthered my project in extremely important ways, I thank Eva-Lynn Jagoe and the Latin American Studies program at the University of Toronto; Sarah Abrevaya

Stein and the Maurice Amado Sephardic Studies Chair at UCLA; Ariana Vigil and the Latin/a-Jewish Studies Working Group at the University of North Carolina, Chapel Hill; Yael Halevi-Wise at McGill University; and Eduardo Manzana Moreno at CSIC (Consejo superior de investigaciones científicas) in Madrid for hosting and co-organizing our seminar on *convivencia* and multiculturalism.

I learned so much also from collaborating with the following great colleagues: Sarah Casteel, Tabea Linhard, and Michal Friedman, who co-organized seminars in Sephardi studies at CSIC, the American Comparative Literature Association (ACLA), and the CUNY Graduate Center; and Michal Friedman, Daniela Flesler, Adrián Pérez Melgosa, Stacy Beckwith, Tabea Linhard, and Asher Salah for putting together and enriching panels at ALCES (Asociación internacional de literatura y cine españoles, Siglo XXI), the ACLA, and the Association of Jewish Studies. The initiative and gentle leadership of Michal Friedman in several of these adventures were precious, as were the many professional and personal exchanges, travels, and laughs. Gracias to José Manuel Fajardo for inspiring us all with his work, commitment, and uplifting spirit and sense of humor. Fellow panel members and audiences at other conferences, including those of ACLA, ALCES, AJS, and MESEA, moved the work forward. Paloma Díaz-Mas at CSIC has been at some of the same events and also generously shared with me her important, extensive contributions to Judeo-Spanish language and culture. The feedback and the new horizons that opened up during all these exchanges nourished this book in profound ways in recent years, as did the earlier encounters with groundbreaking scholarship in Sephardi and Mizrahi studies, especially by Ella Shohat, Ammiel Alcalay, Aron Rodrigue, Esther Benbassa, and Sarah Abrevaya Stein. Directly and indirectly, they have inspired me to forge ahead in this field.

Late during the writing of this book, I started a new project with Rina Benmayor, who agreed to go on a joint oral history adventure. Unpredictably, my two projects coincided in productive ways that furthered some of the work in this book. Many thanks to Rina for helping me grow and for generously sharing her vast knowledge and experience in oral history, backing my overall work, and for our delicious exchanges in "muestro espanyol."

I owe a huge debt to the work of the many Sephardi and Mizrahi studies scholars who traced the fascinating Sephardi routes; to the African

Americanist and queer studies scholars who have changed our questions regarding history, returns, and archives; to the Latinx critique of mixture, race, and transamericanism, which is vast and has informed my endeavors since graduate school; to the research in memory and memorialization in Jewish, Spanish, and comparative studies; and to the study of difference in the context of Turkey and its past. Too numerous to identify here, they have been named in the pages to come and made their mark on this book. My years at the Department of Comparative Literature at New York University, where I received my Ph.D. with the formative influence of Sylvia Molloy, Richard Sieburth, and Jennifer Wicke, continue still, after all this time, to shape my outlook and encourage my impulse to connect the dots across languages and numerous boundaries. I remain grateful for that time and place.

My colleagues in the English Department, College of Staten Island (CUNY), Maryann Feola, Ellen Goldner, and Janet Ng, have inspired me, for too many years to count, with their own work and with their exceptional care for the collective. They have also been by my side throughout *mi vida loca* as a moving target while writing and teaching. Many thanks for all the rides too, Ellen! I am so thankful to have Sohomjit Ray's intellectual stimulation, humor, and friendship at the department as well as at nerds' night out at the Strand. Terry Rowden is a cherished colleague and friend who lifted my spirits and intellectually challenged me. I thank our chairs, Ashley Dawson and Lee Papa, who consistently used their capacity as long-term chairs to back my needs and projects. Together with the outstanding administrative team of Annmarie Franzese, Fredericka Grasso, Wendy Pearson, and Rita Rampullo, the chairs and members of the department have made it possible to have a peaceful and functional work environment, whatever challenges we face—this is something one cannot take for granted and has been essential to both teaching and scholarship. Thanks also to my colleagues in other departments, including especially to Bilge Yeşil, along with those in the Women and Gender Studies and Latin American, Caribbean, and Latina/o/x programs (especially to Sarah Pollack, Rafael de la Dehesa, Ismael García Colón, Álvaro Baquero Pecino, Oswaldo Zavala, Alyson Bardsley, and Matt Brim for running it all) for their collegiality and hard work in making our fields relevant to our students.

At Stanford University Press, series editors David Biale and Sarah Abrevaya Stein and acquisitions editor Margo Irvin have backed this project and, along with Jessica Ling, seen to a smooth process. I am grateful for their commitment and prowess. My thanks also go to Mimi Braverman for excellent copy editing. The blind peer reviewers helped me put the book in better shape; I appreciated especially Reviewer 1 for taking the time to make detailed comments and provide constructive criticism. Shara Concepción, doctoral student and research assistant at the Graduate Center, helped revise part of the Works Cited list.

My one and only life companion, Robert Latham, has supported me intellectually and emotionally through the several incarnations of this book; for this patience and love and everything else that he has given me, I am immeasurably grateful and lucky. And of course, I am lucky for having all the other extraordinary people by my side. I thank all of you from the bottom of my heart: my devoted mother Beki Kandiyoti, whose multilingual verbal creativity inspires me every day and is the reason for my love of languages; and my far-flung, brilliant, and cherished sisters who move and inspire me—Sonia Bakar, Amila Buturović, Anita Gilodo, Aylin Gözübüyük, Shari Huhndorf, Eva-Lynn Jagoe, Helen Lee, Arzu Öztürkmen, Kerri Sakamoto, Valentina Napolitano, Kathy Wazana, and Pınar Yılmaz. My special gratitude in critical times over the last few years to Kerri, for the utmost in sensitive loving care as well as her special stamp on this book; and to Anita, for always having the warmest home and being so supportive; and all my sisters, for their extra time, wisdom, and nurturing; Richard Fung, for my first garden, many first tastes, and deep generosity and hospitality; Gökbörü Sarp Tanyıldız and Selmin Kara for friendship and joyful, collective reading of Turkish literature; my supportive cousins Vanda Kandiyoti Şalom, Nedi Kohen, and Aliza Eluaşvili Kohen; my very dear, wise, and loving uncle and aunts Rıfat Kandiyoti, Jizel Kohen, and Deniz Kandiyoti; and my precious children and loves of my life, Alegra Kandiyoti and Shiran Kandiyoti, whose warmth and insight nourish me every day. You have each sustained me in many profound ways that would take another book to explain. Suffice it to say that you give the kind of meaning to my life without which nothing else can happen.

THE CONVERSO'S RETURN

⟨ INTRODUCTION ⟩

LOST AND FOUND?
The Afterlives of Conversion

QUESTION: By the end of 2018, what did an incoming Democratic congresswoman from New York, a Republican Hispanic American, and an Evangelical Christian Zionist media figure have in common? The answer: All four claimed Sephardi roots reaching back to Iberian Jews who converted to Christianity in medieval times, settled in the Americas, and kept their forbidden former identities secret.

Although she received much attention for her December 2018 declaration of Jewish converso background, part of Puerto Rico's amalgam of African, indigenous, and Spanish origins, Alexandria Ocasio-Cortez is not the first mostly Hispanic/Latinx-identified public figure in the Americas who has acknowledged Sephardi origins. Several years earlier, on the other side of the political spectrum, Linda Chavez, the Reagan-Bush era conservative with New Mexican roots who served in Republican administrations, had the results of her genetic ancestry testing revealed on Henry Louis Gates's popular television show *Finding Your Roots*. Chavez even traveled to archives in Seville to confirm her converso heritage. And when the Christian Zionist media personality Laurie Cardoza-Moore criticized Ocasio-Cortez's views on Israel in early 2019, she accused the congresswoman of betraying their common Sephardi roots and ties to "Hispania." Coincidentally, a scientific study gained international newspaper coverage shortly after Ocasio-Cortez's remarks for its findings regarding Latin Americans' DNA profiles, which match to a certain extent those of Turkish Sephardi Jews. This study, not the first of its kind, suggests that as much as 23% of Latin Americans could be of converso origin.[1]

Whether the intentions are political, personal, or scientific, such public revelations are not obscure curiosities but part of a larger movement in the Latinx, Hispanic, Latin American, and Iberian worlds to assert previously submerged Jewish origins. These identifications, which have emerged more openly in the last few decades in the Americas and Iberia especially, have expanded further since the popularization of genetic ancestry testing and, more recently, since the 2015 Spanish and Portuguese laws granting citizenship to descendants of Sephardi Jews.

The largely forced conversions of Jews to Catholicism in fourteenth- and fifteenth-century Spain and Portugal and the dispersal of their descendants in Europe, the Middle East, North Africa, and Americas have been known, especially in the Jewish and Hispanic worlds, as phenomena of the distant past. However, especially since the 1980s and 1990s, we have witnessed a return of converso history to our present in media, literature, politics, scholarship, and testimonies. In variations of the more famous examples just noted, countless individuals have told tales of growing up in the Catholic Church and eventually discovering their ancestors' secret or unknown Jewish identity and past. Although many people, like Ocasio-Cortez, only have affinity for the ancestry and do not profess current Jewish identity, others embrace the Judaism of their remote ancestors. Commonly, individuals shared their sense that their families had always been "different." Some had practices strange to their (usually Catholic) larger milieu, such as Friday cleaning, mirror covering during mourning, or avoidance of pork.

The emergence as though from underground of such familial whispers and secrets and hidden residual Jewish practices has been narrated frequently as an uncanny survival of what has been presumed dead and buried. In addition to testimonials of individuals who disclosed such family confidences, revealed to them upon reaching adolescence or by accident, other striking stories also surfaced in the media. For example, a young woman who was drawn to Judaism hid her conversion because she deeply feared rejection, but once she was found out, older family members admitted Jewish heritage. Another convert to Judaism by personal choice inherited Jewish relics after her grandmother's death. A woman in Barcelona was exhorted by her grandfather on his deathbed to "return" to a Judaism of which she had had no knowledge. Then there was the story of a legendary Puerto Rican musician who brokered a famous truce between rival New York City gangs in 1971. At around the same time, he discovered his Sephardi origins and spent his later years as a fervent Jewish believer. An Albuquerque Catholic priest who verified rumors about his ancestry through genetic testing continued to be a man of the Church, albeit one who sported a Star of David around his neck and openly acknowledged Jewish heritage.[2]

Less publicly but no less insistently, Brazilians, Colombians, Ecuadorans, Catalans, Spaniards, Portuguese, and many others in the Luso-Hispanic worlds of the Americas and Europe have reported suspecting and verifying Sephardi converso roots, despite the doubts of some scholars as to their veracity, as I explain later. Even without familial revelations or special practices, they have explained, they deduced their Jewish roots based on their family's alienation from Catholicism, unusual surnames, or provenance from towns known to have had a significant Jewish or converso population, and sometimes, by just knowing it "in their bones."

The scientific findings of genetic genealogy that have been reported by major publications have circulated further in blogs and social media and spurred new ancestral pursuits. Although for some individuals identity exploration through DNA testing is a hobby, albeit sometimes a meaningful and occasionally a life-changing one, hidden Sephardi heritage has also been presented as doubly charged for some Latinx in the United States, who were told, controversially, that they are carriers of the Jewish genetic mutation that causes breast and ovarian cancer (Wheelwright 2012).

A community that is not immediately identified with descent from Jewish converts to Christianity but in fact has some roots in that group is the *dönme*, also known as Sabbatean or Salonican descendants in Turkey. Some of the *dönme* have Spanish and Portuguese Jewish ancestors who converted to Christianity and returned to Judaism in the Ottoman Empire and subsequently became followers of the Ottoman rabbi Sabbatai Sevi in the seventeenth century. Sevi, the self-declared messiah who sought to transform Judaism, was known to have converted under duress to Islam, along with many of his adherents. The endogamous Ottoman *dönme* families who lived publicly as Muslims were often known to the larger society and attracted negative attention in different periods. Starting in the 1990s, roughly in the same years when media attention was directed to claimants of crypto-Jewish background in the Americas and Iberia, known families of Sabbatean descent in Turkey became the target of widespread stigmatization. A few chose open identification as Sabbateans or as having Jewish ancestry or both. Because some *dönme*, like many normative Sephardis, also had ancestors who were Christians for a time, those who have knowledge of the community bring together multiple conversions in telling their stories.

As a surviving emblem of the bitter end of *convivencia* (medieval Iberian coexistence of Christian, Muslim, and Jewish cultures) in its various forms, the converso reappears when we are most concerned about endings, including of democracy and its fragile promises of conviviality (Gilroy 2004), *and* when we expand and transform our practices of return. In her important monograph *Figurative Inquisitions*, which is also one of the only lengthy treatments of conversos in contemporary Hispanophone and Lusophone literature, Erin Graff Zivin explains that "the Marrano subject matters to us—here, now—because it signals, from the beginning, the *other side* of reunification, nationalism, and colonialism, as well as the necessary failure of these modern political, religious, and identitary projects" (Graff Zivin 2014, 23). Our own return, in contemporary thought and literature, *to* the conversos as illustrations of the impossibility and dangers of unitary and authentic identities is accompanied, as I show in this book, by questions about returns *of* the conversos or, rather, their descendants.

Widespread interest in converso pasts, speaks in part to a particular need today for stories of survival under repression. We *want* to know about "hidden transcripts" (Scott 1990) and survivals that have been submerged but are imbued with a spirit of resistance to hegemonic powers. Built in is also a curiosity about *how* survival might have taken place: Given our heightened awareness of surveillance and control, evasion and circumvention as modes of resistance capture the imagination and are inscribed in texts about conversos as figures who built lives, identities, and communities by hiding, mixing, masquerading, and moving.

Iberian forced conversions and the Inquisition have been treated in modern literature at least since the nineteenth century, but the past few decades have seen an unprecedented number and array of fictional texts and testimonials on both sides of the Atlantic. These works are written in many languages by authors whose own origins may be close to or at a distance from this history. The return of this past and its reverberations in many cultures and bodies of writing teach us that the converso narrative is located not only in Jewish memory and historical consciousness but also elsewhere, including in unexpected contexts. As several key scholars have pointed out, Sephardi history, like the Holocaust (Rothberg 2009), may appear in the multiple literatures that are not considered Jewish per se, whether Caribbean (Casteel 2016), Latin American (Graff Zivin 2014; Halevi-Wise 2012a), or Iberian (e.g., Linhard 2014). Although crypto-Jewishness has sparked the imagination of literary writers on several continents and descendants of conversos have made identity claims in the Americas and Iberia, leaving their mark on local and global histories and cultures, the multifaceted resurgence of conversion stories has not been studied sufficiently as a literary and cultural phenomenon. Yet it merits attention for what it reveals about the afterlives of past events, the cultural politics of history, and contemporary world narrative.

Although conversion has been a chosen or forced tool of conformity to past and current dominant ideological agendas and modern biopolitics, it also can be widely unsettling. In her important study of colonial conversions, Gauri Viswanathan observes that conversion, individual or mass, interior or public, poses a "severe challenge to the demarcation of identities set by the laws that govern everyday life and practice (1998, 75). Similarly, for Ira Katznelson and Miri Rubin, conversion "is a radical deed" entailing "movements" in social status and to new institutions as well as "interior states of mind ... and new options for economic and political standing. Conversion can be 'riddled with pain' and disruptive as it occasions separations from people and places" (2014, 3).

Revivals of ancient identities born of conversions are no less demanding and disruptive in word or deed. Nor can they be bracketed off from contemporaneous transnational political and social exigencies, even when they seem to be individual or narrowly localized choices based on distant pasts. The texts I have chosen to examine eschew bounded and regressive versions of returns and remnants; indeed, their representations of the converso condition challenge precisely the kind of interpellation of historicized collective identity that produces new certainties and boundaries.

In *The Converso's Return* I examine literary fiction and memoirs that show how remote histories can animate contemporary identities and cultural politics. Recent literary narratives about the migrations of secret Jews to the Americas and the Ottoman Empire—such as the Latinx American, French, Spanish, and Turkish novels and autobiographical texts by Achy Obejas, Kathleen Alcalá, José Manuel Fajardo, Doreen Carvajal, Edgar Morin, Victor Perera, Elif Shafak, and Yeshim Ternar—not only represent converso history but also enable new reflections on the wider issues of genealogy, history, memory, and archives. These works raise questions that preoccupy communities with traumatic histories of genocide, slavery, forced conversion, and expulsion: How does one recuperate a past that has little documentation and extant evidence besides what was generated by the perpetrators, in which victims' perspectives and experiences are erased?

Conversos left an imprint on early modern Spanish literature, and those who returned to Judaism outside Iberia after the fifteenth century, in the early modern period, left behind a wealth of writing several generations after 1492. But little remains about how ordinary converso descendants, especially the crypto-Jews with secret identities or practices, conducted their lives in the Americas, and still less remains anywhere of this legacy of secrecy after the early modern era. Contemporary literary texts inflected by distant and suppressed histories, such as the novels and memoirs about converso descent in this book, tell stories about what we know and what we do not know about the past or its remnants. Thus they not only expand the themes and plots of the narrative universe but also offer a sense of what this history *and* its unknowns mean today and reflect on the ways in which conversos entered contemporary discourse.

My analysis shows how the "missing archives" of the past are presented in narrative. First, in complex ways, literary writing imagines what is unknown but "might have been" (Ricoeur 1988) and calls attention to the narrative and political conditions of disappearance and secrecy of origins, underlining the reasons for the absence of archives. Moreover, despite the loss of records and erasures of experiences, both fiction and memoirs notably and insistently point to remnants, whether in written texts (books and files), oral traditions (e.g., family lore or gossip), or what we can think of as the embodied archive (e.g., the revelations of genetic ancestry testing). At times, this means not only finding extant traces to write about but also involving what I refer to as the *production* of remnants. By "production" I do not mean to evoke a falsification. Rather, I aim to characterize the particular processes of authors' autobiographical or fictional narrations about the recovery of ancient converso or crypto-Jewish identities. These processes require following historiographic, familial, religious, genealogical, and genetic trails and involve a deliberate assertion of survival contra disappearance. "Production" also evokes the selection that may be involved in all genealogy: Some ancestors hold more weight than others, and descendants might engage in an active process of choice—they "clip" some roots and "stretch" and "prune" others (Zerubavel 2012)—if the right social conditions permit it. New or preexisting affiliations (such as with Jewishness) and emotions and political ideas about large-scale traumatic events become intertwined with filiation and perceptions of descent.

The idea that collective traumas cannot be contained in the past but remain with us, leaking into our present secretly or invisibly, affecting our chemistry, and sometimes rearing their heads unexpectedly, has been popularized through therapeutic and historical discourses. The narrative by or about someone who feels strongly that at some point they had a secretly Jewish ancestor of Iberian descent can reveal how the quest for the past can be both productive and problematic. The desire to recuperate buried histories can essentialize identities by reaching back to supposedly authentic and fixed definitions, including those interpretations in which certain looks, behaviors, talents, and choices are marked as "Jewish" and serve as evidence. At the same time, such personal and imaginative narratives can assert what the hegemonic religious, political, and economic powers have long suppressed. And, as Viswanathan (1998) argues, they can effectively destabilize essentializing categories, such as uninterrupted religious (e.g., Catholic or Jewish) or national identities. Reinstatements can also open doors to thinking in terms of convergences, such as the circulations, overlaps, and crossings of convert, Jewish, Christian, Muslim, and indigenous histories throughout the Atlantic that are the subjects of the novels and memoirs in this book. But partitions also emerge. For example, the relinquishing or valorization of one affiliation over another, "truer" one can congeal autarchic identitarianisms, despite the warning that history is necessary not to restore but "to dispel the chimeras of the origin" (Foucault 2013, 80). In the fictional and nonfictional texts that are the subject of *The Converso's Return*, we find reflection on both tendencies, though convergences are foregrounded.

Contemporary discourses about crypto-Jews and crypto-Jewishness include not only historical and genealogical reconstructions of Sepharad (Hebrew for Spain) and plausible converso worlds but also ideas about the metaphorical or representative status of this history. As we will see in the coming chapters, the crypto-Jewish "condition" is presented as a past phenomenon that anticipates and is instructive for the present; it prefigures the internally divided modern subjectivity or modernity's compulsion toward assimilation. Jacques Derrida suggested that we

> figuratively call Marrano anyone who remains faithful to a secret that he has not chosen, in the very place, where he lives, in the home of the inhabitant or of the occupant, in the home of the first or of the second arrivant, in the very place where he stays without saying not but without identifying himself as belonging to.... This secret keeps the Marrano even before the Marrano keeps it. (Derrida 1993, 81)

This figurative approach to the crypto-Jewish condition is shared by many critics. As Erin Graff Zivin observes, "Derrida is interested in not so much identifying historical instances of cultural marranismo—which he declares to be 'finished' (*Aporias*, 74)—but rather in the Marrano as metonym" and of the "right to secrecy" (Graff Zivin 2014, 20). In the complementary views of Argentine critic Ricardo Forster, "The Marrano represents the alter ego of the modern subject [and] exposes the impossibility of the modern Cartesian subject's claim to wholeness, rationality, and autonomy" (quoted in Graff Zivin 2014, 23). Indeed, for Forster, the marrano is a fiction whose origins are unavailable, because there is no fixed point at which the individual becomes a

Catholic or returns to Judaism, the "real identity." "The art of the simulacra" is available for those who insist on knowing origins (Forster 2003, 136).

The recent testimonies and ancestry narratives of crypto-Jewish descendants and of those who have been writing about marranism, *marranismo* (in Spanish), and *marranisme* (in French) in terms of the metaphorical *figure* of the crypto-Jew are contemporaneous, appearing at around the same time. But between them is a tremendous gulf: Many claims to descent in the Americas and most of Europe are motivated by a recovery of authentic identity that contrasts with the concept of "Marrano as metaphor" (Marks 1996) or as metonym (Graff Zivin 2014). The metonym approach deploys "the marrano" (a term in increasing disuse, as I explain in the Preface) precisely in the opposing manner, that is, in order to underline the *indeterminacy* of the marrano, who is not a defined historical crypto-Jew but rather a condition that is similar to or a part of modern subjectivity (Graff Zivin 2014, 2017; Moreiras 2012, 2017). Although those who identify as contemporary crypto-Jewish descendants raised as Christians from Nuevo León to New Mexico and Barcelona take pains to counter skepticism and prove that they are not a "fiction," theorists valorize precisely the constructed quality of the marrano figure without a true or singular identity. In a further difference, in much of recent Hispanophone and Francophone thinking on crypto-Jews, suffering and martyrdom are not always at the center (though indeterminate or divided subjectivity is), whereas many descendants who have come out recently and most fictional and scholarly narratives highlight the oppressions, secrecy, and fear as historical experiences and legacies.

The authors I analyze in this book occupy a different place in this landscape of sometimes contentious, diametrically opposed approaches, validating many of them and conforming to none. Without overturning the possibility that there is something *un*finished about crypto-Jewishness in the contemporary period, Alcalá, Obejas, Fajardo, Shafak, Ternar, Morin, Perera, and other authors I study also valorize its comparative and figurative possibilities. Although the other observers do not necessarily draw on Sephardi history or culture even when conversos are the focus, our authors do; and they examine conversos from within this engagement. Some scholars and critics dismiss figurative and critical analyses and others overlook the possibility of the continuity of the history and its costs, but the literary texts in this study shed light on all approaches. In doing so, they expand on the potential of the crypto-Jewish story, which would otherwise be more limited to the metaphoric import, ideological implications, genealogical fixities, or literary pyrotechnics around crypto-Jews' and conversos' quasi-gothic internal dualities and dissimulations.

The goal of my analyses is not the delineation or verification of crypto-Jewish or converso identities in the present. Rather, I ask what kind of contribution the reemergence of crypto-Jewishness makes to literature and I investigate its shaping of the imaginaries of Sephardi identity and history, the known and unknown ties between Jewish and other histories, and the larger discussions around multiplicity, convergences, entanglements, historical consciousness, (absent) archives, and critical genealogies.

Particulars and Convergences

Rather than providing an overview of the entire corpus of literary works on the topic of converso history's return to our culture, I have chosen to draw attention to texts that I refer to as narratives of convergence. They are not only informed by the particular Jewish histories at play but are also *deliberately* connected to known and submerged intersections among Spanish, Jewish, indigenous, Latin American, Muslim, Christian, and other pasts. This might be expected. The works I study are about Iberian Jewish conversos who have circulated through continents, and they inevitably mark the multiple attachments, languages, provenances, and faith practices of their often wandering, changing subjects. Indeed, multiplicity, whether incongruous, productive, dangerous, or adaptive—or all of these at once—is a prevailing characterization of converso identity for contemporary authors and scholars. The texts do register extensively the effects of intolerance and persecution. But the uncovering of possible, albeit undocumented, connections—such as crypto-Jewish–indigenous encounters in the Americas, normative Sephardi turns to conversos as ancestors, or little-known converso-Sabbatean-Muslim overlaps—is central to the narratives, even as they also make visible the boundaries and persecutions that, paradoxically, led to the forging of such worldly convergences.

Connectivity, along with its dark underbelly of exclusion and expulsion, complicates the idealization or the reduction of the converso to stereotypes commonly found in literature and culture: an eternal Jew untouched by other identities, the embodiment of cosmopolitanism and modernity, an abject martyr, or a suspect opportunist. The notion of incompleteness, of crypto-Jewish subjectivity or history, also looms. Rey Chow has asked a suggestive question in her work on entanglements: "What kind of entanglements might be conceivable through partition and partiality rather than conjunction and intersection, and through disparity rather than equivalence?" (2012, 1). The question is inspired by the idea in physics of quantum entanglements, which are not always created by proximity. This conceptualization of *convergences produced by separations and partiality* is key to the emblematic works we will encounter. The crypto-Jewish story as conceived by each author constitutes an exemplary instance of how convergences of culture, religion, and language, however partial, can be mutually constitutive with boundaries and exclusions.

Likely because they have been writing at a time of ever greater boundaries, borders, exclusions, and even threats to institute more of each, our authors are compelled, against the grain, to create works that reflect and produce multiplicities and crossings across nations and oceans. Crypto-Jews and their returns to public view are positioned as a lens onto a type of worldliness forged in suffering, forgetting, and belated remembrances but also in terms of connection to others. Conversions are particularly apt stories for the world novel's aesthetic of convergence that we find in narratives of the late twentieth century and the twenty-first century. As we will see in Chapter 1, formally, such connectivities are advanced in our texts through undemarcated, decentered temporalities, settings, and perspectives, as befitting the converso trajectory.

What I suggest regarding "narratives of convergence" is in the spirit of Michael Rothberg's influential concept of "multidirectional works," fictions that demonstrate "the dynamic transfers that take place between diverse places and times during the act of remembrance" and the ways "remembrance cuts across and binds together diverse spatial, temporal, and cultural sites" (Rothberg 2009, 11). Rothberg fruitfully parses literary and philosophical treatments of such seemingly disparate traumatic pasts as Atlantic slavery, the Holocaust, and colonialism and decolonization to indicate "dynamic transfers" among the events. Such correspondences provide alternatives to ideas about incommensurability that arise in "comparing" or juxtaposing large-scale traumatic circumstances.

Like Rothberg, I examine the contemporary crystallization of a particular set of historical events and their aftermath: Iberian conversions and expulsions in writing and culture from different parts of the world and in various languages. I chose works that focus on the intersections of the historical circumstances rather than on their singularity. What is specific to the authors I study is that they imagine the fallout from existing historical intersections of kin events and people under the Spanish Empire and in its aftermath. I use the term *kin* deliberately to refer to the connections made visible among events and cultural moments, such as the way the indigenous and Jews are imagined in the early years of the Conquest of the Americas or possible Morisco-Judeoconverso solidarities. Importantly, with the language of relation, I mean to evoke also the genealogical discourses through which the Christians, Jews, Muslims, and indigenous people have been and continue to be imagined in the context of Iberian and Sephardi history.

Not only do the works present the various victims under the same sign of particular imperial or national structures, but they also underline the ancestral links among them. The discourses of genealogy and organic linkages, with all their discontents, and of fellow victimhood and solidarity, rather than analogies, juxtapositions, and comparisons of events considered more distant to each other, are key elements that distinguish the narratives of convergence. Another feature of narratives of convergence reflects the historical consciousness of our current moment, in which the past and the present are often twinned, so that ancient experiences mirror, parallel, or (uncannily) show up in the contemporary. In addition, a sense of lost knowledge of the converso past and its intersections informs the texts that have inspired *The Converso's Return*. Therefore unknowability, dissimulation, archival gaps, and uncanny recurrences play a central and distinct role in shaping the entanglements of conversion legacies.

In reaching for converso history through convergence and multidirectionality, our particular authors enact a world making in terms that literary theorist Pheng Cheah has written about: World literature "is a type of world-making activity that enables us to imagine a world" (2008, 26). It "is not merely a product of the human imagination or something that is derived from, represents, or duplicates material reality. Literature is the force of a passage, an experience through which we are given and receive any determinable reality" (25).

Literature, then, affects how we see the world and has what Cheah calls a "normative" and not just representative or descriptive force. The intertextuality, multilingualism, and genre mixing of such works, Cheah explains, have to do with conveying the plurality in the making of histories (2016). The converso narratives of convergence, which rely on known histories and the insertion of unknown solidarities and crossings among people, present a normative, ethical view of the world.

Some of the buried and interlocking histories in the narratives draw on the general documentation about the postexpulsion and conversion centuries, whereas others are imagined. The works discussed in the next chapters offer what Paul Ricoeur argues is the contribution of historically inflected literature: to "free retrospectively certain possibilities that were not actualized in the historical past . . . [and] to perform a liberating function. . . . What 'might have been' . . . includes both the potentialities of the 'real' past and the 'unreal' possibilities of pure fiction" (Ricoeur 1988, 191–92). But even though they undertake Ricoeur's "what might have been," the texts come closer to Lisa Lowe's "past conditional temporality," or what she refers to as the "what could have been" in the writing of history. Lowe's formulation is undergirded by an ethical impulse to emphasize the loss of "the intimacies of the four continents, to engage slavery, genocide, indenture, and liberalism *as a conjunction*" (Lowe 2016, 40; emphasis added). Similarly, I suggest, the authors who have inspired this book imaginatively recuperate, comment on, and transform our ideas about obscured converso pasts less to reify singular legacies of one group (and its oppressors) and more to present them as a node in the convergence of historical processes of persecution, migration, and diasporization across continents, peoples, religions, cultures, and politics.

History's Missing Archives and Literature

The recuperation of crypto-Jewish identities centuries after their disappearance, the result of persecution and compulsory assimilation, builds on few publicly or privately documented details. Most of the knowledge of survival in modern times is orally or, according to some, biologically or genetically transmitted. Yet the narratives that are the subject of *The Converso's Return* appeared at a moment that is deeply saturated with heightened historical consciousness. Contemporary writers' and artists' works have exhibited an "archival impulse" to "make historical information, often lost or displaced, physically present" (Foster 2004, 21–22), perhaps as never before. Uncovering or recovering past records and creating new archives from suppressed knowledge, identities, and experiences of the disappeared have become aesthetic and political priorities (Azoulay 2011). Walter Benjamin's "Theses on the Philosophy of History" remains influential for its argument about the past as a source of hope, particularly "in a moment of danger," and "the dead" as being in need of rescue from "the enemy" (Benjamin 1969, 255). Like Benjamin, authors, activists, and scholars have insisted that the past cannot be ontologically separated from the present, despite the assertions to the contrary of the progress narrative. Recent antihistoricist thinking about the infusion of the traumatic past in particular into the present is encapsulated in Saidiya Hartman's idea of "the time of slavery" as the present: "We are coeval with the dead" (1997, 6).

What the historical record has excised has also been a part of recent historical consciousness. In addition to forging democratic, feminist, antiracist, and anti-authoritarian projects to recover suppressed voices, knowledge, and documents, scholars are increasingly reflecting on archives that have never existed and cannot be recovered. What can we do about those missing archives, whose absence gives the lie to the truthfulness of History? The contemporary "archive fever," the obsession with capturing an undefinable past with its futurity in mind (Derrida 1996), makes us aware not only of the existing record but also of *un*archived events and experiences.

In the United States, African Americanist thought regarding missing archives of the enslaved has offered the most notable and extensive reflection on both what is and cannot be recovered in documents that overwhelmingly present the conquerors' and slavers' point of view (e.g., Hartman 2007, 2008). Authors' and scholars' returns to sites and histories of slavery, often propelled by the desire for a restoration of identity, community, and psychic and political resources, might yield little. Hence we have the ongoing important debates regarding how to know and honor the dead who have been excised from history.[3]

In queer studies as well, the dearth of queer presence in the record has led to alternative conceptualizations of archives (e.g., Cvetkovich 2015). Reflecting on the missing archive of the "queer borderlands," Chicana historian Emma Pérez (2003) expressed an impossible wish: to find documents of women who loved women in the U.S.-Mexico border region. In their absence, she suggests queering the existing archive by reading its assumptions and exclusions against the grain, including by joining separate bodies of knowledge in queer and borderlands historical inquiry. Such desires to "exceed . . . the fictions of history" (Hartman 2008, 9) question the validity and "factuality" of the historical record (Nyong'o 2018). If it is missing so much, how true or legitimate is the archive?

And what role do fiction and memoirs play in refining and addressing the voices of the past that are not recuperable? One scholar writing in the influential journal *New Literary History* observed that "raw facts of history can be revitalized with a human touch" through literature, which allows us to "have a better understanding of the fantasies, beliefs, fears, and loves of the people" (Pasco 2004, 388). But in the case of persecutions, drastic severances from memory, and exclusion from annals, the preserved "raw facts of history" can obscure rather than illuminate. The memoirs and personal narratives I examine, such as Doreen Carvajal's *The Forgetting River* (2012a) and Victor Perera's *The Cross and the Pear Tree* (1995), express the horror vacui upon not finding evidence of belonging and "the psychic costs of repeated encounters with the 'empty archive,'" as Heather Love wrote in the context of queer history (2009, 42). The missing archives of secret Jewish origins or continuity, especially in the Americas, are a gap that literature fills by blending the few available facts with the plausible. The cross-pollination and intertwining of fiction and documented history take place in part through the replacement and invention of the missing characters, objects, emotions, and events.

Authors writing about converso pasts and their current refractions also mine the available oral and folk archives of rumors, gossip, and contemporary testimony about crypto-Jewishness, reimagining them in a conjuncture of other histories. Moreover, in interviews and in their writing, authors make it evident that they have done historical research and have knowledge of the relevant scholarship. In addition to replacing the missing archives through their historical and literary imagination and research, they also reflect metafictionally on the use of history and its gaps. José Manuel Fajardo's *Mi nombre es Jamaica* (My Name Is Jamaica) (2010), a key novel for the present study, does just this through its depiction of someone besotted by history to the point that he imagines himself to be a character from seventeenth-century events: a Don Quixote who loses his mind not to fiction but to the historical archive. Fajardo's character is a contemporary historian who fictionalizes himself by claiming to have "Jewish blood" running in his Christian Spanish veins and by assuming the persona of an indigenous converso who wrote a testimony (invented by Fajardo) in seventeenth-century Peru. Crafting an extreme, Cervantine example to various effects, Fajardo considers the pitfalls of the dominant appropriations of history. He also compels us to reflect on the misuses of the new historical consciousness, in which the erasure of the boundaries between past and present is sometimes put to work not to question the center of historical knowledge but to appropriate its periphery.

Literature that returns to submerged pasts and their afterlives in the present offers us a "neo-archive," or "fiction that creates history in the face of its absence" (Johnson 2014, 156). But it also goes beyond filling the blanks to shape our historical consciousness about unknowns and absences of past events and people. We may have little evidence about the lives, beliefs, and destinies of crypto-Jews or converso descendants inhabiting the U.S.-Mexico borderlands in the nineteenth century. But in her novel *Spirits of the Ordinary* Kathleen Alcalá imagines "what could have been" (Lowe 2016) by putting together traces and fragments of knowledge about the migrations and continuity in the Americas of crypto-Jews as a Chicana author who identifies with the converso history of her northern Mexican family and with the indigenous people of the borderlands (see Chapter 2).

The fictional works do not serve as evidence but raise awareness about the *making* of an archive filled with remnant stories, yearnings, and curiosities. Beyond imaginatively replacing an archive, fiction and other encounters with voids help us to understand, then, what it *means* for entanglements to have been disappeared (in the Latin American sense) and their archives absented.

In addition to performing recreations of history, narratives like the ones examined here are also textual remnants for the future of *how and why we have returned to converso histories* at a particular point, in our case the post-1992 years in which our texts were written. Literary writing offers accurate or plausible experiences of the past as well as a set of perspectives, ideas, and representations that generate the *present's* view, its historical consciousness of the largely unknowable past. In the near future we will view the fictional works and memoirs of Obejas, Alcalá, Carvajal, Fajardo, Perera, Morin, and Shafak, among others, as an archive of the revival of converso history in the literature of the late twentieth and early twenty-first centuries. Moreover, literary texts, especially but not only metafictions such as those of Fajardo and self-aware memoirs such as Carvajal's (see Chapter 3), act as archives of the present and of a contemporary historical consciousness, if not History.[4]

If traditional history is "the translation of archives into narratives," as Dominick LaCapra has suggested (2009, 36), then literary history perhaps involves the transformation of narratives into archives, whose facticity is not their most prominent or telling aspect, however close to historical "facts" they might get. What emerges from the fictional (and often autobiographical) contemporary archives of converso history instead is "historical consciousness," in Amos Funkenstein's sense, expressing "the degree of creative freedom in the use and interpretation of the contents of collective memory" (Funkenstein 1989, 11). It is also historicity in the anthropologists' sense, that is, the "cultural perceptions" and construction of the past as well as the "techniques" (ritual, performance, genre) through which we learn and express historical consciousness (Stewart 2016). Peter Seixas's capacious definition of historical consciousness, which includes not only collective memory (instead of opposing it) but also feelings and ideas about history at a particular moment, comes closest to my own working definition (see Seixas 2004). I use the term and draw on these various ideas about historical consciousness not to evoke periodicity or the awareness of time and successive eras, following Hans Gadamer or Wilhelm Dilthey (see Seixas 2004), but rather to suggest that the return of converso history not only reproduces and imagines the past but also reflects the contemporary moment's historical consciousness, that is, the sense of the past, whether as history, memory, visions, or rumor.

Survival and Paramemories

Because they return crypto-Jewish stories to the present, literary texts operate on an impulse to highlight or *produce* converso survivals in our day. Contemporary narratives that look back in order to reconstruct both a present and a past out of the shards of experience and knowledge register a tension between the acknowledgment of destruction and disappearance on one hand and the assertion of the past's remnants in the present on the other. The impulse to assert "They/we have been erased" and "They/we are still here" informs converso returns in fiction. Weak strands of knowledge and absent artifacts of conversion nevertheless spur acts of imagination strong enough to reconnect Sephardi and converso survival routes from Spain to the Ottoman Empire and the Americas. These regenerating acts depend not only on the recuperation of ancient identities but also on the production of new affiliations and the *creation of new remnants*.

We think of a remnant as what has survived. Yet in many imaginative acts of return, remnants of the past are not found but *produced*. Narratives of recovery often resignify what may not have been previously perceived or experienced as a remnant, whether it is a Catholic Latinx body that (re)claims Jewishness through genetics or an ordinary unmarked street in a Spanish village that we surmise to be the former site of a converso family's house. What is not "found" and lacks widely accepted physical, documentary, or genetic evidence is produced in narrative, such as in scenes of return to ancient sites, the representation of embodied, symptomatic responses, and the insertion of the "missing" converso element into the historical imaginary. An animating question of *The Converso's Return* is, What are the imaginative and literary means by which remnants are *produced* in the present? Although the scientific, literary, and cultural discourses of genealogy are central to most of the narratives I examine, I show that descent, inheritance, rehabilitation of identity, and the meanings of conversion are neither stable nor fixed in the fictional or autobiographical works. This is not to deny the discursive importance of historical heritage and recovery but to sharpen the focus on its underpinnings, uses, and resignifications.

Narratives that foreground the problem of the missing archives of history and memory and the difficult searches for traces and signs stage their substitution through other elements, including the body, affect, and existing historical knowledge. Knowing through the body is common in this writing. The characters and narrators who are converso descendants in the works studied here, especially those of Obejas, Carvajal, Fajardo, Perera, and Shafak, sense and feel the past. As I explain in "The Crypto-Jewish Body" section of Chapter 1, they experience nervousness, dread, and even terror as they confront known but unacknowledged sites of converso lives and disappearances in Spain and in converso exile sites, such as Havana, Safed, and Chicago. Narratives about converso lives must be constructed without a proximate generation's memories or contemporary memorializations. Even in Spain, where the state has undertaken tremendous efforts to recover and often remake "Jewish Spain" with many new tourist and cultural institutions and "Sephardi" sites all over the country (Flesler and Pérez Melgosa 2008, 2020; Linhard 2014), forced conversions and their aftermath barely register.

With all these gaps in transmission, literary works often produce a *paramemory* of sorts (*para* indicating both "beyond" and "beside"), which avails itself of memory but is beyond it. The only critic, to my knowledge, who has also used this term suggested it as short for "paranormal memory," that is, "a form of memory that, like other paranormal phenomena or events, lies beyond the scope of normal scientific understanding and is often condemned as superstition" (Gratton 2005, 4). My meaning is different; I do not refer only to intuition and the channeling of an other's experience, or a *voyance* (a sort of vision) (Gratton 2005, 6). What the texts demonstrate is similar to but also distinct from Sigmund Freud's understanding of transgenerational transmission of memory. In his astounding final work, *Moses and Monotheism*, Freud argues that Moses, originally an Egyptian, was murdered by his followers, whose descendants fused Moses's teachings with others and, out of guilt, repressed the murder and instead invented another narrative of origins, the one more familiar to us. In this speculative work, Freud sowed the seeds of ideas about transgenerational transmission that have gained currency in a variety of fields from psychoanalysis to epigenetics (Abraham and Torok 1994; Freud 1959; Slavet 2009). The ancient Jews, Freud argued, have a "mental residue of those primeval times" that "has become a heritage which, with each new generation, needs only to be reawakened" (1959, 170). Much of this work concerns the *unconscious* transmission of traumas and other past events across generations through what has been characterized as the "transgenerational phantom" (Abraham and Torok 1994).

Paramemory as staged in our fiction and testimonies is born of conscious deliberations about secret family histories. Narrators might recount a void in the family story, do historical and genealogical research, and undertake visits to sites in which Jewish history was made and unmade. The body might exhibit the unconscious traumas, but the narration reflects a deliberate pursuit of origins and past traumas. The notion of paramemory is close to Marianne Hirsch's concepts of postmemory and secondary memory. As

Hirsch explains, postmemory "is distinguished from memory by generational distance and from history by deep personal connection. Postmemory is a powerful and very particular form of memory precisely because its connection to its object or sources is mediated not through recollection but through an imaginative investment and creation" (Hirsch 1997, 22). "Generational distance" and the mediated "imaginative investment and creation" in lieu of recollection—this is the stuff of crypto-Jewish memory as represented in fiction and first-person reflections.

But if the time lag is centuries long, rather than belonging to "lived time" and the "second generation," the "belatedness of memory" takes on a variant meaning in memoirs and fiction about recovering suppressed knowledge or returns to their putative sites. Rather, it is a recovery, usually based on inferences, public knowledge, and archives, which are, as in the case of Carvajal, general rather than specific, given that public and even private cultural memory of convert origins is scant.[5] Occasionally, a few individuals can trace their genealogy amply (e.g., Milgrom 2012), but especially for the mixed populations of the Americas, this is a difficult task for most, and the results do not bespeak many more details than a few names and places from centuries ago. To document an undocumented past, many seekers turn to genetic testing, which for some serves as "proof" of belonging and of a historical narrative that raises questions and concerns I address later.

Hence the representation of traumatic symptoms in the present based on events that are several hundred years old, such as those we find in narratives about crypto-Jews, suggests a transtemporal transmission, mediated by archives, rather than primarily an unconscious "transgenerational" transmission (Abraham and Torok 1994), which usually refers to just a few generations and not centuries. The term *paramemories* is meant to incorporate all the various sources in documented history, historiography, genetic technology of transtemporal transmission, and symptomatic encounters with the crypto-Jewish past. Out of the impulse to *make* archives and memories in the present are born new narratives that contribute to our contemporary historical imaginary without victims or witnesses known to us. The notion of the self as a remnant of a little-known past that is nevertheless sensed and, sometimes, "experienced" through the body recurs across narratives of crypto-Jewishness.

Historical Background and the Contemporary Context

Each of the texts I analyze has a particular purchase on these concepts, which demonstrate the promises and pitfalls of intertwined historical and genealogical imaginations, past and present. The particular Sephardi history that the narratives return to is the period of forced conversions of Jews and Muslims in medieval Iberia, both before but especially after the Spanish Inquisition was established in 1478. The mission of the Holy Office was to root out heresy, particularly that of suspected "insincere" converts from Judaism and Islam who were publicly professing Christianity but secretly continuing their ancestral faiths. After 1492, along with other "heretics," these converts, and not the banished Jews or Muslims, were the targets of the Holy Office. Medieval Jews who converted to Christianity in Spain did not quickly disappear into Christian society, even under the pressures of *limpieza de sangre* (purity of blood) statutes, which were created to exclude Christians with Islamic or Jewish origins from a wide of range of rights and privileges in what was essentially a racialization and biologization of religion. Known converted Jews and Muslims and their descendants, whose ancestral religions, languages, and literary cultures were banned along with their adherents, were often perceived as an insincere fifth column, tainting Christian purity of lineage.

The "genealogical obsession" continued for centuries (García Arenal 2013, 2; Nirenberg 2002). It began with the pogroms and compulsory conversions of Jews in 1391 and persisted through the Christians' distinction between *cristianos de natura* ("Old Christians") and Jews, finally leading to the *limpieza de sangre* statutes. Frequent accusations of non-Christian customs or beliefs led to expropriation, torture, imprisonment, and burnings at the stake, even though many converts did assimilate successfully by hiding well their origins, including through marriage or falsified certificates of blood purity. Formerly Jewish New Christians were suspected, targeted, and persecuted for "Judaizing," that is, for retaining Jewish faith and practices not only in Spain but also wherever the Inquisition established itself, from Europe to the Americas. This continued for centuries after the most significant periods of forced conversions in 1391 and 1492 in Spain and 1497 in Portugal.

Inquisition records are replete with details of the everyday lives of accused individuals and families of New Christian origin from Lisbon to Lima. The accused were charged for telltale offenses, such as Friday night candle lighting or the substitution of pork with other meats. These and many other such details have furnished us with knowledge about inquisitorial fears and cruelty and with an idea about possible continuing Jewish practices. The fear of loyalty to Judaism and Islam haunted the Spanish Empire long after the persecutions, conversions, and the violent purge of Jews and Muslims as of 1492 and of the Moriscos (converts from Islam) in 1609.

Individuals and their descendants were identified as converts generations after the act of conversion usually because of perceptions about their ambivalence toward becoming Christians. Often, this identity persisted also because the accusers wanted to undermine the political and economic power of families or individuals, even when the latter's attachment to familial pre-conversion identities and practices were weak or nonexistent. But despite claims to the contrary (Netanyahu 1995), crypto-practices did exist among descendants of Jews and Muslims who converted, and some returned to Judaism and Islam in the Netherlands, Italy, the Ottoman Empire, Morocco, and elsewhere. Those of judeoconverso background were banned from Spain's and Portugal's empires in the Americas, but the exclusion from the conquered territories did not stop the many who hid their origins and blended in as Old Christians, though hundreds accused of Judaizing were murdered in the American inquisitions, which began in the early 1570s.

This inquisitorial practice continued throughout the Spanish Americas, from Mexico City to Lima, often against Portuguese New Christians, known as the *Nação* (the Nation), many of whom were influential traders. The *Nação* were accused and persecuted by the Holy Office and then conveniently dispossessed and expropriated (Elkin 1996). Among the most notorious acts of this American Inquisition targeting conversos were the trials and executions of members of the Carvajal family. The remarkable writings of Luis de Carvajal the Younger survive from the end of the sixteenth century.[6] The autobiographer bears witness not only to the torture and executions of his family members but also to the secret and syncretic customs, beliefs, and rhetoric of crypto-Jewish life, which went beyond a condition that was "publicly Catholic, secretly Jewish" (M. Cohen 1973; Perelis 2017).

But the vast majority of the Jewish converts who stayed in Iberia or migrated to the Americas as Catholics were largely presumed to be lost to the Christian world, at best just lurking in Iberian blood. Outside of a few communities in Mallorca, Spain, and in Northern Portugal, where some groups were known as descendants of New Christians and were racialized or saw themselves as Jews (see later discussion), the knowledge about converso or crypto-Jewish presence in the Americas or Europe dating to Iberian conversions often circulated in families as secrets or rumors.

The debates about the Jewish continuity of conversos have been extensive in the Americas, where New Christians, secretly Jewish or not, were considered extinct even before the end of the colonial periods of the Iberian empires and certainly after. The supposition is that in the Americas crypto-Jews moved to remote areas after the establishment of the Inquisition in New Spain in 1571, which rooted out Judaizing families. As a result, the argument goes, "surviving Judaizers went into deep cover" (Gitlitz 2002, 56) and moved to far-flung areas, such as today's Mexican states of Nuevo Léon and Coahuila and what became the U.S. regions of New Mexico and Texas. And once out of the sight of the centers of power, families continued certain traditions secretly and, after a time, hardly knowing why (Alberro 2001; Hordes 2008). In *The Faith of Remembrance*, Nathan Wachtel (2013) argues that in Mexico and Brazil some people of formerly Jewish origins maintained forms of practice and "remembrance" until the eighteenth century, with surviving remnants today in northern Brazil.

But about later continuities, some scholars put credence in the testimonies and evidence provided by descendants, whereas others reject stories of continuity and beyond. Along with those asserting the eventual death of crypto-Judaism in New Spain (e.g., M. Cohen 1972; Gitlitz 2002), historian Judith Laikin Elkin declares that all over Latin America, the "tradition" about crypto-Jewish continuity "proved to be without substance. All manifestations of a colonial Jewish presence were *legally extinguished and genetically submerged*" (Elkin 1980, 20; emphasis added). Hence, for many, extinction became the norm through which to consider crypto-Jewishness in the Americas until more recently, when other historians (Gitlitz 2002; Hordes 2008; Wachtel 2001) declared, sometimes with great confidence, that in fact today it is possible to identify descendants, some of whose practices have Jewish origins, often unbeknown to them. Vehement refutations of New Mexicans' own claims to crypto-Jewish continuity (Neulander 1994, 1996) and media exposés (Ferry and Nathan 2000) created controversy and also led to the increasing visibility of communities and issues not widely known.

The claims of late-twentieth- and early-twenty-first-century Christians with ties to medieval Iberia who not only found Jewish roots but also returned to them, such as those whose stories I sketched briefly at the outset of this Introduction, met with divergent attitudes, not only from academics and the media but also from religious and cultural Jewish entities. Responses ranged from skepticism and rejection to the welcoming and cultivation of Latinx, Hispanic, and Iberian individuals returning to Jewish identity. Whatever the nature of the reception, the self-presentation of Christians (and some Muslims) as Jewish by ancestry and the claims and testimonies only seem to be increasing in number and widening in scope, slowly becoming a more familiar part of the larger Jewish and Hispanic narratives.

"Lost Tribes" and "Found" Remnants

Stories that stage the quest for largely undocumented pasts that may have survived residually or in a ghostly fashion speak to our fascination with extinction and survival. In Jewish and related traditions there is a long-standing rejection of extinction and quests for recovery and return. For example, claims about the discovery of the ten lost tribes of Israel, said to have been driven afar by Assyrians in the eighth century BCE, have long invigorated Jewish (as well as Muslim and Christian) thought and lore (see Ben-Dor 2013), including, most relevantly here, the converso imagination: One of the best-known works of the early modern converso renaissance outside Iberia written by the returnees to Judaism in Amsterdam, who were familiar with both Jewish and Christian theologies, literature, and rhetoric, was *Hope of Israel*. This 1650 text, by the influential Menasseh ben Israel of Amsterdam, made a hero of Antonio Montezinos, another returned converso who left Portugal for Holland and met, he alleged, one of the lost tribes when he was in "deep" South America (Colombia) and heard a group recite the Shema, the central prayer of Judaism. This claim that an indigenous group was practicing Judaism was met with great and widespread enthusiasm among Jews, Anglo-Protestants (eager for both the Second Coming and rationalizing

Native Americans' conversion), and others in an era of extensive millenarianism and messianism (Popkin 1989).

The quest for and "discoveries" of lost tribes has been consistent in many periods (Ben-Dor 2013) and continues today: in Africa, from Ethiopia to Uganda and South Africa (see, e.g., Parfitt and Egorova 2006; Tamarkin 2014); and in Asia (e.g., the Bnei Menashe of India; see Egorova 2015). Iberian and Latin American crypto-Jewish descendants are also often configured from within and without as though they were a lost tribe (if not one of *the* lost tribes), which accounts for a part of the interest in their story. Such recuperations seem irresistible, not least for the "proof" they provide of resilience and survival contra expulsion, persecution, and genocide, especially following the Holocaust, which has shaped the contemporary Jewish world's focus on both annihilation and survival against all odds.

Further, all such revivals pose crucial questions about the authenticity and parameters of identity that might disturb or reinforce existing boundaries. When the returns involve Israel, the stakes in such questions are high. Often, they are politicized with an obvious agenda: to have the "lost and found" in Asia, Africa, and the Americas become settlers in the West Bank, or to use people of color as buffers or allies abroad, though some scholars take pains to underline also the agency of the self-identifying returnees (see Egorova 2015; Tamarkin 2014). The conception of lost tribes makes us think about the assumptions regarding history and identity: Do they posit biological or cultural continuities? Must existing definitions of Jewishness and even Judaism change to accommodate the found and returned? How do we adjust our understanding of historical rupture and disappearance, and how do we conceive of historical continuity when seeking returns and returnees?

Rather than being an obscure interest in an ancient and forgotten piece of the past, the revival of what has been presumed dead is informed both within and outside the Jewish world by recent global and local practices and inquiries about history, memory, and belonging and by imaginative acts. Such practices lay bare our current thinking on those issues, pointing to their limits and better possibilities. To understand this particular reappearance of conversos and what remains of their history, it is important to take stock of processes internal to various Jewish contexts but also of the wider world's contemporary focus on the past and its erasures, in which such returns have become a key practice and idea. In what follows, I briefly situate the interest in conversion's remnants within the contemporary preoccupation with returns.

Returns in Contemporary Culture and Literature

Return and conversion are linked etymologically: The word *conversion* comes from the Latin *convertere* (*com*, meaning "with," and *vertere*, meaning "turn"). In the Jewish context, return and conversion are linked ideologically: *Tshuvah* indicates returning to the Jewish faith, a reconversion. But the positioning of the self and community as remnants and the recovery of ancient identities are made possible at a particular *contemporary* conjuncture where the past has come to the fore. The twentieth-century grand-scale mass returns that had the largest impact were spurred by wars and decolonization, in which ethnoracial-religious homogeneity and state consolidation were major goals, and both history and religion were deployed to justify "returns." Just a few examples from the past hundred years are the displacement and return of Asia Minor Greeks and Muslims in Greece to their presumed homelands in Greece and Turkey in the 1923 population exchange; the uprooting and return of Muslims and Hindus to the new states dominated by their coreligionists after the India-Pakistan partition of 1947; the mass return of worldwide Jews to Palestine after millennia and the partition of Israel/Palestine; and the expulsion and return of ethnic Germans of Eastern Europe to Germany after World War II.

Narratives and ideologies of return are also part of what the scholar Andreas Huyssen calls "the memory boom" (2003, 18). This is a reference to both the grassroots and state-led valorization of the idea of the past, collective memory, and the rise in the culture of memorialization in the past few decades. In the early part of the twentieth century our notions of modernity and progress positioned the past as something to recover from and leave behind, with history largely a subject for historians and some state institutions (Huyssen 2003, 21–38). But in the last few decades we have had an outpouring of remembrance of the past, from genocide museums to grand memorials to conferences and literary and artistic productions, most frequently commemorating large-scale traumatic events. The ascendance of global human rights and transitional justice discourses of recent times, which in great part gave rise to the memory boom, generated a whole set of *re-*'s involving the past, among them, reparation, redress, restitution, recognition, restoration, repatriation, reconciliation, redemption. And of course, what is implied by all of these: returns both metaphoric and literal.

As Marianne Hirsch and Nancy Miller write in the introduction to the important volume *Rites of Return: Diaspora Poetics and the Politics of Memory*, "Far from waning ... in the twenty-first century, the desire for return to origins and to sites of communal suffering has progressively intensified" (2011, 3). Hirsch and Miller date the "longing" and the "quest for a direct link to deep roots and family bloodlines" (3) to Alex Haley's 1976 U.S. book and television series *Roots*, though such practices were also common in other parts of the world. Moreover, returns to known and supposed ancient homelands that involve travel, as well as accounts of these travels, particularly narratives of survivors or descendants of victims of atrocities, have proliferated in the past decades. African diasporic returns to Ghana and its slavery-related sites, Jewish returns to European towns and World War II concentration camps, and Armenian returns to the former territories of the Ottoman Empire are a few examples among many. In the particularly large-scale case of those with African origins in the Americas, the emergence of stories of group survival, transnational and transatlantic continuities, and resistance have been embedded in the idea of return and reunification, symbolic and otherwise, with origins in civil rights, anticolonial, and other leftist movements worldwide. Intellectual and symbolic returns to Africa since twentieth-century Afrocentric or pan-African thought took hold have been complemented by historical and ancestral quests carried out through travels to the continent, genetic ancestry testing, and cultural immersion.

Further on, I explore the controversies specifically around converso returns, including the critique of Jewish identity biologization through genetics and genealogy. More broadly, it is worth noting that, although returns to ancient identities can fulfill essentialist and territorialist functions, they can also figure as opposition to preponderant notions of progress and temporality, as Elizabeth Freeman explains from a queer theory perspective. In the discourses of compulsive repetition (Freud) and degeneration (Lombroso), there is a "certain stalling of any smooth movement from the past to the present." For Freeman, "*compulsive returns, movement backward to reenter prior historical* *moment*s rather than inward or outward to circumvent historical time," exist in queer time and align "blacks, homosexuals, and other deviants with threats to the forward movement of individual or civilizational development" (2010, 22–23; emphasis added). The inevitability of the present (defined as the state of market capitalism and individual freedom) and the irrelevance of the past, described by Francis Fukuyama as the end of history, are subverted. Returns, then, can be identified both with what Freeman means by a queerness that disrupts civilizational temporality and with a regressive desire for a nonexistent, exclusionary, and falsely redemptive wholeness in the past. Freeman proposes that we can concur with the "willingness to be warmed by the afterglow of the forgotten" (2010, 498) but not imagine "a prior wholeness locatable in a time and place we ought to 'get back to'" (499).

As I explain in the chapters to come, I have chosen texts for analysis that perform returns to crypto-Jewish and converso stories but ask to be read precisely for a particular kind of backward look that not only eschews imagining a prior wholeness but productively fragments and troubles dominant Latinx, Latin American, Jewish, Sephardi, Turkish, and Iberian discourses of history and identity. They also join them through stories that make times and spaces converge in unexpected ways.

Fictions of Return

Contemporary fictional and autobiographical narratives that engage in collective memory and history, particularly those of the traumatic kind, have been exploring the meanings of return as a means of confronting, correcting, or rewriting the past and remaking it as a part of the present. In postcolonial literature the trope of return affords recuperative or critical perspectives on precolonial political and cultural formations; it also reflects on the nature of contact and conflict between colonial and postcolonial cultures and subjectivities. The returns following wars, migrations, and transcontinental adoptions have also been the subject of memoirs and novels. In the Americas neo-slave narratives have recovered and adapted nineteenth-century testimonial, autobiographical, and other writing by slaves, fugitives, and former slaves and have staged carefully researched and imaginatively rendered returns in the times and places of slavery. In recent Jewish fiction and memoir, returns and (often fruitless) quests for traces and remains in pre-Holocaust Europe are writ large, especially in Jewish American writing. Returns to Iberia are also prominent in contemporary Sephardi memoirs and fiction. In Latin America and Iberia, twentieth-century traumas created by dictatorship, state terror, civil war, mass murders, and disappearances have held a key place in recent writing, in which exiles' returns and returns to sites of family trauma caused by politics often play a central role. Cinematic, testimonial, and fictional narratives about the willful quest to return to the past that uncover secrets of collaborations, unite stolen children with their biological families, or continue quests for material remains of bodies have abounded in recent years.

The proliferation of these kinds of narratives renders the past as proximate, despite its ostensible imperceptibility in our daily lives, but the past cannot be apprehended and "presented" intact: More often than not in return narratives, the past is not only in great part lost but also unfinished and, frequently, debilitating. The "myth of the redemptive return" can be "one of the most profound mythic structures of the New World," as Stuart Hall has argued (2003, 39), but the preoccupation with memory and returning to the places, times, and archives of the past in the Americas or elsewhere is rarely felicitous or recuperative in most contemporary fiction. The past continues to shape us, but it also cripples us (such as in the haunting image of Dana's arm in Octavia Butler's powerful novel *Kindred*). The return to place as a means of accessing the past can cement the sense of loss instead of repairing it, as diasporic subjects confront the lack of human, material, and other remains and traces of collective pasts, or, like Saidiya Hartman in Ghana, they find remains but no stories (Hartman 2007). The return to Sephardi memory in Iberia and in dispersal partakes of these tropes of loss and lack of remains and stories.

The Returns of Sephardism

The contemporary returns to converso stories unfold not only in the era of global memory but also in the context of contemporary Sephardism. Yael Halevi-Wise asserts that "the Marrano" is "one of Sephardism's main constructs" (2012a, 12), which is true especially in reference to normative medieval and postexpulsion Sephardis, given the compulsion to convert. The tragedy of the expulsion itself was twin to mass conversion, and these two events together defined the Iberian past while seemingly severing the connection between the converted and the expelled after a certain time. Around 1992, the quincentennial year of the expulsion of Jews from Spain, which coincided with the fall of Granada and the departure of Muslims and with the conquest of the Americas, much attention was drawn to the Spanish Jewish world and its extinction in Iberia as well as its afterlife in the Ottoman Empire, Morocco, and the Americas. This interest was manifested not only in the multifarious commemorative events of the year but also in literary and cultural productions just before and well after 1992, including publication of countless novels, plays, and poetry anthologies, the creation of dozens of new neo-Sephardi or Judeo-Andalusian, Judeo-Ottoman, and multicultural music groups, and various related theatrical and musical productions in Europe, the Americas, the Middle East, and North Africa.

The quincentenary benefited images of nation-states, especially Spain and Turkey. In Spain this was spurred by the recognition of the expulsion in 1991 by King Juan Carlos at a Madrid synagogue and the invitation to Sephardi Jews to return and acquire citizenship as a form of restitution and as a way of cleansing its past. By promoting its post-Franco tolerance through a (conditional) citizenship as a form of reconciliation and by emphasizing its (actually contested) role as a haven for Jews during World War II, official philo-Semitism also served to market Spain's medieval *convivencia* to increase tourism (see Flesler et al. 2015; Flesler and Pérez Melgosa 2020). In postdictatorship Portugal, President Mario Soares made a public apology, asking for pardon from Portuguese Jews. And in Turkey around 1992, Jewish community leaders, in partnership with state officials, also promoted the country's status, from the Ottoman Empire to the Turkish Republic, as a 500-year refuge for the 1492 exiles. Such state-produced, politically and economically expedient hegemonic collective memories spurred both consenting and dissenting literary and cultural productions about the Sephardi past and present. "Circum-1992" is a shorthand we can use to point to the period of this rise in literary and cultural production about the expulsion and its aftermath in Latin America, Spain, Turkey, and France; it can also refer to the resuscitation of the largely unknown histories of Jewish converts to Christianity who dispersed into Europe, the Americas, and the Ottoman Empire.

Of course, modern returns to Sepharad took place at other points and in other contexts as well. The philosophers, authors, and historians of the eighteenth-century German Jewish Haskalah, or Enlightenment, recuperated a glorious Spanish Jewish history of cultural, literary, and philosophical integration in the medieval era and revindicated a Judeo-Muslim symbiosis that was extolled in many publications and materialized in the Moorish fashion of synagogue architecture (see also Chapter 1). In late-nineteenth-century Latin America, Jewish immigrants, Sephardi or not, availed themselves of Sephardi history to appear more "native" to the dominant Christian Hispanophone cultures in which they found themselves (Aizenberg 2002; Halevi-Wise 2012a). In Spain the early twentieth century saw the "discovery" of "Spaniards without a homeland," a result of the Spanish colonization of northern Morocco and Spaniards' encounter with Spanish-speaking Jews, descendants of Iberian exiles.

A period of political, economic, cultural, and literary interest in the debated Spanishness of Sephardi Jews in the first decades of the twentieth century led to a new search for knowledge about Spanish Jews and various discourses about their possible return to Spain. This attention also resulted in studies of Judeo-Spanish written and oral expression. Most of these and other reclamations of obscured histories and their attendant philo-Sephardisms did not outlive the needs of their particular historical and ideological conjunctures. But in Spain and Portugal the academic stage was set for future writing about Sephardi Jewry and its reincorporation into Iberia through the special nationality laws of 2015 for Sephardi descendants.

One of the main differences of the more recent return to Sephardi identities and histories is the synchronic spread across regions, cultures, and languages. Global processes such as "the memory boom" (Huyssen 2003), changing conceptions of Jewishness, the rise of interest in religion(s) and therefore in conversion, the analogizing of the tragedies of the Inquisition and expulsion to the Holocaust, and contemporary political repressions are among the many factors that have played a role in cultural production. These include fiction, drama, poetry, testimonies, documentaries, social media sites, and popular and academic histories from Turkey and Europe to the Americas about Spanish Jews. As scholarship of the last two decades has shown, the acknowledgment and awareness of the Nazi genocide perpetrated against

European Jewry have been a key paradigm through which people have understood Jewish history. The visibility of the Holocaust since the late 1960s and 1970s has also been instrumental for other groups subjected to mass trauma in terms of recognition and redress (see, e.g., Barkan 2000; Huyssen 2003; Rothberg 2009; Torpey 2003). Given the transactional construction of collective memory, other events, such as the Algerian War of Independence for the French, can also revive and revitalize Holocaust memory, as Michael Rothberg has shown (2009). It is not surprising that, with reference to contemporary writing and culture, medieval and postmedieval Iberian Jewish traumas have been connected to, copresented with, and interpreted through the Nazi genocide, as Sarah Casteel's (2016) and Tabea Linhard's (2014) key works on the Caribbean and Spain make evident. The expulsion and the Inquisition have been presented as a prefiguration that is also analogous and structurally similar to the Holocaust. All the different kinds of association with the Holocaust, then, have also contributed to the increased visibility of Sephardi historical traumas.

In addition, this particular efflorescence of attention to Sepharad and its afterlives has been taking place with the awareness of decolonization and multiculturalism struggles in a post–cold war world system that could not abide them. This hostility, acute already in the 1980s and 1990s with civilizational discourses rearing their heads forcefully again (as propagated most notably in Samuel Huntington's book *The Clash of Civilizations*), intensified after September 11, 2001.

The search for models of coexistence led to al-Andalus as well as to Sepharad within it—that is, to an Arab/Moorish Spain and the Jewish world that survived and flourished therein. Instead of the glorification of one or the other culture or community of medieval Iberia that characterized some ethnonationalist Jewish, Christian, or Muslim approaches, it was *convivencia*, or coexistence, itself that seemed inspiring in a world of permanent wars that have been cast as conflicts of religion and civilization. Medieval *convivencia* was presented as a model of multiculturalism, hybridity, and universality *avant la lettre*, and its end serves as a cautionary tale. John Docker summarizes 1492 as the beginning of "sinister intolerance and xenophobia" and the end of a Moorish Spain characterized "in subsequent narrative and legend and desire to be open, heterogeneous, tolerant of difference, pluralistic:

multi-ethnic, multi-religious, multicultural" (2001, 190). The contemporary Spanish state's positioning of the Alhambra Decree as "one of the most important historic mistakes" and the offer of citizenship to Sephardis as "redress" (Jessurun d'Oliveira 2015, 15) downplay the *systemic* role of expulsion and racialization.

Latin Americanist decolonial scholars who have positioned 1492 as the year that simultaneously began the conquest of the Americas and the modern world system (Mignolo 2002; Quijano 2000) have contributed greatly to our understanding of the role of racialization in the Americas in this process. But they largely omit the role of expulsion and a racialized "cleansing" of religions in state formation (Kedar 1996) and empire that took place within Iberia itself (see Boyarin 2009). As Ella Shohat has argued cogently, the "multiple 1492s" connecting expulsion, forcible conversion, reconquest and conquest, genocide, and slavery unleashed on both sides of the Atlantic against indigenous, African, Jewish, and Muslim people need to be considered in conjuncture (Shohat 2006; Shohat and Stam 2012). Many of the narratives examined in *The Converso's Return* engage the "1492s" through imaginative revelations of various links, overlaps, and circulations among Native Americans, the Spain of Jews, Muslims, and Christians, and the Ottoman Empire, with conversos as nodes of convergences born of expulsion and conquest.

Converso Returns Then and Now

Although in the last few decades we have been witnessing a fascinating new chapter in the wider context of the resurgence of returns and contemporary Sephardism, converts' returns to Judaism have long been endemic to post-Iberian Sephardi trajectories. In the sixteenth and seventeenth centuries many conversos went back to their ancestral Judaism in the safety of Amsterdam, Venice, Ferrara, Livorno, the Ottoman Empire, and elsewhere. After one, two, or even more generations as Christians, descendants recovered a Judaism attenuated or lost in Iberia by undergoing reconversions, although many rabbis who admitted those referred to as New Christians into their congregations viewed them as never having ceased being Jewish (Goldish 2008). The returnees to Judaism formed, as scholars of early modern Portuguese New Christians explain, "an idiosyncratically rich and vibrant

Jewish-Iberian symbiosis in a Western Portuguese–Sephardic diaspora" (Feitler and Stuczynski 2018, 4).

As for the more recent period, the 1980s and 1990s were not the first time in the twentieth century that attention was drawn to hidden or unknown roots in Iberian Jewish conversion. The most publicized case was the uncovering in the 1920s of the largely endogamous converso community in the Trás-os-Montes region of northern Portugal. Members of this community identified as and were identified by others as Jews and New Christians and had practiced Catholicism as well as a syncretic crypto-Judaism for centuries (see, e.g., Pignatelli 2019). A few of their cultural aspects that the normative Jewish world learned about in the first decades of the century were secret unleavened bread making for Passover, references to Queen Esther (considered a conversa) as "our Lady," and many prayers and songs that survived and were adapted over the centuries.

Although works on crypto-Jewish continuity in Portugal were published in the nineteenth century, Polish Ashkenazi mining engineer Samuel Schwarz's "accidental discovery" of the region's Belmonte community in the 1920s attracted unprecedented attention. Schwarz, who was living in Lisbon at the time, encountered the remote and secretive community while traveling on business. Despite initial discretion and wariness on the part of the group's members, he was able to earn their trust and their permission to tell their stories; he even took their photographs. What Schwarz wrote about their secret practices, largely upheld by women, was revealed in the popular press and had reverberations in Portugal and in the Jewish world. Much of the attention centered around helping the Portuguese communities and individuals, known variously in different languages as New Christians, Marranos, *judeus* (Jews), and crypto-Jews, return to normative Judaism. Non-Iberian Jewish visitors and sponsors proliferated.

At around the same time, the Portuguese army officer Artur Carlos de Barros Basto, "the Apostle of the Marranos," as the historian Cecil Roth referred to him (1930), openly declared himself a crypto-Jewish descendant, converted to Judaism in Morocco, had himself circumcised, and took the name Abraham Ben-Rosh. He also worked to establish a community of other descendants, with substantial interest and financial support from Europe and the United States, founding the large new synagogue of Porto, which is in use today. Barros Basto found himself dishonorably discharged by the Salazar regime for allegedly immoral behavior and adherence to communism. Soon enough, growing anti-Semitism and the influx of mostly Eastern European Jewish refugees into Portugal drove the crypto-Jewish issue underground for another few decades.

In the same period, but a continent away, Mexicans in Venta Prieta, Hidalgo, claimed crypto-Jewish descent and attracted some attention and exoticizing tourism around "Indian Jews." But they were quickly delegitimized by journalists and scholars, who discredited their claims and pointed to their hybrid Catholic traditions alongside the dietary and other Jewish customs and their possible Protestant leanings, which the Venta Prietans denied in vain.

The Portuguese and the Venta Prietan communities that "came out" in the 1930s still exist, and they have gone through fascinating transformations (see, e.g., Cook 2001). But in the first half of the twentieth century they were subjected to external detractions and threats and, in Portugal, internal divisions. After the 1930s, with the onset of the war and the Holocaust, they attracted little sustained cultural and literary attention outside of a few Jewish and local contexts. Several decades later, however, those claiming converso and crypto-Jewish descent, particularly in the American Southwest and to a certain extent in Iberia (especially in Portugal; see Leite 2017) received much more continuous attention than ever, which has been accompanied by, as before, suspicious scrutiny.

The memory boom of the late twentieth century opened a space for converso stories, though factors beyond the desire to bring to light old and repressed traumas played a role as well. These factors include the globalized search for lost tribes and new Jews. The quests were spurred variously by Israel's interests and the increased flexibility of identities under late capitalism that allowed new belongings through research and technology (especially genetic ancestry tests). Iberian and Latin American postdictatorship historical disclosures and revisionism also led to partial confrontations with oppressions in both remote and nearer periods. In Spain, for example, discrimination against descendants of forced converts of the fifteenth century in Mallorca, the Chuetas or Chuecas, was recognized. The Chuetas are a largely endogamous group and were ghettoized until the twentieth century (Moore, cited in Melammed 2004, 141). Jewish missionary efforts to return to Judaism these Christians, whose families were persecuted for their Jewish blood, have been celebrated in contemporary Jewish media.

In Portugal the Belmonte community came to the fore again after the 1980s, after having retreated to their private and secretive ways following the exposures of the 1930s. *Les derniers marranes* (The Last Marranos), a 1991 film by the renowned French Jewish filmmaker and photographer Frédric Brenner, and a book of the same title made their story visible again. Eminent scholars, such as Yosef Yerushalmi, historian of conversos, and the philosopher Jacques Derrida, commented on Brenner's book and the meanings of marrano continuity. In the 1990s efforts to convert the Belmonte New Christian descendants (over a hundred people, about 10% of the total population) to Orthodoxy and to seek their support of Israel redoubled; the Jewish Agency, rabbis, and others descended on the community, whose older members, preferring to continue concealment, were not as enthusiastic about official conversion to Judaism as the younger. Scholars of converso history criticized the imposition of traditional Judaism and the demand for the eradication of secret and syncretic practices. Yirmiyahu Yovel, author of extensive studies of conversos, suggested that the community was subjected to a second "marranism," this time in hiding from Jewish Orthodoxy (2009, 386).

Nevertheless, tourism and a particular kind of Orthodoxization under the influence of the Chabad organization continued hand in hand: 2016 saw the opening of a kosher hotel in Belmonte, and Jewish papers reported the presence of Hasidim singing in the streets. Even the saga of the controversial figure Barros Basto has been revived. Although the accusations that led to his dismissal from the army had begun because of discontented members and other leaders of the new community he had formed to revitalize Judaism in Portugal, the Portuguese parliament deemed in 2012 that the charge against him was anti-Semitic and rehabilitated him posthumously to the Portuguese army. The synagogue that he had established in Porto and that continues to serve the current Porto community welcomes recent Portuguese converts to Judaism. Along with the community in Lisbon, this congregation has been designated to certify Sephardi Jews' applications for Portuguese nationality, although, ironically, its stringent requirements of Orthodox belonging make citizenship difficult to attain for converso descendants who have not returned to Judaism (Leite 2017).

In Portugal, in general, where knowledge of the Jewish past and ancestry in the blood of most Portuguese is widespread, there are many returnees to Jewish identity and/or faith who base their return on the perception of suppressed familial (and national) pasts, through formal conversion or personal acknowledgment (see Leite 2017). In Spain the recognition of the converso past and presence in the gene pool is more muted than in Portugal, although it is certainly not negligible (Flesler and Pérez Melgosa 2020). Elsewhere, there are associations, communities, and annual conferences, for example, the Brazilian Association of Descendants of Jews of the Inquisition (ABR-ADJIN), based in Minas Gerais and claiming over 1,000 members, and the Society for Crypto-Judaic Studies (SCJS) of the United States, which has well-attended yearly meetings and an active publishing arm. In the realm of letters about secret Hispanic and Latinx Jews in the United States and Latin America, testimonies, plays, poetry books, novels, young adult fiction, even children's books, such as *Abuelita's Secret Matzahs* (2005), have multiplied since the outset of individuals' and groups' visibility in the 1980s. A tremendous number of news items have circulated in Latinx Jewish and mainstream media since that time. Those and other stories have made their mark on visual culture too: in documentary films, besides Brenner's influential *Les derniers marranes*, such as Simcha Jacobovici's *Expulsion and Memory: Descendants of the Hidden Jews* (1996), Gabriela Böhm's *The Longing: Forgotten Jews of South America* (2007), the Yaron Avitov's *La Tribu Perdida de Loja* (The Lost Tribe of Loja [Peru], 2010), and Joseph Lovett's *Children of the Inquisition* (2018); and in photography books, such as the aforementioned Brenner work and Cary Herz's *New Mexico's Crypto-Jews: Image and Memory* (2007). New media, such as blogs and discussion lists, online journals, and websites and social media pages of such organizations as the SCJS, Kulanu, Shavei Israel, Name Your Roots, Reconectar, and dozens of Jewish and other genealogy and genetic ancestry testing sites and companies, have been important tools in disseminating narratives and in identity building with various political and cultural purposes.

Controversies of the Genealogical and Historical Imaginations

Clearly genealogy and blood play a tremendous role in the return of the converso to the contemporary imagination, leading to both interesting new openings and considerable controversy. Most of the current debates are around the legitimacy and authenticity of the claimants, which has precedents in early periods of converso returns to Jewish identity. Sixteenth- and seventeenth-century conversos who sought to be integrated into Jewish communities after leaving Iberia (Portugal, overwhelmingly) were often welcomed back as halakhic Jews, but at other times they faced resistance. Some of those whose families had lived for more than a generation as New Christians were able to integrate into Sephardi communities, despite having Catholicized and having lost contact with Jewish institutions and much learning. But sometimes the dualities they exhibited caused problems. This was the case, for example, in the strict Amsterdam Sephardi community of the seventeenth century, the site of a complex return to Jewish life by Portuguese and Spanish conversos; the returnees continued their Iberian culture, commerce, and faith under the watchful "tolerance" of the Dutch.[7]

Returned conversos were not always engaged in apologetics to downplay their Christian past; two of those who did not are Baruch Spinoza and Uriel da Costa, the excommunicated dissenters. Skeptics as well as believers were part of the Amsterdam community of formerly Christianized conversos and crypto-Jews, as were, for a short period in the 1600s, Sabbateans, all of whom presented simply as "Jews" to the Dutch. But the re-Judaization or fusion of the conversos with normative Sephardi communities was not seamless. The arrival, return, and integration of New Christians led to rabbinic debates also in the Ottoman Empire (Goldish 2008) with some responsae of the period also indicating refusals to integrate claimants. These rejections, though far from routine, coupled with the problematics of relying on the veracity of Inquisition records about crypto-Jewish practices, led some scholars to assert that marranos ceased to be Jews fairly quickly.[8]

The accusation of insincerity haunted Muslim and Jewish converts under the Inquisition and indigenous people in the Americas. The possibility of false conversion, dual allegiance, or syncretic beliefs posed a threat to conversion as a tool of conquest and state formation on both sides of the Atlantic. A similar charge, albeit with a different motivation, could fall on those who considered their ancestors to be victims of the Inquisition. Latinx and Latin Americans who have asserted crypto-Jewish identity in the Americas have had supporters as well as detractors among religious leaders and scholars. Some rabbis and congregations have refused to include descendants who seek to be part of halakhically Jewish communities (as documented in part, for example, in Böhm's 2007 film about Latin American conversions). Many in the United States, however, have backed and even espoused the cause for returnees' admittance into normative Judaism, allowing more liberal conversions.

In terms of academic research on the contemporary period, most specialists, who are from outside these groups, though some are not (e.g., Richard Santos, author of "Chicanos of Jewish Descent in Texas" [1983]), have been sympathetic to the idea of remnant communities and practices. They have collected evidence and delineated elements of crypto-Jewish identity based on oral reports and have verified the claims. But others have made opposing arguments that undermine the authenticity of the oral lore and claimants' stories, attributing the assertions of crypto-Jewish custom and identity to Protestant influence, pressure and suggestion from Ashkenazi Jewish historians, or, in the United States, the desire of people of color for racial upward mobility by means of a whitened Jewish identity.[9] These groups and the academics who advanced (or, according to some, created) their cause objected to the charge that some of those who returned to converso identity exchanged one form of whiteness and blood discourse (an oxymoronic "pure Spanishness") for another (white Jewishness). This intention has been attributed by some scholars to Latinx, Chicanx, and Hispanas/os en masse (Carroll 2002; Neulander 1994, 1996).

Given the nationwide demonization of Latinx and Hispanic communities in the United States, distancing the association with the "Mexican" (standing in for Spanish or Latinx/Hispanic) or the long-denigrated Native and aligning with nonthreatening and more prestigious Iberianness and Jewishness is advantageous in the harsh landscape of U.S. racial hierarchy. The charge about whitening makes sense to outsiders who know the history of New Mexican racialization, historical Hispano claims to (noble) Spanishness (Nieto-Phillips 2004), and more generally the high cost of nonwhite racialization in the United States. However, ascribing such goals to those who maintain entirely different motivations implies a manipulation of facts or fanciful delusion, which crypto-Jewish-identifying individuals find patronizing and hurtful (see, e.g., Valerio 2001; Society for Crypto-Judaic Studies, n.d.). Moreover, although the claim to "Spanish" (therefore white) identity is strong in the Southwest, many, including those who claim crypto-Jewish descent, acknowledge not only whiteness but also multiple origins; in academic studies, many or most have asserted multi-ethnoracial backgrounds, including especially Native ancestry (Kunin 2009, 62–63).

Further, some scholars have pointed out the irony in the charge of whitewashing Latin identity through Jewishness in the context of the Southwest, which differs from much of the mainstream concepts of U.S. ethnoracial formations. Reporting on the NPR program *Hidden Jews of Mexico*, Victor Valle wrote in a *Los Angeles Times* article that "conversos subvert the myth [that] the 'sangre pura,' or pure Castilian blood, runs in the veins of New Mexico's Hispanics." Adding to the implication that the Jewish element detracts from rather than coincides with whiteness, Valle argued that the show's content was "an important reminder and negation of what the late Carey McWilliams called the Spanish 'fantasy heritage' of the Southwest. Unfortunately, the myth lives on in our midst in those who would pretend to make themselves Hispanic, or European, and ultimately more palatable" (1988, n.p.). This view does not negate the fact that most Jews in the United States identify and/or are identified as white; however, in the context of Spanishness in the Americas, Sephardi heritage changes the terms of Hispano (Christian) whiteness. In terms of racial thinking, it is also ironic that Latinx are accused of whitening themselves through Jewishness, when genetic ancestry testing has (albeit controversially and ideologically) located Jewish origins in the Middle East (Ostrer 2012). For white supremacists "the Jew's ancient secretive mask has finally forever been lifted by recent advances in genetic science, and the farce of the Jew masquerading as the White Man ended once and for all" (Parfitt and Egorova 2006, 41). The very technology that traces Jews to the Middle East can de-whiten them, with vastly varying implications.

Skepticism has continued, however. For some scholars, professional ethics and the verifiability of findings as well as the dissociation of Jewishness from blood logics, biologization, and race are the main motivations for questioning crypto-Jewish survival. Sometimes these intentions come at the cost of understanding the complexity of the intentions and practices of the people in question. Another motivation is the attempt to reveal underlying racism against Native and Latinx identities by subjects who deny these heritages in favor of the Jewish one (Carroll 2002; Neulander 1994, 1996). In addition, Aviva Ben-Ur, historian of Sephardi Jewry in the Americas, points to a lack of concern on the part of "the Ashkenazic mediators of the modern crypto-Jewish movement" over the stereotyping of Jews articulated by some descendants in interviews. Ben-Ur further suggests that the prodding by some scholars of Jewish identity in some Hispanics is an expression of an exoticizing Jewish American interest in heroic Sephardi continuity and a means of remedying contemporary concerns about assimilation and loss of identity (2009, 186–87). At the same time, Ben-Ur surmises, the Jewish American community's interest in crypto-Jewish returns signals the expansion of the definition of Jewishness to include multiple and mixed races (189). This particular change is not established, given the ongoing colorism within Jewish communities in the Americas, which might partly explain the exclusion of some returning or "new" Jews or crypto-Jewish descent claims (Daniel and Greenberg 2019; Kaye/Kantrowitz 2007).

These debates matter. Returning converso descendants—whether they are perceived, variously, as courageous seekers, carriers of buried stories, exotic remnants, suspect interlopers, aspirational fabulists, or unlikely new candidates to "increase Israel"—raise a familiar issue about Jewish peoplehood and its basis in blood and culture. Because the genealogical imagination within and outside the Jewish world is so charged with regard to the boundaries of inclusion and the role of biology in/over culture, the legitimacy of ancient-identity claims and the concept of authenticity frequently come to the fore. For some, genealogical returns help reinstate the idea of Jewish peoplehood as one based on blood, that is, biology and descent, rather than religious and cultural belonging and affiliation. This assumption conjures the discourse of race, especially in the Americas, where racialization is key to the production and maintenance of power relations; but it also brings up the relation to Nazi and other fascist racializations. Critics also argue that "the logic of *limpieza de sangre* is revived "in demanding evidence of unbroken or unmediated descent," which evinces "how perdurable a racialist understanding of identity remains" (Freedman 2010, 197).[10]

Indeed, on the other side of the Atlantic, the potential perils of asserting continuous Jewish descent, thereby discursively invalidating conversion, were revealed in the reemergence of secretive groups such as the *dönme* in Turkey's public agenda, which coincided approximately with the coming out of crypto-Jews in the Southwest. The *dönme* have been scapegoated because of their preconversion status as Jews and their presumed postconversion deception and dissimulation, even though most Jewish identities and practices have transformed, diminished, or disappeared among Sabbateans of today's Turkey, many of whom have Iberian converso origins. The *dönme*, also known as Salonicans, practiced their faith (which sought to reform Judaism, contra Orthodoxy) in secrecy for centuries. Most of their descendants, whether practicing or not, concealed their origins and have largely assimilated into the Sunni majority. Yet, as we will see in Chapter 5, they have been targeted widely in racial terms as a fifth column of conspiratorial Jews passing as Muslims. They are an exemplary but not unique case of how the presumed duality and duplicity of the convert can persist over time under colonialism, conquest, war, racial states, religious persecution, and other situations involving forced or instrumental conversion, causing much suspicion within the social body and persecution by the state, sometimes for centuries.

In such genetic thinking, the idea of Jewish inconvertibility is unleashed. Conversion is ignored: Once a Jew, always a Jew, with or without Judaism or Jewish identity, knowledge, or practice. This is different from what the philosopher Hannah Arendt observed about the transition from anti-Judaism, which was based on religion in pre-Enlightenment Europe, to anti-Semitism as a racial discourse thereafter, in which unchanging and naturalized features defined Jews. Whereas previously Jews could convert (albeit, as we know, to varying effects), in the race thinking of Europe's secular era, there was no converting out of Jewishness defined as racial: "Jews had been able to escape from Judaism into conversion; from Jewishness there was no escape" (Arendt 1973, 87). But the Iberian mistrust in Jewish and Muslim conversions and its disastrous consequences are elided here, as it is in much European and Latin American thought that posits the European Enlightenment period, rather than the Iberian medieval and imperial one, as the fount of coloniality and racialist thinking (Boyarin 2009; Mignolo 2002; Quijano 2000; Shohat and Stam 2012). Whatever the context, we can see how returning to ancient identities through genealogically or genetically claimed remote ancestry can imply that there is an incontrovertible essence to Jewishness, one transmitted intact through the body and through the centuries, a notion explored in its widely varying facets in my analyses.

But the identification of biological descent does not appear in a predictable or homogeneous fashion. And it is not simply external to the Jewish world in the context of racism or genocide but embedded *within* it. First, the descent- and kinship-based definition of inclusion in Jewish law, that is, the matrilineal requirement, has a biological basis, one that has recently been charged with the implication of racism in a British court case (Graham 2014). The requirement of matrilineal Jewishness can also become a problem for non-Orthodox converts, though recently even the Israeli rabbinate has resorted to DNA testing for the verification of Jewishness. Moreover, forms of Judaism may ethnicize Jewishness beyond religion, but blood-based (i.e., kinship-based) definitions of identity have also been seen widely in other Jewish thought, including strategic uses of "racial thinking" and "blood logic," especially in the modern period and in the conception of modern Jewish peoplehood and Zionism (Abu El Haj 2012; Anidjar 2014; Biale 2009; Glenn 2002; Hart 2009; Kahn 2013; Pianko 2015; Sand 2009).

In her study of Sigmund Freud's *Moses and Monotheism*, Eliza Slavet also delineates a "racial thinking" beyond racism. She refers to "racial fever," which is "the irrepressible desire of individuals and communities to define themselves and others through genealogy, to discover (and sometimes invent) ancestral memories that can somehow explain the tensions and compulsions of the present and to reconstruct and return to these narratives as if they were indisputable history and palpable facts" (2009, 6). The equation of genealogy with race is far from uncontroversial, but the genealogical basis of Jewishness is considered a constant: "For at least fifteen centuries, certain individuals have been defined as Jewish because of the belief that they have genealogically inherited Jewishness" (167). New self-definitions based on rediscovered genealogy, as with the contemporary crypto-Jewish descent claims, acknowledge gaps and twists in the genealogical thread and create a new genealogical memory that takes into account the unknowns and the breaches, but they still emphasize continuity and contemporary subjects as remnants.

Genetic genealogy has added new twists to the controversies around the biologization and consolidation, and returns of identities. Although genetic scientists such as Harry Ostrer, who has asserted that Jews constitute a genetically coherent group, distance themselves from eugenics and spurious "race science," the nationalist conclusions are presented as uncontroversial: Jews are a people because there is some genetic evidence that many have ancient origins in the Levant (Ostrer 2012). As Susan Martha Kahn observes in her critique of Ostrer, genetic evidence is made to coincide with the Jewish oral tradition of common origins in the Middle East (Kahn 2013), with the consequence of biologization of group identity.[11] It is not an accident that the greater visibility of converso descendants in the Jewish and the wider world coincides with the rise of genetic studies that seek to prove that Jews are a people indigenous to the Middle East, with the obvious geopolitical conclusions legitimizing the claims to Israel/Palestine (Abu El Haj 2012; Kahn 2013).

Iberian and Latin American claims to crypto-Jewish descent based on genetic testing or deep genealogical research also confirm the peoplehood of the Jews and are meant to prove the oral traditions—the familial and communal conjectures about secret Jewish origins and customs of Luso-Hispanic Catholics on both sides of the Atlantic. Sometimes, however, ancestry research retrofits individuals' sense of being different, despite the lack of familial lore about different roots. At other times, the findings are simply the result of a purposive molecular inquiry, such as the quest for Jewish forebears to acquire Spanish or Portuguese citizenship, as with the case of many Latin Americans and U.S. Latinx applying for nationality on the basis of genealogical and genetic research.[12] Ancestry research seemingly "finds" a variety of "lost" particular histories.

Participants in such pursuits to locate hidden origins vary greatly in their knowledge of and affinity with Jewishness and are drawn into politics, sometimes in ways unbeknown to them, when they are hailed as returnees. As we can see, individual identifications with Jewish roots are mediated not only by cultural and scientific discourses but also by states. Spain and Portugal offer the opportunity for nationality based on Sephardi *descent* and not current identification as Jewish.

The demographic and political interests of Israel have also been playing a much larger role in the visibility of and support for crypto-Jewish descendants.

The Bnei Anusim of the Luso-Hispanic world are seen as being part of "the next stage of Zionism," with a Knesset caucus dedicated to the "reconnection with the descendants of Spanish and Portuguese communities" (Perry 2016, n.p.). Like the older Kulanu and Shavei Israel, newer organizations are dedicated to promoting the Jewish ancestry of a putative "tens of millions" descendants in the Americas and funding their and others' restoration to the Jewish people or the Jewish State.[13] In the United States these efforts supplement earlier ones to connect Latinx and Jews on the basis of their common immigrant status (see Kandiyoti 2012). This putative analogy between "two immigrant groups" has changed to a discourse of intersection of Latinx and Jews by means of Sephardi identity in mainstream organized Jewish American life, in which Sephardis are usually marginalized. "Latino-Jewish" events have multiplied across synagogues and Jewish organizations in the United States in the past few years, and they now frequently include previously absent references to converso returnees, Jewish blood, and Jewish-Christian (often without reference to the Muslim) coexistence in Iberia, with efforts even extending to bridge building with Israel-supporting Christian Zionist Latinx.

The quest for the archaic can consolidate a discourse of authentic origins, which is why returns have often been viewed as regressions. States can impose returns on unwilling subjects to form a purer national identity, or they can recruit willing returnees to displace or exclude the unwanted. When the historical and genealogical imaginations are joined for such purposes, they recuperate and reinforce identitarian closures from a version of the past that can be superimposed on the present and deployed to exclude and expropriate. On an individual level, returns through selective genealogy (Zerubavel 2012) and curated pasts can have divergent consequences: While biologizing and essentializing identity, they can also overturn presently existing exclusionary identity categories. For example, the widely used ancestry testing results can be deployed to affirm identities that have been delegitimized, suppressed, or lost in the catastrophes of slavery and war (see, e.g., Nash 2004; Nelson 2008, 2016). These include Jewish identities of Christians from Iberia and the Americas and Sabbateans and Muslims from Turkey, whose revelations can have significant social, cultural, and political consequences. As Derrida has explained, "The break with tradition, uprooting, the inaccessibility of histories, amnesia, indecipherability and so on: all of these unleash the genealogical drive" (1998, 59–60). This drive can propel new kinship and tribal discourses that are as liberating as they are exclusionary. Whatever the tendency of such stories, their reappearance in recent times is a testament to the interest in returns and the need for narratives, such as those we will encounter in this book, to examine how historical and genealogical consciousness together shape identities in the present.

Rather than briefly cover a large swath of all the literary writing of recent decades on past conversos and their present-day descendants, I have chosen a smaller number of texts and contexts in which Sephardi history and culture and the converso diasporas are connected and converge with other histories explicitly. I did not aim to be exhaustive, and I only included texts in the four languages of my competence. More work certainly needs to be done, especially in the Lusophone and other contemporary contexts.

Chapter 1 provides the background to the themes and tropes about conversos in contemporary literature, many of which are found in the same or other forms in fiction and thought since the nineteenth century. I begin by explaining how contemporary thinkers and scholars have viewed and deconstructed crypto-Jews in particular ways, whether as religious martyrs, "cultural commuters" (Melammed 2010), or resistant secularists. The crypto-Jew as a figure of internal division and analogous status to contemporary assimilation is part of this discussion. It is important to understand something about current scholars' approaches, not least because novelists draw on these and enter into dialogue with them. I also provide an overview of common tropes in the representation of crypto-Jewishness in French thought and in literature from the Americas and Europe since the nineteenth century, the examination ranging in scope from national literary contexts and genres and the cultural import of lineage and genealogy to "the crypto-Jewish body" and the uncanny. The ideas and tropes reviewed in Chapter 1 will help position the representations of converso lives in the rest of the book.

In Chapter 2 I focus on U.S. Latinx literature's particular investment in Sephardi and crypto-Jewish storytelling, which is fused with borderland, diasporic, and indigenous histories. Studying mainly Achy Obejas and Kathleen Alcalá but touching on other writers from both Latinx and

Sephardi studies perspectives, I explore how absent archives of conversos in the Americas are replaced by speculative and fictional ones. I argue that Latinx writers include conversos as one of the many entanglements of borderlands and transamerican spaces. In Obejas's novel, Cuban exile discourses are refracted, uniquely, through converso history. These fates and their discourses are both overlapping and analogical. Self-division, assimilation, and other themes examined in Chapter 1 cross with exile figurations of homeland, race, and belonging. For Alcalá, the contentious issue of *mestizaje* and the representation of the historic U.S.-Mexico borderlands make a place for converso history. Genealogy is fraught, as we will see in almost every chapter, when documentation is scant, and authenticity becomes a battleground in the texts analyzed in both Chapters 2 and 3.

In Chapter 3 the central texts are Doreen Carvajal's 2012 memoir *The Forgetting River* and José Manuel Fajardo's 2010 novel, *Mi nombre es Jamaica* (My Name Is Jamaica). The works concern the claiming of converso and Jewish identity by an American of Costa Rican background (Carvajal) and a fictional Catholic Spaniard (Fajardo), though much of Chapter 3 focuses on Fajardo's novel after a briefer analysis of Carvajal's memoir. Both protagonists, the fictional and the nonfictional, return to sites of ongoing and erased Sephardi memory and assert Jewish belonging. Carvajal's memoir is an ancestry quest reminiscent of other contemporary returnees, whereas Fajardo's project is a metafictional one that questions the nature of such returns, particularly in the Spanish context, with astute and creative forays into convergences of overlapping Atlantic, indigenous, and Sephardi histories. The discourse of blood, common to most of the works in this book, helps constitute what I call paramemories, an intersection also addressed by Alcalá, as I discuss in Chapter 2. Key issues are the claims of descent from conversos in the context of state philo-Sephardism in Spain's recent reconfiguration of official memory and the definition of Jewishness in terms of suffering and martyrdom.

The selective nature of the genealogical imagination is also highlighted in Chapter 4, in which I discuss the Sephardi Guatemalan author Victor Perera and the eminent French intellectual Edgar Morin, who, as normative Sephardis of Salonican background, choose to position themselves as marranos in their autobiographical and essayistic writing, an impulse common in Morin's French intellectual milieu since the 1990s. This penchant of the normative Sephardi to identify as crypto-Jewish, in a seeming reversal of the identity quests in previous chapters, is born of a desire to resist ethnic, religious, and national categories. The crypto-Jew serves as a means of overturning these categories, albeit from within a set of Sephardi experiences and worldviews that are essential to what Morin calls *poly-enracinement* (polyrootedness).

This suggestive concept complements my emphasis on convergences and entanglements afforded by the engagement of crypto-Jewish histories, which I emphasize in every chapter of *The Converso's Return*. Such entanglements include, in the final chapter, crypto-Jewish–Muslim–*dönme*–Turkish encounters, which are less commonly found in literature than all the others. I read historical novels by Elif Shafak and Yeshim Ternar about conversos and the *dönme* in Spain, Amsterdam, Istanbul, and Montreal, written in Turkish and English, respectively, in light of European images of the "terrible Turk," claims about the conspiracies of Jews and Muslims against Christians in literary history, and images of conversos and Sabbateans in Ottoman and Turkish culture. I also draw attention to Muslim-Jewish and Morisco-Judeoconverso solidarities and convergences as well as converso-Sabbatean continuities that are rarely addressed in literature. Chapters 4 and 5, by connecting the eastward and westward routes, reattach the Luso-Hispanic world and the Middle East via crypto-Jewish routes.

(CHAPTER 1)

DOUBLES, DISGUISES, SPLITS
Conversos in Modern Literature and Thought

SOMETHING IN THE PRESENT MOMENT has returned us to the converso, a presumed extinct identity with few remains. The history and the trope of the converso appear in so many different ways that they seem to work like a linguistic shifter, taking on different significations according to the perspectives and contexts in which they appear. Stereotypes abound: Often conversos are abject, tragic marrano victims, as they are still called, or else they are chameleonic and multilingual "port Jew" types.

Outside of fixed and clichéd representations, there are two principal overlapping ways in which the histories and identities of conversos, until recently presumed to be a long-past phenomenon, have appeared in recent decades in contemporary culture, scholarship, and literature. On the one hand, the converso appears as a figuration of a divided subjectivity that is the hallmark of Western modernity, and, on the other, the converso is a representative victim of oppression and intolerance and lives in secrecy. As emblems of internal division, the converso and the crypto-Jew are mourned *or* celebrated as figures of a universal subjectivity in which "we are our own foreigners" and "strangers to ourselves" (Kristeva 1991, 181). As abject victims, they are embodied cautionary tales about and illustrations of the ideological bases of past religious extremism, racism, and nationalism, which can also serve as analogies to and explanations for contemporary repressions.

In this chapter, I consider these and other generative and wide-ranging tropes and ideas in literature since the nineteenth century and in recent scholarship and thought; these are relevant to the afterlives of this history and the body of writing I study in the next chapters. The synthesis of historical, literary, and theoretical ideas on the subject will be useful, it is hoped, to both specialists and nonspecialists.

Converso writings from the sixteenth and seventeenth centuries have been studied extensively. Part of the synthesis here includes contemporary scholars' perceptions of that period and their characterization of converso consciousness and identity. Importantly, these recent academic investigations have also served contemporary fiction and memoir writers, especially those featured in this study, who have constructed their narratives based on and departing from the work of historians. The larger focus of this chapter is on the less examined modern period and tropes and themes in fiction, scholarship, and criticism in which the converso is a subject and productive "concept." As others have observed, there is scarcely a means of or justification for fixing ideas about "protean and heterogenous" (Ferrutta 2013, 53) crypto-Jews and conversos through the ages. Instead, I present a landscape of ideas about and literary history of the converso past without specifying a particular representation as definitive. But I do turn at the end of the chapter to the particular writings of converso identity that produce a new set of questions and convergent histories and identities.

Doubles, Disguises, and Splits

Prominent in the conceptualizations of conversos by recent historians and literary scholars of the sixteenth to eighteenth centuries is the duality of converso and crypto-Jewish status and consciousness. According to many specialists, the internal division (vis-à-vis religions, belongings, and subjectivities) that distinguishes early modern conversos is partly due to the public profession of the licit faith and the private, secret, enduring allegiances to the outlawed one and also owing to the role of discrimination and persecution in producing duality, whatever the actual loyalties. Their sincerity questioned by Old Christians, Jews "threatened to undermine the salvific power of conversion whenever they refused, reneged, or worse revealed themselves to have converted under false pretenses" (Shoulson 2013, 3). Conversos, whether practicing crypto-Jews or not, were suspect under these conditions of mistrust no matter what their "real" practices and beliefs, because their actual or presumed affective ties to and memories of the original religion posed a great threat.

Drawing on Jean-Paul Sartre's argument that it is anti-Semitism that creates "the Jew," Solange Alberro has asserted that the Inquisition created crypto-Jews through constant reminders of heritage (Alberro 2001). For David Graizbord, author of the tellingly titled *Souls in Dispute*, "The central predicament of early modern judeoconversos . . . lay in the fact that they inhabited a cultural threshold . . . at once a boundary and a crossroads between the Christian and Jewish worlds" (2003, 2). Yosef Yerushalmi, perhaps the most influential historian of conversos, argued for the modernity of the marrano partly on this basis. "One dimension of Marranism," he argued, was "existential": "This was the duality, the profound tearing-apart, that divided their life, and which I continue to think is a contemporary dimension. The Marranos were perhaps the first Jews who had to live in two radically different universes at once, with all the inner tensions and conflicts that resulted from this" (quoted in Birnbaum 2008, 341). Anita Novinsky, scholar of Brazilian conversos, claimed that *marranismo* is less about practicing secret Judaism and more about being a universal outsider (2001, 226).

The crypto-Jew or the marrano also appears in Yirmiyahu Yovel's work as the embodiment of a secularizing, modern subjectivity in tension with itself. Yovel explains that the "semi-christianized Judaizing Marranos were split between two [incompatible] rival traditions and paths to salvation . . . [and were] living in an irresolvable ambivalence and tension" (2009, 87) that is characteristic of modern selfhood. Because the inner self became a problem, "Marranos unwittingly sowed the seeds of a new principle—*inner conscience*" (88; emphasis in the original), the nonintegral split self (343–44), and led the charge on religious skepticism, atheism, pluralism, and proto-universalism. This particular characterization of converts is found also in the different context of Ottoman Sabbatean history, which, depending on the perspective, accuses or credits Sabbatean communities with significant participation in secularization and liberalization and the demise of the Ottoman caliphate (see M. D. Baer 2009; Şişman 2015).

Natalia Muchnik is more specific about divided beings and loyalties. She attributes crypto-Jewish characteristics to universalizing ideas about selfhood.

> The crypto-Jew developed a personal style by making use of alterity, discreet and occasionally deliberate omission of detail, and compromise. . . . Should the Judaizers only be—and be conceived of as—"dual" beings with a life of perpetual inner conflict? Or were they not, rather, the prototype of human beings torn between contradictory identities? In fact, however, what they really were was an extreme case of the fragmentation of self and, hence, a proof of the illusion of the self's indivisible unity. (Muchnik 2011, 170)

For Yerushalmi and so many other scholars, crypto-Jews and conversos "stand out as perhaps the first modern *Jews*" (Yerushalmi 1981, 44; emphasis added). The tendency of scholars to define new conversos and crypto-Jews as well as their descendants as Jews, no matter what the source of their Jewishness (in faith and/or peoplehood) and whatever evidence exists (frequently, Inquisition records), has been criticized as "essentialist" (Graizbord and Stuczynski 2011) in more recent scholarship. Others have suggested more complicated notions than either blood or faith to understand the formation of crypto-Jewishness. In Yovel's assessment, being a marrano was not simply a secret way of being Jewish but a "new way of being other," in which former Jews and their descendants joined the Christian social body but remained other within it, especially when, as New Christians, they rose to enviable positions (Yovel 2009, 72) and became targets. "Identity passions" propelled by *limpieza de sangre* statutes also became instruments of class war and uplift so that, Yovel points out, even Cervantes's lowly Sancho Panza thinks he has the right to be a governor, because he is an Old Christian and of pure blood (Yovel 2009, 74).

For Yovel and others, conversos were distinguished by duality, because the two parts were "in competition" (Yovel 2009, 87). In the mystical verses singing of deserts and the "loving fire's light" by João Pinto Delgado, who published his works in 1627 in the safer city of Rouen, France, rather than in his own Lisbon, Yovel reads "a Jewish heart" that "is implanted into its Christian body" (327). Pinto Delgado's poetic references to Moses's desert and the burning bush are seen through Spanish imagery. In much of the substantial seventeenth-century literary output of the post-converso community that returned to Judaism, authors, writing in Spanish and Portuguese, relied on Iberian rhetorical and literary conventions of their time, from Baroque tropes to the reproduction of Catholic moralizing in Jewish instruction meant to educate other returning conversos, in choices that Yosef Kaplan calls "antagonistic mimesis" (quoted in van den Boer 2000). Nathan Wachtel's work about the Americas also emphasizes "dual sincerities" (2001, 164) involved in the Christianization of Judaism (with their "Saint Moses" and apocalyptic language) and the de-Christianizing of Catholicism (refusal of image worship and sometimes pork). But Wachtel distinguishes "Marrano religiosity," stressing above all its syncretic aspects, from crypto-Judaism, that is, the secret maintenance of an unadulterated Jewish tradition (2001).

According to some of these historians, the competing elements of the duality or the hidden syncretism coexisted in the heart, the mind, and the soul of the converso and were threatening to normative Christians as well as to Jews. In Portugal, where New Christians formed a group strong in numbers (10–20% of the total population) and influence after the forced conversions of 1497, the sixteenth-century "religious life of the Judaizing Marranos had taken up a heterodox content. It was impregnated with Christian elements while missing essential Jewish ones. . . . To outsiders, nearly all Portuguese New Christians were Jews; but to the Jews, even the Judaizers were questionable brethren," with practices not "strictly Jewish," despite their "persistent *esperanza*" (Yovel 2009, 204). Across the generations, New Christians developed a "Marrano theology," which was "meager but persistent" in its fragments of retention and its de-Christianizing of language and the Bible (229). But they also Christianized, not just in Portugal but also in Spain, although they emphasized an "internal" Christianity, "attained through the interior self," and insisted "on personal conscience and subjectivity—their inherited Marrano speciality—as the locus of religious truth" (244, 245). In Portugal the New Christians were a *nação*, or "nation," apart, as they came to be called in the middle of the sixteenth century; they were so numerous and prominent that they became associated with Portugueseness itself to non-Portuguese.

The New Christians who chose to leave Portugal, mostly in the mid-sixteenth century, had been relatively free, unlike in Spain, to retain a form of Jewish practice until the establishment of the Inquisition in 1536, which compelled migration and refuge in Western Europe or in the Muslim world.

Outside the Iberian peninsula, the members of the *nação* had to (re)integrate into Jewish communities by publicly proving their purification, "self-transformation," and denunciation of Iberia, to which they were not allowed to return and faced years of penance and exclusion from the Jewish community if they did (Graizbord 2003, 3, 72). Especially as New Christians but even as returned Jews, they had to suppress parts of themselves or risk the pain of exclusion. Even where Judaism was not outlawed, as in Bayonne and Bordeaux, the wary former conversos did not build a synagogue for a long time until after their settlement (Melammed 2010). In some places, including the Americas, the tradition of secrecy and dissimulation continued even in some conditions of relative safety in more recent times.

In contemporary scholarly studies and in fiction, the marranos, as figures of masks, secrecies, and internal divisions, are also "cultural commuters" (Glick 1997), "shuttling" between Christian and Jewish worlds (J. Schorsch 2009, 1: 63–67), languages, and perspectives (Melammed 2004). Their intermediary status as financiers, traders, tax collectors, and brokers for the Spanish and Portuguese empires was amplified by a distinct rise to important positions, at least until the mid-sixteenth century in Portugal, before the persecutions and greater dangers. The well-networked Portuguese New Christians were also associated with expansion and the slave trade as well as with slaveholding, a matter of controversy (see, e.g., Israel 2002; J. Schorsch 2009) that is rarely addressed in the recent literary return to this history.

In another realm, conversos marked Spain's seventeenth-century golden age in letters. Yovel argues that, unlike earlier influential Spanish critics such as Américo Castro and Angel Alcalá, the renowned Spanish novelists, playwrights, and mystics of the Golden Age of the seventeenth century with known or surmised converso roots were no longer really Jews. But Yovel maintains that there was a distinct converso (rather than Jewish) approach to life and faith that was characterized by irony, distance from and skepticism about official religion, and a tendency toward the personal and mystical; these attitudes provided the grounds for the creativity with which they were associated in Iberia (Yovel 2009, 240–43).

As we can see in this brief overview of what is a vast body of contemporary scholarship, such influential recent interpretations of converso history attribute intermediary, dual (or syncretic, depending on the perspective), ambivalent, ambiguous, and performative characteristics to the converts and their descendants. These aspects are also presented as explanatory factors in conversos' ability to survive, cope, and sometimes even thrive in multiple contexts and situations. Examples abound of conversos carrying double names and even wholly double identities: one for their home country and one or more for travels abroad for work (including forbidden travels to Iberia). Even though crypto-Jews have long been associated with suffering and martyrdom because of the persecutions and murders they endured, converso identity as a whole has been endowed with more agency in recent interpretations that have emphasized necessary and inevitable "cultural commuting." Scholarship on "port Jews" (Sorkin 1999) and Atlantic conversos has positioned the (mostly Portuguese) converso *nação* as a multisited and closely networked initiator of "the tentacular process known today as globalization" (Wachtel 2013, 2), which deployed family and community connections from Livorno and Salonica to the Caribbean and Mexico to advance commerce.

Much contemporary fiction also features recent historians' assessments of conversos' constant resort to secrecy, dissimulation, and continuous self-production. These images tend to focus on the dangers and grief that persecution and hiding produced and on the "worldliness" and entangled multiplicities of converso outlook and customs. In a dissenting view the historian Miriam Bodian qualifies this set of representations, or what Yovel calls "Marrano patterns" in his earlier book, *Spinoza and Other Heretics* (1989). In her critique of current Euro-American scholarship on marranism, which questions its formulation of converso consciousness as a radical response to repression, Bodian argues that although some (ex-)conversos exhibited radical or alternative thinking, others became traditionalists in their writing and lives and did not exhibit "split religious identities," "a metaphysical skepticism," "opposition to official doctrine," or "equivocation" (Yovel 1989, ix–x). Bodian also suggests that their inner quest might have been informed by other factors than the converso experience, for example, Erasmianism and humanism. She further observes that the identification of some thinkers as being converso, such as Montaigne, whose status in this regard is moot despite some converso lineage, is a stretch and the mark of a desire to find "ideological ancestors" (Bodian 2017, 3). Bodian challenges here the totalizing view of conversos as a particular illustration of resistance or ideology without dismissing the notion that some thinking by (ex-)conversos developed along the lines suggested by Yerushalmi, Yovel, and others.

Conversion and Contemporary Assimilation

The "converso condition" as signaled by many, though not all, contemporary historians has shaped much contemporary literary work of the kind I study in *The Converso's Return*, most likely because authors, whether of converso descent or not, have also been exposed to the main ideas of the historical scholarship. But just as important, the themes of divided or multiple selves and survival under repression, rather than the admission of extinction or claims of adherence to absolute identities (steadfast secret Jewishness *or* forgetful assimilation), are compelling for the literary and social imagination. The mixing of official and occluded practices, the alienation from more than one bounded identity, and the need for protective passing (e.g., as a "pure Christian") have all resonated with contemporary authors and thinkers who have gone beyond the imaginative representation of the past in traditional historical novels and deployed the troubled multiplicity of the Iberian converts as cautionary analogies to the conditions under modernity's social regimes.

The parallel between historical conversos and more recent Jews and other minority groups rests on the analogy between hidden and illegitimate identities under the Inquisition and the homogenizing modern, secularized nation-state's requirement of assimilation. The latter regime, like the Inquisition, albeit in quite different ways, drives unofficial and nonmajority faiths, nationalities, ethnicities, and genders into the private sphere and compels hiding and, when possible, "passing" in the public sphere. In the West and in the Ottoman Empire, the French Revolution, the Tanzimat reform period, and Emancipation were decisive grand-scale events that changed the social life of some minorities. Many Jews, along with others, chose to largely relinquish or minimize their practices, beliefs, and identities to claim, variously, new economic and political identities as Westerners, civilized Europeans, citizens (rather than subjects) with potential for upward mobility, atheists, freethinkers, Masons, or passionate socialists and communists. Crypto-Jews and conversos, seen as largely extinct or disappeared, should have had little significance in these new formulations and practices of belonging and assimilation, but their history did not lie dormant.

Already in 1897, at the First Zionist Congress in Basel, Max Nordau, the influential author and Zionist, unfavorably likened the "emancipated Jew" to marranos.

> The emancipated Jew is insecure in his relations with his fellow-beings, timid with strangers, suspicious even toward the secret feeling of his friends. His best powers are exhausted in the suppression, or at least in the difficult concealment of his own real character. For he fears that this character might be recognized as Jewish, and he has never the satisfaction of showing himself as he is in all his thoughts and sentiments. *He becomes an inner cripple, and externally unreal*, and thereby always ridiculous and hateful to all higher feeling men, as is everything that is unreal. . . . In this way *there arises a new Marrano, who is worse than the old.* The latter had an idealistic direction—a secret desire for truth or a heartbreaking distress of conscience, and they often sought for pardon and purification through Martyrdom. The new Marranos leave Judaism with rage and bitterness, but in their innermost heart, although not acknowledged by themselves, they carry with them their own humiliation, their own dishonesty, and hatred also toward Christianity which has forced them to lie. I think with horror of the future development of this race of new Marranos, who are normally sustained by no tradition and whose soul is poisoned by hostility toward their own and strange blood, and whose self-respect is destroyed through the ever present consciousness of a fundamental lie. (Nordau 1897, 60–61; emphasis added)

In the vituperative rhetoric of Nordau, who here hurls the marrano metaphor as an insult, we see the familiar anti-Diaspora bent of Zionist thinking. Nordau creates both a parallel and a contrast through this vision of crypto-Jews as "often" seeking martyrdom and emancipated (or assimilated) Jews as a horribly damaged and fraudulent "race."

About a century later, Sephardi and other European thinkers, including Edgar Morin, referred to this phenomenon of assimilation into non-Jewish communities, societies, and ideologies as *marranisme*, but to opposite ends. As we will see in Chapter 4, Morin prefers to describe this phenomenon as secularization rather than assimilation, providing the examples of the early modern Livornese and their influence on other Jews wherever they settled after Tuscany, from Salonica to Tunis. Morin calls them "neo-Marranos" (and *judéo-gentils*, or Judeo-Gentiles) because they "were secularized rather than Christianized" in their Western dress, shaven beards, Italian language, and university education, though they maintained endogamous marriage practices and practiced religion lightly. In this, Morin partly coincides with fiction writers but also with such historians as Yovel and Wachtel. They understand conversos and their legacy not as obscure vestiges of something old and forsaken, serving as a dire warning, a role model of long-standing faithfulness, or else a prototype for abject, tormented inauthenticity. Instead, conversos present as part and parcel of secularizing modernity. Wachtel, for example, concludes that the contradictions in converso practice, theology, and worldview contributed to the emergence of modernity and the idea of nation as a secularized one, resting on moral obligations, ancestry, solidarity, and memory rather than religion.

In the nonfictional work of Morin, as with many of the novels I examine, these views on Iberian Jewish converts as modernity's ushers appear together with the concept of "marranos as metaphor," to borrow the title of Elaine Marks's volume (1996). As we saw in the Introduction, metaphorization dominates especially in contemporary Francophone and Hispanophone *marranisme* and *marranismo* but also in other contexts. Literary critics have noted the tendency of fiction writers to have the converso stand in for and figure as an aspect of contemporary concerns. Erin Graff Zivin explains this succinctly: "The converso is the body on which the broader values and preoccupations of the writer and his culture can be inscribed" (2008, 120).

In the narratives I examine, crypto-Jews are also figures of undocumented but plausible overlaps of histories. Most of the crossings and convergences that are the subject of the Latinx, Spanish, French, and Turkish narratives are born of repression, not of *convivencia* or hybridity. As such, they also serve as metaphors for the tendency of social and political regimes to pave the way to multiplicity on the one hand and, on the other, to cruelly shatter it. We will see how narratives about conversos and crypto-Jews are instructive in their contradictory ways of exclusion and expulsion. The abolishment of difference (e.g., through forced conversion) can create new covert versions of difference, whereas environments that self-define in terms of tolerance and mixture, such as "immigrant nations" or "multicultural societies," can annihilate difference (e.g., through the potent ideology of assimilation in Western democracies). The writings about the afterlives of expulsion and conversion of Spanish Jewry address the vagaries of multiplicity just as they foreground overlooked entanglements and solidarities born of conversions.

Conversos in Late-Twentieth-Century Thought: French *Marranisme* and Beyond

Even though the circum-1992 surge of interest in Sephardism and crypto-Jewishness has been remarkable in many places, the highly contentious nature of integration, secularism, and nationalism in France is a likely reason for the special and widespread hold that ideas about conversos had over French intellectuals in the 1990s and 2000s. Around this time many authors and thinkers—most of them, though not all, Sephardi or Ashkenazi—found recourse to *marranisme* to explain modernity's prevalent social, psychic, ontological, and even political condition as well as its undefinabilities and ambiguities. As immigrants of color began demanding radical inclusions and liberties, and the secular French state and large swaths of the public resented or refused them, *marranisme*'s analogical import to conditions under regimes of compulsory assimilation and self-alienation became more relevant. For the more radical thinkers, the marrano's resistance to identitarianism, rather than fearful concealment or existential duality, came to the fore. Daniel Bensaïd, Daniel Lindenberg, Edgar Morin, Shmuel Trigano, and Elaine Marks are among the many authors and thinkers who have drawn on the history and concept of *le marrane* and *marranisme* from Francophone perspectives about assimilation and resistance, though best-known are Jacques Derrida's formulations. Derrida, a Sephardi born and raised in Algeria, explained in many places, albeit briefly, his identification with a marrano condition, which he defined in terms of open secrets and indeterminacy. He associated *marranisme* with a secrecy that no longer hides a truth and therefore foregrounds doubt: "I am one of those Marranes who no longer say they are Jews even in the secret of their own hearts, not so as to be authenticated Marranes on both sides of the public frontier, but because they doubt everything" (Bennington and Derrida 1993, 170–71).

The parallel between the contemporary assimilated or secularized person of Jewish origins and historical crypto-Jews is key to contemporary writing about this history. The assimilated Jew's distance from Jewish language, knowledge, and ritual is one of the keys to Derrida's self-identification as a *marrane*. It is also encapsulated in French author and theorist Hélène Cixous's understanding regarding the epistemological aspect of Derrida as a Jew: his "lack" regarding his Jewishness, such as his ignorance of Hebrew and Jewish tradition, as a form of *marranisme*, a not-knowing of the content of the secret he keeps, "the disinheritor, guardian of the book he doesn't know how to read" (Cixous, quoted in Wolfson 2014, 160).

Further, Sarah Hammerschlag observes that "to be a Marrano is, for Derrida, an intensification of what it is to be a Jew, or at least it is an intensification of the dynamic of deracination, appearing as a form of betrayal or breach of contract" (2010, 245). Similarly, Marc Goldschmit suggests that the *marrane*'s doubleness is "not a dual belonging but rather a dual estrangement, a double presence crossed with a double disappearance" ("pas une double appurtenance, mais plutôt une double étrangeté, une double apparition croisée avec une double disparation"; Goldschmit 2008, 143), like Derrida's own Jewishness and like the assimilable others of modern societies.

Relatedly and somewhat amusingly, Derrida also asks: What if we think that "not only Spinoza but Marx himself, Marx the liberated ontologist, was a Marrano? A sort of clandestine immigrant, a Hispano-Portuguese disguised as German Jew who, we will assume, pretended to have converted to Protestantism, and even to be a shade anti-Semitic? Now that would really be something!" (1999, 262). For Derrida, "the supreme twist … the absolute surplus value" would be that Marx's children "would have been Marranos who were so well disguised, so perfectly encrypted that they themselves never suspected that that's what they were!—or else had forgotten the fact that they were Marranos, repressed it, denied it, disavowed it" (262). This whimsical suggestion, reminiscent of Freud's *Moses and Monotheism* (1959), illustrates part of Derrida's position that "real" marranos do not know their own marranoness and would no longer be marranos if they avowed that identity. Derrida follows with the rejection of the "claim … that the question of marranism was recently closed for good." He asserts, "I don't believe it for a second. There are still sons—and daughters—who, unbeknownst to themselves, incarnate or metempsychosize the ventriloquist specters of their ancestors" (Derrida 1999, 262). Yet earlier, Derrida had considered *marranisme* to be "finished" (quoted in Graff Zivin 2014, 20).

It is not only marrano practice, then, but also its *undetected but present* inheritance that is relevant to Derrida and other thinkers. These include Edgar Morin, our own subject of Chapter 4, and Daniel Bensaïd, the closely related but lesser known figure outside of Europe and the global left. Bensaïd, the Sephardi-identified son of Algerian parents, was a renowned Trotskyite student leader in 1968 and became an esteemed leftist philosopher. He also drew on the marrano metaphor in the 1990s, arguing that *le marrane* is distinguished by a "double identity without duplicity," "passing" between worlds, and an "ambivalence" that is "refractory to roots and rootedness" (2013, 312). The challenge of marranism, Bensaïd suggests, is to locate "an exit that is neither a return to the self nor an accord with the victors but an evasion, a flight, an opening to the excluded third realm. This unstable equilibrium between the particular and the universal [is] a question of life and survival; a tenacious gift for letting a text live beneath another, and yet another under that one. A hide-and-seek game that evades tyrannical identities" (Bensaïd 2001, 120; my translation). It is interesting that an internationalist leftist thinker should valorize evasion, which is not conventionally perceived as a mass movement builder. The politics of evasion and dissimulation as alternative modes of resistance have long been a tactic of the vulnerable and surveilled (see, e.g., Scott 1985, 30), valorized also by Alberto Moreiras's "Marrano" infrapolitics (see later discussion).

The deployment of *marranisme* in the work of Derrida, Bensaïd, and Morin, among others, evinces a particularly French inflection: the dominant critique of (indeed, recoiling from) "tyrannical identities," which is a rejection of *communitarisme*, shared by the left and the right, albeit with different terms and goals. But Bensaïd's *marrane* does not fold into nationalist anti-*communitarisme* or anti-identitarianism. He draws instead on an understanding of subjectivity as formed along a "line of contrariness" in which the self is split, without "the comfort of reconciliation." The *marrane*, explains Bensaïd, patiently digs "like a mole" and inhabits a doubleness without duplicity and passes from one world to the other and from one epoch to the other." Further, the *marrane* signifies "an unfaithful faith" that "opposes ... all fantasy of purism" (Bensaïd 2002, 121). The figure of the mole, *la taupe*, from which Bensaïd invents *la taupologie* in his book entitled *Résistance* (2001), is a well-known Marxian reference to revolution but a striking association with the converso or crypto-Jew. Further, Bensaïd suggests, "Perhaps political Marranism leads in this way to an outcome between identitarian panics and the undifferentiated diversity of commodity cosmopolitanism. To a reinvented internationalism" (2013, 313). But Bensaïd does mention that the attributes he describes, of "unbelonged belonging," a "training in modern liberty, and the "ambivalence refractory to roots and rootings," belong to "the figure of the *imaginary* Marrano" (2013, 312; emphasis added).

Like Derrida's, Morin and Bensaïd's *marranes* are stand-ins for other terms invented for the secular Jews of modernity: Morin's are *judéo-gentils* (Jewish Gentiles) and Spinozants, whereas others draw on Isaac Deutscher's "non-Jewish Jew" (1968). All these terms are different shortcuts to describe the condition of identifying as Jewish without being thoroughly observant of or believing in Judaism, or of partaking of "the curious fidelity of nonreligious secular Jews to a sense of their Jewishness" (Marks 1996, xvii). Even though this label is applied usually to Jews in the Christian world, including in Marks's book, it has also been true of Jews past and present in Muslim-majority countries that have had their own secularization processes, however varied, in which many Jews participated, including in both the Ottoman and Republican Turkish eras and in colonized North Africa or Iraq, for example.

For thinkers on the left, the indeterminacy, secularism, and anti-belonging of the *marrane* is more invested than the assimilated secular Jew with subversive and even revolutionary bearing that deconstructs the subject itself and the current order's faux differentiations. The analogies extend beyond the self to particular eras: 2005 saw the launching of the online journal *Les Temps Marranes*, whose title evokes the eminent *Les Temps Modernes* as well as the link between the *marrane* and the modern. In its first issue its editors ended their introduction by asserting that we are in "marrano times" of rupture, confusion, and displacement but also of hopeful confrontations with "intimate contradictions [and] unexpected convertibilities" in a state that is "dialectical and in suspension" (Corman and Pérez 2005).

The French approaches overlap in some ways, directly or indirectly, with the thinking of scholars in Hispanophone and comparative studies. Alberto Moreiras extracts a particular meaning from converso and crypto-Jewish histories and distinguishes between *marranismo* and Judaism: "Literal *marranismo* applies only to *conversos* who, tired, bored, or desperate with the strictures of the Spanish or Portuguese atmosphere, decided to return to the Jewish fold with larger or lesser possibilities of success" (Moreiras 2012, n.p.). In defining the marrano, Moreiras contrasts it to the converso so as to invest the marrano with an originary and indelible doubleness and the converso with "identitarian" thinking.

> The *Marrano* register is the abandonment of what was previously one's own and the embrace of the dominant state of the situation, and at the same time the abandonment of the state of the situation without the recovery of what was previously mine. Whatever was mine, if anything ever was, is blocked forever. The identitarian register, by contrast, is the embrace of what was previously mine insofar as I identify it in the state of the situation and the militant abandonment of the alien as non-dominant. Whatever was mine stays mine and will always be mine. (Moreiras 2012, n.p.)

Recovery and return, then, are possessive and, dangerous, because the "identitarian register ... reproduces and internalizes mechanisms of dominance" (Moreiras 2012, n.p.). For Moreiras, the marrano is at a remove from identity; indeed, it is the name he gives to anti-identity. His marrano is elusive. It is precisely in marrano-like elisions that resistance and freedom emerge.

To further this particular concept, Moreiras draws on and associates with the marrano James Scott's notion of infrapolitics, the "unobtrusive realm of political struggle" (Scott 1990, 183) found in daily acts or evasion, "the twin sister" of "open resistance to domination" (184). Moreiras does not address the ways in which converso subjectivities and consciousness have been and continue to be positioned, not singly but as decidedly changeable, vacillating and shifting from identitarian to non- or anti-identitarian modes. Instead, he extracts a usable kernel from ideas about conversos and offers the marrano as a syndrome to critique identitarian politics, including, among other things, multiculturalism and its identity-based equivalencies. In some important ways, his antihegemonic approach is similar to the approaches of leftist French thinkers, including Edgar Morin (Chapter 4), Daniel Bensaïd, and Daniel Lindenberg, who derive a politics from the history of conversos.

The indeterminacy of the converso or the *dönme*, which has caused so much consternation in the past and present, can also be a mode of resistant freedom from the nationalist and other hegemonic identity politics that are strong and often virulent in France, Turkey, and elsewhere. The notion of the illegibility and mootness of converso or crypto-Jewish consciousness also informs the work of Erin Graff Zivin, who has written extensively about the topic. She focuses on the metonymic import of the marrano, whose analysis, she explains, exposes "the limits of modern subjectivity, sovereignty, and hegemony" (Graff Zivin 2014, 20), concepts that are the basis of an "Inquisitional logic" (xi–xiv, passim). This logic is revealed in her examination of scenes of torture past and present (post-2001) and the presumed extraction of "truth" in which a fictional process of interrogation and confession produces only the discourse of power. Furthering this work in her edited volume *The Marrano Specter: Derrida and Hispanism*, Graff Zivin argues for a "Marrano ethics," in which indeterminacy, opacity, untranslatability, and misreading are bases for an ethical relation to the other (2017a).

As I began to suggest in the Introduction, the metaphorical and metonymic uses of the term *marrano* in contemporary thought might seem at odds with the cultural phenomenon of return to ancient converso and Sephardi identities. Such returns sometimes, though certainly not always, seek determined identities in lieu of indeterminacy, religion instead of secularity, visibility instead of "infra-existence," and nationalist certainties instead of internationalist resistance. On the other hand, the conceptualization of the figurative marranos and *marranes* can seem to elide or even counter the "real" crypto-Jews and their descendants. Yet, of course, the figurative and the real-life conversos of the past and present are not separable, no matter what facticities are attached to them, given the role of the imagination in returns and what I refer to as the production of remnants. As narratives that engage the contemporary imaginaries of converso afterlives, the texts I study in the following chapters draw on "the imaginary Marrano" in Bensaïd's words. But this is not separable from what we know about crypto-Jewish experiences. There are, of course, various ways of imagining conversos today. The one relevant to a liberatory approach can mobilize politics and ethics in the present to subvert bounded certainties of nation and religion; this path undermines the idea that the return to a converso consciousness is only an occasion for uncovering its Jewish remnant to restore a purifying preforgetting and preconversion identity. Instead, we have a non-Jewish/Jewish portal to skepticism and openness to difference.

Further, in most of the French or other European considerations, *marranisme* does not come from an engagement with Sephardi or Atlantic history but from the "mesmerizing and symbolic force" of the marrano for modern thought (Bielik-Robson 2014, 15). But the memoirs and fictions that are the subject of *The Converso's Return* combine their interest in Sephardi history and identity with the extensive allegorical and political purchase of multiple converso and crypto-Jewish conditions.

Conversos in Nineteenth-Century to Present-Day Literary History: Lineage, Martyrdom, Melodrama, Multiplicity

Contemporary literary representations of conversos do not just draw on and reconfigure ideas in recent scholarship and thought. They are also incarnations of previous fiction by or about conversos. In this section I provide a brief overview of conversos in fiction since the nineteenth century, when themes of the Inquisition and conversos returned to literature in Europe and the Americas in the burgeoning form of the novel. I also address more contemporary works to help us situate the contemporary novel of Sephardi and converso entanglements in a broader literary historical context.

In her helpful overview and analysis of major trends in Sephardism in literary history, Yael Halevi-Wise writes about the import of conversos, explaining that "the ambiguity and doubleness that characterize the Marrano's New Christian condition" provides nuance to the binary manner in which Iberian Sephardi history and culture are often presented: a long-lost idealized experience of *convivencia* or else a chain of persecutions and martyrdom (Halevi-Wise 2012a, 27). But, as Halevi-Wise also observes, many other tropes and ideas have been circulating for centuries in the vast body of writing by and about conversos. The most prominent recent works deal with indeterminacy resulting from troubled and complex genealogy and blood and the perdurable themes of suffering, evasion, and resistance. I suggest that, most significantly, converso history has been the material and launching pad for signaling submerged convergences.

The converso's return to literary history, like converso identities themselves, is shaped by genealogical discourses and definitions of belonging. As we will see in the next chapters, descent and lineage continue to be preoccupations for the fictional and nonfictional subjects of contemporary literature. Some of these protagonists try to make sense of mixed and clandestine inheritance, whereas others infuse their normative Sephardi or Christian Spanish identities with subversive converso ancestors (see Chapters 3 and 4). Conversion's extinguishing of former belongings, coupled with the prohibition of these affiliations in toto in the Iberian case, gave birth first to narratives that build on genealogical trouble, such as the Spanish picaresque, and later to narratives of dramatic revelations and recoveries.

A key genre whose significance to Spanish and other European literature cannot be overestimated, the sixteenth-century picaresque had wide-ranging and long-lasting influence. The *picaresco*'s preoccupations with heredity followed from an extensive genealogical tradition in European writing, but some of the genre's later interpreters in Spain were particularly emphatic about its double meanings of lineage. Critics eager to return to Spain's suppressed Jewish and Muslim histories and literary and cultural significance include Amador de los Ríos in the nineteenth century and Américo Castro, a key twentieth-century intellectual.[1] Castro was exiled during the Franco era, and his work was continued by others, such as Julio Caro Baroca.

Such critics x-rayed canonical, presumably Catholic picaresque Spanish texts of the sixteenth century, for example, the anonymous *Life of Lazarillo de Tormes* and Mateo Alemán's *Guzmán de Alfarache*, and pored over the writings of countless other canonical authors, among them Cervantes and Fernando de la Rojas, to find converso traces in them. Some scholars argue that, given the *pureza de sangre* (purity of blood) obsessions of the Spanish state and culture and the converso's anxieties regarding the detection of Jewish blood and its drastic consequences, the *pícaro*'s characteristic mockery of lineage and his own lowly birth, in addition to other characteristics, are marked by a converso consciousness (Yovel 2009, 264–66; Halevi-Wise 2012a). This includes the anonymous writer of *Lazarillo*, who is possibly of converso descent.

But the genealogy of authorship and literary influence in texts propelled by subversions of lineage discourses is itself contested. Spanish scholars of the last century who emphatically underlined a converso presence in Golden

Age Spanish letters largely rejected claims to any Jewish aspect of the converso text, arguing that the Sephardi origins, not continuity, led to a particular worldview that was secularizing, skeptical, individualist, and so on. Hence they returned to Spanish literary history not "the Jew" but a de-Judaized converso descendant. Castro asserts a Jewish inflection to his brand of Hispanism but without taking into account, as I. S. Révah accuses him, of the crypto-Jewishness of some conversos (Bodian 2017, 9). As Miriam Bodian points out, Castro's early modern Jews are decidedly not crypto-Jews. He declared that he had no interest in crypto-Jews because "no crypto-Jew in Spain created anything that endures today" (quoted in Bodian 2017, 11).

Lineage never ceased to be central to converso narratives and their analysis, including in the nineteenth century, which saw a return to the crypto-Jew that is reminiscent of the current proliferation of narratives. The towering figure of Benito Pérez Galdós, who treated various Sephardi and conversion themes, wrote novels (1889–1895) about Torquemada the Inquisitor as a descendant of converts and included conversos as minor characters in the 1887 *Fortunato and Jacinta*. Vicente Blasco Ibañez, who also reincorporated Jews into Spanish literature, albeit in a manner riddled with stereotyping, was the first novelist to write about the Chuetas of Mallorca in *Los muertes mandan* (The Dead Command; 1909). He imparts to his readers ideas about the continuation of racialism even in more liberalized Spain, the absurdity of blood purity, and the discrimination against converso descendants.

Interestingly, Blasco Ibañez points to a particular "revulsion" against the Chuetas voiced by his main protagonist, a fallen man of wealth and title from the island who did not feel such disgust toward "real Hebrews," that is, Jews in other European countries where he had business dealings. It was the origins in conversion that repelled him. They were a "race" apart, stunted for centuries and cowardly; yet his good friend was a Chueta who saved him (and reminded him of *his* descent from Inquisitors). The Chuetas are vindicated in *Los muertes mandan* as victims of discrimination who nevertheless retain pride, though their role is primarily to critique Spanish elitism and racism whose dead still "command." Beyond anti-Semitism, the revulsion that Chuetas, who have been Christians for centuries as a group, elicit is characteristic of the response to conversions and other metamorphoses of gender and culture that cannot and are not allowed to erase or supersede origins. A genetic stamp is forever deemed detectable. A later treatment is Ana María Matute's haunting *Primera memoria* (1959), one of many Spanish coming-of-age novels about the beginnings of the Franco dictatorship, in which the Chuetas, objects of derision, discrimination, and violence, continue to serve as scapegoats in the Franquista era, as they always had.

Genealogical melodramas, involving tragic separations, devastating revelations, and enduring racializations that are aspects of popular novels today, are characteristic also of nineteenth-century literature in Latin America and elsewhere in Europe. Some novels even became "foundational fictions" (D. Sommer 1991) of the relatively new Latin American nations, including Colombian Jorge Isaacs's 1867 *María*. In this novel the eponymous convert's Jewishness is an exotic and racial one, but she is still presented as a Judeo-Christian hybrid (Graff Zivin 2008, 34). The first Mexican historical novel is Justo Sierra O'Reilly's mid-nineteenth-century *La hija del judío* (The Daughter of the Jew). It concerns the Inquisition and Jews and conversos as one cursed, unhappy race. Sierra O'Reilly, like other Latin American authors, including Machado de Assis, was anti-indigenous to a fault and displaced his preoccupations with mixture and racialized nationhood onto the bodies and souls of their fictional conversos and conversas (Graff Zivin 2008).

The discourse of the *raza hebrea* (Hebrew race) persisted in nineteenth-century Latin American writing in denial of conversion, whether or not the authors were sympathetic to Jews and conversos. Then, as now, returns from conversion and recoveries of Jewishness sometimes suppress entanglements and transformations, emphasizing instead genealogy and inheritance, which also may overlap with racializing blood discourses. George Eliot's remarkable *Daniel Deronda* (1876) is rightly noted for its rejection of anti-Semitism and the Anglo-Protestant conversionary compulsion. The sympathetic British author's eponymous protagonist returns to a biological Jewishness he discovers, but, as Michael Ragussis argues, Eliot, along with others, "conflates Marranos with converts"; that is, like many, she fails to distinguish the crypto-Jews, who continue some identity or practice, from those converts and their descendants who have retained neither. Ragussis views this as a "flattening out of the difference" echoing "the means by which religious affiliation became overwritten in Spain by racial genealogy" (1995, 29) in nineteenth-century British literature.

Racial definitions of Jewishness were used to different ends in the German Haskalah (Jewish Enlightenment) movement's philo-Sephardism of the early nineteenth century. The *maskilim*, followers of the Haskalah, deployed medieval Jewish Spain as a model of high culture and integration without cultural loss. They presented Spanish Jews as a purer stock with a more defined Israelite descent that represented a noble Hebrew race, subverting European racializing of Jews, albeit through European racial terms (Efron 2016). In the vast and varied philo-Sephardi thought and writing of the period, conversos played a special role (Feiner 1996; Schapkow 2015, 63; Skolnik 2014). In his *German Jewry and the Allure of the Sephardi*, John Efron (2016) explains the "phenomenal success" of the "first Sephardi-themed novel," the 1837 *Die Marranen* (The Marranos) by Ludwig Philippson, and differentiates between the attitudes toward crypto-Jews in German writing, which varied from sympathetic to critical (the Sephardis were too quick to convert, some observed).

Just as they would in the twentieth century, the *marranen* served as emblems of assimilation and a melancholy loss of faith and self for the *maskilim*. Heinrich Heine considered himself a *marrane* (Veit 1974, 148), partly because he returned to Judaism after conversion. He also considered that the "partial authenticity" of conversos made them "ideal exemplars of modern Jews," with "their multiple identities, their straddling of Jewish and non-Jewish cultures, even their pride mixed with shame" (Efron 2016, 181). In Heine's play *Almansor*, the crypto-Jewish condition is transposed onto the Moorish Muslim subject and settings. Impostors and apostates are at the center of Heine's works about conversos who pass, most famously in *The Rabbi of Bacharach* and "Dona Clara" (Veit 1974; Skolnik 2014). "Dona Clara" is a poem about Spaniards that strikes at the heart of the dominant majority's racial fear about the disguised other's infiltration and sexual contamination of the German body. As David Biale (1982) suggests in an essay on the German philo-Semite Leopold von Sacher-Masoch, sexuality is also a preoccupation in the fascination with another kind of convert, Sabbatai Sevi, whose followers included many with converso backgrounds. With all their vagaries, the conversos were part of German Jewish imaginary genealogies and were assimilated into their fantasies about race, descent, and belonging.

Discourses of martyrdom and heroic suffering are as much a part of Haskalah literature's varied representation of conversos as their figuration in terms of partiality, ambiguity, or disloyalty. Indeed, the heroic narrative is found in all periods and places in which conversion is a fictional or autobiographical topic and serves as an alternative archive to the main body of knowledge about postconversion lives, that is, the records of the Holy Office. It is certainly not just the German-language literature that exalts and pities the maligned but faithful crypto-Jew. *The Siege of Tulchyn* (1888), the signature play of Russian author Nikolai Minskii (or Minsky), who converted to Orthodox Christianity from Judaism, is about the massacres of Jews during the 1648 Khmelnytsky Uprising in Ukraine. In the play a Portuguese "marrano" character is figured as a savior of Jews from Cossacks. As Amelia Glaser explains, a quasi-erotic relationship to his beloved, martyred crypto-Jewish friend Pedro, compels the return of Josif de Kastro to Judaism. After he moves to Amsterdam, he decides to go to Tulchyn and defend "his people" from the Cossacks (Glaser 2015, 130–36). Featuring both martyrdom, the most common representation of crypto-Jews, and military heroism, more unusual, this play's invented character is a testament to the uses of conversos in modern literature, including, in this case, as analogies for assimilation and philo-Sephardi role models of resistance.

German Jewish fiction also includes stories about anonymous suffering marranos, Jewish Inquisitors faithful to their secret religion, and well-known real-life conversos such as Diego de Aguilar and Jacob Tirado. Other famous heroes and martyrs, especially Baruch Spinoza, Luis de Carvajal, and Dona Gracia Mendes Nasi, continuously appear in contemporary novels from Mexico to France and Turkey. Also known as La Sinyora, Mendes Nasi flourished in and ended her days in the Ottoman Empire. She and other conversos appear in the plethora of late-twentieth-century Turkish historical novels about the Ottoman Empire, which often highlight pre-Ottoman sufferings of minorities, including under rival empires. This approach of valorizing a particular period through its tragic anterior history is characteristic of earlier fiction as well, including that of the remarkable Grace Aguilar, an English writer of Portuguese converso background whose non-Jewish works were bestsellers à la Dickens. Her 1850 *Vale of Cedars, or the Martyr* is a melodramatic and unique novel that contrasts inquisitorial Spain to tolerant England, foregrounding most of all the commitment-to-the-death of fifteenth-century crypto-Jews to Judaism. Later, the martyr, as in Aguilar's title, shows up in "the historiography of Spanish Jews: martyrs as heroes and converts as cowardly opportunists and hypocrites" (Ragussis 1995, 29).

As Esther Benbassa (2003) has argued, Haskalah and other writers "left no place" for the rest of Sephardi history that was not European and that continued in the Ottoman and Muslim world of the Balkans, the Middle East, and North Africa, gradually detaching itself from Iberia in many respects. Paloma Díaz-Mas (2009) and Elena Romero (1983), prominent Spanish scholars who have made many important contributions to Sephardi literary and philological studies, have explained that the Westernization of Ottoman Sephardis and the Spanish colonial and liberal turn to Sephardi people and history led to some re-engagement in the Judeo-Spanish-speaking Balkan and Middle Eastern and North African world with a Spain long left behind as a "homeland," however much it lived on in language, song, cuisine, rite, ritual, and naming, coupled with the adaptation, of course, to the local home.

The undoing of Inquisition records and anti-Semitism through the fictional investigation of converso fates appears in Judeo-Spanish writing at the end of the nineteenth and beginning of the twentieth centuries. The interest in Spain in the Judeo-Spanish press was limited and confined to elites; it featured both a positive memory of Jewish ascendance in al-Andalus and representations of the Black Legend in late-nineteenth-century theater, poetry, and journalism (Díaz-Mas 2009, 227–28). Among other works are narratives in the romance novel genre, such as *Salvada del convento* (Saved from the Convent; 1901), published in an Izmir Judeo-Spanish newspaper; novels from 1885 and a few decades later that were published in Romania and elsewhere about Christians (e.g., the legendary Baron Diego de Aguilar and Miguel San Salvador) discovering and returning to Jewish roots; *El Seder de Madrid*, about secret converso seders; and several plays with various versions of the title *Los Maranos* performed until the 1930s (Romero 1982, 1983). Michael Studemund-Halévy explains that historical fiction and plays "set at the time of the Marranos" were also popular around the same time among Vienna's Sephardi community, which produced best-seller feuilletons, including several about Diego de Aguilar (Moses López Pereira), a returned Portuguese Christian and influential businessman of the eighteenth century who is said to have founded the Viennese Sephardi community (Studemund-Halévy and Collin 2013). Ottoman and European letters, then, whether Jewish or not, incorporate the Inquisition and its aftermath to assert persecution but also to highlight Jewish continuity and survival, especially in the stories of converso descendants' crypto-Judaism or returns following revelations of origins.

The surge of interest in converso and crypto-Jewish histories in the nation- and community-defining literature of Latin America, Europe, and the Ottoman Empire in the nineteenth and early twentieth centuries has had its equivalent in what I refer to as circum-1992 fiction and memoirs by authors writing in the Americas, Europe, and Turkey, including postcolonial diasporic authors hailing from other continents, such as Salman Rushdie and Tariq Ali. Many of the ideas and representations found in earlier writing are also present in literature of the quincentenary period. The commemorations in 1992 of the 1492 expulsions took place at a moment of wider preoccupations with migrations, diasporas, and multiculturalism that found their echoes in Iberian *convivencia* and its terrible ending.

The quincentennial also occasioned a wide-ranging production of culture that partly or wholly involved Sephardi and converso history. Much of the fiction on converso and Sephardi pasts published in the United States, Europe, and Turkey falls within the genre of the historical novel, which saw a tremendous burgeoning in the last decades of the twentieth century (Anderson 2011). According to some critics, the "postmodernity" of these novels is not about the alleged "end of history" but a return to history, specifically, to those who had been suppressed (Labanyi 2002, 7–9). Although many of the fictional works are traditional linear narratives, others shuttle between centuries and multiple settings, and some bear the characteristics of "historiographic metafiction" (Hutcheon 1989), which reflects on the constructed nature of the past and its narration.

Both traditional linear historical fiction and its postmodern metafictional new formations also appear in significant ways in contemporary Latin American literature about conversos, as the important works by Erin Graff Zivin (2008, 2014), Kimberle López (2002), and Yael Halevi-Wise (2012a) show. These scholars focus on authors from Argentina, Brazil, and Mexico, such as Homeros Aridjis, Marcos Aguinis, Sabine Berman, Angelina

Muñiz-Huberman, and Moacyr Scliar. Many other Latin American authors give important if secondary roles to converso characters in their historical fiction (K. López 2002), further cementing the role of this submerged history and its known and undocumented possible trajectories in the making of the Americas. In many texts, converso history, with the Inquisition at center stage, is an allegory for present repressions, including especially Latin American dictatorships of the 1960s and 1970s. The Inquisition story also serves as an illustration of the ongoing coloniality, the historically ingrained inequality and violence of power, and the unstable nature of truth (Graff Zivin 2014). Few authors, however, write from within an engagement with Sephardi or converso culture and history or stray from historical fiction to write about descendants and contemporary returns to identities.[2]

In Anglophone and Francophone Caribbean literature, conversos appear in relation to both colonial and postcolonial contexts, as Sarah Casteel shows in her invaluable *Calypso Jews: Jewishness in the Caribbean Literary Imagination*. Renowned Caribbean authors such as Caryl Phillips, Maryse Condé, Michelle Cliff, and Myriam Chancy feature various kinds of Sephardi characters in their novels of the 1990s and after, including especially crypto-Jews, who appear as secondary characters but are significant not least in terms of the convergences with other Caribbean conditions. As Casteel shows, the interest of these authors in conversos has multiple sources, including actual Caribbean history and the role of conversos and Sephardis in it as well as discourses and literature about the Holocaust, which Caribbean authors have engaged.

But Casteel's original readings also uncover, for example, the unique links that authors make between Maroons (or *marrons* or *cimarrones*), which reference the key Caribbean and African diasporic historical circumstance under regimes of slavery, and marranos. Casteel argues for a "governing analogy between the Marrano and the Maroon, which is based in part on their common ability to escape detection" (2016, 92). The association of the marrano with the *cimarrón* (Maroon) has roots in the seventeenth-century narrative of Antonio Montezinos, as Jonathan Schorsch explains. Montezinos's narrative details his encounter and identification with Native people, whom he deems a "lost" and "found" Jewish tribe, in a remote location in the Americas when indigenous rebellions were widespread (J. Schorsch 2009, 2: 444–47).

In addition, as Casteel shows, Michelle Cliff and other writers draw analogies, not uncommon in the Caribbean, between "the Jew and the light-skinned Creole by associating marranism with the Creole's racial instability" (2016, 94). Moreover, "marranism, which shares with creoleness the potential for disguise, passing, and double vision" (94), allows Cliff to recast the Creole. Although Cliff is an exemplary author of connective historical fiction, Casteel critiques the novelist because she "conflates the historical figures of the Marrano and the Maroon in order to celebrate survival, resistance, and the preservation of difference" and because of her "treatment of marranism as a surrogate for maroonage [as] at risk for reducing Marrano experience to the status of metaphor" (98). Derek Walcott's work about the Sephardi Caribbean painter Camille Pissarro (descendant of conversos) is more nuanced, Casteel asserts, and is steeped in Sephardi history. Whatever the differences in approach of various authors, the overlaps and analogies among Caribbean historical formations and concepts of identity (such as creolization) often include Sephardis' converso history as being embedded within the Caribbean and its postcolonial literature, as Casteel demonstrates lucidly. Minor and secondary characters in such works illuminate Caribbean identities in alternative ways and, like the other elements in the novels, forge trans-Caribbean links.

As we can see, racial and other indeterminacy and partiality resulting from genealogical blurs and historical entanglements among Jews and others (and not just Iberian Christians) are integral to such contemporary literature, though they were present under different terms in the nineteenth century as well. In other postcolonial writing and visual culture, conversos help develop ideas around convergences and entanglements as well as secrecy in marronage contexts. According to Robert Stam, there is evidence that, along with blacks, Jews and Muslims were also in Palmares, the famous Maroon society of Brazil (1989, 42). Carlos Diegues's 1984 film *Quilombo*, about that community, includes the character Samuel, a Sephardi Jew, as well as Muslims. In Alejo Carpentier's short story "Camino de Santiago," a Spaniard who has just made the pilgrimage to Santiago de Compostela ends up in sixteenth-century Cuba and joins a *palenque* (Maroon society) composed mostly of slave escapees, or *cimarrones*. This particular *palenque* is full of the mixtures that Spain has expunged and expelled and includes Mandigas, Yolofas, Jews, and Protestants. Carpentier has the Spaniard Juan, the Jew, and the Calvinist return to Spain to signal, through a double of the Juan character, that the Atlantic journeys and their cultural and economic underpinnings, expulsions, and exploitations are cyclical.

The genealogical and historical consciousness in late-twentieth-century Spain's own converso narratives have to be considered in the context of its latest philo-Sephardi wave. There are antecedents in the earlier twentieth century, already mentioned briefly, when, notably, the interest in Spain's Jewish and Muslim past coincided with the country's colonial project. Liberal intellectuals made efforts to acknowledge the "Semitic" contributions to the country, to forge connections with local Spanish-speaking Jews in its colonial North African territories, and to assert a more tolerant, liberal image for a Spain stained by its inquisitorial history (Linhard 2014; Ojeda-Mata 2018).

The circum-1992 era was a new period in the long and complicated relationship that Spain forged with Sephardi Jews throughout the twentieth century by means of state-sponsored philo-Sephardism (Flesler et al. 2015; Friedman 2011b; Linhard 2014; Rozenberg 2006; Tardieu Touboul 2009). This engagement reached a peak in the twenty-first century, with the legal, public relations, and economic development agendas fostering return and reconciliation through nationality dispensation and tourism efforts and recovery (of a sanitized medieval Spain). The plight of the converso, a minor concern in earlier writing, came to the fore in such novels as Carme Riera's 1994 Catalan-language *Dins el darrer blau* (In the Last Blue), about the background of the Chuetas evoked earlier in Matute, and Antonio Muñoz Molina's polyphonic *Sepharad* (2001); it also appears prominently in more popular literature, as the overviews and analyses by Paloma Díaz-Mas (2007), Stacy Beckwith (2012), and others show.

Catalan authors have a special investment in Sephardism, because they were maligned as co-conspirators of or as descendants of Jews by Franco and others during the dictatorship years and thus were eager to underscore their opposition to Spanishness (Illas 2015) as defined in terms of blood purity and anti-Semitism and anti-Islamism. Although many of these "symbolic return to Sefarad" narratives (Flesler et al. 2015, 2) exalt a lost Spanish multiculturalism, others, such as Riera and Muñoz Molina's texts, center on persecution and the Inquisition when the subject is conversos and their descendants.

Many authors also take pains to link the Inquisition to the Holocaust through settings and plots that toggle between the inquisitorial past and the genocidal twentieth century, most famously in Antonio Muñoz Molina's 2001 *Sepharad* but also in works less well known outside the country, such as *La saga de los malditos* (Saga of the Damned; 2003) by Chuffo Lloréns (Beckwith 2020) and the 2001 novel *Velódromo de invierno* (Winter Velodrome) by Juana Salabert (Beckwith 2020; Linhard 2014). Linhard's indispensable study, *Jewish Spain: A Mediterranean Memory* (2014), ably exposes the motivations and limits of forging such connections in culture and literature. In addition to the particular Spanish reason to turn to Sepharad and conversos, such circum-1992 writing partakes also of the recent global novel's impulse, propelled by memory culture, to connect various catastrophes, cultures, and histories across time and space.

In the United States, Jewish-themed works have a larger market than in most other countries, and historical fiction about the Inquisition and converso lives is widely read. Some of these texts convey the complexity of historical circumstances compellingly and without reductiveness, with David Liss's 2003 *Coffee Trader* about conversos returning to Judaism in seventeenth-century Amsterdam being a good example. Other works, such as Noah Gordon's popular *The Last Jew: A Novel of the Inquisition* (2000), center on romance and adventure, and still others, for example, the Portugal-based U.S. author Richard Zimler's widely read *The Last Kabbalist of Lisbon* (1996), are structured as murder mysteries, all in the midst of persecution.

Following some of these genres but set in the contemporary period is *El Iluminado* by Ilan Stavans, the prolific critic and author of many books on Hispanic cultures in the Americas as well as of an anthology of Sephardi writing. Stavans's graphic novel braids several genres to tell a story of crypto-Jews in Mexico. Autobiographically inflected through the central character, Ilan Stavans, a fictional version of the author, the text is also a mystery involving fictional secret documents about the Jewish origins of New Mexicans and the murder committed for their possession. The book treats the authenticity debates regarding crypto-Jewish descendants in the Southwest (see the "Introduction" and Chapter 2) through staged debates between Stavans and other New Mexicans and transmits knowledge about persecutions of New Christians (especially the Carvajals) in the Americas. In a lighthearted, often self-mocking narrative, the author culls crypto-Jewish history through the tropes of the missing documents and unresolvable origin claims and provides a sense of the pervasive belief about secret Jewishness in New Mexico's oral culture. Outside of some exceptions and the Latinx authors I discuss in the next chapter, who have contributed significantly to U.S. fiction about conversos, much, though not all, of the production of fiction in the United States has been by authors who are not deeply invested in Sephardi or converso pasts but are captivated by it as a Jewish topic (sometimes as a precedent or equivalent of the Holocaust) or else as an intriguing slice of history. Frequently, such historical novels mirror Grace Aguilar's racial melodramas of martyrdom.

In an interesting development, contemporary Jewish fiction for young adult readers published in the United States has also seized heroic imagery of the crypto-Jew. Novels such as *Incantation* (2006) by Alice Hoffman and *Out of Many Waters* (1988) by Jacqueline Greene are complex in some ways, but, in an effort to protect young readers ("spare the child") and didactically shepherd them to thinking in terms of pride rather than abjection, they foreground acts of heroic redemption. The crypto-Jewish individuals and families here are brave, loyal, and self-sacrificing. As soon as the adolescents born to converso families lose their innocence through the revelation of their heritage, they rise to the occasion and immediately acquire and use impressive survival skills to also save others. The conventions of the coming-of-age novel are also adjusted to the crypto-Jewish story of heroism. As Kenneth Kidd has written about children's narratives of the Holocaust, the larger historical narrative is often subsumed to the individual psyche's development (2005). Popular novels in all genres also bolster nationalist narratives, such as the U.S. settlement story on which *Out of Waters* is founded or the depiction of the Jewish homeland as the only safe haven, as with the ending of Naomi Ragen's 1998 *Ghost of Hannah Mendes*. Such works, unlike the narratives we will encounter in the chapters that follow, stabilize the crypto-Jewish story and identity in fixed terms of religion, ethnicity, race, and nationhood.

In fiction, critique, and scholarship, we do continue to see some stock representations of conversos, crypto-Jews, and their descendants developed through centuries of knowledge and belief about marrano consciousness and history. Then and now, crypto-Jews especially but also conversos who have little or no Jewish practice (such as Blasco's and Matute's Chuetas) frequently appear as abject figures who cower in fear and are split internally by self-doubt and self-hatred. We will investigate examples of such representations in works ranging from Cuban American writing to Turkish literature in the coming pages, but in these works many types of crypto-Jewish characterization coexist. As we will see, the converso subject is represented through several contradictory figures, often undermining stereotypes and appearing prismatically rather than in a fixed image.

The Crypto-Jewish Body: Affect, Mind, and Spirit

In addition to the duality, ambiguity, martyrdom, heroism, and other typical figurations of crypto-Jewishness in literature, we also find particular bodies. "The body as an archive," a repository of collective memory, appears as symptomatic in contemporary works about the crypto-Jewish "condition." Frequently, the crypto-Jewish body is an abject and weeping one, characterized also by nervous gestures. Key characters exhibiting these characteristics in the chapters to come are Enrique in Obejas's *Days of Awe*, Santiago in Fajardo's *Mi nombre es Jamaica* (My Name is Jamaica), and Miguel Perera in Elif Shafak's *Şehrin Aynaları* (Mirrors of the City). These protagonists are nervous; they weep; they have visions; they bear their pain on their bodies in involuntary reenactments of their own traumas or those of the crypto-Jews in general. Santiago's reenactment is without a real referent, because, traumatized by another cause (his son's death), he, a Catholic Spaniard, imagines that he is the descendant of conversos and the embodiment of a seventeenth-century warrior who is the product of an indigenous and crypto-Jewish union. As I will show in the coming chapters, although Enrique and Miguel's bodies serve as crypto-Jewish archives of trauma, Santiago's body is a faux archive demonstrating the pitfalls of identification and appropriation.

There are precedents in twentieth-century literature that also feature the somatic converso descendant. Jewish American author Henry Roth's short story "The Surveyor" (1966) is a case in point. The narrative features an American married couple in Seville (he, Jewish; she, Protestant) who want to place a wreath to commemorate the unmarked *quemadero*. The couple is saved from the legal trouble that this act leads to by a Spaniard who reveals to them his converso roots, with which he identifies only in part, as a historical curiosity. However, as one critic has remarked, Roth makes many references to the nervous twitch that makes the Spaniard "wince" and "wrinkle" repeatedly, "as if his face were too close to a hot fire," linking the affect to an ancient ancestral origin (Ricard 2005). Converso "nervousness" transmitted transgenerationally marks the otherwise forgetful body, despite long-standing assimilation and collective repression of memory.

In the 2007 autobiographical novel *Marrane!* by Eduardo Manet, a French author of Cuban origin, the child protagonist inherits crypto-Jewish identity, which is revealed to him in Havana by his Andalusian mother. The narrator makes countless references to the mother's weeping, especially but not only when telling the doleful story of the Jewish fate, which also triggers the boy's tears. Racial melancholy, as David L. Eng and Shinhee Han have written (2000), can resist the order of things by serving, inter alia, as a reminder of racism and persecution. In some narratives, the self-division, fear, and anxiety, including about a Jewishness one does not even know, goes beyond melancholy and leads to madness, as with Elif Shafak's tormented, visionary character Miguel, who was inspired by the real-life mystic Abraham Cardoso. Unsurprisingly perhaps, Miguel becomes a kabbalist and a Sabbatean. In Fajardo's *Mi nombre es Jamaica*, a deconversion or appropriation of converso identity results from the Quixotesque madness of a non-Jewish Sephardi studies professor from Spain.

Mysticism, messianism, and madness bleed into one another in current cultural production about converts and descendants, likely because it is guided by contemporary scholarship arguing for the messianic and mystical outlook of early modern conversos (e.g., Goldish 2001; Barnai 1993). Sabbatai Sevi was adopted as a messiah by his followers, including those who had already been Christians (such as Miguel/Abraham Cardoso), and was known by his detractors as a madman. The charismatic leader's adherents, who followed him on the path away from a normative Judaism, including conversion to Islam and practice of what is considered antinomian apostasy, were also perceived as perverse. Even recently, the Sabbatean association of madness with conversion and heresy has been the subject of art: London-based performance artist Oreet Ashery duplicated in 2008 Sabbatai Sevi's "strange action" (Scholem 2016, 161), his famous walk through Istanbul with a cradled fish in baby clothes to indicate that redemption of the Land of

Israel would be under the sign Pisces.[3] Along with the neurotic body, irrational and inexplicable callings, visions, and hauntings are motifs in narratives about crypto-Jews, fictional or autobiographical.

Uncanny Dark Matter

Conversion frequently produces haunting. All conversions signal the death of the old and the rebirth as the new, but these particular dead are not buried, monumentalized, or museumified. They haunt and remain for some time as an invisible threat. Those who demand the total demise of preconversion entities often imagine them to be stubbornly, secretly, and subversively alive. When the policing and persecution required to achieve absolute extinction is seemingly complete, de-extinction or coming out, as it were, can begin. At that point, converts as a long-standing, invisible undercurrent also return to public discourse. Have they really been disappeared all along?

In Spain and Portugal, although the expulsion of the Jews (and to a much lesser extent, Muslims) has been acknowledged as a "historical mistake," the forced conversions and assimilation of vast numbers of Jews and Muslims are neutralized and barely visible. José Manuel Fajardo, the author of the groundbreaking novel that is the subject of Chapter 3, suggests that the converso is in fact "the dark matter" of Spanish society, undetectable but formative (Fajardo 2018). Literary and documentary exhumations (an appropriate metaphor, especially for a Spain literally and metaphorically occupied at the beginning of the twenty-first century with excavating the remains of the Spanish Civil War), detections, and individual ancestral claims restore visibility and life to what is dead (according to some) or submerged (according to others), with a certain quality of uncanniness.

The return of long-lost and unwanted stories and bodies produces a version of the Freudian uncanny, "the name for everything secret that ought to have remained secret and hidden but has come to light" (Freud 1958, 224). This secret is actually "homely" and familiar but has been repressed, and therefore when it returns and "comes to light," it feels both alien and familiar, producing a feeling of threat, because what was supposed to have been surmounted and forgotten (repressed) in fact is not. A collective uncanny feeling can also result, as some have argued, from the return of those long disappeared from view. In her key book *The Return of the Moor* (2008)

Daniela Flesler examines the representation of North African "Moorish" immigrants in Spanish literature and culture and explains that the presence of contemporary Moroccan immigrants "becomes uncanny because the distinction between the imaginary invading Moor of [ancient] Christian chronicles and the real-life Moroccan dissolves." This argument is inspired by Freud's "The Uncanny": The uncanny effect can also appear when the imagination-reality distinction disappears or "when a symbol takes over the full functions of the thing it symbolizes" (quoted in Flesler 2008, 82). In the context of Spain, the Jewish conversos' uncanny return is much more muted than the Arab/Moorish return that Flesler signals. The Judeoconversos' reappearance is spread transnationally, and even though it is not perceived as an assault to national polities or psyches, it disturbs communities, identity categories, in addition to having, as I indicated earlier, political motivations. Still, as our texts also show, the uncanniness of survival clings to the remnants and returns of converso history.

There is some overlap here with the image of the post-Emancipation Jewish identity in European eyes as uncanny. Susan Shapiro (1997) argues that, hovering between death and life, unable to die and unable to be revived, Jewish presence on the continent is ghostly. I discuss the parallel between assimilation and converso disappearance in relation to the writing of Obejas, Fajardo, Morin, Perera, and Ternar especially, though, as we will see, the particular ways that Latinx Jews of color, Latin Americans, and Iberian Jewish descendants in Turkey are resurrected in narrative and practice seem like unbelievable, uncanny revenants. And there is more to it: As Michael Taussig observes, involuntary memory and unmasking are what lead to

> a type of shock in which the "reading back" ... whiplashes time into an overpowering instant of flooding recall, dripping with possibilities, theatrical and otherwise, for transformation. It is not that something previously unknown is gloriously unveiled for the first time.... Nor is it return of the repressed.... What emerges is not so much an item of remembrance but *something new* that emerges from the charged juxtaposition of present with past, creating ... a mystical fusion of the *imaginary* with the *real*. And it is of course just such a fusion that ensures that a new mystery surfaces as the secret is unmasked. (Taussig 1999, 134; emphasis in the original)

At the same time as converso origins are demystified, they point to continuing unknowables and "new mysteries" that generate *new* narratives of the uncanny, haunting, and paramemories.

Circulations and Comparisons

The representation of crypto-Jewishness is distinguished not only by the symptomatic body and spirit, indeterminacy, haunting secrecy, and spiritual and somatic effects of repression but also by convergences. Returning to these histories in narrative and through embodied converso descendants involves not simply a recovery of lost knowledge but the insertion of imagined and occluded convergences into what is presumed to be primarily a Jewish story of martyrdom. In this effort, the story of conversion partakes contemporary world literature's aesthetic and modes of storytelling. The aesthetics of simultaneity, propinquity, and connectivity, the characteristics long ago of avant-garde writing, and the narrative fragmentation that disrupts transparency and emphasizes instead environmental and systemic links outside individual motivation are now ubiquitous. The "world novel" of the 1990s and early 2000s features decentered narratives with interlocking story lines that are often presented out of chronological sequence, shifting perspectives, myriad locations, and transspatial connectivities, especially of traumas.[4] Similarly, Sephardi but even more specifically converso identity and history are not only themes of contemporary world novels but analogies to contemporary narrative itself: Blending, superimposition, confusion, and multiplicity of perspectives abound and unlikely worlds meet, just as in the content of converso experiences themselves. Narrating convergences, both genealogical and historical, partake of what Pheng Cheah explains as a "world-making" that literature can generate (see the Introduction) by changing our perceptions of an ethical understanding of the "world" (Cheah 2008, 2016).

Although the networks and intersections of the global literary narrative lay bare circulations of cultures and systemic intertwined oppressions, they can also elide specific histories in their analogies and comparisons. Because of its transnational circulations and multiplicities of languages and belongings in much contemporary writing, Sephardi history in literature often *is* comparison to various effects. A good example of the discontents of this approach in the circum-1992 era is the award-winning Spanish writer Antonio

Muñoz Molina's widely translated 2001 novel *Sepharad*, whose subtitle is "A Novel of Novels." *Sepharad*'s focus is exiles of all kinds and most prominently the displaced victims of twentieth-century horrors, primarily Nazism and the Holocaust but also Francoism and Stalinism. The book's aesthetic is one of juxtaposition, primarily of the seventeen independent but also connected segments of varied genres, including citations from European Jewish and other writers and a mixture of real and imagined characters.

And then, of course, there is the title: *Sepharad*, which signals a particular content. It turns out, however, that the experience of Sepharad, Jewish Spain, to which other events are compared, is paradigmatic in name. All exile is called Sepharad; all victims are of Sepharad. Muñoz Molina enacts one of the pitfalls of comparison in his "anthological novel" (Walkowitz 2009), drawing on Sephardi history as a template and but in fact displacing it onto other historical events. When comparison rests on a paradigmatic but underexplored case, it can actually be obscured; raised on a platform, it can still be peripheral. Muñoz Molina's politics of comparison dovetails with other writings that also draw on the comparison between the expulsion of the Jews from Sepharad and the Holocaust, sometimes to argue for causality (with 1492 as foundational to modern European genocide) but sometimes to present an analogy to what is perceived as the main event of Jewish history, the Holocaust (see Casteel 2016; Linhard 2014). What is signaled as the paradigmatic case can become muted, as in Muñoz Molina's novel.

But a work like José Manuel Fajardo's *Mi nombre es Jamaica* (see Chapter 3) reflexively stages the discontents of comparison and returns to history at the same time as it signals the convergences of Sephardi and converso lives and cultures in Spain and across the Atlantic with the indigenous Americas. In Fajardo's work and in the other fiction I examine in the coming chapters, Sephardi conversions' blurred, indeterminate identity productions and historical transformations are foregrounded at the same time as they connect with other worlds.

In the chapters that follow, we will find some representational continuities regarding internal division, assimilation, inauthenticity, martyrdom, abjection, modernity, and multiplicity that echo long-standing and newer thinking about conversos. Conversion's "intersubjective, transactional, translational mode of negotiation between two otherwise irreconcilable world-views" (Viswanathan 1998, 176) fits well the aesthetic of spatial and temporal convergences in contemporary letters, fiction and nonfiction. The texts I analyze also assert in a constructive fashion (Cheah 2014) the meaningful possibilities for coexistence drawn from an imaginative reading of history: Boundaries are destabilized through imaginings of solidarities and unlikely unions within disregarded entanglements. The fictions and memoirs under scrutiny in the next chapters, then, mark occluded connections, signal the workings of entanglements, and expose the dynamics and fault lines of contemporary historical and genealogical consciousness.

{ CHAPTER 2 }

LATINX SEPHARDISM AND THE ABSENT ARCHIVE

Crypto-Jews and the Transamerican Latinx Imagination

OF ALL THE CLAIMS TO crypto-Jewish descent in the Americas, those of U.S. Latinx have been the most visible and controversial, most likely because of the larger numbers, the openly charged nature of race relations in the United States, and the wide reach of media and technology. The volume of and interest in crypto-Jewish identity resurgence in the United States is a fascinating case of the missing archive, imagined through personal revelations and the body-as-evidence as well as through a literary archive, in which contemporary Latinx are presented as the remnant group from a (crypto-) Jewish past. As we saw in the Introduction, what existed for some as a family secret or a rumor about descent within Latinx- and Hispanic-identified communities became public knowledge and a matter of often rancorous debate in the 1980s and 1990s. Whereas the largest number of crypto-Jews is in the Southwest (especially New Mexico), elsewhere in the United States too Catholic and Protestant Chicanx and Latinx, including Mexican and Cuban Americans, Dominicans, Puerto Ricans, and Colombians, have reported awareness of their own crypto-Jewish origins. Some explain long-standing familial knowledge and discreetly shared transmission of secret Jewish roots, including, for example, through dramatic death-bed confessions of elders. Others learned independently that certain practices and aspects of family history, such as some slaughtering practices and funerary conventions, might be Jewish (Gitlitz 2002; Golden et al. 2005; Halevy 1999; Hordes 2008;

Jacobs 2002). Those without such knowledge or practices in their families but who always felt different and alienated from Catholicism also investigated and declared Jewish identification and converso or crypto-Jewish descent. I discuss one example of the latter, the prominent memoir by Doreen Carvajal, in Chapter 3.[1] Media attention, especially a program on National Public Radio in 1988 about New Mexicans, increased the number of stories about and storytellers with possible or asserted crypto-Jewish origins. Some of those who conducted historical, genealogical, and DNA research to ascertain such roots brought their findings to light publicly.

Well-known writers, such as Demetria Martínez, Denise Chávez, Kathleen Alcalá, Achy Obejas, and Richard Montoya, whose most visible, literary, and institutionalized identities have been Latinx, Chicanx, or Cuban, have also drawn attention to Sephardi history as a part of their heritage. Demetria Martínez, the highly acclaimed New Mexican poet, novelist, and journalist for the *Catholic Reporter*, has talked about discovering her crypto-Jewish roots, considered converting to Judaism, and reflected on her "obligation to my Sephardic ancestors" (Gutiérrez y Muhs 2006, 66). Denise Chávez, another renowned Chicana author, referred to working on a book about her Sephardi roots; she had already touched on the topic of converso New Mexicans in her novel *Loving Pedro Infante* (2001). Like Martínez and Chávez, Kathleen Alcalá and Achy Obejas, the authors I discuss extensively in this chapter, also discovered Jewish roots and identity as adults, though their works continue to be known and marketed primarily as Latinx, Cuban, or Chicanx writing and less as Jewish or Jewish American literature.[2]

How these public figures and other Chicanx and Latinx ascertain crypto-Jewish descent after so many centuries was, for a period, a vexed question. As we saw in the Introduction, historical and ethnographic research about crypto-Jewish migration to the Americas led mostly to possibilities rather than certainties, though it is not disputed that conversos had a presence in the Americas and that many converts in Iberia blended into the dominant society and produced today's Spaniards and Portuguese. But the questions of evidence and authenticity haunt conversion's afterlives: On the one side, we have the dearth and controversial nature of the proof of survival; and on the other side, we have accusations about Latinx' intentions, truthfulness, or ability to make historical claims and distinguish facts from myth.

The texts I have chosen to analyze, Kathleen Alcalá's *Spirits of the Ordinary: A Tale of Casas Grandes* (1996) and Achy Obejas's *Days of Awe* (2002), as well as a few others I touch on, have the distinction of allowing a variety of views, historical possibilities, and imaginaries to coexist and come into conflict. This is not the case with all writing that treats the topic of crypto-Judaism. Unlike many studies, activist agendas, and testimonies, the works here offer few conclusions and definitive answers; instead, they open a range of possibilities and interpretations that act as an archive, less of actual crypto-Jewish life and more of the *implications* of reviving this suppressed history in the Americas. They also help us explore the reasons that the afterlives of such conversions are important and relevant in the current cultural moment, with reference to history and historical consciousness. Alcalá and Obejas, who themselves identify as descendants of crypto-Jews, Latina/o, Chicana/o, Mexican, Cuban, Sephardi, and/or queer, complicate simplistic definitions or accusations, such as Latinx whitening in the United States. They also expose but reflect on some Jewish formulations about martyrdom, unbroken continuities, and organic connection to Jewish people or Israel.

As works about diaspora, exile, indigenous people, crypto-Jews, conversos, and others in Cuba, Mexico, and the United States, Obejas and Alcalá's novels are transamerican and transatlantic in their vision, opening up and connecting little-known, secret, and lost histories to greater questions of Latinidad, Jewishness, and their overlaps. As imaginative returns to undocumented histories, they remind us of some of the many 1492s (Shohat 2006; Shohat and Stam 2012): They connect expulsion and conquest in narrating the fates of converted Jews from the other side of the Atlantic, expelled from their roots, as they intersected with the conquered and conquering populations of the Americas (given that a few of the conquerors were known or rumored to be conversos). As part of the civil rights era assertion of historical oppression and difference, the project of recovering and rewriting official stories is well established in the Chicanx-Latinx world of ideas and literature. Writing about conversos and crypto-Jews cannot necessarily recover lost knowledge, but it can produce a speculative, fictional archive. This approach dovetails with the work of the Chicana historian Emma Pérez, who called for queering the borderlands and "excavating the invisible and unheard"—that which is not found in documentation but is sure to have existed (2003, 122).

Exploring the Sephardi component of the history of the Americas is also a natural extension of the long-standing Latinx practices of imagining nondominant forms of *mestizaje* to recover, transform, and effectively continue to reimagine Latinx identities and stories. *Mestizaje*, a contested and charged term that has been widely criticized (see Alonso 2004; Klor de Alva 1995; Saldaña-Portillo 2001; Torres-Saillant 2002), has varying and problematic applications and histories in the Latinx diaspora context and in different Latin American countries. But the writers' positioning of the appearance of crypto-Jewishness in Latinx literature in terms of *mestizaje* nods to the convergence of histories and the unstable and unpredictable processes and forms that result, rather than to the mixture of three stable and unequal categories, as in official Mexican and other similar kinds of *mestizaje*. As Sephardi-identified authors, Obejas and Alcalá also contribute to the world of Jewish letters by making visible obscured aspects of Sephardi history and, with their unique transamerican perspectives, transforming the category of "Jewish literature."

What is most salient and distinctive about the writing of the lost archive of the crypto-Jew in the Americas is the authors' production of histories and its remnants in terms of occluded multiplicities, which I also refer to as convergences and overlaps rather than a signaling of unitary or unified categories. Whiteness, Jewishness, indigeneity, and so on are not autonomous sources of identity, culture, and storytelling; rather, they appear as entangled categories in-the-making along the course of history. In the case of missing memories and knowledge, it is important that historical crossings of collectivities (e.g., Native, Cuban, and crypto-Jewish/Sephardi) are informed primarily by what is partial and suppressed. The overlaps and entanglements I refer to in this chapter are the authors' imagined looping together of elements through partitions *and* suppressions of knowledge and identity, which are included, as we saw in the Introduction, in Rey Chow's understanding of "entanglement" (2012, 1). Convergences *and* boundaries coexist and are mutually constitutive in contemporary narratives about crypto-Jews and conversos. Unlike the compulsion of the early modern Jewish returnees to assert complete belonging in and superiority of the Jewish faith (see Chapter 1) or their contemporary equivalents, our narratives present partial and convergent knowledges and belongings rather than intact and discrete ones.

Transamerican Journeys

Achy Obejas, the renowned author and translator, wrote *Days of Awe* (2002) after a book of short stories, *We Came All the Way from Cuba So You Could Dress Like This?* (1998), and the novel *Memory Mambo* (2001). Both earlier works garnered critical acclaim for their telling of the Cuban American exile story and earned Obejas a solid place in Latinx and Cuban diaspora letters. Obejas, who has identified as a converso descendant since the 1990s, belongs to the artistic and literary Cuban generation in the United States that openly built bridges with Cuba in the 1990s, breaking with the embargo culture of disengagement that characterized the first decades after the revolution. *Days of Awe* is another connective effort, one that recasts once more the alternative worlds of the Americas that Obejas created in her previous works, which are populated with exiles from and rebels against political and gendered norms.

The narrator of *Days of Awe*, Alejandra San José, belongs to a Cuban crypto-Jewish family that emigrates to the United States on the eve of the Cuban revolution. As one critic explains, Alejandra is born in a transition of new beginnings and endings, bound thereafter to a "paradoxical relationship with time and history" (Goldman 2004, 63). The complexity of historical consciousness, a feature of many Cuban exile narratives caught between prerevolutionary, revolutionary, and diaspora temporalities, is further compounded by the unstoried trajectory of Caribbean crypto-Jewishness, a parallel but secret and unknown history. Beginning with year 0 of the revolution, Obejas's narrator traces her unusual family's origins in Cuba from the seventeenth to the twentieth centuries, in the process discovering her origins and remaking her own identity. The narrative exhibits the features of the global aesthetic of convergence (Chapter 1) in its spatial and historical alternations between the present and the remote and more proximate pasts and locations. Throughout the novel Alejandra struggles with uncovering family secrets regarding crypto-Jewishness, but she also wrestles with the eponymous Days of Awe, the period between the Jewish new year (Rosh Hashanah) and the Day of Atonement (Yom Kippur). This is a time, among other things, of repentance, forgiveness, and reconciliation with others; in this case, Alejandra reconciles with her diasporic condition and her father's predicament as a crypto-Jewish Cuban, and, according to Iraida López, experiences a "rebirth" (2015, 185) (see also Goldman 2004).

Spirits of the Ordinary (originally published in 1988) is Alcalá's first novel and the initial volume in the trilogy that rewrites and reimagines the history of the U.S.-Mexico borderlands. The work is the fruit of the author's biography and recognition of the Sephardi ancestry of her immigrant family of Protestant Mexicans from the northern Mexico city of Saltillo, Coahuila, where other crypto-Jews might have taken refuge. Alcalá was born and raised in California, where her parents immigrated. Her first book was a well-received, acclaimed short story collection, *Mrs. Vargas and the Dead Naturalist* (1992), which was praised by Ursula K. Le Guin as being "original and totally unpredictable," akin to Borges and García Márquez but in a "landscape of desert towns and dreaming hearts" (Le Guin 1992). *Mrs. Vargas*, hailed as a work of magical realism, also served as a basis for the trilogy. For its first volume, Alcalá extensively researched the history of Saltillo and the converso and indigenous origins of her own family.

Spirits of the Ordinary imagines the lives of the crypto-Jewish Caravals, descendants of the historical Carvajals who were murdered during the Mexican Inquisition, as well as the fates of the Catholic and indigenous (Opata) families to whom they are linked. The historical novel is set in late-nineteenth-century Saltillo, which experienced tremendous instability under the regime of Porfirio Díaz (the Porfiriato) and is located 200 miles from the U.S. border, all too close to the Texas Rangers. Like Obejas's characters, the Caraval family is internally divided with regard to their (crypto-)Jewishness. Each has a separate spiritual and religious journey; Zacarías, the son, and his mother partake of the borderlands experience of "spiritual mestizaje" (Delgadillo 2011), whereas the father, adhering primarily to Jewish textual tradition, does not.

The novel follows the adventures of Zacarías, the gold prospector, and the impact of his quest on the family of his birth and his wife and progeny. His children are unaware of their Jewish heritage, and his ultra-Catholic wife, Estela, takes a lover in the face of her husband's lack of devotion and prolonged absences looking for gold in the suggestively named Sangre de Cristo (blood of Christ) Mountains. Estela's lover is a doctor and a part of the campaigns in the Porfiriato wars against the indigenous people in the region, with whom Zacarías gets involved. The lyricism of the narrative is heightened with a touch of the mystical and supernatural: Zacarías's father, Julio, is a borderlands kabbalist who studies mystical texts and alchemy in a secret Hebrew library; his mother, Mariana, is mute (following a Judeophobic assault when she was a child) but something of a visionary; Estela's siblings are androgynous twins named Manzana and Membrillo (Apple and Quince) and have otherworldly powers and a language all their own; the Tarahumara and other indigenous people whom Zacarías comes to know have secret, mystical traditions. The perspective of each chapter alternates between the main characters and even includes an outsider, a photographer.

Despite their differences in style, structure, setting, and period, *Days of Awe* and *Spirits of the Ordinary* have something key in common besides the centrality of conversos (who mostly play important but side roles in Latin American and Caribbean writing): the significance they accord to crypto-Jewishness in the transamerican narrative. Obejas and Alcalá integrate Sephardi and converso stories into the narrative of the continental Americas to show how they converge with past and present notions of conquest and dispossession and with transamerican migrations and diasporas. Obejas drives this point home in her narrator's story about conversos who arrived as exiles in Cuba with Columbus and stayed on as crypto-Jews. For her part, Alcalá shifts the terms of syncretism in the borderlands we know from many other Latinx and Latin American narratives through her construction of Mexican history and the Mexico-U.S. borderlands as a crossroads with a formative converso component.

Another connective aspect of Sephardism that Latinx authors have explored in their novels and in interviews is that of kinship. Obejas, Alcalá, Chávez, Martínez, and other authors suggest a genealogical relation between Latinx and Jewish people and underscore the suppressed Jewish origins of Latin Americans. The Latino-Jewish band Hip Hop Hoodios expressed this with rap lyrics in their song "1492": "Well, here's some words that will hit you with a thud: Millions of Latinos got Jewish blood" (2005). Although blood discourse can be used to raise awareness of history, as we saw in the Introduction, kinship or "miscegenation" is only one aspect of the historical, cultural, and spiritual knots in which we find Obejas's and Alcalá's conversos.

These entanglements are extended in what I refer to as the aesthetics of convergence, which is characterized by the overlaps of temporal and spatial representations and by the thematic braiding of histories that might be buried or well-known but have been usually considered separate and distinct.

Obejas's narrative takes place in many different periods, but Alcalá's novel follows a linear chronology, one fantastically blended with borrowings from Kabbalah, Native American spirituality, and representations of miraculous cures and visionaries. *Days of Awe* continuously oscillates between the distant and the nearer past, especially the beginning, middle, and end of the twentieth century's key periods: the birth of Alejandra's father, Enrique, to a crypto-Jewish family in a remote part of Oriente Province, the midcentury's revolution coinciding with her own birth, and the 1980s as the beginning of Alejandra's returns to Cuba. Moving between Cuba and the United States, with parts extending back to Spain and Cuba of the past centuries, *Days of Awe* unravels through its structure the border-crossing, transnational, and divided character of Cuban American, U.S. Latinx, and crypto-Jewish histories and their overlaps.

Similarly, Alcalá's narrative choices include juxtapositions and convergences of settings and perspectives that characterize her approach to secret, lost, but plausible histories of the Americas as crossroads. Although it is the kind of historical novel that stays within one period (the end of the nineteenth century and the beginning of the twentieth century), each chapter of *Spirits of the Ordinary* has several different narrators who inhabit or sojourn the northern Mexico borderlands area. The changes of perspective help project "a strong sense of the still-heterogeneous population of northern Mexico in this period" (Delgadillo 2011, 146) and blend peoples and stories that are not usually represented together.

The omniscient narrator of *Spirits of the Ordinary* connects its subjects, whereas in *Days of Awe* Alejandra the narrator—heir to broken and secret family narratives—pieces together in the first person a hidden history of Sephardi Cuban Jews and other Cuban diasporans. The novels are built on a gradual unraveling of what crypto-Jewish and Sephardi identity means to the generations that have inherited this hidden legacy, but the emphasis is less on individual interiorities than on the interpersonal and historical entanglements. In *Spirits of the Ordinary* Zacarías and his offspring bring together Native and Jewish worlds, and in *Days of Awe* Alejandra comes to inhabit an openly Jewish identity through her attachment to Sephardi and Cuban diasporic worlds, unlike her father, Enrique, the twentieth-century tormented secret Jew.

In both works, as with past and contemporary testimonies and studies of crypto-Jewish life, women play important roles in understanding and narrating converso Jewishness (Jacobs 2002; Melammed 2004). In *Days of Awe* the narrator is a 1.5-generation Cuban woman born on the day of the Cuban revolution and brought to the United States as a 2-year-old. She discovers, keeps, and tells the story of her family's secret. In *Spirits of the Ordinary* Mariana Caraval, who is mute, understands spirituality and Judaism more profoundly than her husband, Julio, who reads sacred Jewish texts most of the day. Both works destigmatize secret Jewish identity and practice, albeit without treating them as fixed, continuous, or consistent.

Converso as Metaphor

Days of Awe and *Spirits of the Ordinary* also have an analogical dimension, mobilizing Sephardi and crypto-Jewish representations as metaphors for other constructs. This comparative impulse is not unique to the U.S. Latinx imagination. As we saw in Chapter 1, many, if not most, recent fictional works that have recreated medieval and postexpulsion Sephardi history draw analogies to other catastrophes, including the Holocaust and the torments of Iberian and Latin American repression and dictatorships. Obejas, whose comparative impulse is explicit and extensive, creates an analogy between Cubans (particularly diaspora and exile Cubans) and Jews through many references to their common sensibilities and condition of exile—for example, Alejandra avers that Cubans are "the Jews of the Caribbean" (Obejas 2002, 104). Obejas also makes parallel stories of the martyrdom of the indigenous in the early days of the Spanish conquest and of the Jews in Masada at the time of the Romans (104–5). She makes the comparison diachronically and transnationally, drawing on her current moment as well, and the novel's structure is based on her narrator's traversal through time and space.

Another analogical moment is set in the United States. In Chicago, where Alejandra's parents settle after fleeing the revolution and where both father and daughter work as translators, Alejandra's Ashkenazi American lover, Leni, wishes to be unmarked as a modern American, but this desire is foiled by her physiognomy and dark complexion, which identifies her as Jewish to outsiders. In a dramatic moment for Leni, a Christian stranger wishes everyone on the bus a merry Christmas and "a happy Hanukkah to you, sister," seriously disturbing Leni, who does not identify as a Jew ("My parents are Jewish," she explains to Alejandra) and does not acknowledge the racialization, not of Jews. Leni's need to be unmarked recalls the crypto-Jewish experience and identity-in-hiding that is the story of Alejandra's own family. Hence we are led to think analogically about the desire for the integrated Jewish American to be undetectable as the impulse of a sort of secular contemporary crypto-Jew, who prefers to be in hiding or invisible, one who would have been the subject of Max Nordau's hostile critique (see the Introduction).

This is parallel to the issue of assimilation raised in much fiction and thought about converso history, as we began to see in Chapter 1. As with many episodes in *Days of Awe*, however, the analogy signifies on many levels. Leni is also one of two "dark" Jews in the book, challenging U.S. and mainstream Jewish narratives about Jews' Europeanness and whiteness. Although Alejandra and her father, Enrique, pass for Spanish and Italian or "nothing" at all, the skin color of Leni and Enrique's grandfather's Lebanese friend, nicknamed "the Moor," betrays the "Orientals" within.[3] Included in the exposure of a pseudo-multicultural, assimilationist society, in which those inhabiting the presumably nonexistent norm are always interpellating others, is a presentation of normative Jewish identity as other-than-white and a critique of Euro-American Jews' embrace of whiteness and sense of entitlement to be invisible.

Leni's rejection of Jewish identity irks Alejandra, likely because it recalls her own father's enduring intransigence about admitting his secret. Although safely ensconced in a Chicago suburb full of Jewish people, Enrique, whose parents lived in Cuba in fear of being discovered as faux Catholics, denies Jewish faith or origin but prays secretly in the basement every Friday night. Leni's rejection of Jewishness based on descent is confident and seems untraumatized. But both Alejandra's coaxing Leni into Jewish identification and the Christian stranger's marking Leni as different transform her into the crypto-Jew she says she is decidedly not, unless one argues that Jewish identity is fixed in the blood and body and not in affinity, belief, or practice. Hence, although Enrique is a perennial crypto-Jew, hiding no matter how low the potential of danger, Leni is interpellated as a crypto-Jew by Alejandra.

Assimilationist cultures do not simply harbor crypto-identities but produce them against the will of their subjects. The self-disavowed or else hidden Jew belies the putative openness of U.S. society. Through the stereotype of the tragic, weeping crypto-Jew (Enrique) and the analogy to the contemporary assimilated crypto-Jew who represses her Jewishness to no avail (the rebellious Leni), Obejas helps us rethink facile notions of U.S. multiculturalism and ethnicity, where one chooses identities and can refashion oneself. Attuned to contemporary racial politics, Obejas returns crypto-Jewish history and identity to the present through her imaginative act. She does not use it only as an analogy to the discontents of contemporary pluralistic societies. She also underlines the ways in which it has survived as a signal of the enduring racialized nature of social relations, even when racial categories shift and are subject to redefinition.

Metaphorization of the so-called Jewish condition has been an object of critique, including by Sander Gilman in his *Multiculturalism and the Jews* (2006). Gilman studies what he calls "multicultural literature by non-Jews," which, in the South African, European, and U.S. contexts to which he refers, encompasses works by people of color or racialized minorities. He sees a problem with images of Jews in the works he identifies, ranging from Achmat Dangor's *Kafka's Curse* to Zadie Smith's *White Teeth* to Gish Jen's *Mona in the Promised Land*, along with many others. Gilman argues that global multicultural literature avails itself of Jewish identities and histories only to reduce them to stereotypical Jewish physiognomy and ahistorical notions of Jewish victimhood, primarily resulting from an ahistorical understanding of the Holocaust. For Gilman, such representations serve the particular purpose of representing the Jewish condition as a metaphor for the assimilation anxieties of other minorities: "Jews seem to have become the touchstone for all of the pitfalls that present themselves to other cultural groups." And he asserts further that "Jews on the brave new frontier of multiculturalism seem always to be the subject of comparison" (Gilman 2006, 151). In other words, comparing ethnicities in fictional narratives or in ethnic studies is a tricky business, because instead of underlining the particularities of ethnicities, comparison can actually erase or obscure difference.

In Obejas and Alcalá, comparison works differently. The authors do use the *converso* experience as an analogy to other experiences of oppression and displacement and to strategies of secrecy that counter sexual taboos, religious criminalization, and racism. Especially in Obejas's case, the analogy of transhistorical Jews to Cubans can sometimes seem forced and stereotypical. But Obejas and Alcalá do not obscure the crypto-Jewish experience by using it only as a metaphor or analogy to other ethnic groups; instead, they place Sephardi and converso stories at the center of their texts. For Obejas, conversos are not just a "touchstone," as Gilman puts it, for a Cuban exilic identity that is the main source of the analogy; in *Days of Awe* conversos are at the foundations of Cuban history itself. Indeed, even though the converso experience is central to these novels, it is not a stable comparable entity because the works relentlessly complicate crypto-Jewish identities. In *Days of Awe*, instead of a figure of "the Jew," "the converso," "the crypto-Jew," or "Sephardis," Obejas creates a multiplicity of characters, who vary in relation to their Jewishness and other belongings. Even among crypto-Jews, there is no fixed identity: Alejandra's great-grandfather, Ytzak, becomes completely invested in his Jewish identity, whereas his daughter Sima and her husband, Luis, are ignorant and indifferent, going through the rituals mechanically and fearfully. Ytzak and Alejandra are interested in openness, with Ytzak, Enrique, and Alejandra particularly obsessed by their origins, whereas Alejandra's mother, Nena, is indifferent to her own family's (the Abravanels) long-buried converso roots in Seville. She sees them as yet another aspect of the Cuban *mestizaje* that produced her and part of her blended practices, which include Santería and Catholicism. The family Alejandra is close to in Havana, the Menachs, is also internally divided as to the import of religion and Judaism to the revolution or to Cuba's and their own identities (Obejas 2002, 335–39).

Enrique, Ytzak's grandson and Alejandra's father, exhibits another, rather tormented kind of relationship to Judaism. Of all the characters in the book, Enrique comes closest to the archetypal crypto-Jew who wears his shame on his body, as do other characters discussed in Chapter 1. Through him *Days of Awe* refutes teleological ideas of modernity and freedom, with each generation moving closer to emancipation than the previous: Although Enrique's grandfather embraces Judaism freely after centuries of hidden, repressed practice, Enrique himself is riddled with shame and crushed under the burden of secrecy. He lies to his daughter, claiming that "we are Catholics like everybody else in Cuba," and continues to be secretive after they go into exile from Cuba. His affect reflects his suffering: He is given to melancholia, which is reflected in his "sad eyes" (Obejas 2002, 43), "nervous breathing" (53), and "timid voice" (54). Enrique suffers from his own "feverish racial memory" (39), in which "voices from centuries before echoed in his heart" (43). Upset, he cries and gesticulates in a way Alejandra calls "cryptic" (266). In fact, Enrique weeps several times in the novel. Once, in a dramatic scene, he is caught praying and applying phylacteries by his daughter and her friend; at the end of this scene Enrique's hand is bloodied from accidentally shattered glass and "his face [is] wet from tears" (109). Enrique, the martyr without a cause, the self-hating crypto-Jew, is a literal embodiment of the "lachrymose" version of Jewish history (Baron 1928). The helpless, disempowered, tearful representative of a hated race, he suffers his secrecy and abjection alone, without recourse to family or networks of crypto-Jews and other Jews.

Critics such as David Eng and Shinhee Han (2000) and Anne Cheng (2000) have argued that racial melancholy is not simply pathological but often a tactic of resistance and a reminder of the permanent injury of racism. But Enrique's passing as purely Catholic complicates his position as an emblem of the injuries of discrimination and intolerance, because it is not transgressive or oppositional or even enacted in the name of survival. Even though passing, always double-edged, can reinforce but also destabilize and flout existing oppressive social categories, Enrique's passing obscures the story of Catholic persecution of Jews *and* the privileged place of white Jews in postwar United States.

Although such an archetypal representation of the crypto-Jew seems transhistorical, Obejas signals the differing attitudes of other family members and the context in which Alejandra's parents carry out an anachronistic secrecy. This confirms that returns to suppressed histories do not necessarily entail consistent findings. Returns open up uncertainties rather than occasioning discoveries and recoveries. The scene of the 1939 burial of Enrique's grandmother in Oriente is one of many telling scenes: Weeping and going "into hysterics" (Obejas 2002, 133), Enrique's mother, Sima, tries to prevent her father, Ytzak, from performing Jewish ritual at the graveside, given the suspicious and watchful eyes of the neighbors and her certainty "that a report about Ytzak's brashness would go out to secret inquisitors who'd make their way to the hilly woods of Oriente and force them to repent" (133). The conflict within the family regarding secrecy and revelation shows that Enrique's parents resort to ancient references and enduring fears about the Inquisition in the twentieth century.

That this is not simply paranoia, however, is indicated in a couple of ways by Obejas: Shortly before this episode, we find out that the family's region "had been the only city besides Havana to have an official tribunal of the Inquisition" and a plaza where "Jews and other nonbelievers had been publicly humiliated and 'relaxed'" (Obejas 2002, 122). Moreover, at the beginning of the twentieth century, "traditions lingered," including of parading effigies of *judíos*, while "Ytzak and the other anusim kept quiet, sometimes even torching the figures themselves" (122). Last, the funeral leading to the interfamilial tension is taking place in 1939, adding the lament of a "sobbing" Enrique that "being Jewish is a fucking curse. Everybody hates us! My God, look at what's happening in Europe—no one cares, no one even believes it" (135). Although fearing the Inquisition is anachronistic, the historical context of the Nazi genocide makes it less delusional. The conflict between the older and younger generations about safety and openness and the uncertain standing of Jews in particular places and times prevent a linear story about the progress toward emancipation. Instead, returns provide a sense of tension and a lack of resolution about the conversos and Jews' fate.

A key aspect of crypto-Jewishness, remnant secrecy, is articulated by Leah, Enrique's grandmother and Ytzak's wife, when Ytzak was still Antonio but trying to be openly Jewish and compelling Leah to stop being "a crypto-Jew, trapped by tradition, habit, and fear": When Ytzak says, "There has to be another way, . . . I can't be pretending I'm only half of who I am," Leah answers, "But this *is* who we are" (Obejas 2002, 148), confirming secrecy and dissimulation as a way of life. But Alejandra's return to secret history is motivated by the need for truth and the destruction of the secret. Such returns disrupt both the present and the past; in this case, Alejandra, who is coming of age by patching together narrative fragments and filling in the gaps, disrupts the essence of the past located in a public secret. As Maya Socolovsky observes, "While the narrative insists on the secrecy of crypto-Judaism, and even tells us that the means for finding out the secret is closed (Enrique won't speak), it lets us know that Alejandra knows the secret. The text thus performs a particular understanding of crypto-Judaism as simultaneously revealed and obscured" (2003, 242).

Alejandra extends her attempts to reveal, out, and display in multiple situations. Although Leni and her Jewish boyfriend deny the existence of a "Jewish race," Leni's "big dark eyes, full lips, and cinnamon skin" make her "exotic" (Latina or Moroccan or Greek in a way Alejandra is not) as well as "Jewish" to the aggressively discerning observer. Alejandra herself scoffs at Leni's "I am not Jewish, my parents are" line with "Oh, you're one of those," calling out her "passing" as problematic but at the same time denying her agency to self-define.

Alejandra's role is that of an inquisitor with her father as well, compelling and even shaming Enrique into "confession." Alejandra confesses, "I secretly envy the inevitability of her [Leni's] Jewishness" because in terms of visibility "I'm this blank space, unconnected to history, bloodless" (Obejas 2002, 182). Frustrated by her own passing as non-Cuban (and non-Jewish), Alejandra tries to refute Leni's own denial of Jewishness as well by trying to "out" her father aggressively. Watching the fall of the Berlin Wall on television, Enrique reacts, once again, with his body: "My father sat motionless, his hands beached on his thighs, heavy and useless. He stared, just stared, his eyes red, his skin flushed" (172). When the screen flashes the swastika on a neo-Nazi's forehead, Alejandra taunts her father: "A little racial memory, Papi? A little trouble with the family secret?" She thinks her father, "the reluctant shame-faced Jew . . . would collapse like the wall into my mother's arms" as usual (173). Surprised by Enrique's much stronger reaction, Alejandra tells us only toward the end of the novel that, growing up in the 1930s, Enrique had witnessed anti-Semitic campaigns in Cuba, including media smears and a daily radio show by Nazis, a Cuban Nazi party, and a Falangist party inspired by Spanish fascism. Both Enrique and Ytzak had been beaten up by German immigrants and other youth. More shockingly, Alejandra finds out, in the midst of an anti-Semitic atmosphere around the time of the rejection of the *St. Louis* carrying Jewish refugees, her father, caught up in a pro-Nazi demonstration, identified and labeled as a Jew, screamed "Heil Hitler" out of desperation, which recalls for the reader the earlier description of the crypto-Jews' torching of effigies of Jews during Holy Week. Enrique "ran through the streets of Old Havana, down Amargura and Luz and Inquisidor," famous and symbolically named parts of the city. This meeting of foreign and homegrown fascism and the Inquisition in Enrique's mind and on the streets of Havana ends with him "swooning" (353), adding the shame of this event to that of being secretly Jewish.

Like Alejandra, Enrique suffers from what he perceives as inauthenticity and mixture as the fount of his identity—for example, he is devastated when he learns that the syncretic crypto-Jewish figure of "Saint Esterika" does not belong to Judaism proper but is instead a hybrid Jewish-Catholic creation. Enrique cannot "confess" to being Jewish no matter how hard his daughter tries to get him to do so. This is not necessarily because he "has a Jewish heart implanted in a Christian body" (Yovel 2009, 327), in terminology analogous to the outdated discourse about gay and lesbian sexuality ("a man in a woman's body" and vice versa). It is not clear where Enrique's true loyalties lie, but he suffers from their division. In his longing for a unified, true, and safe identity, Enrique seizes on Spain as a homeland. A literary person, at night he reads "ancient" authors of Spain; the Sephardi poet Judah Halevi is his favorite. Being a translator, Alejandra tells us, "was a spiritual return to Spain, although he never went there in real life"; in visits to Latin America Enrique's "painstaking manners impressed everyone as old-fashioned and very Spanish" (Obejas 2002, 91). The refrain of his parents that he had adopted without believing in it was, "We are Spanish, descended from nobility" (141).

This notion of distinction and the quest to obscure Jewishness, reminiscent of *limpieza de sangre* discourses, is dismissed by both Ytzak and Alejandra: "When the neo-Nazis come, he and I will both be tossed into the ovens" (Obejas 2002, 174), Ytzak had said. "It was his way," Alejandra explains, "of creating and preserving Spain, of explaining his otherness in the U.S. without the blatant trauma of racism" (91). In some ways Enrique fulfills the stereotype of the Spanish-identifying (i.e., "white") Latino, but his Spain-centrism also conceals crypto-Jewishness at the same time it clandestinely acknowledges it.

Finally, as Maya Socolovsky notes (2003, 234), we are made to understand that Enrique suffers from but denies the profound yearning for a Cuba that has rejected him and projects it instead onto Spain, both a place and "scar tissue" (Obejas 2002, 18). The crypto-Jewish problematics of nondetection, inauthenticity, and indeterminacy (Chapter 1) are parallel. And they coincide with Alejandra's own diasporic, in-between condition as the child of exiles, one central to the Cuban American narrative of Obejas's 1.5 generation, whose search for unified, authentic, single identities is almost always inconclusive. As with Alcalá's *Spirits of the Ordinary*, each character represents a different dimension of these entanglements, which cannot be fixed in singular meanings.

Like Obejas, who invites us to consider the parallels between Sephardi crypto-Judaism and assimilation under modernity, Alcalá also sets up comparisons, especially between the double lives of the crypto-Jews and those of the community around them. For instance, the Catholic family that Zacarías Caraval marries into has plenty of its own secrets and shame, including adultery and androgynous relatives who must hide their identities or leave the community. One chapter is told from the perspective of a female photographer who takes on a male disguise, thus becoming a crypto-female, in order to be able to travel and photograph the Southwest. This chapter not only adds a Jewish dimension to the experience of the borderlands, as do all the chapters in *Spirits of the Ordinary*, but also recalls other representations of female masquerades in iconic masculinist eras and "Western" spaces.[4] Alcalá connects Jewish and gendered fates through contact and conflict zones in the United States and Mexico so that in the novel sexuality crimes and secret genders are analogous to hidden religious "crimes."

In his last attempt to strike gold, Zacarías Caraval leaves behind his crypto-Jewish parents and his stale marriage to Catholic Estela to obsessively pursue his conviction that he is destined to find precious metals. During his final days as a prospector, he settles in Casas Grandes (or Paquimé), the actual site of a well-preserved town of adobe structures in Chihuahua, which reached its peak as a trading center from the thirteenth to the fifteenth centuries and is now a UNESCO World Heritage site. This is where, as I explain later, Zacarías becomes a shaman-like figure to the indigenous people, combining belief systems and providing healing.

In his incisive reading of *Spirits of the Ordinary*, Jonathan Freedman points out that the Casas Grandes community's blending of Christian, Native, and kabbalistic beliefs is an instantiation of a "generative remaking" emblematic of borderlands syncretism. Moreover, Freedman (2008, 233) argues that Alcalá draws on the figure of the Jew, particularly the crypto-Jew, as a trope for the syncretism and the indeterminacy of Mexican racial and religious identity in nation making, serving as a "metonym for a wide variety of secret identities and hidden practices forbidden and feared by Church and state alike that lie roiling under the surface" (236–37). Freedman is not claiming that "the Jew" is deployed as a "mere" and inauthentic metaphor, as Gilman argues about the texts he analyzes. Instead, Freedman suggests that the figure of the crypto-Jew is productive and axial to understanding other secret syncretisms. I agree with Freedman's assessment, but I also want to emphasize that here crypto-Jewishness plays both a comparative role, as he suggests, and a *connective* role. Freedman also suggests that the crypto-Jew is "the only stable entity" while all else is in flux, which is true in one sense and incomplete in another. The crypto-Jew is not primarily an analogy or unchanging paradigm.

Although much in the borderlands is indeterminate, as Freedman (2008) argues, the crypto-Jew is not necessarily a stable figure, especially given the varieties and internal differentiation of them, even within one family. In both *Days of Awe* and *Spirits of the Ordinary*, forms of (crypto-)Jewishness vary considerably within the same family and community; therefore we cannot conclude that the novels deploy the figure of "the Jew" or "the crypto-Jew" as a fixed entity reduced merely to a subject of comparison. Just as in Alejandra's family there is a variety of ways of being crypto-Jewish as well as Cuban, in *Spirits of the Ordinary* family members are at odds with each other's outlook. The father, Julio, the dry book learner and traditionalist, is against syncretism and in fact destroys his New World garden in order to bring it order and make it "civilized." His is not a borderlands perspective. By contrast, the female head of the family, Mariana, is a repository of spirituality. Zacarías, their nonobservant son, is entirely different from his parents (and most everyone else). He has received both Jewish and Christian education but is rebellious "against the name he bore" and has "no love for books, tradition, or of enclosed places" (Alcalá 1996, 23). He is an amalgam of the iconic "frontiersman" on a solitary quest for gold (albeit without the inclinations of a conquistador), a Jewish mystic, and a shamanistic healer. There is no fixed crypto-Jewish identity in either novel.

The two works are informed to a certain degree by an analogical impulse: in *Days of Awe* long-standing crypto-Jewishness is akin to Ashkenazi assimilation or crypto-Cubanness and in *Spirits of the Ordinary* the public secret of intersexuality and cross-dressing has something to do with Jewishness-in-hiding. Both novels reconfigure the terms of their comparisons and signal overlapping practices among the different identities they portray. As Janet R. Jakobsen's discussion of Jewish and queer identities and activism shows, analogies can be forceful in arguing for recognition, rights, and equality through a "logic of equivalence" between one struggle and another (2003, 66). However, Jakobsen also asserts, relying on other scholars' work, that analogies are problematic because they separate the analyzed terms, privileging the first term (the basis) of the analogy and neglecting the second. Like Gilman, Jakobsen suggests that analogies lead to a loss of specificity and differentiation between the compared terms, which are then generalized through discussions of marginalization and minoritization. Jakobsen argues instead for "relational complexity" and "complicity" between "Jews" and "queers" to emphasize the possibilities of intersection, which is precisely Alcalá's and Obejas's construction of Latinx and Jewish histories and identities: "complicitious," overlapping, or nondiscrete. Obejas, for example, is attentive in *Days of Awe* (as she is in all her writing) to the particularities of Cuban history and social formations at large: The revolution, postrevolutionary Havana, and Cuban exile politics shape the novel in equal measure to its Sephardi and crypto-Jewish dimension, so that Jewish and Cuban histories become intertwined.

Two modes coexist in *Days of Awe*. One is the act of comparison that Obejas sometimes deploys, where two objects remain seemingly separate and stable. For example, she parses the anti-Semitic commonplace "Cubans are the Jews of the Caribbean" (Obejas 2002, 103–4) and endows it with new meanings based on parallels of exilic experience. The other mode involves the discourse of entanglement in terms of common historical destiny and kinship with Cuba. When Moisés Menach, the family friend in Havana, asks Alejandra in a letter to be more understanding of her father's closeted crypto-Jewishness, he explains that Enrique is stuck with it: "All that anguish in his blood. It's not unlike your situation as a Cuban in the U.S.: Even if you wanted to assimilate, to become one of them, you would still know in your heart that you are Cuban" (186). Alejandra, born on the night of the revolution, has been marked by the island and its revolution "in a way that no American could possibly know" (186). The crypto-Cubanness of Alejandra, exacerbated by her perceived white rather than Cuban looks, is analogous here to the crypto-Jewish condition. But beyond serving as metaphors for one another, crypto-Jewishness and Cubanness are also entangled, in the story of Alejandra's family and in the history of Cuba.

Caribbean Convergences and Authenticities

Obejas and Alcalá investigate secrecy and find syncretism and multiplicity in a Caribbean and borderlands past generated by intermarriage, migration, and forced or voluntary adaptation. Identifications and histories are so multistranded in both Obejas and Alcalá that crypto-Jewishness alone or even Cuban exile history or Mexico's borderlands indigeneities cannot define the novels separately. Obejas also lays bare, especially through Alejandra, the complexity of the compulsion to produce oneself as a descendant of crypto-Jews, a controversial claim as we have seen. In Alejandra's case, this is closely related to her desire, as a 1.5-generation diasporan belonging fully to neither Cuba nor the United States, to be fully Cuban. And, like so many other Cuban American novels, this desire is told through a narrative of return to the homeland (see I. H. López 2015), which, in the case of *Days of Awe* is also a return to a hidden Jewish past. Alejandra returns repeatedly to Cuba, the site of her intense desire to belong, in lieu of her parents, who refuse to go, in a familiar intergenerational conflict in Cuban American writing. As much as Alejandra wants to acknowledge her Jewish identity, what she yearns for is to be fully Cuban and be identified by others as such, but she is not completely acknowledged this way either phenotypically or culturally.

Still, Cuba remains the "true country" for Alejandra and, despite everything, for Enrique. His predilection for Spain, the novel implies, is a cover for his spurned love for Cuba, where he felt persecuted for being Jewish, especially in the 1930s and 1940s. But at the novel's end, Alejandra fulfills Enrique's deathbed request for her to recite the Kaddish, the mourner's prayer. The second time she does this—the first being at a small Tunisian synagogue despite her status as a woman who is barred from this duty—is at the Havana harbor on a rainy day. There she offers "a different, more appropriate kaddish," which is from a poem by the medieval Spanish Jewish poet Halevi.

Days of Awe concludes with the words, "Judah Halevi may or may not have made it to his Zion, but here, through me, my father is at rest in his" (Obejas 2002, 357). These words solidly locate the crypto-Jew not in a place of remote origins, like Spain or a territorialized "Zion," but in Cuba, the true homeland, even though at that point in the "special period" after the fall of the Berlin Wall, everything is chaotic and uncertain, as Alejandra finds in one of her many returns. After all, as Alejandra told us at the beginning of the novel, Spain "was scar tissue, whereas Cuba was a gaping historical wound" (18), not an idealized homeland. Yet, to Enrique and his grandfather, Ytzak, its capital city was a Zion nevertheless.

The young Alejandra also "held Havana out to myself like a *secret hiding place*, a trump card, the Zion where I'd be welcomed after all my endless, unplanned travels in the diaspora" (Obejas 2002, 55; emphasis added). Alejandra's returns, however, occasion less homecoming and more the convergence of seemingly disparate elements of Cuban life. Just as Alejandra comes out of the womb and is greeted by a mother performing Santería to heal her, a priest blessing her with Catholic prayer, and her father defiantly doing the same in Hebrew on the very eve of the revolution, Enrique is commemorated as Cuban, Sephardi, and Catholic all at once through the scattering of ashes and the words of Halevi in Havana's harbor. Alejandra was not able to out her father, but instead she transgressed all boundaries to honor her father's mixed legacy: She performed a male role in the synagogue, defied the injunction against cremation, "prayed" with poetry, and made the Havana seawall a site of Jewish ritual. Going beyond analogies of Cubanness and Jewishness, Alejandra merges them along with marking the overlapping dilemmas of authenticity as diasporic Cubanness and crypto-Jewishness.

In a further and productive complication, the terms of (in)authenticity themselves have been positioned as containing extensive multiplicities. Jewishness is represented by Sephardi traditions (in which Alejandra participates) and the multinationality of the kind represented in the small synagogue that Alejandra chooses as the most comfortable one to attend. Cubanness begins as a crossroads of traditions at her birth. What is more, Nena is descended not only from the Sephardi and crypto-Jewish Abravanels of Seville and Cuba but also from a slave and a Confederate soldier. Alejandra insists frequently on *mestizaje* as a defining feature of Cuba, including its patron saint, the Virgin of Charity of Cobre, whose pictorial representations and story feature two indigenous boys and a slave youth who discover her statue, miraculously dry, in the Caribbean. This is the Virgin that her mother holds close but shatters in the exilic passage to the United States, to be mended later by Enrique's deft fingers.

There are repeated references to the indigenous and Afro-Cuban character of the island. Structured around returns, *Days of Awe* is about finding multistranded narratives and remnants at the place of origin and exile. Similarly, in *Spirits of the Ordinary*, Alcalá's fictional return to lost crypto-Jewish history involves not only an injection of the repressed Jewish element into the story of the borderlands but also an imaginative insertion of narratives of solidarity and originary entanglements in a transamerican historical context of violence and separations.

Curiously, however, the background of the queer story is missing from *Days of Awe*, a novel that educates its readers about several places and periods. And despite the abundance of other analogies, the obvious one of the crypto-Jewish as queer and vice versa is not used in Obejas's novel. Queer closeting and outing tropes are frequent in writing about crypto-Jews, including in Yirmiyahu Yovel's statement quoted earlier contrasting the impulses of the heart to the strictures of the body. Here, the queer dimension of experience is the only one among the Cuban, diasporan, and crypto-Jewish facets that is almost unproblematic; only one minor incident is presented in terms of analogies and convergences. Queerness mostly exists in its own realm. Alejandra's open bisexuality has no background and is not a cause of internal or familial conflict for her or her lovers. Explicit sex scenes, including Alejandra's triangulated desire for the young female lover of her male lover-to-be, Orlando, in Havana, are presented as uncomplicated. In an interview with critic Ilan Stavans printed in the reader's guide that follows the novel, Obejas has a telling response to Stavans's request that she comment on sexuality as "an essential element" in her work: "I'm not especially interested in assimilation, but I am interested in normalization. . . . In *Days of Awe*, I tried to just let everybody be whatever they were going to be, to live and love according to their hearts rather than any particular label" (Obejas 2002, n.p.).

The freedom for queerness to just "be" does not apply to the other categories in the novel. Cubanness, Cuban diaspora identity, and crypto-Jewishness cannot just "be," even if they overlap with queer discourses past and present, including "negative" queer affects such as shame and melancholy, which stymie Enrique in particular, though they can also be productive. One effect of what Obejas calls normalization is that in this historical novel with many forays into Cuban, crypto-Jewish, and Sephardi history in various periods, there is an "absence of a queer past."[5] Instead, it is crypto-Jews and Cuba that have histories, separate and entangled, "gaping wounds" and sources of resilience. The queer dimension is muted, though it is far from absent: In addition to Alejandra, Celestino, an intertextual reference to the gay Cuban author Reinaldo Arenas's eponymous novel *Celestino antes del alba* (translated as *Singing From the Well*), appears in the character of a countryside boy who learns to read from the younger Enrique, who is teaching while languishing in remote Oriente. Celestino, who writes poetry, much to the distaste of his fellow peasants, is found hanging from a tree. Another reference is to Farruluque, a queer character out of José Lezama Lima's work *Paradise*, one of Cuba's most famous novels. In the interview with Stavans, Obejas enumerates these and several other intertextual references she made in homage to canonical Cuban authors, many of whom, she points out, have been gay. But the queerness of Obejas's text is neutral, unlike anything else in the novel, and compels us to ask about the relation of normalization to the hiding, erasure, and forgetting of pasts that are the very themes of her novel.

New *Mestizaje* in the Borderlands

Alcalá inserts a converso and crypto-Sephardi presence into our borderlands imaginary, going beyond the use of the figure of the crypto-Jew as grounds for understanding syncretism; she links the fates of Native Americans and Sephardi crypto-Jews as two groups who have been targeted for disappearance, to different extents and by different means, contra the official Creole, mestizo, Ladino, and Christian stories that dominate the continent. Through the imagined story of Zacarías's time with the indigenous people of the borderlands, Alcalá creates a moment in time marked by the massacre of both Indians and descendants of crypto-Jews. This is prefigured in Zacarías's conversations at the beginning of the Casas Grandes venture, when the people hear his kabbalistic creation story. Jesusita, an older Tarahumara/Raramuri woman, tells him that they share the messianic vision of "the fourth world" and that, since the Conquest, they too pray in secret and retain their devotion to secret sacred places.

As Theresa Delgadillo explains elegantly in her analysis of the Zohar's relevance to the narrative, Alcalá's works "stage a symbolic mission of returning the voices of the marginalized to history, recognizing the multiple spiritualities and sacred texts of the Americas, and opening the door to further spiritual renewals and revisions" (2011, 166). Just as Obejas weaves a Cuban story out of known and unknown histories and includes the rare Jewish element, Alcalá in *Spirits of the Ordinary* creates a new narrative that leads us to reflect on the missing archive of converso descendants in the borderlands and its convergences.

Zacarías's time in Casas Grandes is the key site and time of the novel. The locus of Zacarías's transformation is what turns out to be not Cíbola, the city of gold of his dreams, but his vision beholding the cliff houses of a city of light "from another world, another time" (Alcalá 1996, 182) that regenerates Zacarías's self and spirituality. This miraculous encounter with the self is interesting for the role that it plays in Zacarías's bond with the indigenous people as a consequence of his perceived powers as a healer, an accidental shaman. Because he is also known as a storyteller of (kabbalistic) miracles, Zacarías acquires a status and a vocation he had not sought and is unsure he is worthy of. Around him grows a community of indigenous people, drawn to his powers and ready to put aside their own differences. They move in droves into the abandoned Casas Grandes in the hopes of being healed by Zacarías, whom they name the Tecolote (owl), and reestablish this site as the crossroads that it once was as a trade center. With them, Zacarías abandons Spanish and speaks exclusively in *el llanero*, a regional trading language, as the narrator tells us. Even Apaches, enemies of many other northern Mexican tribes (including the Opata, subjects of Alcalá's novels, who helped the Mexican army forces fight them), seek help from Zacarías. Although there are shades of "the great white savior" stereotype here, the young Carvajal cannot really "save": The community is destroyed when the government deems it a threat to its project of the brutal suppression of the indigenous people, most infamously of the Yaquis but also of many other groups, such as the Opata. As a result, the Native Americans in Casas Grandes are martyred after they lead their Tecolote to safety.

Before he leaves the area in flight from the Mexican army, Zacarías returns to Saltillo briefly to bid goodbye to his family and to circumcise his infant son with his own hands, despite earlier indifference to his roots. He crosses the Rio Grande in search of sanctuary, like many after him. The journey, however, is punctuated by his discovery of a resting spot in a "new world garden," an oasis of Jewish life identical to his father's; this one belongs to a Jewish family that welcomes him. Yet despite these acts by Zacarías, which signal a return to a Judaism he had previously taken little interest in, the Caravals do not simply adhere to their ancestral faith but continue in the path of mixing that Zacarías established by marrying a Catholic woman, furthered also by contacts he established during his miraculous time in Casas Grandes. Zacarías's half-Catholic, half-crypto-Jewish son becomes a Protestant and marries Rosa, an Opata, and the novel ends with the words, "The time had come to begin again" (Alcalá 1996, 244).

Zacarías's prospecting for gold and his surname's evocation of Luis de Carvajal (as conqueror, a servant of empire and church, and as accused Judaizer, their victim) associate him with *conquistadores*. After all, other conquerors are also reputed, sometimes without evidence, to have had converso forebears. And it is not rare to hear some New Mexicans identifying with crypto-Jewish roots to express pride in conquerors with converso roots as their ancestors, which is only a twist on the Spanish and conquistador identification (Nieto-Phillips 2004) that has long been a part of New Mexican Hispanic culture. But Zacarías's eccentricity and his experience of spiritual *mestizaje* (Delgadillo 2011) at Casas Grandes and the *mestizaje* of his descendants in Native America delink him from the figure of the converso conqueror. Instead of existing in isolation and martyrdom, his crypto-Jewishness is forever entangled with the Opata and other nations. The connection with the diverse Native communities that regathered in Casas Grandes survives in Alcalá's imagination, as we see in her subsequent novels, in which the intertwining of Opata and crypto-Sephardi destinies begun in *Spirits of the Ordinary* continues, albeit in other guises and sites along the U.S.-Mexico borderlands.

Sephardi Jews and indigenous people are connected not only analogically, through the common experience of genocides and forced or voluntary syncretisms, but also as fellow subjects to the *same* genocidal project: racist national identity and colonialism formed around religion and pioneered in fifteenth-century Christian Spain against Jewish and Muslim Spain and disseminated through the Americas. This shared fate as victims of 1492 does not signal discovery and expulsion as equivalent outcomes in the novel; when the Mexican soldiers arrive in Casas Grandes, Zacarías is moved by the Indians to safety and told to leave them to their struggle. Even when a pogrom against Jews and their associates breaks out at the instigation of the Mexican military, which accuses Zacarías of fomenting trouble among Indians, Zacarías and his parents escape separately, whereas the Indians are either murdered or made to return to their forced labor.

But Alcalá also shows how the destinies of the borderlands people overlap, especially in her intertwining of Jewish and Native stories, present in the literature of the Americas but infrequently noted.[6] In Alcalá's oeuvre, Sephardi, crypto-Jewish, Mexican, and Native stories are treated as separate entities that are, moreover, tied together. For example, *The Flower in the Skull* (1998), the second novel in Alcalá's trilogy, places the Opata at the center of a narrative that ends with the marriage of Zacarías and Estela's Protestant son to a Tucsonian of Opata and Mexican heritage (who is also half-Irish by parentage). Alcalá's novels, each a different facet of the prism she has constructed, recast the transamerican imaginary by emphasizing the occluded Native (especially) and converso elements as essential to borderland histories and identities.

Imagining Transamerican Indigenous-Sephardi Fates

Although critics have charged that Chicanx and other Latinx are whitening their identities through Sephardism (see the Introduction), Latinx fiction writers who trace the absent archive of underimagined entanglements assert indigeneity rather than deny it and also link it to the lost crypto-Jewish element of the Americas. A primary aim of Alcalá, Richard Montoya (see later discussion), and Jose Manuel Fajardo (see Chapter 3) is to forge links between indigenous and Sephardi histories. There are historical reasons for making these links. From the very beginning of the conquest of the Americas, Jews, including New Christians suspected of Judaizing, were thought not only to desecrate Christianity or seek Christians for ritual murder but also to conspire with Indians and blacks against the Spanish Empire in the Americas. Indeed, the mid-seventeenth-century narrative of the converso Antonio Montezinos, popularized by Menasseh ben Israel as a true account of the discovery of lost tribes, would not belie such a fear: As Rachel Rubinstein summarizes in her important study of Native Americans in the Jewish imagination, Montezinos's "narrative proposes a Jewish-Indian ancient brotherhood confirmed in the present through rejection of Spanish rule," understandable for both groups, as victims of Spain (2010, 39).

All these subjects were perceived to be fifth columns, and New Christians of Jewish origin, with their suspect sincerity, were seen as corrupting the newly converted Indians, especially because "indios" and "negros" were positioned as simple or barbarous and were therefore more vulnerable to the heresies and anti-Christian conspiracies of the formerly Jewish New Christians. New Christians, it was supposed, could even speak the special languages of slaves and Indians in order to conspire treason. As Irene Silverblatt has pointed out, "For those who believed native peoples were descended from the lost tribes, Jews and indios became natural allies" (2004, 151).

Judaism was also likened to the Indians' "primitive" religion on the unfounded basis of similar practices around circumcision, cannibalism, and so on (Elkin 1996, 135). The two peoples were said to have a similar temperament: In the words of one priest-chronicler, they were "cowardly, ungrateful, lazy, superstitious, crafty liars" who had a talent for magically creating wealth and then disappearing it, as it was supposed the Incas did by hiding their vast treasures underground and refusing to reveal their location (Silverblatt 2004, 151). Similarly, New Christians would rather swallow their wealth than surrender to Spaniards. And, "even those Spaniards who visited the Indies and returned home with significant amounts of accumulated wealth were retyped as *conversos*," writes George Mariscal in an article arguing for contemporary racism's roots in medieval Spain (rather than exclusively in the Conquest era) (1998, 14). Mariscal adds:

> Spanish racial projects, stretching from the late 15th to the 17th centuries, struggled mightily to connect Amerindians and Jews, producing texts such as Gregorio García's *Orígen de los indios del Nuevo mundo y las Indias occidentales* (1607). García attempts to apply long-standing anti-Semitic stereotypes to the "newly discovered" people. Like Jews, he writes, Indians have large noses and speak a guttural language. (Mariscal 1998, 14–15)

As Mariscal shows further, García also claims they have "Jewishy" gestures (15).

A conspiratorial alliance between the "Indians" and the "Portuguese" or New Christians was frequently blamed for indigenous uprisings (Silverblatt 2004, 151). Further, as we saw earlier, the idea that "lost tribes" of Jews could be found among Native Americans was widespread for centuries (Popkin 1989), and it indeed lasted into the nineteenth century. The project of

Mordecai Manuel Noah attests to the enduring idea; in 1825, Noah, an influential U.S.-born Portuguese Jew, attempted but failed to establish a Zion in upstate New York with Native Americans, "descendants of the ten lost tribes of Israel" (Rubinstein 2010, 1).

Obejas and Alcalá are engaged in a rather different project of connecting indigenous people of the Americas and Jews, one in which the question of remnants also plays a role. In one of the many expository sections of *Days of Awe*, the narrator explains toward the end of the novel that those who believe that Jewish remnants among the indigenous persist in symbols, such as the Star of David in pottery, "often see these Jews through an ideal prism: Connected to the earth and spirits, they lived collectively and naturally, their Eden interrupted only when the white men, with their viruses and criminality, upset the balance of their idyllic American environment" (Obejas 2002, 332). Alejandra's beloved family friend Moisés, who is committed to the Cuban revolution, believes that Cuba's indigenous population "spiked the general population with their blood" and that "each Cuban, if not each Latin American, from the Rio Grande to Tierra del Fuego, [is] an unwitting Jew, part of god's plan to save humankind through—what else?—the eventual triumph of Marxist revolution, the embodiment of Talmudic promise" (333). The "judeo-indigenous" (335) story is an alternative to the crypto-Jewish one (arrival with the first European ships). In this narrative, whose unlikeliness the narrator registers, Jewish and Marxist messianism blends with an idealized *mestizaje* that willfully denies extinction (of Indians and conversos/Jews) by asserting its remains "in the blood" and the continuity rather than the disappearance of indigeneity.

The non-indigenous-identified Latin American body as a bearer of indigeneity (by blood) is a widespread view, including among those pursuing genealogy and genetic ancestry testing and those invested in various forms of indigenism in the Caribbean. Although this outlook affirms an indigenous past, it can have, albeit certainly not in all cases, the effect of obscuring the calamities that led to the erasure of Caribbean Native peoples. Alcalá's work is invested in a different approach. It is less an acknowledgment or a critique of notions of *mestizaje* or remnants in the present and more an investment in registering a lesser known Native history of the Opata and Tarahumara as they confront the Mexican and U.S. states and cross artificial borders, their stories mingling with the converso and the crypto-Jewish ones.

In the post-1492 centuries, ideas about connections between Jewishness and indigeneity stopped being prevalent. The New Christian or crypto-Jewish population disappeared or hid, and the indigenous populations met atrocious fates at the hands of Europeans. With the emergence of recent decolonial thinking, the impact of the 1992 quincentenary of conquest and expulsion, and the reinstatement of crypto-Jewish identities among Latinx populations, the fates of Jews, Natives, and their Latinx descendants have been rejoined in fictional narratives, including those by such eminent Native American authors as Gerald Vizenor (see Casteel 2012; Rubinstein 2010). The emergence of these linkages continually redefines, extends, and transforms Latinx identities as well as Jewish identities without asserting commensurability and by incorporating their previously unconsidered dimensions, missing archives, and entanglements. We witness a different transamerican consciousness of history, together with its secrets, disappearances, and unknowns.

Secret Syncretism

As Theresa Delgadillo explains regarding Alcalá's "spiritual *mestizaje*" in *Spirits of the Ordinary*, the inhabitants of Casas Grandes merge kabbalistic and Native belief systems. As a result of their experiences in the community that they created together at the site of an ancient junction of cultures and languages, both the indigenous people and Zacarías change irrevocably. The secret syncretism of the Catholic-Jewish-Native traditions, cultures, and languages presented in these texts speaks to the concept of *mestizaje* used in Chicanx and Latinx critical discourses. *Mestizaje* is a rarely used term in Jewish literary criticism or Sephardi studies, but it characterizes the way in which Alcalá and Obejas position Jewishness at the Mexico-U.S. borderlands, in Cuba, and in the Cuban diaspora. The endurance of Jewish tradition and the resilience of Jewish people under conditions of terror are often emphasized in popular discourses and some scholarship on crypto-Jewishness. The tenacity of group identity and its interpellation across time can indeed be remarkable. But what Obejas's and Alcalá's narratives underline is the mixing that occurred, whether Enrique's tormented dual loyalties and allegiances, Alejandra's own negotiations of Sephardism and contemporary American life, or Zacarías's blending of Native and Jewish worlds.

In her essay collection *Confessions of a Berlitz-Tape Chicana* (whose title, relevantly, points to a struggle with authenticity and mixture), New Mexican Demetria Martínez offers a rare formulation that articulates a Sephardi presence in the Americas in terms of *mestizaje*. She writes of her ancestors, who include Spanish conquerors, Pueblo people, Navajos, and "'conversos' who practiced a mishmash of Jewish and Catholic rituals, mixing Ladino with their Spanish." Martínez explains that "these were a mestizo people creating themselves anew every generation in an unrelenting odyssey away from the Spanish ideal of 'limpia sangre' or pure blood" (2005, 8). Unlike dominant articulations of *mestizaje*, such as the official Mexican stance in which races have mixed harmoniously to produce the mestizo Mexican, the *mestizaje* articulated in Chicanx critical discourses can foreground the historical and ongoing overlaps and conflicts among peoples and histories whose narratives are buried by ruling interests. The borderlands, as Theresa Delgadillo explains, is a crossroads of religions, "a meeting ground . . . where adherents of diverse beliefs meet and are altered by that contact" (2011, 154).

But the converso story is not just a way of adding to existing aspects of *mestizaje*; it plays a role in further complicating the term. Because the continuity of the crypto-Jewish component is secret and unknown and perhaps irrevocably lost from documented history, the idea of dissimulation and unknowability must also be considered a part of *mestizaje*, leaving our imaginations open to its barely visible traces, shards, and ruins. This is Marie Theresa Hernández's project in her brilliant ethnographic study *Delirio: The Fantastic, the Demonic, and the Réel* (2002), which is an examination of the buried histories of the northern Mexican state of Nuevo León. Among other occulted experiences in the history of this region, considered socially and politically remote from the Mexican national imagination, is its Jewish past. Hernández shows that Nuevo León, established by Luis de Carvajal, the historical ancestor of Alcalá's fictional Caravals, is fascinatingly redolent of histories that are denied or absent from the state's official narratives: a Sephardi past (and presence?), Native origins (and continuity), and many other taboo subjects, including grisly murders of women and organized crime.

In her creative ethnography of secrets and absences, Hernández places the anecdotal, the oral, and the trace at center stage, drawing on, among other concepts, Michel De Certeau's understanding of "the story that slips away" only to reappear in fantastic and demonic forms in myths and legends, which Hernández collects. This accords well with the fantastic elements in *Spirits of the Ordinary* (i.e., the powers of Zacarías), which bridge the gap between what we know to be plausible (Sephardi-Native encounters) and what we do not yet know for certain through public history. In such gaps, Hernández identifies narratives of "renunciation," namely, the relinquishing of inconvenient stories in official histories (2002, 189). Like Hernández, the historian Emma Pérez (2003) writes of a lack of documents and "proper" history on the subject of queer borderlands sure to have existed but disappeared from official history. But this history can be examined through a "decolonial imaginary" that critically interrogates what has been retained in the archive (123).

Alcalá's and Obejas's creative acts of tracing the buried Sephardi elements of Latin American and Latinx history and *mestizaje* take place in the context of other such explorations, scholarly and creative, of disappeared, residual, and fantastic knowledges. Their Sephardism hence raises the question of what to do with the unverifiable, suppressed aspects of history, urging us to think about them as an integral part of *mestizaje*, and fiction as a paramemory of the convergent stories that slipped away. We cannot find these lost archives, but literature ignites our imagination about how entanglements were born of boundaries.

This becomes especially clear when Alejandra details several narratives that circulate regarding Jews in Cuba. Besides those who trust the lost tribes theory (more on this later), the notion that crypto-Jews who might have arrived with Columbus's ship and stayed on "hiding behind baptisms and crucifixes but Jews nonetheless" (Obejas 2002, 333) is also popular, according to Alejandra. To demonstrate the enduring circulation of this story in Cuba, Alejandra even cites the venerated Cuban anthropologist Fernando Ortiz as having referred to "such quintessential Cubans as José Martí and Antonio Maceo," who also happened to be among Ytzak's heroes, along with Abraham Lincoln and Hatuey (105), as probable crypto-Jewish descendants. For those inclined to believe this, the crypto-Jews were "not . . . assimilationists but . . . part of an intrepid resistance" (333). This perspective appeals to Deborah, the rebellious artist and daughter of Alejandra's family friends in Havana, for whom secrecy is subversive and revolutionary in a manner reminiscent of Daniel Bensaïd's mole (see Chapter 1), rather than abject and filled with shame.

Without documentation, the secret allows flexibility in representing and interpreting the past. This is of course fodder for the imagination, which registers the differential effects of the secret. Deborah champions it, but members of Alejandra's family mourn it. Melancholy over secrets and absent archives (Best 2012; Cvetkovich 2015) is a common response, shared also by Enrique and to a certain extent Alejandra, whose narrative compensates for the loss of history in an episode that serves as a *mise en abyme* of the contemporary crypto-Jewish condition. When Luis becomes enraged at Ytzak for kidnapping Enrique to circumcise him against his and Sima's wishes, Luis throws the family Bibles into the river. "The books," recounts Alejandra, "spilled their rare ink into the waters, and with it our family history" (Obejas 2002, 125). It then becomes Alejandra's task to recreate that story to the extent that she can in the context of a "shallow" genealogy, but the sense of loss and indeterminacy of crypto-Jewish identity is ubiquitous, despite Alejandra's eventual patching of the narrative.

Because secrets are always public in some sense (Taussig 1999), there is always someone who rebels, seeking to expose them and tear off the shroud in the name of truth, justice, pride, or narrative coherence. In *Days of Awe*, this is Alejandra. In *Spirits of the Ordinary*, Corey, the cross-dressing photographer traveling in the Southwest, assumes this role. The inclusion of her perspective in one of the chapters, even though she is an outsider and not a main protagonist, is significant in terms of understanding various approaches to difference, mixture, and indeterminacy, concepts that are common with Obejas and long-standing in crypto-Jewish representations, as we saw in Chapter 1.

The disguise of Corey, who comes to think about her masquerade in terms of "the Outside Corey" and "the Inside Corey" (Alcalá 1996, 110), is parallel to the crypto-Jewish inside-outside dissimulations, as I have suggested. But this performative gesture does not necessarily lend itself to the recognition and practice of borderland entanglements. A northerner in search of subjects on the verge of disappearance, Corey wants access to secrets and losses, like an early anthropologist. She wants to "capture the west before it is a thing of the past," and two members of Zacarías's strange family attract her interest. These are the twins, Manzana and Membrillo, minor characters endowed with symbolic significance, who have supernatural gifts that are the cause of much gossip. In a book abounding with "public secrets" (Taussig 1999), the twins' intersexuality is a secret that also emblematizes indeterminacy, itself associated with crypto-Jewishness. Corey's instinct is to categorize and de-queer them to "discern which was male and which female but she could not" (116). When the twins recognize *her* secret as a cross-dresser, Corey becomes "determined to have them on glass" (116). The white outsider's gaze on exotic queer subjects of the borderlands needs to fix in imagery what is under erasure and indeterminate.

Multiple 1492s and Latinx Literature

Alcalá's work takes part in the Chicanx revisiting of indigeneity of the 1980s and 1990s and its efforts to move away from the idealizations and appropriations that earlier Chicanx writing has been accused of, as I mentioned earlier. Some of the rewritings have appeared in forms that go well beyond realism and perform pyrotechnical and subversively humorous transamerican projects of reinventing conquests. The convergence of the converso story with the conquest of the Americas is also part of the newer Latinx historical imagination, which includes but goes beyond a genealogical idea of *mestizaje*, emphasizing convergent secrecies and disappearances under the yoke of church and empire.

An example of creative expression that also moves away from the conventions of historical fiction or realism is the work of performer and playwright Richard Montoya, of the widely known Chicano performance group Culture Clash. Montoya has also embraced the crypto-Jewish origins in his New Mexican family and has spoken publicly about his "Sephardi roots" (Pfefferman 2009; *This Stage Magazine* 2012). His unique play, *Palestine, New Mexico*, premiered in Los Angeles in 2009 and bears the hallmark of the humor and absurdism of Montoya and Culture Clash. It is also an example of other Latinx works that imagine Native-Jewish crossing, though Montoya goes a step further both with his satirical style and by extending historical convergences to connect them to present wars and empire.

Set in two deserts in New Mexico and Iraq, Montoya's play concerns conversos, indigenous New Mexicans, and the Iraq war. Investigating the death of one of her soldiers, a U.S. army captain, a white woman, stumbles onto a reservation in what is effectively the borderlands to which the dead man had belonged; she finds out about the conversos who had established a community there and called it Palestine. The miscegenation of crypto-Jews with Natives who are on this reservation is a secret that is eventually unearthed as the play builds on political references to wars and (border) walls, satires of ethnoracial purity, mischievous repartees, ethnic parody, and visual kitsch (e.g., a cactus golem wearing a Star of David running amok onstage).

But more somberly, memories of the Iraq war also erupt on stage unannounced in a ghostly fashion. This is not surprising for Montoya or Culture Clash, which have long traded in combinations of clownish slapstick, political satire, and historical spoof. Montoya, the son of the influential Chicano poet José Montoya, who left an indelible mark on the Chicano movement and was a founder of the art and activist collective the Royal Chicano Air Force, has grappled with various political issues in the same satirical manner. He embraced New Mexican (crypto-)Jewish identity despite the critiques he received from both the Jewish and the Chicanx communities, referring to himself as a "Jewish comedian inside a Chicano body circumcised with a machete" (Pfefferman 2009, n.p.).

Palestine, New Mexico is a parodic homage to the need to fill the gaps in the archive of the Jews of the Southwest and to return to that history to assert continued intersection of domestic minoritization and dispossession with imperial wars. Like José Montoya's renowned bilingual poem "El Louie" and other Latinx poetry, theater, *corridos* (ballads), and novels about Latinos in U.S. wars (see Vigil 2014), Richard Montoya's play pays homage to the fate of minorities serving in the military and signals overlaps between borders at home and wars abroad through stories about ancient oppressions that he makes relevant to the present. Like Obejas and Alcalá, Montoya creates aesthetic and thematic convergences (e.g., a "tribe" of Native Jews; the overlapping of the two deserts; militarization here and there) as well as analogies regarding ethnoracial strife and ethnic purities of yesterday and today; in the Los Angeles production, Montoya played the subversive "half-breed" character Top Hat. By producing himself as a remnant of crypto-Jewish, Native, New Mexican, Chicano, and other histories, Montoya also contributes to connective Chicanx, Latinx, Sephardi, and Jewish American writing all at once.

And Montoya has not been alone in his endeavors. Through a sensibility and aesthetic similar to Montoya's, George Sanchez, a New York–based

Latino performer and author of Peruvian origin, wrote and performed the monologue "Shalom" (also known as "Latindio Dream #3"), about an imagined meeting of a crypto-Jew and an indigenous woman. Sanchez, the character, is defecting from conquistador Pizarro's expedition and is on the run from "capture, auto-da-fes, from religious fervor, from xenophobia, from fanatics, from colonizers, from collusion with European expansion" (Sanchez 2010, n.p.). Lost in Inca territory, he meets and falls in love with an indigenous woman, who is also a runaway from Inca law because of her protestation on behalf of "the sovereignty of other indigenous nations unrecognized by the Inca hierarchy" (n.p.). The piece concludes with a comical identity shuffle, in which the converso tells the Inca woman he is "a Visigoth," and she answers that she is Argentinian. Following these "half-truths or pure lies," they greet each other in their supposedly indigenous languages, beginning the "lineage of the unknown tribe we refer to as Inca Jews" (n.p.).

This parody of sixteenth-century conquest chronicles and dominant origin stories ridicules inquisitorial and contemporary obsessions with blood and mocks the documented lies about race and conquest with its pointed falsifications and equivocations: "Sanchez, who found his escape from Spanish rule as a crew member of the Pinta ... or maybe it was on Pizarro's crew." Like other Latinx authors not only rewriting known stories but also reminding us of historical erasures through faux testimonies, origin stories, and genealogies, Sanchez here mimics and goes beyond the history of dissimulation, mixture, and lost knowledges at the heart of the crypto-Jewish narrative.

The question of authenticity is also at the center of another novel of Obejas's: *Ruins* (2009), written several years after *Days of Awe*, in which crypto-Jewish features are less pronounced than in the earlier work. *Ruins* takes place in the Special Period of Cuba in the 1990s after the fall of the Soviet Union and in a Havana racked with scarcity, penury, and clandestine flights to the United States. Amid all this, the main protagonist, Usnavy, can barely hold onto his revolutionary faith when he makes a discovery that leads him to a secret past. The atmosphere in Cuba is rife with all kinds of secrecy and inauthenticity: The black market thrives, countering and exploiting shortages in revolutionary Cuba; and underhanded exchanges and deals are made by even the most authentic revolutionaries, like Usnavy, who resorts to them out of desperation and hunger. Salvaging Tiffany lamps from the eponymous ruins, the crumbling buildings that dot Havana, Usnavy sells them to an artisan who uses the parts to produce fake new Tiffany lamps as a means of subsistence. This trade is a materialization of questions about the real and the copy that are central to the novel.

Usnavy's converso background is as indeterminate as the originator of Tiffany lamps or the ethics behind fakes and the piecemeal sale of the family heritage. The latter, Usnavy's own lamp, turns out to be a counterfeit made by Jewish artisans who were cheated by Tiffany—forged, then, much like the Christian identity of his mother's family. A revolutionary past and Usnavy's fanciful imagining of African origins because of a Jamaican father, whose whiteness he ignores, and other notions of stable truths, including the fixity of gender (refuted by a trans character), fade away in the setting of the ruins of the city and nation in the bleak 1990s. Although not the central element of *Ruins*, the indeterminacy and unknowability central to converso and crypto-Jewish experiences are nevertheless multiplied analogically and in convergence with other destabilizations and ripple through the political and social fabric of the novel.[7]

Sephardism and Latinx Crypto-Jewish History

Although much contemporary fiction treats crypto-Jewish history as a primarily generic Jewish one (of persecution) with a muted Sephardi particularity, Alcalá and especially Obejas assert Sephardi difference, which is another feature that distinguishes their approach and ties them to most of the other authors I study here. In her book of essays, *The Desert Remembers My Name: On Family and Writing* (2007), Alcalá alludes to rejections of the existence of crypto-Judaism in New Mexico and suggests that it is "the difference in standing between North African/Mediterranean/Latin Jews and the Northern European Ashkenazi Jews that seems to be the subtext to many of the current arguments against the continued existence of crypto-Jews" (95). Alcalá does not elaborate, but it is clear that she is thinking about the contestation of crypto-Jewish identities as part of a general marginalization of the significance of Sephardi Jewry.[8] Of course, Ashkenazi scholars have certainly served as "mediators," as Ben-Ur has called them, and have shown an overwhelming interest (2009, 178). In addition, many descendants have felt welcomed by Ashkenazi rabbis and individuals. But there is a particular sense of Sephardi consciousness on the part of many who, like Alcalá, have returned to a suppressed Judaism and Sephardi history at a time when Sephardi culture in the United States has been declared moribund (Gerber 2012).

Further, together with Latinx and Latin Americans of normative Jewish background, returning descendants of conversos occasion a new Judeo-Hispanism in the United States that falls outside the parameters of mainstream Jewish Americanness (and U.S. Jewish studies) (see Ben-Ur 2009; Kandiyoti 2012). Obejas also affirms Sephardi and *converso* particularity in language, culture, and ritual. Her narrator Alejandra finds herself in the company of Sephardi Jews, to whom she feels closer and who transform the regular Passover seders she attends annually with distinct traditions, though connections with Ashkenazi Jews are also important to her and her family (Obejas 2002, 264–65). Ytzak, Alejandra's great grandfather, encounters a Lebanese Sephardi Jew traveling in Cuba with his merchandise, which becomes a turning point: The salesman, nicknamed El Moro or "The Moor," was openly Jewish in a way he could recognize, unlike the American Jews he had met in the Havana hospital where he was treated for the injury he incurred during Cuba's war of independence. The Moor explains to Ytzak that the American Jews must have been Ashkenazi and different from the two of them, establishing the connection between the lost crypto-Jew and the Arabized Mediterranean Lebanese and their difference from the Jewish American norm. The Lebanese man later helps Ytzak settle in Havana, where Ytzak can feel freer and "let the light glint off his own gold Star of David" (123).

But the limits to the Sephardi sense of belonging come with gender politics. When her father dies, Alejandra looks for a congregation to say the mourners' prayer, the Kaddish, and, though well treated by the Ashkenazi reconstructionists, she prefers the Tunisian storefront temple, where "the men looked like my father and his domino partners: Yemenites, Lebanese, Portuguese.... They could have all been Cubans claiming Spanish ancestors" (Obejas 2002, 306). She is welcomed there, but not after she defies gender roles and starts reciting the Kaddish wearing tefillin (phylacteries). Alejandra creates herself as a Sephardi, transforming herself from a remnant of crypto-Jews into an expansive and multicultural Sephardi identification that is, however, far from being traditional with its bricolage elements and gender nonconformity.

The Sephardi identification is persistent in the novel and in the author's experiences. In interviews Obejas has pointedly declared that most Cuban Jewish history is Sephardi history, although this is frequently ignored by Ashkenazi Cubans in the United States and Ashkenazi Americans who do not favor the Cuban embargo (Sheppard-Brick 2002). Hence, like nonconverso Sephardi authors, Alcalá and Obejas are engaged in a corrective project of recovering and emphasizing the significance of Sephardi presence and history. By doing so, they intervene in the normative and dominant Ashkenazi (often excluding non-Europeans), Sephardi (often excluding converso descendants), and Latinx (often excluding non-Catholics) definitions of belonging.

Do these authors produce a new version of Hispanism, one that partakes of secrecy and unknowability with relation to Sephardi history? The older versions of Hispanism that had to do with Jews in the Americas included Sephardism in Ashkenazi Latin America, which sought a connection and assimilation to the unfamiliar Hispanophone cultures of Argentina or Cuba by way of Iberianist discourses of *convivencia* (Aizenberg 2002). The (philo-)Sephardism in Spain, which has ebbed and flowed for over a century and has added the excluded Jew to the Spanish body, albeit not in uncontested and unproblematic ways, instituted one version of Hispanism (see Friedman 2011a, 2011b), which also shaped the Sephardi intellectual world in the early- to mid-twentieth century United States, as spearheaded by Ladino-speaking Turkish Jewish immigrant scholar Meir José Benardete (Ben-Ur 2007, 2016). All these writers and scholars asserted the Iberianness of Sephardi Jews and, to a certain extent and only by some, the Jewishness of Spanish culture, downplaying or ignoring the import of the converso and the crypto-Jew to the Americas, the making of the "Hispanic/Hispano" Jew (including the many with Portuguese provenance and Spanish roots and culture) across the Atlantic, and the crossings with entities and identities other than the Catholic-Iberian.

The work of our authors, however, is informed by transamerican as well as transatlantic histories and processes, from borderlands cultural formations and the diasporic United States to Caribbean revolutions and wars in the Middle East. The Latinx Sephardism or new Jewish Hispanism of the United States differs from the Spain-centered Sephardi approach of the early and middle decades of the twentieth century (Ben-Ur 2016) and the Israel-oriented goals of organizations reconnecting Latinx to Judaism. It is informed instead by a critique of racialization, civilization, and imperial discourses in the Americas and imagines convergences that the other approaches eschew.

In unraveling the story of the "lost" conversos and crypto-Jews of the Americas, Latinx authors do not recover but reimagine the lost archives of the victims of empire's racializations, expulsions, and forced conversions. Through various means, including the genealogical and the genetic, the fictional, and the interpretively historical, they create something new: a paramemory in a fictional production of remnants that explores what collective memory might have been like if people and cultures had not disappeared. In addition, they record for the future our present historical consciousness about such losses. The works do not resolve the questions of truth and authenticity that trouble declared certainties and revelations about the crypto-Jewish trajectory in the Americas. Through transamerican perspectives afforded by their investment in Latinx cultures, authors such as Obejas, Alcalá, Montoya, and Sanchez examine intangible remains of suppressed histories, which circulate as rumor and gossip across borders, north and south, and produce new borders in their own stories. They *add* questions and mysteries, instead of solving them and fixing an image of the "original" crypto-Jew, while declaring themselves remnants of that history.

Recursions to the past and finding entanglements instead of unitary origins yield mixtures and ambiguities rather than certainties. In fictions such as Obejas's complex and multilayered novel and Alcalá's lyrical braiding of peoples, stories are nestled within other ones in unexpected ways. They stage intertwined fates through analogy, fellow victimhood, and kinship, returning us to the history of the Conquest and its blank spaces in the archive (such as Native–crypto-Jewish crossings). And finally, although the Sephardi world is often pronounced to be past or passing, these critical returns to crypto-Jewishness initiate a new chapter in ongoing Sephardi history and alternative ways of imagining our Americas.

{ CHAPTER 3 }

RETURN TO SEPHARAD

Blood, Convergences, and Embodied Remnants

AS WE HAVE SEEN IN PRECEDING CHAPTERS, returns to homelands, whether ancestral, spiritual, or national, have been persistent tropes and practices in recent times. Laws that were approved in 2015 presented descendants of Sephardi Jews with the possibility of "return" to Portugal and Spain, offering nationality as a form of reconciliation and reparation. These new gestures to reincorporate Sephardis into Iberia provide a special impetus to consider more broadly Jewish returns to Spain, the meaning and import of Jewish Spain/Sepharad today, and the unique place of the converso past with regard to returns. In this chapter I juxtapose a memoir, *The Forgetting River: A Modern Tale of Survival, Identity, and the Inquisition* (2012), by U.S.-born journalist and author Doreen Carvajal, with the novel *Mi nombre es Jamaica* (My Name Is Jamaica; 2010), by the Spanish novelist and journalist José Manuel Fajardo. Carvajal's memoir narrates a Costa Rican American's return to Spain in a quest for converso roots; Fajardo's novel is about a Spaniard's return to Spain's and his own converso past. Each work demonstrates a different facet of reviving dormant histories and genealogies. Further, like Obejas and Alcalá, Carvajal and Fajardo connect the Atlantic worlds of Iberia and the Americas in the search for answers about not only the specifics of the past but also the discontents of making the past our own today.

Returns often take place as a reenactment in the present of an obsession with history. Gilli Bush-Bailey has written about heritage tours, historical reenactments and the generalized "yearning to experience history somatically and emotionally," including as spectators and gallery visitors (2013, 281). In Carvajal's and especially Fajardo's works, history is reenacted and experienced to opposing effects: Carvajal presents transhistorical transmission and the self as a remnant of converso history, whereas Fajardo's novel is devoted to the *problematics* around such a production of the self as a remnant of a submerged past. Issues of authenticity and evidence emerge as the narrator and characters of each work assert themselves as remnants of a secret, unacknowledged past.

For a wealth of reasons, Spain is a particularly appropriate site for narratives about Jewish returns to the past. Spanish officials promote the country's return to its Jewish past, reconceived under the umbrella of medieval Spanish tolerance. The spirit of *convivencia*, or coexistence of the Moorish/Muslim, Jewish, and Christian cultures, which has become a tool of marketing Spain, is the organizing idea behind the efforts to draw large numbers of tourists, Jewish and otherwise (Flesler and Pérez Melgosa 2008, 2020). The endeavors to return Sephardi Jews to Spain and have Spain return to its Jewish past are widespread. In addition to the nationality law, cities from north to south have been filled with markers of *juderías* (Jewish neighborhoods) and with centers, small and large museums, galleries, shops, and "Sephardi" restaurants. In recent years, towns in northern Spain have had Sukkot festivals, and Ribadavia, which had no Jewish residents but has enjoyed a well-attended Sephardi festival every summer since 1994, saw its first kosher Passover seder in hundreds of years (Guttman 2013). Simulacra of "Jewish weddings" are also held as festive events. Another example is found in Hervás, where annual celebrations take place during the Festival of the Converts. The event is attended by thousands, some of whom dress up "as Jews," and features plays about "conversas" with carefully orchestrated plots to minimize guilt and blame for the town inhabitants. The festival compensates for the town's unremarkable and undocumented Jewish heritage or other attractions to draw crowds (Flesler and Pérez Melgosa 2010, 2020).[1]

All this remarkable heritage, commercial, and cultural activity has been taking place after hundreds of years of self-distancing from Jewish and

Muslim pasts, with notable twentieth-century exceptions. These regenerating acts depend not on the recuperation of ancient identities but on the production of new affiliations and the creation of new remnants. As I explained in the Introduction, remnants are what have survived from the past; but in acts of return to history, we do not simply find remains but produce them, resignifying as a remain what was not previously perceived as one (such as towns with dubious Jewish heritage). The Spanish state's efforts to downplay expulsion and the Inquisition and to promote pride in Spanish Jewish history intermingles, to a limited extent, with some Sephardis' interest in origins lost after the catastrophe of 1492, which is mourned by observant Jews every year on the fasting day of Tisha b'Av.

The return as a quest for evidence of ancestral belonging in a Spain that has destroyed or converted almost every material sign of its ancient Jewish life often yields accounts of the "encounter with nothing," in the words of Saidiya Hartman (2007, 16) regarding her own return to Ghana as an African American. This is true of returns by normative Sephardi Jews (see Kandiyoti 2016a; and Chapter 4) but even more so with converso pasts, which are not a significant part of Spain's (or any other entity's) official discourses. In literary and autobiographical writing, such journeys not only are disappointments, because of absent archives and missing sites of memory, but are also presented as destabilizing the basis of identity, which can sometimes lead to a *delirio* (Hernández 2002). In Fajardo's novel a version of *delirio* is enacted by the main protagonist, who claims converso roots and enacts them through his body. Signs of transgenerational transmission and transhistorical affect are also present in Carvajal's memoir, in which the author reports embodied reactions to ancient events in present-day Spain.

These embodied discourses of the converso-descendant narrative are remarkable, not least because of the signs of modernity that have accrued to converted Jews of Iberian background. As we saw in Chapter 1, scholars have emphasized the secularizing, modern, and cosmopolitan outlooks of this group because of their mobility and multiple (if partial) belongings, which is expressed by the term "marranos of reason," the title of a study by Yirmiyahu Yovel (1989). In light of this charged association with reason and the Enlightenment, some contemporary returns to and recoveries of Judeo-converso identities that resort to discourses of blood and genes and argue for the somatic retention of the past might seem to be out of sync with the characteristics of secular modernity.

However, turning the clock back 500 years, recovering something that has not been in evidence for generations, and grafting that piece of the past onto the contemporary self take place under a different umbrella of the modern. We might think of returns as responses to the "disenchantment" embedded in modernity, as described by Max Weber (1946), where "reenchantment" is a return to the mysterious and the suppressed (along with the occult and the magical), which had disappeared with the annihilating bureaucracy, conformity, rationalization, and scientization of our times. Yet, all is not so simple. The leap backward that magically returns history to the present is not just dependent on faith and faint traces but is invigorated, indeed frequently generated, by advanced science and technology. The "genealogical science" (Abu El-Haj 2012) of genetics can also have a reenchanting effect of sorts, as we have seen in our previous discussion of genetic memory and kinship, with its critics often pointing out the technology as a sort of wish fulfillment (for origins) that is based on a selective set of scientific evidence and truth. Carvajal and Fajardo's texts compel us to consider these timely and important questions on the discontents of returns, recoveries, and transhistorical transmissions through their specific lens onto submerged converso pasts.

A Modern Tale

Costa Rican American Doreen Carvajal's memoir *The Forgetting River: A Modern Tale of Survival, Identity, and the Inquisition* skillfully weaves many of the themes, tropes, and issues also found in short testimonials, essays, and other first-person narratives of the return to crypto-Jewish history and Jewish identification found in publications such as *HaLapid* or collected in books (e.g., Golden et al. 2005), though in a sustained and writerly manner. The memoir also bears many of the features of fictional works, including the themes of loss and forgetting, the production of the self as a remnant, the body as an archive, and narrative structure and topics organized around convergences and overlaps. Widely reviewed and well received, *The Forgetting River* is an exemplary quest narrative for converso roots and Sephardi identity that is also remarkably open about the issues around evidence and truth that trouble many such experiences, as we have seen. I pair this work with a Spanish author's novel rather than including it in the chapter on U.S. Latinx narratives because of the central role of Spain in both works and their common theme of reviving previously unknown converso identity today, which is thematically and conceptually different from the works of Alcalá and Obejas.

Carvajal confronts what many other personal and fictional narratives avoid: the question of evidence for converso genealogy. A well-known *New York Times* reporter, Carvajal preempts in the first few pages of *The Forgetting River* the skepticism that her enterprise to ascertain the converso roots of her Costa Rican family would meet. She asserts early on, "Doubt was my religion" (Carvajal 2012a, 3), laying the groundwork for the prism through which she tells her story of a yearning to belong and to find the truth about her Sephardi ancestry. Carvajal, who shares a surname with the most significant known converso family in the history of the Americas, secularizes her quest to find clues to a Jewish ancestry she suspects: From the outset, she distances herself from Judaism as a religion and places herself in the realm of doubt rather than faith, descent rather than belief. She pours tremendous effort into her quest: extended stays in Arcos de la Frontera, an Andalusian town named for its location as a front in the Spanish-Moorish wars of the thirteenth century; archival research in Inquisition records; and other travels and interviews. These endeavors substantiate her instincts about a hidden heritage in her family. Her trips to Spain and her investment in this identity, which she continued to document in articles published after the book, are, for her, returns.

Carvajal's affective encounters with history in Spain, especially of the Inquisition, are balanced with the quest for evidence that would counter the forgetting that informs her title, which is inspired by Arcos de la Frontera's river Guadelete, the Arabized name for Lethe, the Hades river that induces forgetting. The journalistic, modern, skeptical, secular approach to certainty that is a recurrent motif in the text is nevertheless undergirded by a strong sense that there is "something in the blood," as many returning descendants of crypto-Jews put it. Truth quests and claims coexist with folk notions of blood memory or genetic memory that draw descendants to certain affinities associated with Jewishness or Spanishness. In addition, the sense of lurking familial secrets informs both the search for concrete evidence and the call of the blood.

That Carvajal's book features many tropes found in briefer testimonials and in fiction about the return to converso history signals the overlap between fictional and nonfictional discourses. In writing about a desire for the recovery of a past and its intercalation into the layers of the present, Carvajal mobilizes both imaginative and documented sources. However, with her emphasis on a skepticism that forestalls the kind of mistrust that individual testimonies have often elicited, Carvajal does something different from other personal narratives that assert descent and history in a linear narrative of certainty, despite their frequent lack of absolute evidence. Like Obejas's narrator in *Days of Awe* (Chapter 2), Carvajal uses metaphors for the fragmentation, absence, forgetting, and loss she seeks to remedy, including "broken spiritual shards" (Carvajal 2012a, 3), puzzles, "the deep, black holes of family memory" (25), "the missing key" (3), and "discarded Sephardic identity" (123). Also in the manner of *Days of Awe*, Carvajal's time and place shift with each chapter, and the book is structured by linked associations rather than by linear temporality; hence it is very much like fictional narratives of convergence.

In other ways, however, Carvajal's account echoes many other descendants' longing. She describes "a strange yearning for something indefinable, a sense of refuge, of belonging. It was what they called in Spanish a feeling of añoranza, a longing from home, to be whole" (Carvajal 2012a, 24). Like so many others who declare crypto-Jewish descent, Carvajal is partly motivated by always having felt different. But in a metanarrative move, she makes plain how this sense of divergence from her milieu is an impetus for a narrative that involves a mystery, that is, her own account: "I always felt like an outsider—this sense of not being deeply connected to all the branches and roots of my family and always observing from a distance. *So I concocted a classic literary plot* and cast myself as the protagonist. A stranger arrives in an exotic town to dig in the archeological site of memory. Start with the territory. The adventure follows" (17; emphasis added). Already from the outset, Carvajal signals that she will not be sharing certainties and assertions but instead will provide us with a plot that involves a quest. Neither linear nor defensive, *The Forgetting River* is for the most part a self-reflexive narrativization of a longing based on a "genealogical drive" (Derrida 1998, 60) rather than a definitive assertion of converso ancestry, until the end when the author comes to a different conclusion.

Carvajal's sojourn in Arcos de la Frontera and her research in the country's various archives during her months in Spain are frustrating because they yield no proof of her hunch about Sephardi provenance. Although she has returned to an ancestral land, everything of Jewish history has been erased, including in the built environment of the lovely Andalusian town. But the returnee seeks signs in *non-lieux de la mémoire*, nonsites of memory, a term Claude Lanzmann (1990), the director of *Shoah*, used to refer to derelict or invisible World War II sites of extermination. Their material and human tracing may have been deliberately disappeared, but nevertheless the past continuously rises from the grave for Carvajal through free associations with the present. An officious local resident who informs the authorities of illegally parked cars reminds her of those who might have denounced their neighbors as Judaizers in revenge for an insignificant slight. The very whitewash that lends renown to Arcos and other nearby *pueblos blancos* becomes Carvajal's metaphor for the erasures that propel the narrative: "In Arcos de la Frontera, practically anything can be whitewashed—houses, tragedy, history" (Carvajal 2012a, 53). Calle de la Cuna (Street of the Cradle) is supposed to be the old Jewish corner, but the names of Jews who lived there are forgotten.

Carvajal describes various correspondences between past and present as the manifestation of a "parallel world" (2012a, 18), what is visible to the eye today and the past it must have contained. Besides treating time as recursive, Carvajal views space, including nonspaces, as remnants, interpreting her environment through the lens of crypto-Jewish spatiality and finding hidden spaces: an underground passage with a secret trapdoor, unmarked houses of possible conversos (including two authors of sixteenth-century books on melancholy, Andrés Velázquez and Isaac Cardoso), and a cave that became a refuge for the observation of ritual by "Jewish survivors" after a church was built over what had been a synagogue in 1500 (138). (The cave, she reports, is a restaurant, La Taberna de Boabdil, named after the conquered last ruler of Granada, but its mystique has been preserved thanks to its owner's emphasis on the Moorish and Jewish past).

In the absence of spatial markers of converso lives, Carvajal inscribes them in writing and reflects, "The people of this Jewish quarter had died twice: once when they were banished, imprisoned, or punished, and again when they were forgotten. Forgetting is the injustice. My senses sharpened.

I knew the old white houses were observing me. Past and present is an illusion. Places, like people, keep their scars and footprints" (Carvajal 2012a, 19). Through such anthropomorphisms and other means, Carvajal finds continuities everywhere that belie the disruptions of time, though she also maintains the doubt and skepticism she has "faith" in. The two references in her subtitle "modern" (by which she means contemporary) and "the Inquisition," are not simply juxtaposed but presented as continuous and redolent with echoes and simulations of one another.

Notably, the crypto-Jewish quest story has particular tropes around longing, mysterious origins, clues, and detection in its approach to time and narration of a parallel world. But it also shares language and concepts with normative Jewish narratives of the era of Holocaust consciousness and other trauma stories, such as neo-slave fiction and postdictatorial memory of the global "memory boom." By collating and collapsing different periods in individual and collective memory, such narratives make the past proximate and reveal its secrets. As Carvajal expands her understanding of Andalusian culture and the possible residual elements of Jewish life in the region, most significantly the *saeta* song tradition, historical parallels with the Inquisition multiply, including parallels with other repressive periods. Carvajal finds out that Arcos de la Frontera is the site of mass graves from the Civil War era, recently being discovered all over Spain. This leads her to remark on the continuity of murder and brutality in the area and on how "the residents of Arcos live, after all, in daily contact with the spirits of the dead" (Carvajal 2012a, 111).

The work of recovering the ancestral past requires a continual assertion of larger historical continuities and comparisons. Unlike the criticized forms of nostalgia in which the idealized past is contrasted against the present, in many narratives of return the present appears as a replica of the past, at least in its disturbing or else tragic aspects. Indeed, it is primarily the signs of disaster, suffering, and persecution in which parallels are found.

Affect as Evidence

One of the more perplexing aspects of the idea of crypto-Jewish continuity is the body as evidence. Although felicitous versions of normative Jewish life are celebrated in Spain, converso lives are absent from most official stories about *convivencia* and its aftermath. The quest for a Jewish past is riddled with frustrations and nondiscoveries in the archives and in Spanish places. Carvajal builds her narrative from these gaps and "encounters with nothing." In the absence of material remains and discursive acknowledgment, the body becomes a substitute memorial and archive. Emotionally and somatically, Carvajal presents herself as a receptacle of ancient traumas in an interesting example of what I have referred to as the production of the self as a remnant of a previously undisclosed history. Of course, "production" does not imply falsification but points to the ideas and performances that build identity.

Carvajal's first impressions during her sojourn in Spain produce strong affect, which she attributes to a transgenerational kind of recognition and reenactment. Of the house she rented with her family in 2008, she reports, "The minute we stepped into the house, I felt a current trembling on my skin, pulsing out of my fingertips. Sometimes the body recognizes things before the mind catches on" (2012a, 36). This seemingly involuntary somatic reaction is based on fear, which she reports on the second page of the book, when she first describes Arcos and its ancient church bells: "I couldn't shake the dread that something was taking place around me. Something I couldn't understand. Something I couldn't flee" (2). Indeed, her family's entry into the house does not begin with good augur: She, her husband, and her daughter are briefly plagued by bee stings and nightmares about being surrounded by "long-haired men in tunics" with weapons. The author interprets her feelings of unease about the past and reports, "I felt the force of the house and heaviness in the air. Maybe it was trying to communicate something to our family—people who had never lived here before, but whose ancestors may have walked or run along these streets" (38).

But Carvajal is not alone in viewing things in a state of suspense and with dread. Both the locals and the expatriates in the tourist business view houses as active containers of the past, with one family reporting being punched and shoved by spirits in their own house, eventually causing them to move, and others speaking of "powerful energy" in their house. The legend of the Moorish woman who was turned into a vulture that haunts the fortress and other tales compound the eeriness of the built and natural environment in Arcos, where "dank caves constitute a subterranean universe. Secret passageways honeycomb the pueblo's ridges with tunnels leading directly to the sunny courtyards of houses along the ridge. The dark caves are linked to every primeval fear—ghost tales, local superstitions, buried skeletons" (Carvajal 2012a, 41). In some ways, this is a transgenerational experience of the Freudian uncanny, "that class of the terrifying which leads back to something long known to us, once very familiar" (Freud 1958, 123–24). In this case, the familiar is not experiential or known in a personal way but presumed to be ancestral and transmitted through blood and historical consciousness in the sense of both awareness and understanding of the past and its "creative freedom in the use and interpretation" (Funkenstein 1989, 10–11).

Although a secular skepticism guides Carvajal's quest, the presence of the irrational in nature, storytelling, and architecture is felt (though not known) as history. All are signals of a transgenerational recognition that Carvajal states and exemplifies without belaboring. The two approaches are in tension in Carvajal's self-reflexive staging of both reenchantment and secular doubt: The quest for documentable evidence of Jewish ancestry and the doubts that plague her in their absence coexist with the bodily and affective signs of repressed identity. Carvajal's longing for an archive and evidence is expressed from the outset to the very end: "Why didn't my ancestors also leave a message that lingered? Their story always seemed to hover just over the edge of the horizon, a hidden homeland of secret resistance. . . . All I wanted was a scrap of paper. Words. Paragraphs" (Carvajal 2012a, 298–99).

An individual reenactment of the past through the somatic takes place, given what queer theorist Heather Love has referred to in a different context as "the psychic costs of repeated encounters with the 'empty archive'" (2009, 42) and the failure of official or social recognition of crypto-Jewish and Jewish persecution in Spain. Affect serves as a kind of evidence of the collective past (under the Inquisition invoked in the memoir's title) and personal identity; it also constitutes a paramemory, something beyond unconscious transgenerational transmission and mediated by general historical knowledge and, in this case, contained in the body (and the blood) and awakened by physical sites.

Besides reworking the trope of the somatic crypto-Jewish body (see Chapter 1) through the paramemories of descent rather than personal experience, Carvajal's embodied reenactment of the past also speaks indirectly and critically to the efforts of the Spanish government and municipalities to market Spanish Jewish history, as I noted briefly. Spain's income-generating tourist discourse purports to return to and recover a tolerant, tricultural medieval Spain, with celebratory, crowd-pleasing "medieval" events, spaces, foods, museums, festivals, and recreated objects but scant acknowledgment in these memorializations of the dark side of Spain's past. In the section on José Manuel Fajardo later in this chapter, I further discuss Spain's current relationship to history, but it is important to note here that Carvajal's account as a roots-seeking visitor and tourist takes place both within and against Spanish tourism's particular discourses of return. Her reporting of enchantment and corporeal haunting in nonsites of memory contests the lack of material heritage and the official message about a felicitous past. Even the few materialized sites—here a new synagogue on the site of an old one and there a discovered mikvah—can foster forgetting as they promote a particular kind of memory of Jewish Spain.

Forgetting as a second death is a motif in other narratives of return to the scenes of disasters. Using a metaphor that Carvajal and others are also inspired by, Saidiya Hartman comes to a realization in *Lose Your Mother* about West Africa's "own Lethe" (2007, 156), waters that induced forgetting in slaves, also symbolic of Ghana's own project of forgetting of its participation in the slave trade and exploitation of particular ethnic groups in its northern region. As Hartman explains, the Ghanaian Tourism Ministry has launched efforts (which recall Spain's in some ways) to cleanse the image of the slaves and better welcome their American descendants in search of home and wholeness in Africa. Yet, Hartman shows, neither in museums nor in public discourse are the lives of those who became slaves to whites or the lives of the elites who profited from the trade acknowledged.

> "Remembering slavery" became a potent means of silencing the past in the very guise of preserving it, since it effectively curbed all discussion of African slavery and its entailments—class exploitation, gender inequality, ethnic clashes, and regional conflict. The sorcery of the state, like the sorcery of marabouts and herbalists, was also intended to wash away the past (at least those aspects that might create conflict) and to pacify the heirs of slaves, except that now this process was described as memorializing rather than forgetting. (Hartman 2007, 164)

Despite their seeming interrelatedness, then, memory and memorialization can be severed from one another; indeed they are working at cross-purposes. Commemoration, especially in its cleansed, Disneyfied versions recounted critically by Carvajal and by Hartman, can induce forgetting by focusing on celebration and by downplaying or suppressing past and continuing injustice. All of this complicates the memory-forgetting dichotomy and the suggestion that memorialization rectifies or heals.

Forgetting is not the only operation that can cause a "second death," then. Memory work also can help to forget and bury. Hartman's poignant insights into the vacating of memory from memorializing refers to a very different context. However, we can see overlaps in the ways that governments and publics deploy a globalized, institutionalized memory discourse to induce forgetting. They do so under the guise of moving forward and forming new relationships across countries or continents based on a presumed former unity.[2]

Carvajal's own visit to Spain undermines the silences and blind spots of the official tale of Spanish *convivencia*, which is devoid of insights into the actual and profound cross-pollinations that took place (Menocal 2002). But her presentation of embodied paramemories and transhistorical trauma, with a genealogical basis, is equally outside history. The *delirio* (Hernández 2002) that circulates orally about houses and the body as a repository, which seem beyond the rational or plausible, are recourses that validate submerged memories. The returnee's need to be marked recalls for us Obejas's Alejandra and her exilic yearning to be identified with a particular (Cuban) history and identity through her body, language, and desire. At the same time, however, like the desire of Obejas's Alejandra to suppress her diaspora experience and recuperate and continue a pre-exilic identity in Cuba, these longings are fraught with the perils of new erasures and timeless certainties.

Collapsing the Past and the Present

The Forgetting River helps us to consider complex issues regarding the role of the body and conscious transgenerational transmission mediated by historiography, genealogy, and archival research, which I am calling paramemory. DNA testing, another corporeal entryway to the past, fails to provide the proof that Carvajal seeks. The results suggest only faint traces of ancestry and migrations, which leads Carvajal to turn instead to "everyday symbols," such as the last name of her grandmother, Chacón, "salamander," relevant because it is an animal also mentioned in the Talmud. Carvajal explains her skepticism about DNA testing as a source of Jewish identity and faults herself with focusing on DNA at the expense of a labor of interpretation of already existing symbols, though indirectly she also presents her body as evidence. She quotes Einstein's conviction "that the distinction between past, present, and future is only a stubbornly persistent illusion" (Carvajal 2012a, 223).

As we have seen, contemporary narratives of circulation, connectivity, and memory trade in this idea of blurred temporal distinctions that informs Carvajal's enterprise. They tell stories replete with archeological and botanical metaphors of digs and roots of the past coming to the surface to graft themselves onto the present. Yet the search for the persistence of the past, instead of exploding the present, as in Walter Benjamin's historical understanding (Benjamin 1969, 257–58), can be deceptively static, despite the impressive intricacy and expansiveness of temporal and geographic twists and turns. Stephen Best refers to the desire for the redemption of the past as a "refusal or an inability to reckon with the true alterity of the past" (2012, 465). On the one hand, some of these critiques seem to reinstate a problematic historicism and periodization, in which "the past is over and knowable" (Stewart 2017, 139). On the other hand, in their diachronic compulsion, narratives such as Carvajal's sometimes abandon the synchronic: While connecting to the past, other connections in the present are lost from view, including their political implications.

Yet, like many other authors of return narratives, Carvajal politicizes belonging in other ways, including, after the publication of her memoir, knowing that returns to scenes of trauma and recuperation of the past can be subjected to current discourses and practices of power. For example, she criticizes what she perceives as the noninclusion of those of converso or crypto-Jewish descent in Spain's offer to extend citizenship to people of Sephardi origin worldwide (Carvajal 2012b), although this has turned out not to be the case. As Hirsch and Miller ask, "The popularization of return tourism, which has become a familiar activity of our global moment, equally and simultaneously is a matter of rights: who is entitled to return to a home, a homeland, a place to which one once belonged?" (2011, 17). For Carvajal, as for others, the return to converso and Sephardi identity is equated with rights, as it is for the Israel- and U.S.-based organizations regarding the return of conversos and lost tribes. The implications of these new rights in the making and those they exclude (Morisco descendants, today's refugees, Palestinians) are rarely explored.

Like many other contemporary narratives (see Chapter 1), *The Forgetting River* consists of chapters that alternate in space and time. Many are set and written in the period of residence in Arcos de la Frontera, whereas others are sandwiched in-between or after the sections on Arcos in 2008, including France in 2003 and 2009 and Belgrade and Barcelona in 2010, in a mirroring of the temporal recursions and gaps in Carvajal's quest: "I came here to Andalusia for my personal *right of return*, to recapture what might be homeland, to salvage beginnings and an identity that my family forgot" (Carvajal 2012a, 7; emphasis added). Echoing a Zionist narrative that she does not otherwise engage, Carvajal, like authors who have written testimonies, seeks less a territorial return than a temporal continuity that will validate the longings of the present. Arcos de la Frontera, where Carvajal went to experience today's Spain to understand the remote past, is not an opportunity to know a territory but a way to make the past familiar and living.

Although Carvajal's memoir is a story of an encounter and deftly weaves between times and places like so many contemporary novels, it is not what I have been calling a narrative of convergence, because, unlike the other texts analyzed here, it does not thematize the entanglements of otherwise occluded or marginalized histories or imagine their overlaps in the present. However, Carvajal does create analogies between the Iberian and American historical events of direct concern to her and other global events, registering their similarities and implying or stating continuities (though not so much their entanglements). She takes pains in *The Forgetting River* to demonstrate that her quest is not exceptional. If the sites she encounters during her stays in "the territory" of Andalusia are almost always those of nonbelonging, secrecy, and oppression, other places and events are also evocative of the same elements.

For example, Carvajal's professional task as a journalist to report on the missing war criminal Ratko Mladić is an opportunity to explore Sarajevo and consider the region's relevance to her own story. Given the DNA findings that possibly locate her grandmother's origins in the Balkans, she guesses that perhaps her ancestors were in exile there from Iberia. The thematics of the missing, secret, and ancestral links in the past and present of others in the Balkan chapter also reappear when Carvajal is assigned to cover sex abuse in the Belgian Catholic Church; in this case Carvajal looks for a particular victim and draws parallels between past and present repressions, secrets, and crimes related to the Catholic Church, to which she had once belonged.

These consistent links between then and now within and without the Iberian and post-Iberian world finally cure Carvajal of the double life she leads between facts and "spirits" (Carvajal 2012a, 226), skepticism and embodied recognition. Instead of a eureka moment upon the tearing open of an envelope from a genetic ancestry testing company or the miraculous discovery of a genealogical tree or family diary, Carvajal finds answers through an accumulation of possibilities, including familial rumors, symbolic names, and, finally, the discovery of a great-aunt's prayer card featuring on the reverse side a psalm also sung on Shabbat.

Queer criticism is insightful, again, on the uses of buried evidence and the desire for its materialization. Ann Cvetkovich notes that "in the absence of institutionalized documentation or in opposition to official histories, memory becomes a valuable historical resource, and ephemeral and personal collections of objects stand alongside the documents of the dominant culture in order to offer alternative modes of knowledge" (2015, 457–58). But rather than offering an alternative way of thinking about knowledge and evidence, Carvajal solidifies the ephemera to remove ambiguities and gaps: "Doubt," she writes in the final paragraph, "was no longer my religion" (2012a, 301).

On the one hand, then, Carvajal overturns the domesticated official discourses about Jewish Spain that evacuate precisely the d(r)ead of history to present a palatable and commodifiable story of the past. The author removes the whitewash of tourism, reanimating suppressed affect and repressed knowledge (she gets a classic response from a local when she asks about the Inquisition: "We don't talk about those things" [Carvajal 2012a, 9]). Although at the beginning of the book Carvajal has not yet confirmed her origins, bodily symptoms (and other signs she perceives in her daughter) perform a kind of proof, despite her self-avowed skepticism. Returns such as Carvajal's are different from archetypal ones, from Homer's to diasporic fictions that idealize home and homeland, a space of full belonging. Carvajal's return is to a site of expulsion, murder, and postexpulsion states of terror. The desire for belonging is not located in the homeland; instead, the yearning is one for deterritorialized, secularized filiation with a community, specifically a Sephardi Jewish one. Hence it is at a remove from the felicitous returns that Spanish tourism and the offer of nationality seek to elicit and also holds at bay the recruitment of Latinx to the cause of finding and repatriating the lost tribes.

The connection to place in Carvajal's crypto-Jewish narrative of return to Spain, inspired by gaps and unaccounted elements in family history, seems to be mediated through general historical knowledge, which is often the main resource in such genealogical narratives. The known facts, albeit few, are performed through the body in Carvajal as they are for Obejas's Enrique and other figures in fiction and memoirs we have met in the discussion of the crypto-Jewish body (Chapter 1). Carvajal's embodied, affective return, in which the body reacts to the built environment of Arcos, filling in the gaps left by documentation, is a paramemory enacted in cases of absent or faint personal, familial, religious, ethnoracial, and national memory. Unlike the "phantomatic" transgenerational transmission of trauma described by psychoanalysts (Abraham and Torok 1994), the symptoms are not inexplicable or unconscious, though they present unpredictably in context, upon contact with what is perceived to be a crypto-Jewish historical site such as Arcos.

Carvajal does not position her corporeal responses to the environment as mystically unmediated the way some subjects do in their testimonials about returning to a preconversion Sephardi identity. But there is no explicit reference to how the affect (such as the dread experienced in Arcos or the daughter's penchant for flamenco) that Arcos produced was mediated by historiography. The reader could infer, as I am doing, that it was perhaps historical *knowledge* and not just transgenerational haunting of secrets (Abraham and Torok 1994, 171) that led to these sensations, especially because Carvajal does problematize other means of accessing history (e.g., genetic ancestry testing) and explicitly makes "doubt" central to her enterprise. But we are left to think that the body is reenacting an ancient persecution involuntarily. In the face of buried evidence, the body is produced as an archive, a remnant, a carrier of a paramemory.

In *The Forgetting River* Carvajal offers us, then, two irreconcilable modes of memory construction in narrating her return to Spain and to Jewish identity. In one mode there is a diligent and self-reflective skepticism and evidence gathering in archives, DNA tests, familial knowledge, and local lore. None of this evidence, sought through rational modern means, is sufficient or uncontested; however, the mediation inherent in returns and quests for recovery is made explicit. In the other mode, which is more mystical and corporeal than the modern and rational approach, missing archives are replaced in part and inexplicitly with an a priori paramemory residing in the body and surfacing upon return. The body remembers without experience or transmission. That something resides in the body and is triggered on contact in the absence of transmission stabilizes memory to posit a fixed component to identities and memories. In contrast to *Mi nombre es Jamaica*, in which Fajardo seeks precisely to problematize such returns, Carvajal's memoir is more than a return to genetic identities and contains a more nuanced approach that relativizes her quest; she is open about doubts and improbabilities. But in the end these are resolved hastily through a single object of her grandmother's.

The Forgetting River is an exemplary text about self-making as a remnant of the converso past with its evocative writing, sustained tropes about erasures and forgetting, expression of emotion and yearning, and the questions it raises for us in terms of evidence, returns, recoveries, and the production of remnants.

Blood and Convergence

José Manuel Fajardo's *Mi nombre es Jamaica* (2010) problematizes certainties in returns. Winner of the 2011 Alberto Benveniste Award for fiction from the Paris center of Sephardi studies of the same name, the novel incorporates Native, converso, and Spanish contexts, found also in Latinx literature, into other European and Palestine/Israel reference points. Fajardo's other work about Spain's postmedieval, postexpulsion legacies includes *El Converso* (1998), which is about the aftermath of the Morisco expulsion and the Republic of Salé. *Mi nombre es Jamaica*, which has been translated into several languages but not English, is an expansive novel that speaks to the complexity of narratives regarding the histories of conversion and expulsion, philo-Sephardism, and ideas in the past and present about exclusion, minoritization, and genocide. Fajardo's ambitious work is woven with Sephardi, crypto-Jewish, Christian, Muslim, European, indigenous, and other imaginaries and creates a narrative world in which the period after 1492 coincides with the present. Like the Latinx authors already examined, Fajardo represents conversion and conquest in terms of overlapping fates of the disposed and exploited subjects of empire. Whereas in Latinx literature the Americas component of Sephardi and converso history and culture is emphasized, in *Mi nombre es Jamaica* Fajardo aims for a transatlantic, transhistorical meditation on suppressed histories, suffering, and victimization.

Mi nombre es Jamaica also provides a paradigmatic example of the treatment of Sephardi culture and history as an inherently connective enterprise. Knowledge of and appreciation for Sephardi history and culture are evident in the text. But the presentation of the richness of Sephardi literary, philosophical, and theological traditions is far from neutral, as it is framed by the question of how Spain relates to its own history, in relation to both Sephardi life and the fate of the indigenous in the Americas. Appropriately, the exploration of answers is full of conflict, doubt, desire, and denial. In Fajardo's narratives fundamental questions regarding converso and Sephardi history come alive: Christian Spain's "Jewish blood" quantum and its implications; the genealogical imagination and its role in historical consciousness and culture; the ethics of appropriation of others' identity and suffering; authenticity of returns to ancient identities; and how (not) to think about victimhood in relation to Jewishness and how this might resonate with the situation in Israel/Palestine.

In my analysis I focus on the relationship between the novel's narrative of convergence and its narrative of blood. Because *Mi nombre es Jamaica* is about the problematics of recovering origins and reinserting suppressed histories into the present through ("recovered") ancestry, it is preoccupied with blood: national and individual, Jewish and Christian, Spanish and indigenous. The blood narrative, especially the one about Sephardi blood running in Spanish veins, veers toward incommensurability, whereas the narrative of entanglements among Jews, Christians, the indigenous, and so on emphasizes intersections and congruities. In drawing our attention to both the fixities of blood discourse and the overlapping fluidities of traumatic histories, Fajardo's novel ultimately incorporates blood into the convergence narrative in which Spanish, Sephardi Jewish, American indigenous, Palestinian, and Maghrebi French overlap. Blood and convergence narratives and genealogical and historical consciousness have intertwined logics.

Spanish Philo-Sephardism

Fajardo's work contributes to the ongoing grappling with the Muslim and Jewish components of Spanish culture, a highly contentious and multidimensional debate. The tourist discourses I referred to in relation to Carvajal's memoir are only one part of Spain's official recuperation of Sephardi memory. Fajardo is in a long line of revisionists who consider Muslim and Jewish Spain essential to its identity. Américo Castro's revalorization of medieval Spain's "tricultural" past in his 1948 *España en su historia: cristianos, moros y judíos*, written in exile, has been transformed with less nationalistic and more radical aims by the generations after him; most notably, Juan Goytisolo persistently underscored Spain's profound erasures of and debts to its Muslim and Jewish past that were not always made apparent in Castro's vision of *convivencia* (Goytisolo 2002). Scholars have continued the quest to position medieval Iberia in terms of cultural multiplicities, with María Rosa Menocal (2002) emphasizing intercultural imbrication and others highlighting conflict (e.g., Nirenberg 2002).

Castro's contestation of the conversos' disappearance in Spain's Golden Age and Goytisolo (see e.g. 2014) and others' work on converso aspects of Spain's literature have been resisted by many, despite the openings to thinking otherwise about Spanish literature and identity initiated in the twentieth century (see, e.g., Aronson-Friedman and Kaplan 2012; Silverman 1976). Fajardo has suggested that the converso is "the dark matter" of Spain. It cannot be observed, but it is pervasive. Disappearance from view does not entail destruction or extinction, though survival has to be detected.

Indeed, though all Jewish presence in Spain was terminated in 1492, it lived on, mostly in negative stereotypes or else surreptitiously in its literature and popular discourses. The study of Jewish Spain was not revived until the early decades of the nineteenth century, when the elites with liberal convictions sought to effect political change through the readmission of Sephardi history into the Spanish imaginary. These efforts intensified with Spanish defeat in 1898 and the colonization of North Africa.[3] Seeking to align Spain with its Northern European counterparts in liberalization efforts, the Spaniards faced a problem: There were no Jews to emancipate, because they had been converted, killed, or expelled centuries before. In the relative absence of real Jews, Spain's Jewish past was discursively emancipated, at least by certain factions. The uneven process of revising official history to make space for the non-Christian and specifically the Jewish presence continues today. Like many such acts, the developments have been politically or economically motivated, such as the liberal desire to turn the Black Legend into a "Golden Legend" (Tardieu Touboul 2009) and erase the stain of the Inquisition and conquest.

Early-twentieth-century philo-Sephardism also had to do with continuing imperial ventures, especially in North Africa and the encounter there with Judeo-Spanish-speaking Jews, who served as intermediaries with Muslims and opened vistas for trade opportunities afforded by the descendants of the Spanish exiles throughout the Mediterranean (Calderwood 2019; Linhard 2014; Rozenberg 2006; Tardieu Touboul 2009). These efforts did not go uncontested by the various forms of opposition, whether Catholic, monarchist, or nationalist. The liberals tried to persuade the Church to lift the Edict of Expulsion, which was only rescinded in 1968.

Philo-Sephardism in the earlier part of the twentieth century, advocated and practiced by visible political and literary figures such as Américo Castro, Ángel Pulido, and Rafael Cansinos Assens, reinserted Sephardis into the national imaginary. In addition, cultural, political, and commercial efforts (especially around trade in the towns of northern Morocco with Sephardi presence) yielded some fruit. Américo Castro also played a role by challenging, from the 1940s and onward, dominant versions of Spanish national identity in his work and by asserting instead Spanish history as a hybrid Muslim, Jewish, and Christian formation. As Tabea Linhard has written, Castro and subsequent scholars have shown "that a Jewish element is always and unvaryingly present in Spain in the form of remainders, traces, projections, fears, and desires" (2014, 13).

An earlier influence was Ángel Pulido, the senator who "discovered" Judeo-Spanish-speaking Jews in his travels in the colonial territories. He advocated for the reincorporation of these people, whom he called *españoles sin patria* (Spaniards without a homeland), into Spanish hearts and minds. Pulido and others viewed Jews in the Balkans, the Middle East, and North Africa as surviving witnesses to *convivencia*. These Sephardis were the human incarnations of a Golden Age, with an antiquated Spanish flowing from their tongues and Spanish toponyms and pastoral vocabulary ringing in their surnames—Arroyo, Perera, Navarro, Soriano, DeToledo, and hundreds more. Miguel Unamuno's letter to Pulido makes this plain: Judeo-Spanish, he writes, "is the language of our primitives; it is the language of juvenile Spain" (Pulido 1993, 104–5).

As studies of numerous scholars show, such Spanish intellectuals believed that their work ahead was to update Sephardi Spanish and cleanse it of its impurities developed during centuries in exile and contact with non-Spanish languages and to "naturalize" Sephardis through citizenship. In the long decades of Francisco Franco's dictatorship, a strange philo-Semitism coexisted with official anti-Semitism: Although the Franco regime reinstituted Catholicism as the state religion and reversed these earlier revisionist trends, the Instituto Arias Montano for Sephardi studies was established in 1941 even as Nazi discourse about the "Judeo-Masonic conspiracy" became a favorite slur of the regime (Avni 1982; Friedman 2014).[4]

The contemporary period has seen Spain's transition to democracy and its bona fide inclusion in the "new" European identity, with Pedro Almodóvar, Penélope Cruz, Arturo Pérez Reverte, and other icons, not to mention its international fashion brands, disseminating its culture globally as never before in the modern period. The Europeanization of Spain, previously considered other to the continent, brought with it a revival of its past; the post-Franco era has been characterized, as elsewhere in Europe and postdictatorship Latin America, by intense debates around history and memory, culminating legally in 2007 with the Law of Historical Memory. In Spain, as in Latin America, historical writing and fiction have taken stock of twentieth-century dictatorship, repression, and mass murder with reference to their antecedents, including especially in inquisitorial Spain and the colonization of the Americas. As we have seen, the Inquisition served as an allegory for a repressive contemporary period in Latin American novels at the same time as its stories revived consciousness about past violence as always racially, politically, and economically motivated. In post-Franco Spain, reimagining the medieval and Inquisition period was urgent. Writers and artists demanded that the country recognize the entirety of its stained past and acknowledge the Jewish and Muslim stamp on Spanish culture and the key components of conversion and conquest that led to the making of today's Spanish nation and, in part, the Atlantic world.

The proliferation of historical discourses in fiction and nonfiction, some seeking to preserve and others trying to dismantle official histories of today's "Spanish nation," have led to competing narratives. The conservative insistence on the homogeneously ethnicized and Christian national, literary, and cultural identity, which minimizes or denies other religious, cultural, linguistic, and regional formations, continues along with the Europeanization process and global memory's demand of confrontation and reconciliation with the past. The 1992 quincentennial events included a skullcap-wearing King Juan Carlos I acknowledging the expulsion of the Jews in a Madrid synagogue and other overtures.

But many observers have commented on the "refusal of 1992 quincentennial celebrations to confront ethical implications of Spain's colonial past" (Labanyi 2002, 9). This becomes even more obvious in the discourses around Muslim immigration to Spain. Hisham Aidi wrote in 2006 that Spain, after 9/11 and 3/11 (the March 11, 2004, bombings in Madrid), was "facing two directions: searching for a place in the Western world and trying to define its relationship to the Orient, a process that requires the country to reexamine its ties to its historic others—Jews and Moors, two peoples who now have their own states and nationalisms" (2006, 69). In reviewing briefly earlier discourses about "the Moors," Aidi explains that steps toward "reconciliation" were made toward "both Jews and Muslims. The Arab-Israeli peace conference, a major exhibition at the Alhambra, the opening of a mosque in Madrid where King Juan Carlos declared that Arabic culture 'has a special place in our heart' were all meant to display Spain's new relationship with the Arab world" "(Aidi 2006, 75). But, unlike the "return" of Sephardi Jews' descendants, with the accompanying legal dispensation of the possibility of Spanish citizenship between 2015 and 2019, the state-sanctioned "return" of the Morisco descendants did not take place, despite the reconciliatory rhetoric.

Simultaneously, then, leading up to and after 1992, we have a proliferation of nostalgic *convivencia* narratives and opening toward Jews and Muslims, albeit unevenly and with resistance from various quarters, as well as more radical intellectual and artistic approaches to the past in the tradition of José Camilo Cela and Goytisolo, who have provided serious critiques of imperialism, the Inquisition, and other such aspects of Spain's past as they have also valorized the cultures and lingering influences of the expelled and oppressed, a work extended by Fajardo.

The return and welcoming back of the Sephardi Jew leaves both Spain itself and Sephardi Jewish descendants in an ambivalent, strange position of privilege. It is not clear whether the descendants were asked to return through a citizenship offer, which expired in 2019, because they are considered descendants of former "natives," former "native strangers," or, as Maite Ojeda-Mata suggests, "mixtures" of Spaniards and Jews in a "false dichotomy" (2015). Being offered naturalization rather than birthright perhaps provides one answer, but there are more ambiguities: Do they represent for Spaniards the retention of an ancestral and primitive past, in echoes of Unamuno? Is their return a restitution? How exactly does it relate to the so-called "return of the Moor" (Flesler 2008), in which we also see how discourses of return, rehabilitation, and resurrection appear in both discursive and embodied forms that inform one another?[5] North African immigration, positioned as the "return of the Muslims to Iberia," is the most contentious of them all, as Daniela Flesler argues in her key study (2008). Immigration from Arab and Muslim countries raises questions about racism, Islamophobia, and the Christian identity of Spain and Europe.

Conversions of Christian Spaniards to Sephardi Judaism and Islam, which some of the converts view as a return to their origins, also appear as a defiant recovery of sorts that challenges nationalist, homogenizing, xenophobic outlooks and intervenes in the nation's incomplete chronology, though they might reinstate bounded ethnic and religious categories at the same time.[6] Deconversion of all kinds is frequently perceived as regression. Some Muslim Spaniards (among them many converts) have demanded that the Mezquita of Córdoba, a cathedral but referred to in Spanish as the mosque that it once was, accommodate Muslim worship and thus be returned in some measure to its former status. This is but one example of heavily contested returns considered anachronistic by many Christian Spaniards and the Church. Acts viewed as anachronistic become weapons of sorts, and the fight against them reinforces the triumphant Christian Spanish and European narrative. Fajardo's novel concerns just such a deconversion, albeit through a critical lens on Spain's imperial past and the use of Sephardi culture and history by Spaniards.

Despite ambivalences and denials of histories involved in state philo-Sephardism that *Mi nombre es Jamaica* stages, the interest in Spain regarding not only a past Jewish presence, acknowledged through the nationality law, but also Sephardi origins is significant. Popular books such as *Sangre Judía* by Pere Bonnín (1998), which lists 3,000 Iberian Jewish surnames to raise awareness about obscured genealogies, and individual declarations of Judeoconverso family histories (as in the Americas) have brought further visibility to both the converso and the Sephardi past. Particularly interesting is the overlap of philo-Sephardism with Catalan resistance to Spanish-centrism through the reemergence of Judeoconverso identifications in Catalonia. Further, the increased awareness of discrimination against Chuetas, descendants of the Mallorcan conversos who have been the subjects of segregation and subjugation on the island despite their converted status since medieval times, has resulted in new studies and well-received novels, for example, Carme Riera's 1994 Catalan-language *Dins el darrer blau* (In the Last Blue).

In addition, as elsewhere in Europe, the widespread influence of Holocaust history as a template has colored the narratives that Spaniards tell about themselves, including about their Jewish past. Antonio Muñoz Molina's *Sepharad* (2001), discussed in Chapter 1, is a prime, widely read, and much translated example of Sephardi history's increasing prominence in Spain and the universalization of Holocaust awareness.

It may still be the case that for many "the word 'Jew' still evokes medieval Spain, biblical times, or the Israeli-Palestinian conflict, and occasionally, under names such as Anne Frank, the far-away Holocaust" (Ojeda-Mata 2006, 55). But the nationality law of 2015 and the national discourses and counterdiscourses, some of which I have referred to here, as well as Jewish voices within Spain have made the Sephardi question more prominent and at least somewhat more contemporary. The frequent aligning of the current Jews of Spain with Israel, fostered also by Jewish institutions, has made the Sephardi question thorny with respect to Palestine. In this charged context of Spain's revival of its past, Fajardo stages a Christian Spaniard's return to converso identity and Sephardi history in order to complicate some of the most sensitive and key concerns in Spanish and Jewish life and thought: Conversos and their afterlives, Jewish and universal suffering, the body as an archive, paramemories and remains, appropriation of an other's identity, and the continuities and parallels between the past and the present.

Suffering as Identity

The central protagonist of *Mi nombre es Jamaica*, Santiago Boroní, is a Christian (albeit atheist) Spaniard and historian of Jewish Spain teaching in France. He has recently lost his wife to illness and his child to an accident. On a side trip to Safed, Israel, from a Tel Aviv conference on the history of conversos, he has a revelation and becomes a man transformed, indeed possessed. Seemingly out of nowhere, he insists, inexplicably until later, on being called Jamaica, not Santiago, and begins to act aggressively toward those who he thinks are committing injustice. The narrator, Dana, who is a friend of Santiago's deceased wife and a colleague attending the same conference, rescues the misbehaving Santiago from the Israeli police and does what is necessary to return with him to Paris, where they each have a teaching position. Manically and insistently, Santiago tries to persuade Dana, a Sephardi Jew born and raised in France, and others that he is descended from Judeoconversos, something he has "discovered" during his day trip to Safed. Despite her profound skepticism about his revelations, Dana listens to her friend out of concern for his mental and emotional state in the aftermath of his son's death and helps him return from Israel to France, eventually also undertaking a journey with him to Spain. Although Dana at first interprets Santiago's "possession" by a historical figure named Jamaica to be a strange consequence of his extreme pain and personal losses, others surmise early on that he is in a fit of Quixoteism. That is, like Don Quixote, Santiago has been driven mad by his historical readings to the point of believing himself to be living in their world, with symptoms of hysteria and aggressive assertions about his Jewish origins and Jewish victimhood.

The most curious aspect of Santiago's *locura* (craziness) is not that he is possessed by someone named Jamaica and is preoccupied with descent from conversos. He also identifies as Jewish any community and people who are oppressed. Turning around the cliché about all Jews past and present as eternal victims, Fajardo invests his character with the delusion that all victims are Jews. In Jenin, Santiago/Jamaica calls Israeli police "anti-Semites" and "Inquisitioners" and tries to protect "the Jews" (actually the Palestinians) who are being harassed by the Israeli forces. Similarly, in Paris, he appeals to the rebels of Muslim Maghrebi origin of the 2005 riots as Jews. In this too, Santiago/Jamaica is like Aníbal Quijano/Don Quixote: The misrecognitions of the "the knight of sad countenance," who believes prostitutes are damsels in distress and windmills are giants, are probably what is best known about Cervantes's enduringly inspiring character. Not only is Quijano himself as Don Quixote a fiction out of chivalric fictions, but so are, he thinks, other people he encounters. For Santiago/Jamaica, the self is a fiction created out of *non*fictional traumatic histories, but European Jews and Palestinians are fictionalized through misrecognition.

Santiago/Jamaica's *locura* is based on his reading of historical records. Before they set off for Granada from Paris, Dana realizes that Santiago's "crazy" story about his origins corresponds to a document she vaguely remembers having previously read, titled *Relación de la guerra de Bagua*, about the seventeenth-century struggles of the Peruvian indigenous people. This document (imagined by Fajardo) is narrated by Diego Atauchi, the son of a crypto-Jew and an indigenous mother who joins the indigenous insurgency against the Spaniards. Diego becomes a warrior along with Jamaica, a slave from Ceylon brought to the Americas who fights against all colonizing forces. Santiago's own story, style, and even words overlap with those in the document, but he denies having ever known it. When Dana starts reading the testimony, her first-person narrative about herself and Santiago becomes interwoven with her reading of *Relación*, with the older text sometimes appearing verbatim and at other times through Dana's summaries.

At the end of the document and toward the end of *Mi nombre es Jamaica*, Diego's group is defeated in the Bagua war and travels to a different area, its members pretending that they belong to an unthreatening group of indigenous people and denying any relation to the fierce fighters in the war. Once warrior "tigers," they become dissimulators, in an analogy to the condition suffered by Diego's crypto-Jewish father, who, despite his hiding and secrecy, was found out and died at the hands of the Inquisition. By the novel's last pages, both Diego's text and Santiago's thought-provoking but outré pronouncements and behavior in several countries come to an end. Like Don Quixote who recognizes his follies and returns to his real identity before the finale, Santiago realizes that he had an extended period of madness. Like

Cervantes's text, the return to sanity in Fajardo's novel does not negate the important questions raised earlier, in this case regarding the perception and appropriation of the knowable and unknowable past.

Santiago's recovered ancestral memory is supposed to be a matter of madness, as it is diagnosed, on multiple levels. Assertions of Jewish blood in a Christian body, individual or national, do not go uncontested in Spain or elsewhere. This is another reason that Santiago's claims seem delirious. But they also raise issues about the mysterious idea of the collective unconscious recovered by Santiago. His identity claims take place not only in relation to Spain but especially with reference to Jewish worlds and the memory debates therein. By claiming to be Jewish through a remote ancestor, Santiago, a privileged Christian who has suffered no consequences of traumatic history, is putting on the mantle of Spain's victim, in what Dana considers a questionable act of appropriation of Jewish suffering. Moreover, even his own actions make it clear that in the context of the Israel-Palestine situation, the idea of the Jew as an eternal victim has inevitably lost some of its force.

The presumably recovered ancestral memory and return to a fictive seventeenth century and identity draws Santiago and us, the readers, into the fray of global debates on Jewish and other victimization and suffering, which, in the scholarly world was in part unleashed by Pierre Nora's assessment of the radical division, also formulated by many as a competition, between history and memory. Although prominent memory scholars such as Michael Rothberg suggest that "despite the violence that can accompany hegemonic acts of remembrance, memory can also spur solidarity and empathy" (2009, 18), the renowned historian of the Sephardi world, Esther Benbassa argues against "the tyranny of memory" (2010, 163) because of the exclusive and uncontested ways in which it is deployed. Like many others who have responded critically to the global memory boom and France's own nostalgia for memory unleashed by the work of Pierre Nora, Benbassa and other historians have endeavored to prove Nora right in his argument that "history is perpetually suspicious of memory, and its true mission is to suppress and destroy it" (Nora 1989, 9). The presence of memory, which to Nora "is life, borne by living societies," is opposed to history, "the reconstruction, always problematic and incomplete, of what is no longer" (8).

Benbassa's book, translated from the French as *Suffering as Identity* (2010), also pits history against memory, but with history serving as a universal, evidence-based reference point to memory's sacralization, self-isolation, and political dangers. Although they constitute only one possibility for the practices of memory, the dominant formulations of Holocaust memory, with their "obsession with uniqueness" and status as a "religion," explains Benbassa, "contributed, paradoxically, to the de-universalization of the Jews, distancing them from others who suffered and gradually shutting them inside their own pain" (2010, 161). Along with testimonial memory (as in the Eichmann trials), Benbassa argues that the Jewish state was sacralized, with Jewishness also isolated and contained "in the iron cage of endlessly remembered pain" (161), which justifies the treatment of Palestinians.[7]

Rothberg's *Multidirectional Memory* offers a powerful argument in response to such assertions about the dangers of memory, offering instead productive and progressive examples and possibilities of engaging with (Holocaust) memory, though the other uses of memory criticized by Benbassa do continue to exist as well. Relatedly, within memory studies itself, scholars have debated the role of experience; in particular, the idea of transgenerational transmission has been challenged by critics who have argued, for example, that postmemories are entirely different from memories in that the referent in postmemory is the previous generation itself rather than the events that happened to them (Hirsch 2012; Van Alphen 2001).

Interestingly, Santiago's appropriation of Sephardi, converso, and indigenous memory as part of his own experience raises questions that go beyond some of these debates: What happens when there is a past for which *too few* documents exist, such as most historical conversions of Iberians? Issues like transmission and circulation take a back seat to concerns about veracity and evidence. It is one thing to evaluate the history and memory of subjects whose stories feature reference points and evidence, even if tenuous, and another thing to understand those who recover history by renouncing conversion and returning to prior identities that are undocumented. This is a worldwide phenomenon that happens at individual and communal levels, with Colombian and New Mexican Catholics returning to Judaism, Muslim Turks being baptized in the Armenian Church to undo the conversions of c. 1915, and Hindus reconverting to Islam. Stories of submerged pasts and identities are often perceived to be remote from today's concerns, hard to substantiate, and difficult to believe, and yet they too take their cues from the global memory booms and various debated articulations of history and memory.

Return to History As Appropriation

Fictional, testimonial, and embodied returns to preconversion faiths not only are charged with archaism, anachronism, mysticism, and nefarious political intentions (such as reconquest) but are also related to delusion, with Fajardo's protagonist as a limit case. Through its two protagonists, *Mi nombre es Jamaica* stages the clash between recovered memories and their audiences: Santiago's madness of deconversion and return to Judaism is counterposed against Dana's rational and authentic Jewish identity in a kind of Don Quixote–Sancho Panza pairing. Dana stands in for the "real Jews" representing the "true" Sephardis and the skepticism around recovered ancestral memories and identities. If, as Benbassa argues, historically in the Jewish world "the cult of the martyrs and practices connected with death served to reinforce the story of suffering and to preserve the always fragile unity of the community in diaspora" (2010, 40), then, by invoking converso status and seeing all the world's victims as Jews, Santiago claims belonging in a community defined by suffering. He associates being Jewish with victimhood, but he behaves as though all victims were Jews. Santiago's crazy misidentification as Jewish of non-Jewish victims, whether Palestinians or French people with origins in non-Jewish North Africa, extends the community of Jews as victims to include all victims, acknowledging their suffering at the same time as erasing it. Benbassa's argument that the retreat into unique suffering as collective memory, which denies experiences other than that of suffering and nonunique suffering, "deuniversalizes the Jew" is inverted here: Every victim in the world is universalized as Jewish. Rather than simply a delusion, this construct upsets the "suffering as identity" paradigm of Jewishness and demonstrates its pitfalls.

Because Santiago is not really Jewish, his delusions can also be attributed to his lack of full understanding of what Jewishness is. But in his madness he in fact illustrates Jewish problematics around essentializing both Jewishness and victimhood itself. Santiago's confounding of Palestinians harassed by Israeli forces as Jews and his calling the police anti-Semitic Inquisitioners work on multiple levels: He acknowledges that Palestinians are being victimized, which is the position of some Jews. And yet he does not acknowledge the victims in the situation *as* Palestinian, which is the position of some other Jews, who see the Israel-Palestine conflict only in terms of Jewish victimization. Or, even when acknowledging Palestinians, Santiago turns the Palestinian question into a Jewish question. Although he acts mad and out of control, screaming and acting wildly, he is not simply a crazy Christian who does not understand the Jewish condition. He also embodies the unreasonable position that Jews are the principal sufferers in *every* conflict and that Jewishness is equated with suffering: "Los judíos somos un cuerpo de sufrimiento" ("We Jews are a body of suffering"; Fajardo 2010, 107). Dana is deeply disturbed by Santiago's identity claim as a kind of born-again Jew, explaining that Santiago's Jewish suffering is a displacement, merely a cover-up for his real pain over his wife and son.

And yet Santiago's misidentifications, displacements, and lachrymose Jewish history (Baron 1928) reveal the complications of Jewish victimization and collective memory. The novel asks us to consider that *any* totalizing vision of victimization can be a delusion, including but not just through self-definition as a remnant of past victimhood. At the same time as it is a valorization of Sephardi culture and history, Fajardo's novel is also a critique of the insulating aspect of "suffering as identity" and the obsession with the uniqueness of a particular history. The Christian Spaniard's appropriation of Jewish suffering and identity adds another layer and complicates the questions around authenticity in converso returns raised in the discussion of Latinx authors in Chapter 2 and of Carvajal in the present chapter. Although the reduction of Jewish identity to suffering is not unique to philo-Sephardism and philo-Semitism and is also shared by some in the normative Jewish world, Santiago's misguided equations also demonstrate their hazards.

Identity Theft

In addition to voicing the skepticism that is the usual response to self-generated recuperations of identity, Dana also articulates other problematics of mimeticism. For Dana, the converso history that Santiago is possessed by comes too easily. First, she tries to sympathize with him because of his pain over his deceased wife and son. She gently explains that his son Daniel died tragically but that Santiago does not need to transform him into a Jew to bestow him with dignity: "Los judíos podemos ser tan verdugos como víctimas, tú eres ateo como yo y sabes que no somos el pueblo elegido de Dios, eso es sólo un mito" ("We Jews can be executioners as much as victims; you are an atheist like me and you know well that we are not the chosen people of God; this is only a myth"; Fajardo 2010, 100). But Santiago rejects her rational, secularist plea to abandon his madness. Dana shortly loses patience and begins seeing Santiago as a monster of appropriation, the unearned claiming of others' pain and identity. In his manic speeches about hatred for the pious inquisitorial hypocrites, sometimes mixing Castilian with a faulty Judeo-Spanish as though he were speaking in tongues, he is an insulting, disrespectful "impostor" for Dana, who has no patience for paramemories or sudden self-declaration as the remnant of a remote past (115). In a mirroring of authenticity conflicts in U.S. Latinx contexts, Santiago's self-production and self-presentation as a descendant of conversos is distasteful to the normative Jew.

The boundaries around empathy and solidarity dissolve when a complete identification is in question. Santiago's mimetic boundary crossing as a self-proclaimed, born-again Jew is not a reaching out but a violation that effaces the lived experience of others and subverts them. Dana, who is reluctantly helping Santiago, resents that he has chosen her world in which to seek refuge and transform herself.

> Y me incomodaba ver todo eso reflejado en su discurso errático; en sus arrebatos y diatribas; era como mirarse en un espejo de feria que devolvía una imagen grotesca, ridícula, pero que de alguna manera también era la mía. (Fajardo 2010, 200)

> And it bothered me to see all this reflected in his erratic discourse, in his fits and diatribes. It was like looking at oneself in a funhouse mirror that reflected a grotesque, ridiculous image, but one that was also in some way my own.

Dana's words to Santiago undermine both philo-Semitism and anti-Semitism usually involved in identification with or distancing of Jews as a collective.

> Tu hablas de los judíos como si fuéramos una metáfora. No lo somos. No somos mejores ni representamos nada, tan solo somos hijos de nuestra Historia,

como cada cual. Ni somos espíritus puros ni el mínimo común denominador de nada. Ya estoy harta de tener que considerarme un ser especial, especialmente odioso y especialmente admirable. (323–24)

You speak of Jews as though we were a metaphor. We are not. We are not better, and we represent nothing. We are just children of our History, like anyone else. We are neither pure spirits nor the least common denominator of nothing. I am tired of having to consider myself something special, specially odious or specially admirable.

Dana also has other critiques of Santiago's appropriation, whether or not he is possibly a converso descendant. Her response to him regarding authenticity illustrates the resistance to returns to ancient identities through the issue of experience, especially the experience of suffering, that converso descendants and returnees cannot easily claim except through remote ancestors. Before his visit to Safed and the onset of his *locura*, Santiago passionately lectures Dana about the great mystics of Safed and the Sephardi presence in Spanish culture. Dana observes that, though aware of this history, she, being Jewish, does not perceive it in the same way. However, when Santiago later transforms into a Jew, in his own mind, and goes further in his ideas than an overexcited scholar fascinated with otherness, Dana has difficulty tolerating him. She cannot assimilate such abrupt transitions and unfounded claims. Interestingly, although she does not glorify Jewish suffering, she still equates Jewishness with it: For Dana, without scars that have accumulated from Jewish identity, one cannot simply reach back to putative ancestors and identify with victims. Yet Dana's critique is not solely about appropriation of a victim identity but about Santiago's severing of experience from identity. Without detaching suffering from Jewishness, Dana's critique of Santiago's "suddenly Jewish" identity, to refer to the title of a book about such discoveries (Kessel 2000), involves the reinstatement of "lachrymose history."

In Dana's response we see that the rejection of the genealogical blood narrative (i.e., of having "Jewish blood," not just for Santiago but for millions of Spaniards), which is what converso descent narratives often mobilize, does not also entail a rethinking of suffering as identity. In fact, suffering is equated with Jewishness over and above blood. We can see here how critiques of blood and return narratives as essentialist can themselves get mired in essentialism, albeit of a different kind than that produced by genealogy and genetics. Experience, especially painful collective experience, remains key and cannot be divorced from matters of belonging and authenticity. In returning to the past for ancestral places and narratives, Saidiya Hartman explains in the context of African Americans on a roots quest in Africa that "the hope is that return could resolve the old dilemmas, make a victory out of defeat, and engender a new order" (2007, 100). Santiago is someone who belongs to the dominant Christian caste and returns to the past in order to fashion for himself a *defeat out of the victory* to which he owes his present. Two discourses of suffering are at odds, then: the self-declared descendant's story of secrecy and loss of origins is positioned against normative Jewish suffering through the ages. These compete in Dana's mind but converge in Santiago's. Although it is not the principal preoccupation of the novel, this pairing stages many of the conflicts in returns to ancient identities and acceptance of returnees by normative and continuous community members.

Appropriation is a particularly charged issue when traumas and "colonial differences" (Mignolo 2002) are at play. Literature and anthropology, among other realms, have staged colonialist identity play and passing (especially as a person with a power deficit) in the context of conquest, empire, and expulsion. In a different context, scholars who are critical of "secondary witnessing" (Apel 2002) or "witnesses by adoption" (Hartman 1997, 9) have even accused the children and descendants of victims as engaging in "identity theft" in their writings (Franklin 2004). Yet the promotion of identification itself has been a pedagogical tactic in transmitting knowledge of catastrophes. Examples abound: Holocaust museums invite visitors to assume the identity of a random victim; plantations invite role play. Among the critiques of such practices is the claim that they encourage feelings instead of learning (Benbassa 2010). But the subtler, more complex strategies that Marianne Hirsch develops through her idea of postmemory are predicated on distance, for example, of the second generation or of other mediated experiences, like the museumgoer with no personal connection to the exhibits. Hirsch argues for an expression of traumatic affect through the mediated experience, in which, for example, the viewer of visual materials experiences trauma-like symptoms upon encountering disturbing evidence of violence. But she considers this a working-through rather than an identification (Hirsch 1997).

In Santiago's identification with a victimized child in Jenin, Fajardo explores the vexed borderline between empathy, identification, and appropriation. Ultimately, however, we see that the difficulties surrounding histories of minoritization, expulsion, and genocide are not resolved through the narrative of ancestry without experience.

Blood Narrative

The question of Jewish blood in the Christian body does not haunt Spain like it once did or have negative legal and social effects, but it remains a question not simply of how much (as in what percentage of Spaniards and Latin Americans have Jewish heritage) but of what to do about it. The Jamaica that emerges from Diego Atauchi's story, whose identity Santiago takes on, was a slave who knew oppression firsthand, whereas Santiago benefited throughout his life from dominant status but now demands to be recognized not only as a savior warrior but also as a Jew, simply because he might, like millions of Spaniards, carry "Jewish blood." Santiago's outburst to David invokes blood discourse without reservations: "¿Cómo sabes que no llevas sangre judía? ¿Cómo sabes que no la llevo yo?" ("How do you know you don't have Jewish blood? How do you know I don't?"; Fajardo 2010, 113). Even though this is not an outlandish question, what is its meaning and import for the present?

Dana finds it disturbing that Santiago acts "como si todo fuera un asunto de sangre, como si la vida, la cultura, la memoria y las cicatrices familiares no contaran" ("as though it was all a question of blood; as though life, culture, memory, and family scars counted for nothing; 119). Dana's anger represents the widespread disbelief in blood narratives that lead to identity claims solely through (sometimes dubious) buried kinship ties and dubious genealogies, therefore through real or imagined biology rather than through experience or cultural inheritance. Because of the well-known racialist and genocidal effects of blood logics and ancestrally overdetermined identities, nonexperiential "inheritance" of identity, especially in greatly receded versions, as in many post-converso narratives, is often perceived as primitivizing, ridiculous, or politically dangerous. Racializing blood discourses is associated in Jewish contexts with the Holocaust and the destruction of the Ashkenazi, Sephardi, and other Jews of Europe. But the "purity of blood" was mobilized as a policy that caused the earlier catastrophes for Iberian Muslims and Jews, when the "community of Christians [reinvented] itself as the community of blood" (Anidjar 2014, 67).[8]

Santiago disputes the Spanish nation's dominant historical blood stories, in which *limpieza de sangre* is a requisite, ironically also because

> Spain itself became a figure of contamination from which other kingdoms were to protect themselves. Their blood purity, implicit or explicit, could thus be taken for granted. Outside of Spain, and throughout Europe, Spaniards were often called "marranos," and "Portuguese" quickly became a synonym for Jew. In sixteenth-century France, Antoine Arnaud advocated against any Spanish interference in French affairs on the basis of such blood impurity. (Anidjar 2014, 76)

Although Santiago asserts contamination as oppositional, his recourse to the language of blood is fraught with peril, because it evokes these other, older logics even as it raises complex questions about biological heritage and the past.

As we saw in the Introduction, we are not really modern subjects free of the blood narrative. In the case of "Jewish blood," David Biale argues that rather than disappearing after the Holocaust, questions around "a community of Jewish blood" intensified after 1948 and the "ingathering of exiles" (2008, 14). Susan Glenn has shown that "throughout all of the de-racializing stages of twentieth century social thought, Jews have continued to invoke blood logic as a way of defining and maintaining group identity" (quoted in Hart 2009, 2). Such thinking, Mitchell Hart argues, also led to the Jewish participation in European racial thought, though not necessarily in the same terms of dominant racialism or racism, with its causalities and hierarchies, but with an eye to explaining historical conditions and preserving identity (Hart 2011, xxviii).

Dana does not believe in blood narratives; but early in the novel she explains that, although Santiago was drawn to Spanish Jewish studies to rebel against his conservative Catholic family, she herself was attracted to it for the opposite reasons: because of the very *blood* that flowed in her veins and to know a past that was *not* foreign to her; indeed to explore the meaning of "diaspora," the word she had heard since birth (Fajardo 2010, 17). Later in the novel, Diego Atauchi relates in his memoir that when he meets his father the crypto-Jew, who had been unaware for most of young Diego's life that he had a son, the older man confesses his dissimulation, passes on a mezuzah to him, and asks Diego to keep the mezuzah "por más que la tuya sea otra religion, judía es también la sangre que te recorre las venas" ("because although you have another religion, Jewishness is the blood that runs through your veins"; 182). Diego's father dies at the stake soon after their meeting, which puts Diego in terrible danger. Marked as a heretic and a Jew and facing inquisitorial reprisals in his village, Diego has to flee into the Amazonian jungle, where he seeks to fulfill his desire for revenge against the Spaniards, now his enemies twice over for their crimes against the indigenous and against the Jews, "whose prohibited blood was also mine," as he explains (186).

Fajardo's text continuously returns to the issues around blood discourse as a basis of identity. As readers, we cannot simply side with Dana and critique Santiago for appropriation and the mobilization of these putative biological categories, as she engages in them as well. Moreover, as with other narratives of crypto-Jewish identification we have seen, Santiago's claiming of his "contaminated" heritage interrupts homogeneity and the idea of Christian Spain as a pure blood community. Both returns and recuperations and their dismissals are often based on genealogical discourses, which are simultaneously problematic and productive.

Possession by History

Explaining his state of being at Isaac Luria's synagogue in Safed, Santiago exclaims to Dana that he is indeed a Jew: "Yo le sé, le he visto, lo he sentido. Ha sido una revelación" ("I know it; I've seen it; I've felt it. It's been a revelation"; Fajardo 2010, 66). The revelation of Sephardi identity at the synagogue takes place simultaneously with Santiago's transformation, or possession, whereby he decides to become the "tiger" Jamaica, the historical figure avenging the dispossessed. That this transubstantiation takes place in Safed is significant: Considered a holy city, Safed is where in the sixteenth century, exiled Iberian Jews and conversos settled and outnumbered the indigenous Jews. The belief that Safed was the most spiritual place in which to understand the Torah as well as the best place to die was widespread (Chajes 2003, 125). Safed was also where spirit possessions by the dead became the most popular type of possession in Jewish history (126). The Ottoman-ruled city was home to the great kabbalists, who resided there in the sixteenth century, such as Isaac Luria, Hayyim Vital, Isaac Caro, and Moshe Cordovero. Unlike the dybbuk, the evil spirit, the event of *Ibbur*, or impregnation by a spirit, was perceived and even cultivated by the Safed mystics as positive for spiritual growth (Chajes 2005, 100). Not merely a marginal phenomenon, "spirit possession constituted a prominent feature of the mystical religiosity cultivated by the town's preeminent rabbis" (100).

Safed is also the contemporary twin city to Toledo, Spain (where Dana and Santiago travel as well), an iconic site for Spanish Judaism and a cosmopolitan intellectual and cultural *convivencia*. Santiago's "Safed syndrome" (which I am renaming after the Jerusalem syndrome) is a reenchantment, in terms I discussed earlier, displacing the scientific and scholarly approach to Sephardi studies. The rational mind gives way to the mystically possessed mind and transforms knowledge into an imagined experience. Like Carvajal, Santiago responds to a Sephardi *lieu de mémoire* with a self-production as a remnant, turning the body into a symptomatic archive of unrecorded experience through reenchantment. As paramemories take hold of him, his possessed mind and body reenact what has been largely erased from the Spanish national body.

For Paul Ricoeur,

> Everything starts, not from the archives, but from testimony, and that, whatever may be our lack of confidence in principle in such testimony, we have nothing better than testimony, in the final analysis, to assure ourselves that something did happen in the past, which someone attests having witnessed in person, and that the principal, at times our only, recourse, when we lack other types of documentation, remains the confrontation among testimonies. (Ricoeur 2004, 147)

In Latinx narratives the lack of documentation motivates fiction and alternative histories. What about such revelations as Santiago's, which are plausible in light of Spain's history but impossible to verify and their import hard to define? Unconscious transmissions are a way of closing the gap of written evidence, but severed from personal experience, testimonies of ancestral memory, Dana implies, are associated with insanity. For Dana, representing many others, nonwitnessed memory is not just a falsity; with its funhouse reflections, it also reduces the value of "real memories." False memories and false testimonies, as in the Benjamin Wilkomirski incident (see Suleiman 2003), cause outrage and pain, expressed also by Dana in the novel. She cannot accept the reenchanted recovery, even though it takes place seemingly to undo extinction and assert survival, a key motive of converso and other returns.

The binary Fajardo sets up between the real and presumably restored Jew (Dana and Santiago/Jamaica or Sancho Panza and Don Quixote) helps to highlight the complexities of missing archives, converso returns, and genealogical and historical or experiential imaginations' continuing preoccupation with truth and authenticity.

"Todo se superpone" / "Everything Is Superimposed"

As we saw in Chapter 1 and in the analysis of Obejas, Alcalá, and Carvajal so far, contemporary narratives, whether "anthological" (Walkowitz 2009) or "networked" (Bordwell 2006), collate and often collapse borders between times, places, and people. *Mi nombre es Jamaica* does this textually as well, not by separating them visually on the page but by blurring Dana's first-person account in the present with the invented seventeenth-century account of Diego Atauchi. Santiago's possession by Jamaica forges links to Sephardi culture and thought, which he strives to place at the forefront of Spanishness. Indeed, a primary concern in the novel is the revalorization of a critical Sephardi intellectual and cultural tradition. This is not an instrumental philo-Semitism that serves national interests or romantically glorifies the past. When Santiago and Dana are traveling to Granada, Santiago proposes stopping in Toledo, or in "Sepharad," as he calls the iconic city. Despite her skepticism about his ownership of this history, Dana finds that he is right about Jewish people's visit to Spain as a return analogous to the return to Israel. Dana dismisses Santiago's questions about her family's Judeo-Spanish language and stories about keys from Spain. Instead, she tells him about her probable origins in France as an exile going back to the aftermath of the auto-da-fé of a famous crypto-Jewish martyr, Abraham Nuñez de Bernal; she recites a poem dedicated to him, which is reproduced in the novel.

The two historians then launch into a conversation about Spanish Jewish exile poets (e.g., Manuel de Piña and Daniel Levi de Barrios) and Rebecca Correa in a quasi-expository section on Sephardi and converso history. This is not a detached exchange among historians but an expression of a passionate knowledge. Santiago is fulfilling a philo-Sephardi mission begun earlier by the likes of Pulido and Castro, but, unlike them, his purpose is also to connect Sephardi history with other absences and destructions, namely, those in the Americas. Hence in a seemingly contradictory manner to its emphasis on boundaries and separation, Santiago's blood discourse of converso ancestry serves to further a narrative of convergence, which, with its histories and fantasies, is at the heart of the novel. But Fajardo goes a step further by also questioning the temporal and spatial overlaps thematized in world narrative today and reflected in our contemporary ideas about history's persistence in the present.

Not only might Santiago be crazy, but he also expresses others' conviction that the past is not past at all.

> Yo he decidido ser un tigre . . . combatir con uñas y dientes tanta injusticia como me rodea, tomar partido por los perseguidos, y gritar la verdad aunque moleste. Porque la Inquisición no es cosa del pasado, al contrario, es el primer invento de la modernidad, la máquina de moler carne humana que nos lleva haciendo picadillos desde hace siglos, bajo las formas y los nombres más diversos. (Fajardo 2010, 118)

> I decided to be a tiger . . . and combat tooth and nail all this injustice around me, to be on the side of the persecuted and shout out the uncomfortable truth, because the Inquisition is not a thing of the past; on the contrary, it's modernity's primary invention, a machine that grounds human flesh and has made minced meat of us for centuries under different forms and names.

Like Carvajal, but writing beyond Sephardi experiences, Santiago sees insuperable continuities. But in his case these entanglements become more complex and problematic in a different way.

The most important expression of boundary collapsing—between Santiago and Spain's others, between the present and the past, between one set of oppressed people and others—is his realization, as Santiago tells Dana, that "todo se superpone" ("everything is superimposed"). For Santiago, "En la misma tierra, sangre tras sangre, todo se superpone y todo continua, es un círculo sin fin" ("In the same lands, blood upon blood, everything is superimposed and continues. It's an endless cycle"; Fajardo 2010, 58). The recognition of such layerings and convergences, unacknowledged in national discourses, leads to the privileging of Sephardi history and identity, which, after Safed, Santiago embraces with the passion of a madman. He relinquishes the objective detachment of the scholar, becoming one with what was previously an object of study.

But it is not sufficient for Santiago to privilege what makes Spanish blood impure and to accentuate the importance of an ethnoreligious (again, blood-related) culture. His attempt to create correspondences among different oppressions is flawed when it is interpreted through a single paradigm, that all suffering is Jewish. Santiago's rage against the oppression and assassination of minoritized peoples, seen through Jewish suffering, invalidates both his understanding of and empathy for the people and histories in question. When he links the hatred that produced the infamous blood libel case of the "holy child of La Guardia" to the persecution of Palestinians and specifically to the murder of a child, Ahmed, in Jenin by the Israeli forces, he loses legitimacy. This is in keeping with the Quixotesque aspect of Santiago; he is not only deluded in taking his readings literally and personally and imagining that he is a character out of them but also mistakes other people and groups for figures in his books. He insists on calling the Palestinian child Jewish and his murderers anti-Semites (Fajardo 2010, 96–99).

Of course, such comparisons are made on a daily basis, including by Palestinians, dissident Jews, and others who compare Gaza to the Warsaw ghetto, arguing that the historical parallels are real as well as instructive, although many disagree (see Rothberg 2011). However, Santiago's delirium of substitution is an erasure of all specificity of Gaza as Gaza and Jenin as Jenin and Ahmed as Ahmed. Similarly, Santiago invokes Jenin as a "Jewish tragedy" amid the 2005 Paris riots, when he finds himself among young people of Muslim and North African origin. The parallels between diasporic Muslims of varying origins and Palestinians have been made, of course, whether in the context of Islamophobia, racism, or colonialism. However, connecting Paris to Jenin through Jewish victimization (the Maghrebi rioters are also Jews for Santiago) is an illustration of comparison and connection gone wrong. Jewish specificity is erased, as is the French North African. Hence the genealogical compulsion that leads to Santiago's self-declaration as a remnant ("by blood") is not just a critical genealogy that deploys ancestry to overturn common categories of nation and belonging.

As Sander Gilman has argued, some authors represent Jews simplistically as metaphors, often reductively, for non-Jewish problematics (2006). Fajardo, however, *critiques* such metaphorization through Santiago and the problems of ahistorical analogies and comparisons. But he does not dismiss readings based on convergence and connectivity between Jewish and other histories' expulsions, racisms, colonialisms, and genocides. Santiago's declarations of ancestry serve to underline the question of whether one needs to be attendant to repetition of oppression and trauma in order to break the cycle or the specificities of incommensurable events and situations. The productive dilemmas of comparison (to dwell on similarity or difference?) are extended by the reading for convergence and connectivity and by the questions of appropriation and memory, inherited, recovered, or revealed.

Atlantic Convergences

In the legend of Jamaica that Fajardo invents, we are shown a different path to understanding historical, communal, and political convergences, one that does not have a single center. In telling the story of the eponymous Jamaica through Diego Atauchi, the fictional author of the seventeenth-century document, Fajardo, like Alcalá, Montoya, and many Native American authors (Casteel 2012), braids together Sephardi and indigenous histories. I have already explored some dimensions of this connection and the discursive overlaps in Spanish imperial discourses of race and religion (see Chapter 2). In Fajardo's novel these overlaps are echoed in current politics around Israel/Palestine and the colonial background to France's domestic racial and class divides.

Santiago first makes the connection when speaking passionately about the dead boy of Jenin, stretching the boundaries of the tragedy to other places and times: "Los judíos somos como el cuerpo de ese niño, somos un cuerpo desmembrado que trata de recuperar su unidad, que intenta alcanzar al fin la cabeza decapitada, para despertarla a una nueva vida" ("We Jews are like the body of that boy; we are a dismembered body which tries to regain its unity and finally find the decapitated head to reawaken it to a new life"; Fajardo 2010, 107). Dana notes the origins of this image in the Inkarrí legend of the indigenous of Peru, whose leaders' (Atahualpi and Tupac Amarú; see Graziano 1999) bodies were dismembered and buried in different spots, which, once found and reunited, would bring about a new age. But Dana disapproves of Santiago's mixing everything together in a jumble, from Palestine to Paris to Peru, and the way that he makes the "Jewish" (but actually Palestinian) corpse signify universal oppression and suffering under conditions of genocide and colonialism.

Once we become acquainted with the document that Dana finds and incorporates into her own narrative, however, we realize that, despite Santiago's misguided Judeo-centric interpretation, the links that he points to are historically plausible ones that have been difficult to prove. The story of Diego Atauchi, the son of an indigenous woman and a Spanish crypto-Jew who burns at the stake along with his other family members, is one in which indigenous struggles are at the forefront. However, they do not only recall but also connect to the persecution of Jews in various ways, including Diego's parental origins, expulsions and forced conversions, and the postdefeat survival tactic of ethnic dissimulation.

The presence of the past is also indicated textually, in the interlacing of Dana's first-person narrative with Diego's. The more she has to confront Santiago's incessant claims and her own personal issues with her daughter and other family members, the more she enjoys withdrawing into Diego's memoir, beginning with the story of his birth in 1599 and ending with the defeat of the uprising, which she reproduces for us verbatim or in summary. Sometimes Fajardo stages an interruption of her reading, as when she overhears Santiago's conversation with David on the Paris riots, thus linking the events as though by chance. Pretty soon we realize that the rebel Inca group that Diego joins in the jungle has something to do with the rebellion in the French suburbs. There is no historical continuity or structural resemblance other than the continuously transforming workings of coloniality. However, the events of Peru are telescoped: They are not the faint traces of bygone genocides or uprisings. From Diego Atauchi's Peru to Ahmed's Palestine, "everything is superimposed." After all, contemporary struggles over indigeneity, precedence, and justice in Israel/Palestine are positioned often in relation to indigeneity, expulsion, and cleansing in the Americas.

The possibilities for indigenous-Sephardi or indigenous–crypto-Jewish continuities that we have seen in the creative and ethnographic work of Marie Theresa Hernández, Kathleen Alcalá, Richard Montoya, and others in Chapter 2 are here extended to the Middle East, where indigenous,

Christian, Jewish, and Muslim overlaps and conflicts are brought into proximity of one another despite incommensurabilities. The Quixoteism Santiago is afflicted with emerges in Dana as well. Through her reading of Diego Atauchi's memoir, she sees the Paris riots as related to the events in the narrative of a struggle of indigenous people and perhaps some Sephardi Jews: As she drives home from a dramatic event where she gets hurt in a skirmish because Santiago insists on staying around through the violence, she confesses to herself that the events of that day are all mixed up with the *Relación de la guerra del Bagua*; suburban French Aubervilliers is an Amazonian city, and the rioters are fighting against an empire (Fajardo 2010, 217). And despite her feelings of an unreal, intoxicating experience, it is difficult to say that the Paris events are unrelated to the account, time, and place that has absorbed her attention. A glimpse into the world of the rebels has made such sensations of temporal and spatial proximity and convergence possible.

As I remarked earlier, Diego sees the "prohibited blood" of his crypto-Jewish father as his own, which reinforces his previous hatred for Spaniards and determination to seek vengeance as a tiger, his main motivation to go to the Bagua lands and seek out the rebellious groups of different origins uniting against the common enemy hiding in the jungle. Native and African marronage in the Americas, as a form of marranism found also in contemporary Caribbean and Brazilian narratives (Casteel 2016; J. Schorsch 2009), is present in Fajardo as well. Contemporary political thinkers such as Daniel Bensaïd see evasion and dissimulation as forms of resistance (see Chapter 1), an idea also emphasized by Nathan Wachtel, a scholar of the indigenous and crypto-Jewish Americas. Wachtel provides an example from an indigenous-penned chronicle of Peru, the *Relación* of Titu Cusi Yupangui: "Indians," when forced to "be at Christian ceremonies," pretend to be obedient but "secretly, they are to remain faithful to the traditional gods" (Wachtel 1977, 198; Wachtel 2013, 15).

Evasion and masking appear in Fajardo's novel as the last resort of converts under compulsion and the indigenous victims of empire. And in Diego's body and spirit, the "great conspiracy" of "Jews" and "Indians" dreaded by the Spanish Empire and the Catholic Church comes alive in revenge and rebellion. Upon Jamaica's death and his group's defeat, Diego, who has learned about dissimulation as a survival strategy from his father, leads the survivors, who swear to collective secrecy, into a village under the pretense that they have nothing to do with war making but are simple peasants expelled by the warriors. Their evasive imposture works, thanks to a well-woven web of lies. Diego takes on Jamaica's name; and the *Relación* comes to an end. The indigenous rebels of Peru follow the crypto-Jewish path of hidden identities, secrecy, and double names for the sake of survival. This ending validates Santiago's claims to be called Jamaica, after Diego's assumed name, and a descendant of crypto-Jews, because his last name relates to Diego's ancestor, who might have arrived in the Americas with Columbus.

Mi nombre es Jamaica is an exemplary metahistorical novel that, like many contemporary world narratives (see also Chapter 2), exhibits an aesthetics and cultural politics of convergence through its presentation of overlapping times and spaces. But, unlike many other recent works, it questions the implications of collapsing such frames and content. A key idea in this investigation is the discontents of deploying ancestral history as a basis for identity and as a form of resistance to dominant discourses of nations and states. The main protagonists' claims to ancestral or "racial" belonging harken blood narratives and nationalisms that reify origins with memory as their static tool. Such assertions highlight the problems with imaginative genealogies based on historical possibility rather than on documentation, transmission, or experience. And despite the grandiosity of the character as a self-appointed savior of Jewish and converso memory and of all oppressed people's memory, Santiago's temporary transformation into Jamaica also connects the consequences of the destructive and genocidal collusion of church and empire in the Americas, which is still largely omitted from official histories. In lieu of an honest and critical history and collective memory, Santiago makes rhetorical appeals to the body, that is, the likelihood of Jewish blood in his Spanish veins, though ironically, his Quixotesque madness and his claims are in fact spurred by his readings. Blood and text together express entangled histories that have few documents. But the paramemories of Santiago and implicitly of Carvajal bump up against the issues of authenticity and appropriation, which Fajardo problematizes extensively and Carvajal addresses partly.

The texts also address the use of history. In *Mi nombre es Jamaica*, Fajardo creatively presents the madness that can result from historical consciousness of a certain kind. The recuperation of history can lead to a Quixote-like confusion between not only reality and fiction but also past and present. The productive aspects of making the boundaries fluid between these rationally separated categories in the modern period are revealed in texts such as Carvajal's or in accounts of genetic ancestry testing (Nelson 2016). In such testimonies, imagination, affect, and agency step in to fill the gaps of knowledge, producing a nonlinear historical consciousness with overlapping historical periods.

It seems ironic that in *Mi nombre es Jamaica* it is a historian, professionally charged with exploring and narrating the specificity of periods and places, who conjures the past in his own person and is seemingly besotted with unlikely, ahistorical stories of blood and dissimulating racial memory. But this is not bizarre or unprecedented. Not only are nonhistorian individuals claiming Jewish and Muslim identity in today's Spain and Portugal, but scholars and aficionados of Sephardi history have done so as well, including the influential figures of twentieth-century Spain's gradual and conflicted return to Sepharad, Rafael Cansinos Assens and Federico de Onís (see Ben-Ur 2016, 190). Further, Dominick LaCapra (1984) has called "historical transference" the transference to the historian (the "analyst") of his or her object of study (the "analysand"), through a displacement of the past onto the present and the replication of the dynamics studied by the historian in his or her life or work. Even in the case of those who are not historians but are immersed in the past, like the everyday genealogist searching for roots or a period aficionado, the passionate archival quest affects the present conception of the self and the world. Far from being an inert repository, the archive, including the missing archive of what was plausible but lacks material evidence, can interact with and transform consciousness, identity, the body, and practice.

Fajardo stages the skepticism toward decontextualized temporal convergences effected by Santiago's return to converso identity and Atlantic history through Dana's valid objections about experience and appropriation. But the novel does not ultimately reject such convergences in toto. We cannot diminish the importance of the unfinished business of history and memory, though we need to be alert to its excesses and abuses. What *Mi nombre es Jamaica* asks is that we consider exactly *how* we approach historical similarities with regard to power and oppression. Santiago's is one problematic approach: to read the present as the manifestation of an eternal repetition of the past, with a paradigmatic center (in this case, of Jewish suffering). His related mission to make the invisible visible, albeit without evidence or experience, is also troubling for reasons articulated by Dana. However, neither Dana nor the reader can deny the significance of the revolt against the disappearance from view of crossings and mixtures, here symbolized by blood. The motivation to stress parallels and convergences is frequently a counterhegemonic one that acknowledges the consequences of foundational violence and challenges the triumphant linear narrative of progress that hides its skeletons.

The texts lay bare the processes through which selves are produced as remnants of the past. Corporeal, emotional, and mental returns as well as epistemological returns to the past explain and disrupt the certainties and concealments in the present and are witnesses to the "wreckage" of history (Benjamin 1969, 257). At the same time however, the past can be apprehended in problematic ways, and experience can be devalorized in preference to transhistorical ideas about transmission.

As always, returns unleash questions of (the returnee's) authenticity and (ethnic and religious) boundaries and temporalities of belonging. Some narratives about returnees do not necessarily make clear what the persecutions of the past have to do with today's oppressions. How can reminders about and returns to the atrocities of the past in a present that occludes or minimizes them, such as the Inquisition and expulsion, have a role that is other than redemptive? Drawing the line from Peru's rebellious indigenous to the postcolonial migrants rising up in peripheral Paris seems obvious in its demonstration of ongoing colonialities, but what about the return to Jewish blood and its inquisitorial repressions? What is its link to the present? Fajardo's Israel/Palestine setting stands the question on its head and complicates the perception of Jewish suffering today. Ultimately, when converso history ceases to be a "dark matter" (Fajardo 2018) and steps into the contemporary frame, it asks us to reconsider all our "rites of return" (Hirsch and Miller 2011).

(CHAPTER 4)

SEPHARDIS' CONVERSO PASTS
The Critical Genealogical Imagination

THROUGH THE FASCINATING WORKS of two Sephardi-identified authors, Edgar Morin and Victor Perera, in this chapter I deepen our engagement with the *critical* genealogical imagination that has been a key topic but not the emphasis of previous chapters. The ways in which the historical and genealogical imaginaries cross-pollinate inform *The Converso's Return* as a whole and perhaps nowhere more explicitly than in the analysis of the memoirs and other writings of two authors of normative Sephardi backgrounds who have identified with those they refer to as marranos of the past. In previous chapters we focused on works by and/or about Christian or crypto-Jewish descendants who came to identify as Sephardi Jews because of their genealogical and historical research and consciousness. Here, we turn our attention to a seemingly opposite phenomenon in which normative Sephardi writers and thinkers see themselves in historical conversos, who are documented or likely ancestors and also serve as models. Further, in ways that add to the previous chapter on Carvajal and Fajardo, I note that what seemingly partakes of a blood logic, that is, the turn to genealogy, is resignified as a form of historical consciousness. Ironically, this particular resort to genealogy contravenes against the absolutism of blood, including through its treatment of crypto-Jewish consciousness as an ethically desirable position. The Sephardi return to converso roots is a road paved with Jewish and non-Jewish cultural, religious, and ethical entanglements that not only describe a Sephardi-converso world coconstituted by what lies outside it but also make such a world for our cultural and political imagination (Cheah 2014).

Although the paths of some Judeoconversos and unconverted Sephardis separated forever after 1391 and 1492, converso routes after Sepharad have also crossed or united with the normative Sephardi ones in a variety of periods and places. These include the post-Iberian converso migration to and reintegration in Sephardi communities in Muslim lands in the sixteenth and seventeenth centuries, the contact between continuous Sephardis and former conversos and their descendants in Amsterdam or Italy in the seventeenth century, and contemporary descendants of crypto-Jews in the Americas who connect to specifically Sephardi traditions and communities as a return to their roots in Iberia and the early post-Conquest Americas. In these and many other historical and current examples, Spanish Jewish identity is not contained by an abiding, normative belonging and ritual but is shadowed by past conversions submerged in Sephardi collective memory largely as the road not taken.

The less well-known turn in contemporary Sephardi letters toward the crypto-Jewish and converso is exemplified through the key memoirs of Victor Perera, *The Cross and the Pear Tree* (1995) (as well as his 1970 novel *The Conversion*), and Edgar Morin, *Vidal and His Family* (1989). Perera, the Guatemala-born author of Salonican and Jerusalem descent, and Morin, the renowned French scholar also of Salonican background, have engaged deeply with Sephardi history and culture, through which runs a strong converso and crypto-Jewish, or, as Perera and Morin call it, a marrano or *marrane* thread that they assert as both an elective affinity and an ancestral filiation. By connecting the normative Sephardi and converso worlds of the past to the present through their family histories, Perera and Morin participate in a long tradition of reflection on the role of conversos from within the Sephardi communities.

I argued in previous chapters that in narratives about converso returns, a production of remnants, including the self as a remnant, takes place. In a twist on the long tradition from the sixteenth century to today of conversos' descendants' revelation and legitimization of their Sephardi provenance, Morin and Perera, Sephardi Jews through and through, as expressed in their own writing, foreground their ancestral past *and* current identities as conversos and crypto-Jews. Thus they present themselves as the remnants of secret Jews living amid normative Jews and Christians. The early modern question of whether Iberian conversos and their descendants were Jews, which preoccupied Jews, Christians, and those of converso descent, is inverted here and answered in the affirmative: (Some) Sephardis can confirm converso ancestry and also subscribe to what is positioned as a converso outlook.

Perera and Morin's historical (auto)biographies weave personal stories of family and genealogy quests with an analysis of social formations and politics and an exposition of Sephardi history in Iberia, the Ottoman Empire, Europe, and the Americas. Why would individuals and writers with backgrounds in normative Sephardi families and communities return to and identify with the converts in their family line? In what ways is this a recovery or an invention? And even more significantly, why and how does reclaiming and resuscitating converso history and consciousness through genealogical narratives provide a model for Perera and Morin? In exploring these questions, we will see that in the work of each author, the production of the self as a remnant of converso lineage and the presentation of an ethical converso axis challenge hegemonic formulations of Jewish identity as bounded and continuous with an uninterrupted, insular lineage and faith. This production of the self also serves as an archive of a dissident historical consciousness. Moreover, we have another but quite different example of critical genealogies, in which ancestry is deployed to counter, not reproduce, blood discourse. Last, converso history provides a model of worldliness and cultural entanglements with an ethical thrust, including in Morin's term *poly-enracinement* (polyrootedness).

The crypto-Jewish past has figured previously in limited but important ways in recent Sephardi letters as a metaphor for the Jewish condition under anti-Semitism. For example, in André Aciman's widely read reflections on growing up in and exile from Egypt in a bourgeois multilingual family with origins in Turkey and Syria, a telling analogy appears in his reports of post-Suez seders: "After almost three centuries of tolerance, we found ourselves celebrating Passover the way our Marrano ancestors had done under the Spanish Inquisition: in secret, verging on shame, without conviction, in great haste and certainly without a clear notion of what we were celebrating" (Aciman 2000, 109). Historical crypto-Jewishness also evokes exile in a larger sense in Aciman's work. Aciman coined the term "marranism of time" to refer to the act of "living doubly," drawing an analogy between the doubleness of some Iberian converts, publicly Christian but secretly Jewish, and that of exiles, whose double consciousness oscillates between here (in exile) and there (home). Like crypto-Jews and conversos living in "double time" ("real" time and the time in which they burrowed), his own parents decided to lie low (stay) rather than act (leave), even when the future looked bleak and most others had left Egypt (Aciman 2011, 62).

As I have explained elsewhere with regard to Middle Eastern Jewish diaspora writing, Aciman and other contemporary Sephardi authors participate in discourses of "the marrano as metaphor": The historical crypto-Jewish condition is made analogous to assimilation and dual identities produced under modernity (Kandiyoti 2016b). The abject marrano, as we saw in the Introduction and in the Chapter 1 overview of representational continuities, as a metaphor for the fate of Egyptian Jewry, also serves to evoke a permanent story of persecution. But several newer developments have reinvested the Sephardi past as one shot through with conversions that matter in the present: the upsurge in returns of mestizos, Hispanics and Latinx, and Iberians in the Luso-Hispanic worlds of Europe and the Americas; the "diaspora Zionism" (Abu El-Haj 2012) of contemporary groups that recruit and encourage individuals and communities to return to their authentic Jewish selves and recent similar efforts in Israel; and the proliferation of fictional and other narratives about conversos.

In many ways Perera and Morin's approaches to converso history reflect contemporary concerns with secularism, pluralism, difference, and the critique of nationalism and, as such, overlap with the non-Sephardi interest in the aspects of the converso, or, as commonly referred to in Europe and Latin America, the marrano or *le marrane*. Morin's dwelling on *le marrane* is clearly situated in an intellectual context in France that has valorized *marranisme* (see Chapter 1). Perera's approach is a more sui generis treatment, informed by experiences in sites ranging from Jerusalem and Madrid to New York and Guatemala City, but it shares much with Morin's. As Perera and Morin assert their fascination and identification with historical Sephardiness, they also eschew "identitarian logics" (Graff Zivin 2014); indeed, they deploy marranism precisely to intervene in categorical identity constructions. Converso consciousness, as they formulate it, serves as a bridge to and crossroads of personal and Jewish historical connections to *others*. For Morin, it is central to politicized cultural identity in the present.

Morin and Perera's understanding of Sephardi consciousness, shot through with that of the converso, is exemplary of the worldly bent in many narratives of Sephardism. As with most of the texts examined in *The Converso's Return*, Morin and Perera also emphasize multiplicity and convergence with regard to converso and Sephardi pasts. Even though they mobilize nonfictional genealogies and stories of descent, the two authors adapt the genre and discourse of the genealogy memoir that traces familial history, in their case one that is a shifting and complex amalgam of displacements and crossings. In tracing multiple expulsions, exiles, settlements, languages, and belongings across kingdoms, nations, and continents, Morin and Perera's genealogical histories open up the world instead of closing in on family or community. Whereas others might have focused solely on the paths and discontents of normative Sephardi lives, these two authors recruit a critical genealogy to valorize the off-center and connective trajectories of conversos, in some ways for the purposes of self-fashioning but more pointedly toward an ethical goal. Why posit an ethical and entangled view of familial, Jewish, Sephardi, or generally diasporic identity when genealogy can so often reduce history and memory to blood and fixed "arboreal" figurations? I first turn to other scholars of "roots and routes" to help explain.

Historicized Affiliative Self-Fashioning

In her key work on African American "root seekers" who pursue ancestry testing to identify particularized origins in Africa, Alondra Nelson suggests that her subjects do not simply succumb to blood logics and ideas about molecular destinies but engage in "affiliative self-fashioning," a formation of the self that is collectively imagined (Nelson 2008, 771). The term *affiliative* provides a helpful modification of literary critic Stephen Greenblatt's well-known notion of "self-fashioning" (individual identity formation in the Renaissance) to reflect collective and relational formations and "desires for relatedness" (Nelson 2008, 771) in the genetic and genealogical quest.

And relevantly here, Nelson's term is also reminiscent of Edward Said's concept of affiliation. In "Secular Criticism," the introduction to *The World, the Text, and the Critic* (Said 1983), Said contrasts filiation (associated with nature and inheritance) with affiliation (related to culture, ideology, and networks of choice) and advocates, contra the filiative tendency (the linear and conventionally genealogical), an affiliative vision of relations. Whereas the filiative is

> held together by natural bonds and natural forms of authority—involving obedience, fear, love, respect, and instinctual conflict—the new affiliative relationship changes these bonds into what seem to be transpersonal forms—such as guild consciousness, consensus, collegiality, professional respect, class, and the hegemony of a dominant culture. The filiative scheme belongs to the realms of nature and of "life." (Said 1983, 20)

Inspired by Antonio Gramsci here as elsewhere, Said explains that the affiliative can be coercive. Yet it does retain productive potential, including when it is applied to criticism, in which an affiliative interpretation "worlds" the text, contextualizing it in the ideological and material relations of its worlds and thus undermining notions about its autonomy. Like comparative literature, both a way of reading and a description of a type of work, the affiliative can be a mode of criticism as well as a characteristic of texts. Such texts offer "the status of the author, historical moment, conditions of publication, diffusion and reception, values drawn upon, values and ideas assumed, a framework of consensually held tacit assumptions, presumed background" (Said 1983, 174).

Morin and Perera's works are exemplary of this kind of affiliative charge. To interpret them, I borrow from Said's understanding of situatedness and Nelson's reference to the "desires for relatedness." Morin and Perera's texts are personalized reflections about cultural and familial origins and heritage; therefore filiation is not vacated from their project. Rather, in the backward look at their converso ancestors, the authors' genealogical quests to trace family trees and stories become, in great part thanks to their exposition of the converso past, countergenealogical and affiliative writing and practice. Their memoirs are oriented toward the inclusion of occluded cross-affiliations, with larger implications for how we view history, returns, and politics in the present.

By modifying Nelson's term and drawing further on Said, I explain Morin and Perera's project as a "historicized affiliative self-fashioning," because reclaiming and re-presenting a historical archive of conversos—with all its evidence, gaps in documentation, and silences of the oral and written record to fill or to emphasize—is key to the world making of the affiliative vision at the heart of the return to ancient conversions and identities. I further argue that the willed efforts that affiliation entails constitute a world of cultural and ideological entanglements, albeit one based on a particularity, that of Iberian Jewish histories and experiences.

Foregrounding the converso dimensions of identity and history as central to Jewishness not only is antithetical to hegemonic discourses of Jewish continuity and purity but also destabilizing of national narratives that do not take into account the diversions from continuous histories and remnants of conversion within and outside those histories. The willing or compelled Christian identities and practices of former and returned Jews, though a matter of substantial scholarly interest, are largely omitted from many conceptualizations of Jewishness, Hispanism, and Iberianness. In addition to reintegrating the "foreign" and "entangled" elements into Jewish history and belonging, Morin and Perera insert the converso into the Jewish and Iberian present moment. Through critical genealogies, these two authors introduce a fugitive element into preponderant current narratives of peoplehood and nation.

Genealogy and Sephardi Consciousness

Those who know something about Sephardi history and representations of Sephardis in modernity are aware that tracing genealogy is far from being simply an interesting, albeit complicated, individual enterprise or just an affirmation of families and communities long extinguished or currently oppressed or under the sign of extinction. Nor is it a new or modern concern or interest. Sephardi attitudes toward the Jewishness of New Christians after the mass conversions of 1391, which followed genocidal attacks on Jews, and in the wake of the expulsion decree of 1492 had to contend with what Gil Anidjar argues are the "haematological" obsessions of Christians (2014), causing a particular preoccupation with Sephardi Jews. According to some scholars, the ambiguity and chaos created by the mass conversions (before 1391 conversions were few and far between) led to "genealogical thinking" on the part of both Jews and Christians (Nirenberg 2002, 9). After the expulsion and mass conversions, the rabbinic emphasis was mostly on establishing Sephardi lineage for conversos toward their consideration and readmission into Jewish communities (Nirenberg 2002). In the sixteenth century and today, many converso authors and those writing on their behalf argued for a Jewish faith and identity uninterrupted by baptism. Borrowing from Yosef Hayim Yerushalmi, David Graizbord explains that for the rabbi Jacob Sasportas in 1655, for example, conversos who fled the Iberian Peninsula "seek the nearness of God... and they reckon their lives as nothing in accepting the yoke of the kingdom of heaven lovingly" (Graizbord 2008, 33). Deliberations on the religious status of conversos were not always so generous, and the stakes were high.

Iberian Sephardis have long been associated with superiority claims in reference to genealogical origins. Some scholars have repeatedly emphasized that Iberian Jews, especially the Portuguese New Christians who returned to Judaism in freer lands outside Iberia, used the very ideology of descent and purity of lineage that was deployed to oppress or destroy them. They did this, it has been argued, to prop up their own postexile identities and positions; at times, they even used it against non-Sephardis. Some U.S. and Spanish scholars have stressed a Sephardi obsession with lineage and superiority, wielding it to bring down to size Sephardi origins and history, and not just with regard to the medieval and early modern periods (Endelman 1996; Kaplan 1997; Roth 1955; I. Schorsch 1989) though sometimes, as David Nirenberg has argued, they present no evidence at all (Nirenberg 2002, 5).

There are examples of this perception of Sephardi obsessions with genealogy in fiction as well. Israel Zangwill's 1893 novella *King of the Schnorrers* presents a comic character to mock Sephardi lineage discourses. The main protagonist is the wily low-life Manasseh Bueno Barzillai Azevedo de Acosta of London, whose mendicant status clashes risibly with his pretensions to a noble Sephardi identity emblematized by his exaggerated name.

In a related vein, some Spanish academics, such as the renowned Carlos Sánchez Albornoz and Américo Castro, went one step further about the blood obsessions of the Sephardis. Although their agendas vary (one being a Spanish apologist and the other a philo-Semite), they have argued for Judaism as a *source* for the Inquisition. Sánchez Albornoz and Castro contended that it was from Jews that Iberians learned exclusionary logics which were based on the purity of blood laws, and Sephardis paid the heavy price of having these ideas turned against them, a notion that some U.S. scholars have contested (Nirenberg 2002).

In either approach, Sephardi genealogy is a problem, especially with regard to conversos, because it seems to replicate the categories and ideas of Catholic orthodoxy's blood logics. Yet much of the evidence from the sixteenth and seventeenth centuries demonstrates that the lineage argument was used to effect a return to and a reincorporation into Sephardi communities after decades of distancing from Judaism. Also, Jewish identity in Spain was nourished by the belief in the community's noble descent from King David and Hebrew exiles, a pedigree admired even by Church officials. Therefore Spanish Jewish pride, which they carried with them from Iberia into exile, may have had more to do with a long-standing valorization of this Hebrew lineage than with Iberian *limpieza de sangre* and the unmediated absorption of the Christian Spanish predilection for blood discourse (Matt Goldish, personal communication, September 18, 2017).[1] Joseph Shatzmiller (1985) asserts that the same genealogical bent is present among medieval Ashkenazi Jewry, as a reaction to Christian discrimination, and there are also arguments about the influence of the Muslim Andalusian predilection for pedigree as an influence on non-Muslims (Gerber 2015). Further, not only are the medieval genealogical concerns that transformed and reappeared after conversion and expulsion not uniquely Sephardi, but they also dovetail with halakhic notions of maternal descent.

Being willingly or unwillingly distanced from Jewish and especially talmudic observance and knowledge, many New Christians could still return to Judaism. Some became Jewish ("again") because of intolerable persecutions, despite their Christian status and/or due to their ongoing, if partial and secret adherence to the "old" faith. Often, if they were not born into a legal Jewish identity but were descendants of converts, they had recourse to authentication as Sephardi Jews through lineage. Descent from Iberian Jewry became essential to welcoming the converted and their descendants back into the fold, as rabbis attested in their responsae of the period (Goldish 2008) and as the former conversos did in their writings.

Of course, many complications arose in the process of relinking, including how to account for baptized children, property left behind, and marriages in Iberia (Goldish 2008; Yerushalmi 1981). Blood logics and ancestral rather than experiential or faith-based identifications are not unique to Iberian conversos of the early modern period. As Eviatar Zerubavel has observed pointedly in his work referring generally to genealogies:

> Rather than simply passively documenting who our ancestors were, they are the narratives we construct to actually *make* them our ancestors. As such, they often entail deliberate manipulations as well as actual distortions of the historical realities they supposedly document. By selectively highlighting certain ancestors (and therefore also our ties to other individuals or groups presumably descending from them) while ignoring, downplaying, or even outright suppressing others, for example, we tactically expand and collapse genealogies to accommodate personal as well as collective strategic agenda of inclusion and exclusion. (Zerubavel 2012, 10)

How and what kind of strategic uses of genealogy are put into place is what concerns self-reflexive authors like Morin and Perera.

With regard to the investment in genealogy in our own times, we can hear echoes of contemporary discourses of secular or non-Orthodox Jewish identity based on kinship (Glenn 2002) as well as modern citizenship's own foundation in blood: legal belonging and inclusion thanks to *jus sanguinis* through a select group of ancestors and maternal or paternal lineage (which, according to Anidjar, has a basis in Christian theology [2014, 64, 95]). But, as the discussion of Fajardo's *Mi nombre es Jamaica* showed, blood narratives can work to subvert existing exclusions and boundaries even as they reestablish others.

Perera and Morin's efforts to insert converso history and identity into the normative Sephardi past reconfigure the recourse to lineage by using ancestry and heritage not to claim and reinstate existing categories of identity but to overturn them. Unlike many other genealogical discourses, Morin and Perera's are portals to a historical consciousness in which imaginative affiliations and critical filiations replace discrete, exclusive ancestral and communal identity. Often, though, elective affinities have nothing to do with genealogy. Like Daniel Bensaïd (see also Chapter 1), Edgar Morin also includes un-"related" predecessors and inspirations as "kin" and these forebears and some relatives as "non-Jewish Jews," in Isaac Deutscher's well-known formulation.

In his autobiography Bensaïd writes about growing up with his parents, who were liberated of shame regarding Jewishness and free of Arabophobia, though they were not religiously observant.[2] As Bensaïd sees it, his father, with his leftist politics, brought Bensaïd closer to the *marranisme* that he and other French thinkers assimilated into their experience of Jewishness. Genealogically, though, Bensaïd writes in his memoir *An Impatient Life*, he saw himself as an heir to "a splendid gallery of ancestors," such as Isaac Deutscher, Henri Curiel, Rosa Luxemburg, and of course Bronstein (Trotsky), just as Morin sees himself as heir to Spinoza, Cervantes, Freud, and Marx in many works, including the earlier *Le vif du sujet* (1969). Bensaïd explains, "In an unstable equilibrium between their milieu of origin and inclination to universality these miscreant mutant Jews stubbornly strive to believe in an international emancipation" (2013, 274–75). He remarks that this endeavor has historical roots in "the critical marrano" of Amsterdam, such as Uriel da Costa or Baruch Spinoza, who, "having tasted Christian universalism" cannot "return to the closed particularism of the chosen people. He is condemned, then, to the solitude of exile and spiritual exodus, the errance between two worlds, two uncertain identities" (Bensaïd 2001, 85).

In a similar spirit but drawing seemingly on the more traditional notion of genealogy, Morin self-fashions as being of marrano descent, combining filiation and affiliation to subversive ends. Historicized affiliative self-fashioning in his case is the production of the self as a remnant of conversos' secret multiplicities and skepticism. These, rather than the certainties created in conventional genealogies with a single fount of blood and belonging, undergird polyrootedness.

Converso-Sephardi Intimacies and the Historical Memoir

For Morin and Perera, the Sephardi and converso fates are intertwined genealogically and historically. Perera, writing in English, and Morin, writing in French, also interpret the diasporic indeterminacy and secularization of the Balkan and Ottoman Sephardis and of the Sephardi communities in France and the Americas as belonging to the same logic as the condition of the historical converso. Far from serving only as a metaphor for modernity, repression, secularism, or the assimilation of the secular Jewish or other minority subjects, decontextualized from their origins, Morin and Perera's marranos emerge out of the depths of Sephardi history and culture, which they have written about passionately, intimately, and historically in their memoirs: Morin in the autobiography of his father, Vidal, *Vidal et les siens*

(1989), or *Vidal and His Family: From Salonica to Paris* (2009), and more briefly in the 1994 book of essays *Mes démons* (My Demons) and elsewhere. Perera's *The Cross and the Pear Tree* (1995) is a mixed-genre work chronicling his search for the story of the Perera family through Portugal and Spain; it is interspersed with anecdotes from the familial past and the present. Perera engages Sephardi culture also in his 1970 novel *The Conversion*, in his 1986 *Rites*, a memoir of growing up in Guatemala City, and in many essays.

Covering vast swaths of history in Iberia and beyond (including Salonica, Livorno, France, Palestine, Israel, and Guatemala), Perera and Morin constantly move among expository, intimate, and reflective modes in the presentation of their historicized and affiliative present. Morin's *neo-marranisme* is complicated and overlaps to a certain extent with the extensive use of the marrano as metaphor by European (and especially French) and Latin American thinkers, as we have seen; but unlike in many readings of such *marranismo*, the converso past is fed by Sephardi history and thought. Morin's model for the *neo-marrane* is not only Freud or Einstein but the Jews of Livorno/Leghorn who ostensibly returned to Judaism but were in fact beyond both Judaism and Christianity, like his other model, Spinoza. The Livornese and their influence on other Jews wherever they settled after Tuscany, whether Salonica, Tunis, or elsewhere in the Ottoman Empire, have been extensive. Morin calls them *neo-marranes* because they "were secularized rather than Christianized" in their Western dress, shaven beards, Italian language, and university education but maintained endogamous marriage practices and practiced religion lightly, blurring somewhat their converso pasts and Jewish present.

Even though they hail from different parts of the world, Morin and Perera's deliberately patchy, multigenre narratives in the first person are hallmarks of their own style and of the writing of the period in which the works, especially Perera's, were published. Particularly but not only in the United States, a context more relevant to Perera's writing, mixed-genre and personalized reflections on history and culture became prominent in the unique and enormously influential border-crossing work of U.S. feminists of color such as Gloria Anzaldúa, Cherrié Moraga, and Audre Lorde, who led the charge with influential texts written at the crossroads of poetry, history, memoir, and theoretical reflection. Perera and Morin's books are not quite as radical in form; however, they too challenge both the memoir and history as genres, blending them so that neither takes a back seat to the other.

Intimacy is a method for opening up history: *The Cross and the Pear Tree* begins with a Ladino curse that Perera's mother lobbed at him when he was a child in Guatemala City; in that sentence, which also includes Italian and Mayan words in Spanish syntax, a whole Sephardi and Perera family world is contained. It also serves as a portal to the picaresque journey to Iberia and elsewhere that Perera chronicles in *The Cross and the Pear Tree* and in his fictional *Conversion*, a novel based on but also going beyond that journey. The language and trappings of intimacy as history is a method as well as a theme. Similarly, Morin intersperses his expository passages about Salonican life with quotes from his father, the eponymous Vidal, and with his own biography and experiences.

Autobiographical discourse is informed by conversion's structure and rhetoric insofar as it marks "turning points" and transformations (Riley 2004, 1). As Patrick Riley explains, "Conversion's rhetoric and logic of rebirth are particularly suited to the autobiographer's explanation of the foundational moment in which he or she adopts a new philosophical system, worldview, or vocation" (2). The conversion of the Sephardi to crypto-Jewish or converso identification represents a turning point in Morin and Perera's individual histories as well as a shift in the perception of Sephardi and converso history more broadly. But the two memoirs differ from what is traditionally classified as Western autobiography, characterized by a conversionary impulse, most famously, though certainly not only, in the classic works of St. Augustine and Jean-Jacques Rousseau. In Perera and Morin, autobiographical discourse is intertwined with the historical and the (allo-)biographical and does not center on a dramatic central moment, a conversion à la Augustine. But the works do trace, through filiation and affiliation, a turn toward the nonunitariness associated with crypto-Jewish experiences.

Doubleness is ascribed to all conversion experiences: the ambivalences and self-searching before the moment of conversion *and* the continuing questioning of the self and faith for some time after. But the representation of crypto-Jewish experience is really one of multiplicity rather than duality; it is characterized more by various displacements and re-formations of allegiances and belongings and less by rebirth. "As one version of the self is buried, another is born and begins to speak" is how Riley explains Paul de Man's notion of prosopopoeia and autobiography as "the voice-from-beyond-the-grave" (Riley 2004, 16). In the case of the crypto-Jew as conceived by most of our authors, there is no "dead" preconversion self but a multiplicity of selves in various half-formations and partialities, which also inform the generic unconventionality and self-reflexivity of the memoirs.

The Cross and the Pear Tree

Polyrootedness is one of Morin's many concepts that I assume would have delighted Victor Perera, who set out to explore precisely this in *The Cross and the Pear Tree*. Perera was born in Guatemala City in 1934 to Sephardi parents from Jerusalem with origins in Salonica; he moved to New York with his family in his adolescent years. Besides the aforementioned works, Perera is also the author of two books on the Lacandon Maya. *The Cross and the Pear Tree* and *The Conversion* overlap in some ways, but the memoir evinces a converso consciousness that the novel simplifies somewhat by evoking primarily persecution and martyrdom regarding converso and Sephardi history.

Some of the events and characters are shared by the two works. Stanley Bendana, the main protagonist of *The Conversion*, a fictionalized narrative of a return to Spain, is a Sephardi American who is in Spain to write a comparative literature master's thesis on the "Byzantine traces in Cervantes and their influence on English Pastoral Poetry," a rarefied project that he abandons rather quickly. His surname is identical to the original name of Victor Perera's ancestors, Abendana/Bendana (from the Arabic *ibn* and the Hebrew *ben* for "son of"; hence, "son of Dana" as we find out in *The Cross and the Pear Tree*). Stanley is "the first Bendana to return (so far as he knew) since 1492" after the expulsion and dispersion of his ancestors to Lisbon, Salonica, Istanbul, Beirut, Alexandria, and Palestine. He "half expected to be rent in two by the fury of his wracked, unavenged ancestors" (Perera 1970, 14) for this return and is even called a masochist by an Eastern European Jew he eventually meets.

The novel's central episode, which stages the Spanish Jewish condition along a historical continuum, is also recounted in *The Cross and the Pear Tree* so that in a few parts the experiences of the fictional Stanley Bendana in *The Conversion* and Victor Perera the memoirist are almost identical. I refer to both texts in my discussion of this episode. At the outset of the novel,

Bendana experiences no wrath against Spain and feels right at home in Málaga, southern Spain, observing that it "still belonged to Cervantes" and was "untouched" (Perera 1970, 15). Bendana participates in the travel discourse common to readers, for whom beloved books are the primary referent and the travel experience is largely an unfolding of landscapes, speech, and attitudes that have already been experienced textually. However, subsequent events awaken Bendana to the continuity of a different kind of textual past, one out of Inquisition records and Iberian refugee narratives.

In this picaresque, comic novel constructed around the hapless protagonist's encounters with strange characters in the Franco era in the 1960s, the commercial philo-Semitism that marks today's Spain, with its Jewish-themed festivals and museums, is still a few decades away. At the level of the populace, centuries of erasure have had their effect. Perera writes in his memoir that "The Jew himself, the open, avowed Jew, was reduced to an almost mythic abstraction, a bogeyman invoked to intimidate misbehaving children. In 1958 I would meet many Spaniards who had no idea of the connection between the state of Israel and Jews, whom they believed to have disappeared centuries earlier" (1995, 90). Because of his family history but also because of the repressive atmosphere of Franco-era Spain, which, in Perera's words, was in a posttraumatic "trance" state after the Civil War and preserved the Middle Ages "like fly in amber," the novel's Stanley Bendana hides his Jewish identity.

Performing Crypto-Jewishness

For the fictional Bendana of *The Conversion*, as for the real Perera of the memoir, befriending the minor canon of Málaga metaphorically returns the traveler to inquisitorial Spain. The novel's protagonist's name seems deliberately almost identical with the real Father Francisco Bandeña, but he also appears in *The Cross and the Pear Tree* as a real person. At first, the novel's Stanley is intrigued by Father Bandeña's attention and relishes the Christian disguise he has adopted, a twentieth-century masquerade of the original crypto-Jew, who grows "enamored of his own conversion" (Perera 1970, 30). But Father Bandeña, more developed in *The Conversion* as a persona than in the memoir, tends to rhapsodize about the utopian impulse of the Inquisition and has written many pamphlets on converting Jews, even though, or perhaps precisely because, he is convinced that his mother was a crypto-Jew.

Father Bandeña also lends Stanley books that are supposedly by Jewish converts from Milan, Hamburg, and beyond who tell their stories about leaving the old religion and finding the right path to salvation.

Stanley first plays the role of the fellow Christian and then confesses, falsely, to being a Christian with one Jewish grandmother. Strangely, the canon then declares, because of the similarity of their names (Bendana/Bandeña), that he and Stanley are long-lost cousins, though he has discovered that the younger man is Jewish. But Stanley becomes perturbed by the canon, who asks him to listen for the "brightly plumed messenger" and "the soft flutter of its wings" (Perera 1970, 34), and finally realizes that the cleric's persistence on this friendship stems primarily from his ardent desire to convert a Jew: "Through some quirky evangelical algebra, I would be returned to the fold as a devout Christian, and he would expiate the Jewish blot in his inheritance" (Perera 1995, 91).

Stanley has nightmares about the priest, who calls him a "religious mestizo" (Perera 1970, 38), invoking a category borrowed from conquest and colonialism in the Americas about the mixing of the racially privileged with the unprivileged, but the priest declares him a kinsman nonetheless. Stanley's confession to the priest is meant to end the masquerade and convince him of his "one hundred percent" Jewishness. Through the family history of the Abendanas of Toledo, which included converts, Stanley avows that he enjoyed pretending he had an interest in converting "to feel ... what it was like" for his ancestors. But he finds out that Father Bandeña has known his true identity all along: The cleric had sent Stanley's roommate as a spy to check for the mark of Jewishness on Stanley's body and to search for other signs as well. At this point, Stanley becomes so disturbed as to walk "beside him with a creeping dread. He felt linked to the canon's ankle by an invisible chain" (45). He finally flees Málaga after what he calls the priest's own "little Inquisition," which also includes extensive genealogical research into the Abendanas.

In this episode, elaborate in the novel and briefer in the memoir, we witness a perversion of the recognition that returns to former homelands involve, the Sephardi Jew's desire to capture crypto-Jewish consciousness, and the dangers of particular kinds of genealogical discourse. In *The Cross and the Pear Tree*, a memoir of travel to the multiple diasporic spaces of Sephardis, Perera writes of his visits to Spain after 1958 and "the ghostly sense of familiarity I always experience there" (Perera 1995, 35). Homecoming is based on recognition, as Barbara Cassin (2016) argues in her work on nostalgia. Although Stanley expects that the wrath of his ancestors will envelop him for returning to Spain, which they might have called "a land of idolatry" in the seventeenth century, instead he experiences "gentle" déjà vus and "felt right at home" with Andalusians, their landscape, and their sunlight. But this sensation does not last long. Like Odysseus, the returning subject must recognize, which Stanley does, but also be recognized, a process Stanley deliberately and strategically blocks by hiding his Jewish identity. He engages in what we might call temporal masquerade, to adapt Elizabeth Freeman's concept of "temporal drag." For Freeman, the past might be incorporated into the queer present as a "counter-genealogical practice of archiving culture's throwaway objects, including the outmoded masculinities and femininities from which usable pasts may be extracted" (Freeman 2010, xxiii).

Stanley performs a presumably outmoded crypto-Jewish identity, with its inside-outside, secret-public distinctions, and for a time enjoys dissimulating as a Christian. But his masquerade becomes real, with the reenactment taking on a literal dimension. We can link this to Fajardo and his character Santiago/Jamaica's declaration that he is a descendant of conversos. Perera's context, which is Franco's Spain, and Fajardo's twenty-first-century Israel, Spain, and France are of course different. So are the thematizations of voluntary versus involuntary conversion, possession, and masquerade. But both authors' works instruct us on various aspects of marranism and identity performance.

In both of Perera's interrelated works, the narrators performatively resuscitate the crypto-Jew in the very place of conversos' origins. Although they enjoy inhabiting and performing this ancient, ancestral identity in secret, the reenactment itself turns abject once recognition comes into play. Being recognized by the canon and his spy is a forced unveiling of the Sephardi Jew's Christian mask. Performative crypto-Jewishness turns sinister in Franco's Spain, which proves not to be a home over and over throughout the novel. And in the memoir it is a place that restricts access to the genealogist: Perera likens a haughty Madrid librarian impeding his access to materials to Torquemada. Stanley's return produces *not* the recognition that facilitates homecoming but the kind of putative recognition and its consequences that produced exile in the first place: the demand for the truth of identity and the demand for conversion.

In texts like Perera's, where the descendant of the expelled flees in a manner reminiscent of his ancestors, this time from dictatorial rather than inquisitorial Spain, Spanish-Sephardi recognition consists of enduring absolute difference, and the recovery implied in the rite of return is interrupted.

It is important to underline Stanley's and Perera's flight as an understandable reaction in the Franco years. Even though rumors have floated about the dictator's secret Sephardi background and although he is credited with "helping" Jews during World War II, recent research indicates that these characterizations are false or exaggerated (Linhard 2014; Ojeda-Mata 2018; Rohr 2007). In 2010 evidence emerged that Franco had provided a list of 6,000 Jews in Spain, including their political affiliations, to Heinrich Himmler; the list was compiled on the dictator's order. In the provinces governors had to search high and low for Sephardi Jews, because, according to the 1941 order, "Their adaptation to our environment and their similar temperament allow them to hide their origins more easily" ("General Franco" 2010). This was no mere Inquisition allegory, but a serious modern hunt for Sephardis, positioned as crypto-Jews, who were not handed over by Spain only because Franco found it more advantageous to stay neutral. Although these particular acts were not known when *The Converso* was written, it is not just ancestral memory and "temporal masquerade" (Freeman 2010), then, that lead Stanley to hide his identity and run when he is discovered. Largely, he is conforming to the repressive reality for Jews and any other nonnormative or dissident individuals and groups in that period in Spain.

At the same time, Stanley plays a role in the return to the crypto-Jewish identity of some of his ancestors, wittingly and unwittingly. He pursues the relationship with the canon despite his unsavoriness, tests and enjoys the power of the masquerade, and then, when his masquerade is turned against him, experiences a brief *delirio* (Hernández 2002). From the tension of being under surveillance, the novel's protagonist acts peculiar: He starts laughing maniacally, speaks English to the dumbfounded priest, and takes flight abruptly. The discourse of abjection takes over: Stanley feels enchained, tricked, and trapped through most of the rest of his (mis)adventures in Spain. His self-respect dissolved, he leaves the country "having understood now that Spain had sapped his vitality and undermined his confidence; it had tried to make him reject his seed and nearly succeeded in turning him, as it had the more craven of his ancestors, into a fugitive crypto-Jew: a Marrano" (Perera 1970, 197). The Spanish-Sephardi recognition is perverted, and the Sephardi's transformation into the eponymous converso is complete.

Wrongs of Returns

Many other contemporary novels, especially those set in the years before state-sponsored philo-Sephardism, stress the disappointments of the return to Sepharad and the failures of recognition. In Salman Rushdie's well-known 1995 novel *The Moor's Last Sigh*, Moraes Zogoiby of Bombay, who has reclaimed his Sephardi roots, gazes out on the Spanish vista: "I tried to imagine this landscape as it might have been when our remote ancestors had been here.... I am a Jew from Spain, like the philosopher Maimonides, I told myself, to see if the words rang true. They sounded hollow. Maimonides's ghost laughed at me. I had reached an anti-Jerusalem: not a home, but an away. A place that did not bind, but dissolved" (Rushdie 1995, 388). In Antonio Muñoz Molina's novel *Sepharad*, a Sephardi Holocaust survivor reflects from Tangiers, Morocco, his place of refuge, that "Spain is a stone's throw away [but] is so remote that it is nearly nonexistent, an inaccessible, unknown, thankless country they called Sepharad, longing for it with a melancholy without basis or excuse." The character Salama is "the only one of all his line to fulfill the hereditary dream of return, only to be expelled once again, and this time definitively" (Muñoz Molina 2003, 111).

The difference between the pre- and post-1990s era in terms of Sephardi returns to Spain is striking, as exemplified in two essays about the return to Spain by the renowned anthropologist and author Ruth Behar. Behar holds the Victor Haim Perera Collegiate Professorship in Anthropology at the University of Michigan, a title she chose for Perera's influence on her with regard to Sephardi culture. As a young anthropologist in the immediate post-Franco years, when political and social conservatism had yet to loosen its grip, Behar hid her Jewish identity from the otherwise kind Catholic villagers she was studying. She slept under a cross (which she secretly took down nightly) while living above a family's pigs, inevitably invoking her own marrano condition (which evokes both "pig" and, albeit controversially, the converso). This particular journey is earlier and rather different from her later account of worldwide Behars' felicitous return to Béjar, Spain, in search of origins (Kandiyoti 2016a) during the ongoing period of state philo-Semitism in the early twenty-first century.

In *The Conversion* Stanley's crypto-Jewishness seems more deliberately performative and multifaceted. His act is comfortable and familiar initially and becomes more tenuous gradually; within a short time he turns abject, reflecting the converso condition as terribly oppressed in some contexts and, in others, as multisited, multilingual "cultural commuting," in which different identities are strategically performed (Melammed 2010). Stanley's dissimulation is at first somewhat empowering—masquerading as fully Christian and later as part-Jew—is an intriguing experiment in fooling the conservative Catholic and enacting in seeming safety the experience of some of his ancestors. Later, when he becomes subject to what Perera calls in his memoir a *proceso* (trial), Stanley's identification with his converso ancestors takes on flesh.

Ironically, Perera's long sojourn in Spain was compelled by his mentor at Brooklyn College, Mair José Benardete. A 1920s immigrant to New York born in Çanakkale (Dardanelles) and later a renowned professor of Sephardi culture and language in New York, Benardete bridged Sephardi studies and Hispanic studies of his period. Benardete pushed Perera toward scholarship in Spanish literature and Spain as a "cure" for Perera's desire to be a writer. The scholar faulted the young Perera for having been "corrupted by Yiddishistic values" when he did not show interest in "the Marrano nuances of Fernando Rojas's sixteenth-century classic, *La Celestina*" (Perera 1995, 87). But Spain proved to be less a locus of rehabilitation through glorious Hispanic/Sephardi culture and more a brush with the converso within and Judeo-phobia without. The "Marrano nuances" of his own life, family, and community history, together with the canon's avowal of converso ancestry (as a reason for his zeal for converting Jews), were no longer a subtext, as in Benardete's classroom, but at the very surface, though no less dramatic for it. From the margin of Perera's ancestry, the conversos surge to the center.

In *The Conversion* the return to this history is less a recovery of belonging than a retraumatization in the context of the social and historical residues of conversionary zeal in Iberia. Although Stanley does not consider converso history a central part of his identity, he converts from being a normative Sephardi Jew to a hidden one and, as such, represents a remnant of past crypto-Jewish histories. The masquerade, then, *produces* a remnant, albeit not a willing one: His performance of a contemporary crypto-Jew through a citational parody leads to existential dilemma, embodying crypto-Jewish ancestry. Stanley's adventure reminds us, among other things, of conversos, subjects from most Spanish and Jewish contexts who have until recently been erased.

Perera's Genealogical Quest

The Cross and the Pear Tree, the later work and fruit of much genealogical and historical research, is a unique and generically hybrid foray into Sephardi pasts that undoes erasures. Positioned as a quest for roots, Perera chronicles travels and archival visits in several countries to find something most Sephardis cannot: records of ancestry predating the nineteenth century. Expulsions, movements, and the attendant problems around record conservation make this task impossible for most. Writing accessibly, Perera describes the impossibilities inherent in this search, tracing the Pereras' journey in twelve chapters, each titled geographically to reflect their movements. In following the routes he took to trace his family's multiple paths, the narrative shifts from the personal to the factual, weaving in stories of Perera's childhood or anecdotes about his friends made during the journeys. The author distills with ease the scholarly and archival research. The personal is not confessional, though not remote; the motor of the narrative is to recount the remarkable crossings, travels, and travails of Sephardis through the thread of the Pereiras. *The Cross and the Pear Tree* is a return narrative to not one but multiple homelands of Sephardi experiences, from Spain and Portugal to Amsterdam, Salonica, Istanbul, Jerusalem, and Guatemala City; hence there is no central locus or final resting place and resolution, unlike in popular historical novels that tie together the strands of migrations and settlements.

The centrality of conversion in Perera's work, evident from the titles of both the novel and the memoir, becomes more complete and less focused on crypto-Jewish identity as being primarily a product of anti-Semitism. In previous chapters we saw how fictional and autobiographical subjects produce themselves as remnants of Sepharad. In *The Conversion*, however, Stanley gets interpellated as a Jew against his will and despite his mask. Although the memoir, like *The Conversion*, includes accounts of Spanish sojourns that repeat the scenario of such maleficent recognition, from the beginning it is invested in placing conversos at the heart rather than at the margin of Sephardi history and Perera's own identity.

A personal explanation for this is familial, post-Salonica roots in Jerusalem and Perera's great-grandfather's testament, framed and transmitted to descendants, forbidding his children and grandchildren to leave the Holy Land at the cost of excommunication. The author's father and grandfather defy this covenant by settling in "lands of idolatry," including Guatemala, where Perera was born and raised. Their endangered status as Jews leads to the author's "symbolic castration" at a young age: Perera is circumcised twice by the orders of a father compelled to go above and beyond the law to compensate for his own deviation. A sacrificial figure born to errant Jews, Perera writes that he "conceived an affinity with Pere(i)ras who had converted to Christianity to escape the Inquisition, only to reconfront their Jewishness after they fled from Spain and Portugal" (1995, 17).

Spurred on by the Jerusalem-based director of the World Sephardi Federation, Perera embarks on a search far and wide to trace the many strands of the dispersed Spanish Pereras and the Portuguese and Dutch Pereiras. Although the archives of his direct lineage, postconversion survival circumstances, re-Judaizations, and personalized accounts are missing, Perera constructs himself as a remnant of conversos based on more general knowledge. He finds that his family name, whose meaning lends the tree name to the book title, was originally Abendana, the fictional Stanley's surname in *The Conversion*. Perera traces the Abendanas to Toledo, where they were chandlers and vintners, with the last of them, Suleman Abendanno, leaving in 1492. Before launching into the specifics of the Jews' and his ancestors' trajectories in Iberia and beyond, Perera explains the role of the Arabic language in Spanish culture and concludes that "a Sephardi is still marked by the inner dialogue between the ancestral Jew and the Christian and Arab 'others' who inhabit his psyche." For Perera, the "triadic bond defines the Sephardi's role in the modern world" (1995, 42).

This definition of Sephardiness as shaped by its presumed others informs Perera's and Morin's work, with conversos at the center of a Sephardi identity conceived as a crossroads rather than as a linear Jewish heritage, and, in Morin's case, an ethical outlook. The converso deviation, unlike in some narratives of absolute faith and return (to Judaism), is incorporated into the narrative of self and family. Returns and genealogical self-fashioning as remains, then, serve to underline not fixed origins and neat trajectories but detours and disparities.

After a chapter that explains familial background and motivations for writing, Perera's impressively wide-ranging journey through Sephardi history begins almost immediately with the persecution of New Christians in Toledo in the more general context of the city's "narrow, labyrinthine Moorish alleys and cobbled plazas [still] shadowed by the hatred of neighbor for neighbor, by suspicions of mala raza, tainted blood and imported ideologies. The blood not only of Jews and Marranos but of thousands of Muslims and Christians has reddened the brown waters of the Tagus in the recurring slaughters variously named Reconquest, Inquisition, and Civil War" (Perera 1995, 17). Despite the sense of familiarity he writes of about Spain, the oppressions that have crossed communities and centuries inform Perera's sojourns in Iberian landscapes and archives. Conversion haunts his very name, transformed from "son of Dana" to "pear orchard," and his documentable family records are largely in the lands once synonymous with converted Jews: Portugal.

According to a 1934 study, the Pereiras could claim descent from a medieval nobleman and a Renaissance-era count and perhaps a king, but Perera's own investigations present a much more motley crew. They include the "unfaithful" seventeenth-century translator of Yehuda Halevi's *Kuzari* in Amsterdam, who perhaps avenged his own converso past by omitting the Christian part of the medieval Spanish author's imaginary dialogue among representatives of the three Abrahamic faiths. Among the hundreds of Pereiras tried just in the Portuguese city of Évora in an almost three-century span are a laborer's wife who died in an auto-da-fé; a fugitive from the Portuguese Inquisition who wrote a book about his experiences; one who burned at the stake in 1595 Mexico; 15-year-old Ana, daughter of a merchant, whose torments in the *casa santa* (the "holy house," as the torture chambers were called) Perera imagines extensively; and in Amsterdam the community leader returnee Abraham Israel Pereira (who probably participated in the ex-communication of Baruch Spinoza) and other "reclaimed" Pereiras who "lived in close proximity to the Abendanas, bound together by their presumptive descent from a common ancestor" (Perera 1995, 39).

Most of the figures in Perera's selective genealogy are conversos, some of them ordinary and others notable. One of the more distinguished ancestors is Abraham Israel Pereira, formerly Tomás Rodriguez Perera, who was close to Menasseh ben Israel, a wealthy trader, author of two books, and a convinced Sabbatean until the disillusionment with Sevi's conversion to Islam. In trying to narrow down and identify his direct ancestors, Perera encounters many obstacles, which he recounts in many chapters that weave together his archival travails and discoveries of his variegated relatives with relevant expository segments on Jewish thought in Spain and in exile.

The identification with crypto-Jews emerges as a paramemory in certain situations, with symptoms of fright, sadness, or anger, and at other times as an analogy to the loss of tradition and assimilation, which I have discussed regarding other authors, especially Achy Obejas. At the security checkpoint in front of the Lisbon synagogue, where he was asked for "Jewish credentials," Perera reports that he was used to such procedures, but "a sadness lingered. Had I been a Marrano seeking his Jewish roots after centuries of anonymity, would I have been able to get past the gate?" (Perera 1995, 71). The experience inside the temple, where Perera cannot keep up with the ritual and is "overcome by a familiar sense of inadequacy and intimidation," is due to the fact that "Father turned his back on the religious orthodoxy of his forebears; and he all but turned me into a Marrano. It was a fate shared by many Sephardim of my generation," whose parents abandoned observance in the Americas (72). The crypto-Jew's detachment from tradition for reasons beyond his control is not just a metaphor; in that experience are the seeds of the search for ideological purity.

In Abraham Israel Pereira, our author discovers a forebear much more than in name. This renowned former crypto-Jew shares a didacticism born of guilt for the Christian past with Perera's forbidding great-grandfather, Yitzhak Moshe, and Yitzhak's own father's writing. The "generations of ancestors who practiced a furtive crypto-Judaism burned alike in the souls of both authors" (Perera 1995, 127). Moreover, the testament of the patriarch against leaving Jerusalem is signed with an "ST," which stands for *Sephardi Tahor* ("pure Sephardi"), "as though to distance himself not only from Oriental Jews with no link to Spain but also from Marranos whose Jewish identity remained suspect. And this shared Inquisitorial memory apparently led Yitzhak Moshe Perera to pronounce the Kabbalistic injunction . . . that prohibited his sons and their descendants from ever again departing Jerusalem for the 'lands of idolatry'" (127). Interestingly, then, Perera attributes his patriarchal relative's demand for commitment to an insecurity born of converso roots, despite the declaration of purity in the "ST" signature.

This testament, ironically the founding document of his family's uprootedness, because Perera's immediate forebears defied it, is key not only to family history and its discontents but also to Perera's genealogical quest. Because of it, he seeks to understand Sephardis' dispersal as well as their persecution. At the heart of the document, Perera asserts, the history of the Pereras and Sephardi pasts in general are converso experiences. Perera does not just make marranos central to his own and other Sephardi pasts; he also explains post-converso Jewish lives as those lived in the shadow of insecurity and inauthenticity of the "mixed baggage" (Perera 1995, 117). The effects of conversion and hidden identities persist, despite the certainties that deconversion and return to Judaism promise, as in the title of the Abraham Perera's 1666 work, *La certeza del camino* (The Certainty of the Path).

Although the expansive cultural productions and rituals of Sephardis, conversos, and returned Jews are the subject of *The Cross and the Pear Tree*, Perera's valorization of converso experiences also connects him to his other work and a commitment that go well beyond the Jewish world. Perera wrote two key works on the Lacandon Maya, an oppressed indigenous group in Central America, where he was born and raised. His awareness of the Lacandon dates to the moment when Perera, as a 5-year-old in Guatemala City, sees caged indigenous Lacandon people on display at a festival. This event, which he could not forget, coupled with the murder of his Christian Mayan caregiver by her lover, marks Perera and orients him toward the dispossessed. Long used in academic research on the Lacandon, Perera's book, as with his oeuvre more widely, coheres in its impulse toward convergences, whether genealogical, historical or spiritual.

This focus on convergences is also obvious in the last essay Perera wrote, published posthumously in 2003, the year of his death. In it Perera reviews his peregrinations through time and place: the search for ancestry and familial legacy in Sepharad and its exilic spaces; a kindred spirit (which he found in his wife, a Brahmin writer from India); and his multiple seasons in the Mayas' rainforest. These seemingly disparate experiences merged for him in myriad ways, including his wife's family origins in Ur, Abraham's city; the historical precedent of Antonio Montezinos, who connected to the Peruvian indigenous people under the imagined premises of the lost tribe; Lacandon parables that could have been straight out of the Zohar; and the Mayan leader Chan K'in, a surrogate grandfather for whom Perera recited the Kaddish at his passing.

Perera's Sephardi legacy is one that he tried to keep at a distance, he relates, but that kept catching up with him by way of other journeys. During the writing of the chronicle, the author was "closing a circle opened by my Perera ancestors centuries ago; ... at the midpoint of my journey I would find myself inside the circle looking out, in a mirror image of where I began" (Perera 2003). Earlier, in a piece on the 1992 commemorations, "Columbus and the Jews," Perera distanced himself from Columbus, despite the latter's soi-disant converso roots. Pointing to the destruction and greed that the explorer had unleashed, Perera wrote instead of his Guatemalan and Sephardi upbringing as informed by the Mayans he was surrounded by, one of whom was planning a demonstration and ritual in New York to "Return the Gift" of conquest.

By connecting the Americas with his own Sepharad from critical perspectives, like other Latinx authors we have examined, Perera's quest for elsewhere, as with so many others' quests, leads him home, but only through its entanglements with what lies outside it. Worlds that would not otherwise have come into contact without the affiliative vision and critical genealogies of Perera coincide and reveal their particularities as well as their porosity and associative constitution. The converso is one important conduit for this kind of worlding that Perera performs. As former Christians and Muslims claim ancestral Jewish faith and Sephardi belonging, Perera himself in *The Cross and the Pear Tree* and his fictional counterpart Stanley Bendana in *The Conversion* do the reverse. They create a usable past through a kind of "temporal masquerade" (Freeman 2010) and critical genealogy projects of reviving, performing, and writing conversos for today to locate them in the worldliness of the tangled web stretching from Jerusalem and Salonica to the Americas.

The Complexity of Morin

The work of Edgar Morin, a towering figure of the French intellectual and academic world, includes but is certainly not limited to several dozen books. Morin is well known all over the world, with the exception of Anglophone areas. Universities in Mexico, Peru, France, and Italy have dedicated research centers and chairs in his name and work in various programs, which is only one indication of his transnational, cross-disciplinary influence on the natural and social sciences and the humanities. Morin was born in Paris in 1921 and was living a productive old age in his late 90s in Paris at the time of this writing. He is the son of Vidal Nahum, a Salonican immigrant to France, and Luna Beressi, also of Livornese and Salonican origins. During his years as a communist in the Resistance, he changed his family name from Nahum to Morin, which is a distortion of Manin, after the Risorgimiento leader and patriot Daniele Manin (notably, Manin himself belonged to a family that had been Jewish until a mid-eighteenth-century conversion). Morin kept his new name following the war, including after his falling out with Stalinism and ostracism from the party, and all through his life as a renowned scholar and the first of many things—for example, the first *verité* film, with Jean Rouche, *Chronique d'une été* (Chronicle of a Summer, 1961), and the first and still-influential studies of the "star system" in cinema and popular culture. In addition, Morin wrote many hugely influential volumes on "method" and disciplinarity as well as on political thought, including a co-authored volume with Stéphane Hessel, one of the inspirations behind the Occupy/*indignés*/*indignados* movements. These are only a few of his endeavors. One of Morin's signature contributions is the *pensée complexe*, or complex thought, a critique of atomistic, rationalist disciplinary science that advocates for unity and relationality of knowledge. The goal of complex thinking is to underline the linkages among knowledges and the partiality of all knowledge.

Morin's Sephardism and *marranisme* constitute but one part of his lifetime work and yet are key to it in their politicization of identity, creative use of genre (biography as history and autobiography in *Vidal et les siens*), and a personalized approach that is unorthodox in most academic endeavors but runs through Morin's scholarship. The intimacy with and of which he writes is one of the chief characteristics of his work: This is a scholar of cinema, disciplinary method, and complex systems who published not only a biography of his father in *Vidal* but also his diaries of his time in California, an homage to his wife, and, in 2017, at the age of 96, a novel about the early, defining loss of his mother. It is not surprising, then, that a moving biography of his father, seemingly an ordinary man, is also a history of and reflection on the ordinary worldliness and polyrootedness of Sephardi lives and culture, which is, in Morin's presentation, nourished by the submerged converso past and what he considers the *neo-marrane* present.

Morin and French *Marranisme*

Although Morin's configurations of Sephardi and converso history are unique, they are also continuous with French thought involving *le marrane* of recent decades, as reviewed in Chapter 1. Some French thinkers adhere to marrano consciousness as an exemplary lack and condition of unidentity, as it were. For others, as with scholars and authors from other regions, Sephardi crypto-Jewish history becomes an explanatory paradigm for the modern condition and, especially in the case of Morin, an ethical position.

As I have explained, marranos and modernity have been considered isometric, intersecting, analogous, or even causal (i.e., we have modernity thanks in part to marranos) in Latin Americanist and European (particularly Spanish and French) critical thinking and scholarship. But perhaps this association is nowhere more emphatic and relevant than in France. The modern double consciousness or self-alienation exemplified by the crypto-Jew, or *le marrane*, is furthered by the uniquely rigid anticommunitarian Republicanism that rather unsuccessfully, though ever more combatively, requires a strict separation between the public and the private and between ethnoreligious affiliations and national selves. Perhaps this is one key reason that the secrecy, dissimulation, and assimilation coexisting with the estrangement of the crypto-Jew has served as a particularly apt paradigm in French thought, whether or not informed primarily by Jewish perspectives. *Marranismo* has reverberated in the Hispanophone and Lusophone worlds too in the past few decades, but despite the historical connection, it does not come close to the prevalence of French *marranisme*.

For Shmuel Trigano (2000), a French Sephardi author, the condition of the modern Jew (in France) is the condition of the *marrane* because of the pressure to assimilate. But writers and academics on the left position the marrano difference otherwise, often going beyond Jewishness. Indeed, Élisabeth Roudinesco, the well-known French philosopher, puts it pithily: "The term 'marrano' [in French, *marrane*], in fact, is still used today to define an inner mode of resistance to an oppressive institution" (2013, 189n13)). And further: "Marranism can be defined structurally as a passing or transition between two existences. The Marrano subject was forever a convert, and everywhere an outsider, divided against himself and a prisoner of his past as well as of his future: he was a Jew to the Christians and a Christian to the Jews. This proved a real opportunity either for fomenting rebellious ideas about faith, religion, and dogma or else for turning out real dogma-driven fanatics" (14).

Daniel Bensaïd's *marranisme* was discussed in Chapter 1 as a politics of refusal, with the practices of elision and evasion as attendant forms of resistance, and in the context of an anticapitalist cosmopolitan internationalism. For Bensaïd, "the intrinsic duality of crypto-Jewish existence, a duplicity recalcitrant toward communitarian closure" is a "rupture," one that "furnished the organic intellectuals with a universalist Judaism that is non-confessional; Jews without Judaism; falsely Jewish after having been falsely Christian" (Bensaïd 2001, 86). In Bensaïd's formulations, as with Morin's, the *marrane*'s polyrootedness does not simply reside in a tragic or (proto-)modernist self-division but in difference. Like Alberto Moreiras (2012, 2017), Erin Graff Zivin (2014, 2017b), and others who associate a version of an elusive, non-possessive *marrane* with an infrapolitical, anti-identitarian position, French thinkers notably trace emancipatory politics to converso history. Morin is aligned with these positions, albeit from a different textual practice and cultural perspective.

"Oriental-Occidental Poly-Identities"

Vidal et les siens (1989), translated as *Vidal and His Family* (Morin 2009), is a quirky biography of Morin's Salonican father as well as a wide foray, like Perera's, into Sephardi history. The book is also only one of the texts in which Morin offers his own brand of *marranisme*. Like much of Morin's oeuvre, *Vidal* is a mixed-genre work, combining details of the large Salonican family and father-son intimacies with expository segments, letters, reflections, and more. The father is referred to by his first name and not by his familial role or surname, and Morin himself appears only in the third person as "his son" or

"Edgar." In some ways, this choice distances both father and son as representative of Sephardi destinies rather than particular subjects. But at the same time, it imparts affection, dignity, and respect for someone who would have otherwise gone unnoted. The city of Salonica is described lovingly as a cosmopolis with a Jewish majority harboring his extended family, the Nahums of Livorno. Indeed, Salonica and Vidal himself are paradigms of Mediterranean complexity and mixture of filiation and affiliation.

> L'Orient et l'Occident s'étaient étrangement combines en lui et Salonique fut la matrice de cette combinaison. Pendant quinze siècles, les séfarades avaient gardé en Espagne leures rite d'Orient, mais s'étaient intégrés dans le monde occidental médiéval, chrétien et musulman; puis ils avaient emporté et conservé en Orient, dans l'Empire ottoman, la langue occidentale qu'était l'espagnol. Plus encore, les familles Toscanisées des Nahum, Frances, Beressi, Mosseri avaient reçu, dés le XVIIIe siècle, les premiers éléments de la culture laïque de l'Occident moderne. A Salonique même, à partir du XIXe siècle, ces mêmes familles s'étaient profondément laïcisées, ells étaient entrés dans le movement du «Progrès». (Morin 1989, 356)

> The East and West were strangely combined in him, and Salonica was the matrix of this combination. For fifteen centuries, the Sephardis had continued to practice their Eastern rites in Spain, but they had also been integrated into the Western world of the Middle Ages, which was both Christian and Muslim. Afterwards, they had taken with them and kept alive the Spanish language of the West in the Ottoman Empire of the East. In addition, Tuscanized families like the Nahums, Frances, Beressis and Mosseris had begun to absorb the first elements of the modern West's secular culture as early as the 18th century. In Salonica itself, these same families were profoundly marked by secular ideas during the 19th century, when they joined the "Progress" movement. (Morin 2009, 292)

Early on, regarding Vidal's nostalgia for Salonica and the Ottoman past, Morin explains what he calls his father's "Oriental-Occidental poly-identity."

> Salonicien d'abord; Salonicien surtout, enfant de Salonique, petite mais vraie patrie devenue paradis perdu, d'essence irréductible à toute autre dans le monde séfarade, il était en même temps spécifiquement judéo-espagnol, plus

largement fils du people hébreu, plus largement encore méditerranéen, et il devint français par hazard et predilection. Il fut salonicien, séfarade, méditerranéen, français de façon concentrique et enchevêtrée. Il ne fut jamais d'un «lieu» unique. Il ne fut ni nomade ni sédentaire, mais sédentarisé et nomadisable. (Morin 1989, 357)

Although he was first and foremost a Salonician, a child of Salonica, his small but true homeland turned paradise lost, essentially irreducible to any other place in the Sephardi world, he was also specifically Judeo-Spanish, more broadly a son of the Jewish people, and more broadly still Mediterranean, and he became a Frenchman both by chance and by predilection. He was Salonician, Sephardi, Mediterranean and French in a concentric and interwoven fashion. He was never from a single "place." He was neither nomadic nor sedentary, but sedentarized and nomadizable. (Morin 2009, 294)

Morin attributes the *poly-enracinement*, polyrootedness, of his father to a Salonica "marked by Marranism, Shabbataism, and we would add, Livornoism, all of which in their way broke with the constraints of the Mosaic Law" (299). Morin describes Salonica as a city that "had become a new Sepharad in miniature" with its Muslim-Christian-Jewish coexistence and a "microcosm of Spain," where Jews of different Spanish regions and North Africa and Ashkenazis had their own congregations, "Castilianizing" newcomers through culture and *djidyo* (Jewish), that is, Judeo-Spanish.

The concept of polyrootedness, in my view, is key to Morin's Sephardism, which is irrigated by the multiplicity of the converso experience. In Morin's formidably influential *Method*, *poly-enracinement* is the basis of knowledge itself (Morin 1986, 231). The title of this six-volume work is deliberately misleading, because it is not about "the" method but a multiplicity of methods and a transdisciplinarity that recognizes the relationality of systems and understanding, characterized by a complexity that is, in the repeating key words of Morin, "complementary, concurrent, and antagonistic" (Morin 1992, 53). What Morin calls the "dialogic" (containing contradiction) principle is apparent in his interest in the movements of converso history and identity as being based on polyrootedness in concurrent, complementary, and antagonistic sources, including Christian, Jewish, and Muslim cultures, multiple languages, and multiple locations. Already in the prologue of *Vidal*, which provides the crucial historical background on Spain, Livorno, Salonica, the Ottoman Empire, and so on, Morin incorporates a section on "Marranism and Shabbataism" into his lovingly described and analyzed Sephardism not as a side note but as an integral part of Salonican and Sephardi identity.

In *Vidal, marranisme* appears in several ways. First of all, like Perera, Morin finds converso ancestors whose journeys brought his own ancestors to Salonica, and he writes in detail about their trajectories. Also like Perera, Morin deploys this filiation to show its continuities in modern times, including in his personal history, in which he learned dissimulation after the untimely death of his mother when he was a boy, trying to seem "normal" despite the terrible pain. This intimate doubleness is also connected to other features metaphorically, literally, and spiritually, linking the Nahums and Morin to crypto-Jewishness, including Vidal's identifying with while not knowing very much about Judaism and his lack of ritual observance, which produced Morin's own lack. Hence Morin threw himself into the study of the Sephardi world in terms of its undefinability.

Of his father, "Was he Greek?" people asked. "No, Salonica was Turkish," Morin answered. They went on. "'Was he Turkish?' 'No, he was of Spanish origin.' 'Was he Spanish?' 'No.... Actually, he was Salonican,'" thus identifying his father with the cosmopolitan city, an "anti-ghetto" with a 60% Jewish population, and the pleasures and dangers of not belonging ethnically or nationally. The Sephardi condition in its original lands of exile dovetails with Vidal's historical consciousness, with a similar conception of the *marrane* proposed by Derrida, of not knowing one's own Jewishness or one's own secret (see Chapter 1). For Morin, maintaining a loose and composite identity is in itself not only a Sephardi condition but also specifically a *neo-marrane* condition.

Morin "became strongly aware of his neo-marranism at the age of 40," writes Morin of himself in the third person in the Epilogue, continuing to remark that

> il l'assuma comme plenitude et non comme insuffisance.... Il n'a pas rompu avec Vidal, il l'a continue: sa «déculturation» est une conséquence logique de la laïcisation commencée à Livourne au XVIIIe siècle, développée et quasi accomplice à Salonique dans les années 1870–1900, puis de l'émigration,

elle-même logique, en France, et enfin de la désintégration de la famille à sa génération. *De même, en assumant une doublé identité, non pas camouflée à la façon des deunmès ou de Jacob Frank, mais à demi ouverte et à demi fermée, Edgar prolonge sur le mode laïque le marranisme et le sabbétaïsme salonicien.* Même après avoir perdu la foi dans le salut terrestre, il n'a cessé dêtre traversé par ce «messianisme» qui s'empare de ceux qui rompent avec le monde des juifs sans pourtant entrer dans le monde des gentils, et qui veulent un nouveau monde où, comme disait Paul de Tarse, autre modèle de doublé identité, il n'y aurait plus ni juifs ni gentils. (Morin 1989, 364; emphasis added)

He did not see neo-Marranism as incomplete in some way, but instead embraced its richness. . . . His life does not represent a break with Vidal's, but a continuation of it; his loss of culture is a logical consequence of the process of secularization that began in Livorno in the 18th century, and grew until it became almost complete in Salonica in the years between 1870 and 1900, followed by the emigration, itself logical, to France, and finally by the disintegration of the family of his generation. In the same way, by *assuming a double identity, not a hidden one like that of the Dönmes or Jacob Frank, but half-open and half-closed, Edgar has taken Salonician Marranism and Shabbataism into the secular world.* Even though he has lost his faith in earthly salvation, he has never ceased to be deeply moved by the "Messianism" that inspires those who break with the Jewish world without entering that of the gentiles, and who hope for a new world where—as Paul of Tarsus, another example of double identity, said—there would no longer be either Jews or gentiles. Edgar has fully retained Vidal's Mediterranean tropism. (Morin 2009, 301, emphasis added)

In *Mes démons*, a collection of autobiographical intellectual reflections on some of the events and ideas of his times, Morin elaborates on his ideas regarding what he calls *marranisme*, *neo-marranisme*, and *post-marranisme*, providing a genealogy of his own thinking. He cites an essay from the early 1960s, in which we see that he was already invested in varieties of crypto-Jewishness or suppressed converso pasts beyond what was reflected in, for example, the authenticity of the Jewish or Christian faiths of the conversos. Rather, what reattached Morin to Sephardism and *marranisme* were the seemingly opposing tendencies toward rationalism and mysticism—the passion of Teresa d'Avila and the skepticism born to a heritage of irreconcilable religions in the work of Montaigne and Spinoza. Having traced conversion and reincorporated it into family and Sephardi history in *Vidal et les siens*, Morin seizes once again in *Més demons* the duality of the convert in a countergenealogical move that divorces it from ancestry and filiation and reorients it toward an ethical position of historical and worldly affiliations and entanglements.

Although Morin shares the impulses of other French thinkers, such as Jacques Derrida, he is somewhat less invested in promoting crypto-Jewish conversion as a paradigm of indeterminacy of being or of modernity and is more interested in mobilizing it as a goal. Just as he had followed the thread of converts in his own genealogy, Morin traces in *Mes démons* his own intellectual and political trajectory through changing ideas around *marranisme*. Seeing the holes in Marxism regarding the "problems and torments of the human soul" (Morin 1994, 155), Morin turns to the transgressive messianism of Sabbateanism, only to abandon all messianism, including the Marxian, following the disillusionments of the 1950s (Stalinism, party politics, etc.). Instead, he establishes himself in "neo-marranisme" (155) as a "stranger" to all notions of "the chosen" who rejects the idea of a conquered "promised land" and what is done in its name.

Neither "Jew" (because he prefers Sabbatai Sevi and Jesus to Moses and Paul to Saul) nor "Christian" (because, he explains, Christians had yet to renounce the persecution of Jews that Christianity allows), Morin continues his quest, which takes him in 1963 to Israel, where he finds not a Mediterranean culture but an unfamiliar Ashkenazi one and an intolerable partition from Arab Palestinians. Morin's politics on the Israel-Palestine issue led to a court case for a 2002 op-ed piece that was critical of Israel's policies. In the essay, Morin suggested a partial remedy through the increase in contact among Arabs and Jews in France, no doubt an outrageous proposal to the conservative Jewish politics at the bottom of the court case against him.

Given the increasingly sclerotic views of the conservative and nationalist Jewish communities in France, despite the concomitant widespread rise of dissidence, Morin's long-standing refuge in *neo-marranisme* has in part to do with his self-distancing from Zionism and other nationalisms and exclusive communities. Instead, Morin formulates his own divergent trajectory of identification with the converso and the secularizing heart of Italian, Spanish,

French, and Salonican Sephardi "singularity" (rather than Jewish specificity), including through the knowledge about his Livorno ancestry (Morin 2009, 161). Having previously claimed communism, rather than Judaism, as his "religion," Morin moved to the *neo-marrane* position in the 1960s and 1970s as significant portions of French Jewish institutions hurtled toward their present state largely, though not wholly, on the side of conservative or right-wing Judeo-centrism and nationalism. The double move of returning to Sephardi sources through the biography of his father and reattaching to a "mediterraneité marked by marranisme and Tuscan laicism" (Morin 2009, 161) is a historicized affiliative vision that departs from filiation (without completely abandoning it); Morin is more invested in the complex network of entanglements in which Jewishness is continuously created than in an autonomous and linear identity.

Those who reacted to *Vidal et les siens* with "So you too are returning to Judaism," as many French Jews on the left did, did not understand, Morin explains, that "the familial sources" in fact freed him from certain forms of *le judaisme* (in French the term refers to both Jewishness and Judaism), including its postwar *enfermement* (enclosure) and "becoming-machine" for Israel, save for its identity as a minority with a history of persecution (Morin 1994). Born in particularity, this history can also move toward awareness of other persecutions and can, in a seeming paradox, distance the Jewish person from the Bible and nationalism. Arguing that the "Jewish genius" of the great musicians, authors, scientists, and so on emerges not from Jewish isolation but from contact with Gentile culture and the insecurities and contradiction that Gentile culture produced, Morin makes it clear that these assimilations, full of uncertainty and betrayal, are also entanglements that have something to do with the condition of the *marrane*, a position he explicitly elaborates on and politicizes.

Unlike some other versions of French *marranisme*, in which the repression of Jewish specificity and the compulsions of assimilation are mourned, Morin's *neo-marranisme* is in part a response to politicized Jewish identitarianism in the last decades of the twentieth century. But, having characterized the *neo-marrane* as a double identity born of instability and interrogation, with sources variously in mysticism and rationalist humanism, and tied to his identification not with inclusion but with exclusion, Morin defines himself: He is not "deracinated" as a result of his standing apart from both the Jewish and Gentile worlds, but "poly-enraciné dans la Mediterranee," polyrooted in the Mediterranean (Morin 1994, 183). Situating himself in convergences and multiplicities, emblematized by the Mediterranean and particularly its Iberian, Italian, Salonican, and Balkan heritage, "the post-marrane" is a "permanent interrogation about the mystery of the world, of life, and humanity" and a reflection on contradiction. Ultimately, explains Morin, joining his life's work with his Sephardi thought, "the supreme state" of "la pensée complexe" is the "supreme state" of *marranisme* in its integration of "different, and sometimes antagonistic points of view, including the point of view of rationality, mysticism, and faith" (Morin 1994, 184).

Throughout his work on Jewish identity, Morin converts *le judaisme* into *marranisme*, just as Perera redirects his investigation's critical genealogical memory toward crypto-Jews. The normative and the marginal or transgressive are transposed. In some ways, Morin merges the idea of what Isaac Deutscher called the "non-Jewish Jew" (which Morin also calls himself) with his own understanding of Sephardism: The "non-Jewish Jewish" transcending of Judaism is embedded within (converso and other) aspects of Sephardi history itself and is no obstacle to the proclaiming of Jewish identities or affiliations.

Sephardi French *marranistes* and *neo-marranistes*—along with contemporary descendants of conversos who grew up as Christians and, in fewer cases, Muslims and are now reasserting themselves not only as Jews but particularly as *Sephardis*—are reviving (despite the use of conflicting terminologies and different backgrounds) and not overturning Spanish Jewish history, which has absorbed and been marked by cultures of conversion (and deconversion) for more than half a millennia. The biographical and intellectual contexts of Perera and Morin, as members of normative Sephardi Jewish families and communities and as inheritors of generations of Sephardi memory that are personal legacies as well as sources of critical and creative work, are different from those of the Latinx authors discussed in Chapter 2. For Chicanx and Latinx writers such as Obejas, Alcalá, and Montoya, as for others who identify with converso or crypto-Jewish descent, the sources of Sephardi identification are various: from enduring New Mexican rumors and stories of Jewish provenance in the region, to personal quests based on researched conclusions, to clues and residual communal or familial practices. Perera and

Morin's familial and communal narratives are seemingly more based on certainties: They narrate lived and directly transmitted Sephardi experiences of language, custom, and ritual.

Yet the differences between Perera and Morin and the Latinx authors who have acknowledged or asserted an ancestral Jewish past (with or without returning to identification) and who have written about it in their fictional works are not great in other respects. Perera and Morin, like Alcalá, Obejas, and Montoya, draw on converso history and their own selective converso genealogies to reinstate occluded convergences and crossings of boundaries (in their case, between Christian, Muslim, and Jew, believer and skeptic, victim and victimizer, Iberian and Ottoman, and many more) and to demonstrate the transversality of converso lives and subjectivities that they find relevant to contemporary projects of connectivity among seemingly disparate social and aesthetic formations.

Just as the Latinx identified authors insert the converso past into the foundations of the Americas, Morin and Perera move the converso and the crypto-Jew from the margin to the center of the Sephardi narrative, led by their particular understanding of Sephardi and crypto-Jewish or converso culture and history. In his 2003 op-ed piece, Perera again observes "the Sephardi's ties with his Christian and Muslim peers—wound together like an arabesque" and "the historic Sephardi" who "lives in a state of flux between his Jewish origins and the Muslim and Christian 'others' who inhabit his psyche." The contradictions between Sephardis' tendency "to be polyglot and multicultural from infancy, as they crisscross religious and ethnic boundaries with deceptive ease" and what Perera sees as their stubborn insularity and unyielding customs are noted extensively. Perera's historicized affiliative self-fashioning is isometric with his interpretation of Sephardi and converso filiation, not as a genealogical closure but as an opening, whether as Judeo-Muslim intertwinings or indigenous cosmologies. His return to Sepharad and its genealogies and the resulting self-production as a remnant of conversos are a conduit for understanding the past and identities in terms of entanglements rather than the insularities that are his subject of critique. Perera shares with Morin a critical genealogical and anti-identitarian vision of converso history, which comes in substantial part from within a particular view of Sephardism rather than from a universalist or generic perspective.

Going one step further, Morin seizes on the *marrane* model as a fount of politics and identity in the present. Both Perera and Morin engage in Sephardism, including through its converso pasts, without subscribing to bounded or exclusive notions of Sephardi identity and history and by constructing a paramemory of converso and crypto-Jewish pasts. They achieve this less through the genealogized body (as with Carvajal and Fajardo's works) and more through historicized affiliation. Through Sephardism, their critical genealogical narratives transform filiation into affiliation, making present the obscured converso ancestors, a filiation rejected or simplified in the telling of a linear Jewish narrative of martyrdom and continuous belonging. Weaving together the intimacies of family, the selective backward look at ancestry, Sephardi historical spirals, and ethical and political urgencies, Morin and Perera present themselves as latter-day conversos and *become* remnants of an occluded legacy. The purpose is to make subversive use of genealogy and to reorient its customary exclusions toward polyrootedness and alternative historical consciousness that accounts for entangled and contradictory formations of historical identities.

Of course, Sephardi *marranisme* that does not emphasize martyrdom to the exclusion of ambivalence and agency can have its own problematic aspects, including, contrarily, understating persecution to valorize the skepticism, multiplicity, and indeterminacy inherent in converso consciousness and subjectivity. Moreover, the genealogical quest, especially for Perera, is patrilineal, which reinforces the "father's progenitorial legitimacy" and "female-line genealogical amnesia" (Zerubavel 2003, 68).

Last, in Morin's work, all references to Gentile culture as the locus of assimilation belong to the high culture of Europe, without extensive referents in the Muslim world, which is curious for someone steeped in Sephardi history, even if a large part of it concerns "Western Sephardis," because neither the "Western Sephardis" nor the Salonican heritage or experiences are divorced from the Ottoman or the Muslim experience. In fact, the first sentence of *Vidal and His Family* is a date, but it is neither 1492 nor 1391, the two key years of catastrophic turning points for Spanish Jews. It is 1453, the year of the conquest of Constantinople, where the "defeated Christian population is tolerated" (Morin 2009, 1). The paragraph that follows this turns first to 1492 for contrast, establishing from the outset Sephardi and

Salonican fates in the opposing Christian and Muslim contexts, despite the author's immersion in and identification with great parts of (Christian) Western culture and thought.

Morin also explains Vidal's nostalgia for his past in Salonica, resurgent in his later days and expressed in sayings and song, as "mixed up with his regret for the Ottoman Empire, which had given the Sephardis a warm reception, protection, autonomy, prosperity and peace, and whose collapse had brought ruin, war, and ultimately the death of Sephardi Salonica" ("confondit avec le regret de l'Empire ottoman, qui avait apporté aux séfarades accueil, protection, autonomie, prospérité, paix, et dont l'écroulement apporta ruine, guerre, et finalement mort de la Salonique Sépharade") (Morin 2009, 293). There is a suggestion of polyrootedness in the worlds of the three religions but without the significant historical or cultural dimensions of the third, Muslim, one.

In the next chapter I examine precisely the largely neglected Sephardi-converso-Muslim conjunctures and consider the writing of the crypto-Jew in the context of Jewish-Muslim and Ottoman-Western crossings and confluences, touching also on their *dönme* or Sabbatean extensions.

(CHAPTER 5)

OTTOMAN-SPANISH AND JEWISH-MUSLIM ENTANGLEMENTS

Conversos in Contemporary Turkish Fiction

AFTER TOUCHING on the trajectory of the crypto-Jewish Iberians in the Balkans through Edgar Morin's work, we now turn our attention more fully to Ottoman and Turkish Sephardi Jews and conversos in Turkish cultural discourses and fiction. A full history and analysis of Jewishness and crypto-Jewishness in Turkish writing remains to be written. This chapter is devoted to the neglected topic of Iberian crypto-Jews in contemporary literature about Turkey and the Ottoman era. In the context of contemporary discourses in Turkey around multiculturalism, cosmopolitanism, Jews, conversos, and Sabbateanism, I analyze two fictional works by Turkish authors now living abroad: Elif Shafak's *Şehrin Aynaları* (Mirrors of the City, 1999), written in Turkish; and Yeshim Ternar's *Rembrandt's Model* (1998), composed in English. Although Shafak's novel receives most of the attention, we will see how both works, as well as a few other examples, trace Iberian conversos' path to the Ottoman Empire and how they connect the Spanish exiles with the followers of Sabbatai Sevi and their descendants. The analysis of the context in the recent cultural politics of Turkey locates our two texts' ideas, themes, and genres within the wider literary and cultural landscape. In imagining the links among multiple conversions and exiles, Shafak and Ternar incorporate the representation of conversos in the Ottoman Empire and Judeo-Christian-Muslim-Sabbatean histories in ways that are unique to literature and cultural politics in Turkey and in world literature. The connective literary and historical enterprise of both novels, which link various ethnic, religious, and national narratives within and without Turkey, helps us to consider also how converso stories have traveled in the past and present.

Shafak and Ternar's texts reveal key aspects of contemporary Turkish discourses about the larger Jewish histories in Ottoman lands and Iberia in the aftermath of the expulsions and Ottoman refuge. The authors help destabilize contemporary categories of "Jew" and "Muslim" by foregrounding ambiguous conversions, hidden syncretisms, and secret sympathies that overturn identity norms in their representations of Jewish and Muslim conversos (Moriscos, that is, Muslim converts to Christianity), "Jewish Christians," and "Jewish Muslims." In addition to challenging ethnoreligious boundaries, the texts have a normative force, often double-edged, in shaping our perceptions, especially of Jewish-Muslim crossings. These fictional texts remedy to a certain extent the dearth of knowledge about Judeoconverso-Morisco and converso-Sabbatean-Morisco overlaps and interactions.

Historian Natalia Muchnik has found it

> curious that relations among judeoconversos, Marranos and Moriscos within Spain have been so little studied. There are several barriers to such analysis: *a lack of non-inquisitorial sources (and even those from the Inquisition are scarce)*; a discourse contaminated by stigmas that reduce both conversos and Moriscos to stereotypes; the attribution of one group's traits to the other, etc. It is reasonable to suppose that the groups maintained mutual relations, just as each did with Old Christians. (Muchnik 2014, 236; emphasis added).

Shafak and Ternar, whose texts also evince knowledge of the relevant historiographic scholarship, imaginatively redress the gaps in knowledge about such plausible but nondocumented convergences among converts from Islam and Judaism. The construction of the conversions and reconversions of Muslims and Jews under the sign of two empires helps us also to reflect on "past conditional temporality" (Lowe 2016) and on what is missing from the archives and why. Further, Shafak and Ternar transform these multiplicities into not only historical overlaps and genealogical links but also solidarities between Jews, Muslims, and those in-between or nonconforming to these categories. At the same time, the texts reveal their cultural moment's investment in the multiculturalist interpretation of the past, especially but not only in Turkey. They impart a version of the popular historical consciousness in Turkey regarding the Ottoman Empire's redemptive "cosmopolitan" values.

Shafak and Ternar engage with the conjuncture of Spanish-Jewish-Ottoman history and contemporary discourses about this past and its remains, which have been largely unexplored in fiction until recently. In doing so, they enable us to evaluate new approaches to the place of Jewish Iberians in the Muslim world and in the contemporary imagination. The works belong to a particular moment in the 1990s and 2000s, when revisiting ideas and practices of coexistence and repression in Ottoman, Republican Turkish, and European history converged in Turkish writing with the global memory boom, the world novel's new forms and themes, and newer Turkish conceptions of multiculturalism and cosmopolitanism. The texts expose not the facticity but the "historical consciousness" (Stewart 2016) and historical imagination (Funkenstein 1989) of the last decades of the twentieth century, as revealed by the debates around these concepts. They combine the known, the speculated, and the fantastic in multisited narratives about entangled empires, religions, and cultures, past and present.

Shafak, Ternar, Conversos, Sabbateans, Muslims, and Jews

Elif Shafak, a household name in Turkey and a literary and popular phenomenon, is also one of the few contemporary Turkish authors on the world scene. Impressively prolific, she began publishing novels in the 1990s, when she was in her 20s. To date, Shafak has more than a dozen books in print, with several of them bestsellers. Their subjects range from the politically inflammatory topic of Armenian and Turkish identities and history in *The Bastard of Istanbul*, to the story of the mystics Rumi and Shams in *Forty Rules of Love*, to an essay about postpartum depression (*Black Milk*).

Shafak's presence in world literature is largely thanks to *The Bastard of Istanbul* (2006), which received both terrific acclaim and terrible condemnation. Originally written in English, *The Bastard of Istanbul* was the reason that Shafak was taken to court for violating the infamous Article 301 of the Turkish penal code, which makes it a crime to "insult Turkishness." Although the charges were ultimately dropped, thanks to local efforts, the case contributed significantly to Shafak's status as a Turkish literary celebrity, second only to Nobel prize winner Orhan Pamuk, who was also accused under the same code and, like Shafak, acquitted.

Shafak's biography is well known, perhaps more than her works. Much discussed and criticized are her childhood spent in Europe as the daughter of a single mother, who was a career diplomat; her multilingual cosmopolitanism; her extremely disapproved choice to write novels in English and to then translate or rewrite them in Turkish; her Ottoman-laden Turkish, which features an antiquated vocabulary long out of circulation; the spelling of her name on these books as the transliterated Shafak rather than Şafak for easier pronunciation and recognition in the English-speaking world; her frequent media presence and self-promotion; her somewhat dramatic court case in the last weeks of her first pregnancy; her husband's political affiliations; accusations of proximity to the political regime, of which she later became openly critical; writing and speaking from London in the 2010s; and her coming out as bisexual.

Along with her changing persona, Shafak's wide-ranging oeuvre crosses literary and popular genres and has a significant place in the literature of Turkey, whatever one thinks of her literary prowess or political vision. In this chapter I examine *Şehrin Aynaları* (Mirrors of the City), which has received less attention than her other work. Published in 1999, the novel concerns seventeenth-century Spanish conversos and their many Muslim and Christian friends and foes. Several of Shafak's works have key Jewish characters, including the Jewish American Ella Rubinstein in the bestselling *Forty Rules of Love* and Turkish and other Jewish characters in her early novels *Araf* (The Saint of Incipient Insanities, 2004) and *Bit Palas* (Flea Palace, 2002). Shafak's inclusion of minor and major Jewish characters is not a simple philo-Semitism but emerges from her own brand of cosmopolitanism, which has a place in both Turkish and Euro-American multicultural globalizing fiction, where previously stereotyped or neglected ethnic and minoritized subjects are featured prominently, often to foster an obscured pluralism in the context of its reputed passing. Hence all kinds of minority subjects have a place in Shafak's fiction, including most significantly in *The Bastard of Istanbul*, which not only is about Armenians but also reveals the secret Armenian origins of Muslim Turks. Along with the neo-Ottomanist (see later discussion) and multiculturalist appetite for minority narratives in Turkey and worldwide in the 1990s and 2000s, which was critiqued by some as the "global commodification of cultural difference" (Huggan 2002), Shafak's self-presentation as cosmopolitan helped pave the way for the author's commercial and popular success at home and abroad.

Mirrors of the City is one of her few works published in Turkish but not in English. Shafak spent a considerable time of her youth in Spain, one of the several countries in which her mother worked as a diplomat, which is one likely source of inspiration for the novel's subject of Spanish Jewish history. Shafak explains in an interview that the references to mysticism that pervade her writing are owed to her years in Spain, where she learned about Jewish mysticism before Muslim mysticism and began reading mystics of the two traditions (Shafak 2004), with the medieval Andalusian Muslim scholar Ibn Arabi becoming an important influence. Shafak's novel appeared as interest in historical novels in Turkey and in 1492 in the Atlantic world were at their zenith and just a year before Solmaz Kâmuran's epic and very different novel about Jews and conversos, also discussed briefly in this chapter, was published.

Questions of identity rather than historical verisimilitude are at the heart of *Mirrors of the City*, as with other contemporary literary historical novels. In the better-known and well-regarded historical fictions by Orhan Pamuk these issues are frequently presented allegorically in terms of the East-West dichotomy and the ambiguous positioning of the Ottoman or the Turk within it, but in Shafak's novel it is the discontents of internally conflicted Judeoconverso and Morisco identities that become more universalized. The novel is also informed variously by the specific histories of Muslim and Jewish converts in Spain, Sabbatean messianism, Sufi ideas, and Jewish folklore and is replete with historical figures ranging from the painter Diego Velázquez to Philip II to the Ottoman Queen Mother Kösem Sultan. Moreover, Muslim and Sephardi fates are often intertwined, and the characters are presented as fellow victims and resisters to the hegemonic power of the church and the state.

Linking imperial, religious, and ethnic histories across the Mediterranean from Madrid to Venice to Istanbul, *Mirrors of the City* also partakes in forms of the world novel both formally and thematically. Like other fictions of entanglement and convergence, this work, like Shafak's oeuvre as a whole, connects multiple historical and cultural worlds and registers. Supernatural events and characters, such as speaking body parts, djinns, and spirits, some of which are derived from sacred texts, mingle with and accentuate the known histories of Jewish and, to a certain extent, Muslim conversos. The novel simultaneously represents relevant historical events and undermines factual approaches through the supernatural and the recourse to deliberate anachronisms. Like other historically inflected works that I have discussed, *Mirrors of the City* does not simply *reflect* our world's human and ideological routes and crisscrossings but attempts to *make* a cosmopolitan world *through* narrative (Cheah 2014). The convergences staged by Shafak, particularly the Judeo-Muslim one, convey postexpulsion solidarities and cultural overlaps.

Such entanglements take place against the novel's thematization of the extreme boundary creation, secrecy, and expulsion under repressive regimes such as the Spanish Empire and the Inquisition. The chapters alternate between the story of self-hating Alonso Perez de Hereira of Avila, an Inquisitor, and the crypto-Jewish Pereira family of Madrid, whose main character is the wayward Miguel, the young man in love with Isabel, the wife of his more respectable brother Antonio the physician. Eventually, the Pereiras are denounced as Judaizers by a woman who covets Isabel's son, conceived most likely with Miguel. The family falls apart and is dispersed. Isabel is jailed; after her release, she, like Miguel, ends up in Istanbul, the eponymous city of mirrors, while Antonio stays in Venice, where he has fled. All return to Judaism outside Iberia and take on new biblical names.

The narrative alternates among several locations (Spain, Venice, Istanbul) and sets of characters. In the Ottoman capital, Miguel, who becomes Isak there, pursues mysticism and messianism. As for Isabel, thanks to the supernatural gifts she acquired while still in Spain from a Morisco woman of Plasencia del Monte, she becomes associated with Kösem Sultan, the formidable seventeenth-century ruler in the "Sultanate of Women," who reigned alongside or acted as regents for their husbands and sons. Although the de Herrera and Pereira families are separated as prey and predator, they are equally plagued by secrets. Alonso is profoundly ashamed of his discovery of Jewish ancestors and unclean blood and of his personal shortcomings, whereas the Pereiras' secrets include continuous Jewish identification and blurred bloodlines because of in-marriage and adultery. Miguel and Alonso's identity dilemmas draw on gothic and supernatural sequences.

Anyone familiar with the fascinating story of Abraham (born Miguel) Cardoso and his brother Isaac (born Fernando), seventeenth-century conversos who left Spain for the safer lands of the Mediterranean and who wrote influentially on Jewish and Sabbatean subjects, will recognize them in Shafak's novel, despite the many factual alterations. The brothers' trajectories are recorded and analyzed in the classic study of Isaac/Fernando by Yosef Yerushalmi (1981), which Shafak most likely has read, and in Gerschom Scholem's early article on Abraham/Miguel that was the building block of his major study of Sabbateanism (Dweck 2016, xxxiv).

The real-life Abraham/Miguel Cardoso, who lived in Madrid with his brother before leaving for Italy, choosing the Judaism of his ancestors and moving on to various other cities such as Tripoli and Cairo, is, in the words of Matt Goldish, "the most important theologian of Sabbateanism," an "astounding spiritual personality," and "one of the most interesting figures with formation in both Catholic and Jewish thought and Spanish culture" (Goldish 2004, 97). Abraham Cardoso went along with Sabbatai Sevi's conversion to Islam and belief in "redemption through sin." In addition to many common basic facts of birth, displacements, and professions shared by Shafak's Pereira brothers and the real-life Cardosos, Shafak attributes to her invented Pereiras the visionary, sexual, and ecstatic qualities that scholars have deduced from Abraham/Miguel Cardoso's messianic writings. The qualities of rationality and tranquility known about Isaac/Fernando Cardoso, the Catholic court physician in Madrid turned normative rabbinic scholar in Venice and Verona, are also present, though Shafak seems to have used part of the Cardoso brothers' names in reverse birth order in the novel and changed other aspects of their biographies.

It is not my intention to trace what Shafak kept and changed about the history of these significant lives. As in many historical novels, the known and the invented coexist. It is extremely unusual for a Turkish fiction writer of any ethnoreligious background to be aware of converso or Jewish thought and to engage such figures at the crossroads of Christian, Jewish, and Muslim histories. But one can see why fictionalizing the Cardosos in particular would be well suited to Shafak's background in Spain, her wide-ranging work's investment in multiplicity and its discontents, the brothers' own wanderings, writings, and penchant for mystical dissidence, and, of course, their protean and conflicted belongings. These features also dovetail with global cultural cosmopolitanism and cultural neo-Ottomanism, whose overlapping literary features Shafak adopted during the late 1990s and early 2000s.

Relatedly, *Mirrors of the City* also stages but questions the idea of the "cosmopolitan converso" of the seventeenth century as a paradigm of adaptability, presenting instead deviance, *delirio* (Hernández 2002), and little-explored solidarities, especially Jewish-Muslim relationships. The latter are markers of shared victimhood and of affinities in Spain and the Ottoman Empire, thereby confirming but also going beyond an affirmation of Ottoman tolerance of Jews and other minorities. The novel's Muslim-Jewish alliance, which has little place in contemporary discourse, dates to inquisitorial Spain and continues in Istanbul, a version of the abiding cooperation that spread terror and revulsion as a conspiracy in the old Christian Europe.

Publishing their novels in the same year in two different cities, Montreal and Istanbul, both Shafak and Ternar, who left Turkey as a young woman and spent many years in Canada and the United States, chose to stage the conversos' journey toward and presence in the lands of the Ottomans. They both thereby link the Spanish and Ottoman Empires through their Jewish and Sabbatean elements, a side theme for Shafak's book and a key one for Ternar's. Like *Mirrors of the City*, Ternar's English-language *Rembrandt's Model* links Ottoman, Spanish, Sephardi, and Venetian histories in the sixteenth and seventeenth centuries through acts of conversion and secrecy, but it also includes the well-known Dutch aspect.

Rembrandt's Model, bookended with chapters about contemporary times, tells the story of a seventeenth-century converso returning to Judaism. Like *Mirrors of the City*, the novel, which draws on the supernatural and the mystical, but with Sabbateans at its center, appeared at the time of the widespread targeting of the *dönme* in popular media in Turkey, as we will see later. Few literary works are available on the *dönme*, despite an abundant sphere of conspiracy fiction in Turkey that demonizes the *dönme* and Jews, among others, though a couple of life stories made their mark, such as the "coming out" title *Evet, Ben Selanikliyim* (Yes, I Am a Salonican) by Ilgaz Zorlu (2000). Ternar wrote *Rembrandt's Model* in a period when Sabbateans' alleged names were being published in lists to publicly identify and presumably undermine their passing as ordinary Sunnis. In the novel Ternar avoids fetishizing one of the main targets in the scapegoating: secrecy, which justifies the group's vilification (Nefes 2014, 155–56) for its presumed propensity for treachery. Instead, she emphasizes the historical, intellectual, and artistic ties, real and imagined, between Sabbateans and conversos. Ternar also refrains from reproducing the familiar typologizing and fixing of Sabbatean identity. What emerges is the space of the imagination and utopian desire that Sabbateanism allowed in the past and its mysterious effects in the present. It is not Sabbatai Sevi's persona and ideas but the entangled histories of his followers and descendants that stand out in Ternar's and my reading of the work in terms of its import to the returns of conversos to contemporary literature.

In the first chapter of *Rembrandt's Model*, told in the third person, we are introduced to Sara, who is a tourist in Istanbul. She meets a mysterious man at a Jewish cemetery that she is visiting on her sightseeing itinerary. In a dreamlike sequence before this encounter, Sara absorbs supernaturally the story of the wife of Sabbatai Sevi by lying on her tomb. The story is fantastical and involves a woman who is transported from the Balkans by gales to meet the messiah, wed him, and become the Queen of Jews. On the way, the woman stops in the iconic converso and Sephardi city of Livorno before she flies to Istanbul. At this point, Sara meets a man named Ali at the cemetery. Ali takes her to an Istanbul island in the inner sea of Marmara, where his house is "the last outpost" on a remote hill. A book she finds in his uncommon library leads the narrative to backtrack in time to tell the stories around the volume's ownership, which involves converso returnees and Sabbateans in seventeenth-century Amsterdam, a former converso who becomes the title's model, and Muslims and Sabbateans in Istanbul. The novel then returns to the contemporary period and Sara's experiences in Montreal.

Weaving together periods and locations, Ternar's novel partakes of the multisited and multitemporal global novel's approach to the afterlives of Iberian conversions. In its blending of gothic, mystical, and supernatural themes that it shares with Shafak, it also partakes of Turkish literature's particular convergence with the internationalized genre of historical fiction through Ottomanism, Sufi themes, and, to a certain extent, minoritized groups that came to the fore in the discussions of multiculturalism and cosmopolitanism in the last decades of the twentieth century.

Post-1980s Multiculturalism

One of the outcomes of the neoliberal overhaul of Turkey that started in the 1980s was a reassertion of Ottoman cosmopolitanism. This was concomitant with the country's opening to foreign investment and the emergence of socially liberal discourses about ethnicity and identity, which ironically occurred simultaneously with the large-scale domestic conflict with Kurdish populations in the country's eastern regions. Other ethnic and religious communities, already diminished or disappeared along the course of the twentieth century, came to the fore in liberal, literary, and cultural discourses, resulting in more media, scholarly, and literary production about non-Muslim "minorities" than ever. With the establishment of the Turkish republic and the Lausanne Treaty of 1923, Christians and Jews, who had been legally equal citizens of the Ottoman Empire since the mid-nineteenth century, became official minorities, a status that protected their rights but distinguished them from Muslims, who, whatever their (many) ethnic, religious, and linguistic provenances and practices, were bestowed undifferentiated Turkish identity.

In much, though not all, of twentieth-century literature, nationalism relegates Greek, Armenian, and Jewish communities to marginal status. The members of these communities are represented largely as minor and minority characters, primarily to reflect the diversity of urban and/or cosmopolitan settings (R. Bali 1999, 2006; Gürsel 1993; Millas 2005), or they are used to populate less savory literary contexts (R. Bali 2006). After the 1980s, the uncovering of some suppressed elements of Turkish republican history allowed for previously disregarded narratives of minorities to emerge in fictional forms and in nonfiction and scholarly works. Ubiquitous liberal discourses feature mourning over the disappearance of non-Muslims, who became viewed as the creators and backbone of a lost cosmopolitan Istanbul or Izmir.

The nostalgia for these multilingual communities is also an urban elite response to the undesired Anatolianization and lumpenization of Istanbul and Izmir as a result of rural-to-urban migrations. Despite the confirmed presence of Armenians and Jews, numbering 100,000 and 15,000–20,000, respectively, these communities and the truly diminished Greeks are part of the "mourning for what one has destroyed" (Rosaldo 1989, 107). The yearning for a lost Ottoman cosmopolitanism and Istanbul as a majority-minority city led to enduring perceptions of multilingual, multifaith communities as being in decay, indeed as remnants. The words of an elderly Greek man I chatted with in the late 1980s in the main bookshop of the largest of the Princess Islands in the Marmara Sea were telling: "We are museum pieces here," he said with a smile. "Everyone wants to interview me, only because I am still here and can be placed in a display window."

The mourning of the disappearance of others and the discursive production of communities as mere remains can serve contradictory purposes: obscuring *or* making visible the causes of diminishment; marking actual continuity and presence *or* ignoring it. Both processes took place throughout the 1990s and early 2000s, which saw, along with the widespread narrative of vanishing, returns to key periods and events through films, fiction, historical studies, and so on. The works that gathered particular attention in the 1980s concerned past injustices toward non-Muslim minorities during World War II, including, for example, the devastating discriminatory and arbitrary taxation imposed on Jews, Armenians, Greeks, and the *dönme*. Yılmaz Karakoyunlu's *Salkım Hanım'ın Taneleri* (Salkım Hanım's Necklace; 1990), a novel about the effects of the tax on Jews and others, had a wide impact, though its film version became controversial for vacating the Jewish content of the award-winning fictional work. Despite the many flaws of the novel and the film, Karakoyunlu's fictional narrative was instrumental in drawing popular attention to this issue and was followed by works by Jewish and other authors—for example, Moris Farhi's *Young Turk* (2004), published first in English in the United Kingdom; Stella Acıman's less well-known but equally important 2006 novel *Bir Masaldı Geçen Yıllar* (The Past Was a Fairy Tale); and Zülfü Livaneli's well-received *Serenad* (Serenade) of 2011. These works helped the fiction-reading public have a better sense of the discriminatory policies of the wartime Turkish regime and its policies toward the fate of European Jewry (such as in the *Struma* boat tragedy of 1941).

Although their readership is limited, memoirs by Turkish Jews in Turkey and in diasporas as well as historical novels have also proliferated. The years since 2000 have seen, among other developments, the opening of an active Turkish Jewish cultural center, international conferences on Jewish Turkish issues, and an annual community celebration of European Jewish culture. Beginning with the outset of the neoliberal era and before the diplomatic hostilities between Israel and Turkey, which began after Israel's attacks on Gaza in 2008 and 2012 and the 2010 *Mavi Marmara* event, official and other openings toward Jews and other minorities, including Muslim ones,[1] and their suppressed histories gained some visibility. Fictional and nonfictional books, films, and other media disseminated narratives of both coexistence and mutuality and minoritization and oppressive practices. The stories of Jews became more public than before (albeit less than those of Armenians, with their more urgent cause in relation to the Turkish state), despite the simultaneous growth of religious and nationalistic hostility against the critical narratives of and about these groups.

It is in this general context, briefly outlined here, of the emergent cognizance of minoritized histories that fictional historical works about Iberians, and specifically conversos and the *dönme*, appeared in the 1990s. These cultural productions also coincided with the 1992 quincentennial commemorations of Sephardi Jews' arrival in Ottoman lands en masse and the transnational turn toward history and collective memory.

As I have mentioned, Shafak's and Ternar's works are also part of the boom in historical fiction that emerged in the 1980s internationally as well as in Turkey. Nobel prize winner Orhan Pamuk, through his works *White Castle* and *My Name Is Red*, two among a plethora of works in Turkish, made the greatest impact on global readership with his decentered, metahistorical approach. Rather than a linear re-presentation of history, Pamuk emphasizes existential quests, formulated also in terms of an East-West dichotomy and Ottoman and Turkish identity questions, which he positions as the central preoccupation of the historical novel.

Pamuk is far from being the only author who has written about Ottoman and Turkish pasts through such literary strategies and themes that underline issues of identity. The less-known fictions that are the focus of this chapter also partake in the global and Turkish approach to fictionalizing the past through polyphonic and metafictional means with questions about individual and collective identities at their center. Central to these works is conversion, which is important also in Pamuk's work (Göknar 2013). Stories about Jewish conversions in particular allow reflection on both the flexibility and repressions of identity in particular times and places. The existential, linguistic, and cultural multiplicities that conversions produce, including those under duress, are linked to the concerns around cosmopolitanism and the remains and survivals that have been prominent in the past few decades.

Turkish- and Ottoman-related fictions allow us to think about the construction of the converso past. The historical novel is a reparative form, in particular, one that seeks to redeem the erasures of minorities and rehabilitate the Ottoman era, much of whose late legacy was denigrated in the modern Kemalist republic. Returns to ancient identities as reparation for the past persecutions of those identities have been the subject of previous chapters. The fictional return to the Iberian Jewish-Ottoman past in particular functions also as a form of recuperation of Jewish-Muslim histories and identities for the present, a feature we find also in other contemporary fiction, including French, Arabic, English, and Spanish writing (Kandiyoti 2017).

The Jew and "The Terrible Turk"

The novels I examine, like many others presenting a cosmopolitan coexistence of the Jew and the Muslim, counter the traditional European Christian conception of the alliance and resemblance between "the Muslim" and "the Jew" and the more recent invention of Jews and Arabs or Muslims as enemies. Since the relatively recent advent of the "Judeo-Christian" and geopolitics established in the twentieth century around Israel and Jewish identity as Western, it is hard for most people to fathom that not so long ago Jews and Muslims were perceived as twin enemies of the Christian world. It was not only the Jews' welcoming of the Muslim invasions of Iberia in the eighth century but also subsequent Judeo-Muslim cultural and political developments in Spain and the larger orbit of Europe that positioned Jews and Muslims as fellow Orientals, allies, and collaborators (against Christians) long before what Gil Anidjar (2008) explains as the nineteenth-century invention of "the Semite." These perceptions were common even during the Crusades, when Jewish and Muslim beliefs and communities were confused with one another, with this misunderstanding even reflected in literary works of much later periods, for example, in the fifteenth-century *Croxton Play of the Sacrament*, in which a Jew worships "Mahomet" (Vitkus 2003, 181).

The bond between "the Turk" and "the Jew" became particularly prominent in European popular and literary discourses when the Ottomans, referred to by Martin Luther as the flesh and body of the anti-Christ, began to pose a serious challenge to the Christian empires. Ottoman military successes and ambitions cemented the perception of Jewish-Muslim equivalency (including in their Orientalism), sympathy, and conspiracy. The idea of the Jew as an enabler of the "terrible Turk" was enshrined in the narrative of acts of conspiracy, such as the Jew who reputedly handed the keys of Buda to the invading Sultan Süleyman in 1526.

The well-known rivalry of the Spanish and Ottoman Empires in the sixteenth and seventeenth centuries, as they, along with other European empires, including most importantly the Venetian, fought for supremacy in the Mediterranean, left crucial traces in European literature. The most notorious example is Miguel de Cervantes, who is known to have lost a hand in battle and earned the title El Manco de Lepanto (the cripple of Lepanto). In Christopher Marlowe's representation of the rivalry between Spain and the Ottomans in *The Jew of Malta* (1592), the Jewish character Barabas is reputedly inspired by the grand figure of Joseph Nasi, a former Portuguese converso banker of tremendous influence among the sixteenth-century Ottomans (as we will see later). Barabas is a heinous figure who betrays everyone but is allied with the Turks for the common purpose of removing Christians from power. Centuries later, Benjamin Disraeli overturned the shared imagery as villainous, which led to the accusation by his enemies that "as a Jew he is a kinsman of the Turk" (B. Lewis 1993, 138) and "an enemy of the Christian" (Ragussis 1995, 208).

Indeed, Disraeli was a Turcophile who in his youth had contemplated joining the Ottoman army. In a book chapter titled "Pro-Islamic Jews," Bernard Lewis explains that Disraeli's "pro-Turkish sentiments were connected with his vestigial Jewishness and are typical of a good deal of Jewish opinion at the time. [Member of Parliament T. P.] O'Connor, despite his malicious exaggerations, was not wrong in speaking of Jews in the nineteenth century as a pro-Turkish and, more generally a pro-Muslim, element" (B. Lewis 1993, 141). In the intellectual sphere, as Lewis and others have shown, Jewish scholars developed Islamic studies in Europe (B. Lewis 1993).

The streams of Iberian Jewish refugees into the Ottoman Empire, the most significant being after the 1492 expulsion but with influxes of Spanish and Portuguese Jews throughout the sixteenth and seventeenth centuries, further solidified the Jewish-Muslim alliance but also forged links between the Muslim and Christian empires. Spanish Jews often served Muslims as allies or bridges in their encounters with Christians, connecting the Spanish and Ottoman Empires in multiple ways, direct and indirect. The indirect ways included the cultural productions of the Iberian exiles in the Ottoman realms, such as the voluminous rabbinic literature of especially the sixteenth and seventeenth centuries. The Sephardi legacy from an Islamo-Christian Spain that articulated with the Ottoman era survives in the Spanish language, Jewish cooking, literature, and music of today's Turkey and in its Sephardi diaspora spaces in the world.

The Jewish-Turkish connection, then, was not forged only in the anti-Muslim and anti-Jewish imagination of Christian Europe. The Jewish community's gratitude toward the Ottomans and the relatively great safety they offered was sincere. This thankfulness was made evident early on, even before the expulsion, in the famous 1430 letter by the rabbi Ishak Sarfati. The rabbi exhorted the European Jews to immigrate to the Ottoman Empire, where "every man may dwell at peace under his own vine and fig-tree," and to leave behind their "accursed lands" in Swabia, the Rhineland, and Hungary (Baron 1952, 21). In the early days of the Turkish republic, the Bodrum-born Jewish scholar and Turkish nationalist Avram Galante (1932) emphasized ancient links between Turks and Jews, including through sources from the Torah (continuing a medieval tradition of viewing Noah's great-grandson Togarmah, the Anatolian, as a Turk) to the Talmud (which includes, Galante claimed, three Turkish words). Galante, a member of the Committee on Union and Progress and a member of the Turkish parliament, was not alone in the first decade of the twentieth century in forging links between a racial Turkism and Judaism in his fervent Turkish nationalism.

Even without the trappings of Ottomanism or Turkism, the discourse of loyalty has continued for centuries within and outside the official Jewish community, though other community voices and historical studies have registered their dissent and critique, especially since 2000 with the rise of scapegoating and racism. In a complex and constantly changing conjuncture, fiction underlines what is absent from official configurations of the past by featuring what is covert or maligned, such as *dönme* or Sabbatean culture and converso history. Further, the representation of motile subjectivities under particular pressures, such as those of converts' lives, serves to question both minoritized and majoritized identity categories. At the same time, the historical setting of the novels studied in this chapter reproduces to a certain extent the backward look for models that characterized cultural discourses at the time of their writing.

Sephardis and Conversos in Contemporary Turkish Cultural Imagination

Turkish literature returned to the historical Sephardi and converso in the 1990s in complex ways, both despite and, ironically, because of the discourses of disappearance about Jews and other minorities and the proliferation of historical discourses and fiction. The mainly Sephardi Jewish community's culturally rich and long-standing history often serves as an official alibi of Ottoman and Turkish tolerance, with the central narrative of rescue in 1492 supplemented by the refuge accorded to European Jewish academics during World War II. For these and other reasons, 1492 and Spanish and Ottoman histories resonate in the Turkish republic's state memory discourses and rituals and in fiction from the 1990s, though the narrative of refuge and gratitude is centuries old. The relative autonomy and security of many minority groups until the late nineteenth and early twentieth centuries in the empire, where Ottoman identity was loosely defined and communities could self-govern to a large extent, has served as the basis for nostalgia.

In Turkey, neo-Ottomanism appeared in part as a critique of the long-dominant monological nation-statist project of modernization known as Kemalism, which sought to assimilate the variegated Ottoman population into a secular republican identity. Kemalism claimed to be inclusive but was ethnoreligiously limited to the Turkish and the Sunni. Under Kemalism, the Ottoman past, other than its glorious early modern period, was jettisoned as a resource and model in favor of a Westernizing, universalizing, modernizing ideology. From the beginning of the republic in 1923 until the late 1980s, there was little sustained, large-scale political and cultural challenge to this model outside of 1950s conservative party ideologies and the leftist movements that were crushed in the 1970s and 1980s. The onset of economic neoliberalism in the late 1980s and the subsequent dismantlings by the ruling Islamist party of the secularist, militarized infrastructures saw the rise of multiculturalist and tolerance discourses in Turkey (Mills 2011), which coincided with their global dissemination but with a distinct model located in the Ottoman past. After decades of what some refer to as the "assassination of collective memory" (e.g., Onar 2009, 235) by Kemalism, the empire was restored to national consciousness as a fount of pride in a magnificent collective heritage. Ottoman lands were also positioned as an *avant la lettre* space of coexistence surpassing contemporary Euro-American multiculturalism (236).

Neo-Ottomanism in Turkish and foreign media is invoked largely to describe the geopolitical aims of Islamist Turkish foreign policy to return to leadership in the region. But the term is also used with reference to cultural productions that foster awe before Ottoman accomplishments, which includes *convivencia*. Neo-Ottomanism, contrary to the earlier Ottomanism, dovetails with contemporary multiculturalism and cosmopolitanism, both the global version and the specifically Turkish version (see Göknar 2006, 2013). As such, it emphasizes not geopolitics but the culturally avant-garde status of Ottoman social worlds, characterized by coexistence and tolerance.

Critical scholars characterize this description of Ottoman cosmopolitanism and multiculturalism, mourned by secular elites, as an inaccurate and anachronistic projection of contemporary values and interests onto the past (e.g., Eldem 2013; Iğsız 2015). This projection presents "elite visions of history that paradoxically refer to minorities even while they obscure minority perspectives of history" (Mills 2011, 190). At the state level, Aslı Iğsız explains that "neo-Ottomanism" is "a discourse on the past intended to legitimize contemporary neoliberal and cultural policies by drawing on anachronistic reinterpretations and the glorification of the Ottoman past in Turkey" (Iğsız 2015, 327; Iğsız 2018). Scholars acknowledge the existence of tolerance, but some argue that it was an Ottoman state practice rather than a value, "a means of rule, of extending, consolidating, and enforcing state power" (Barkey 2008, 10). In other discourses, Ottoman tolerance is presented frequently as particular to Islam, reaching back to the Medina Contract. In situating the novels within this context, my intent is less to answer the question of whether tolerance, cosmopolitanism's sine qua non, existed in a true sense as a system of circulation and exchange among various groups (Eldem 2013), and more to investigate how the contemporary imagination, specifically the fictional one, has reconfigured it.

Even in this brief overview, we can see immediately that neo-Ottomanism has been practiced by varying actors from different positions in the ideological spectrum (Onar 2009; Çolak 2006). Although neo-Ottomanism was and continues to be presented as a countermemory to remedy Kemalist erasures, it has become hegemonic. Still, at least since the 1990s, cultural workers, authors, and artists are recuperating history to glean its most fruitful aspects that are relevant to contemporary life, and they are deploying the Ottoman-Western and Ottoman-Republican tension to ask crucial questions about the state, religion, Turkish identity, Westernization, and collective memory.

Historical fiction, both literary and popular, is only one kind of cultural production among many to uncover, question, or glorify this history that was previously available only in controlled and limited versions. Throughout the 1990s and at the beginning of the twenty-first century, artists and authors were endeavoring in various media to reverse the cultural losses and willful erasures that took place in the process of establishing a republic and effecting a clean break with the imperial past. Those years saw the burgeoning of fiction featuring historical themes, settings, and metahistorical reflection; the inclusion of Ottoman literary genres and art forms in Turkish prose; the return to Ottoman vocabulary, borrowed from Arabic and Persian, which had been purged in the New Turkish of the republic (see also Göknar 2006, 38); and Sufi themes and ideas as mediating between the dichotomy of Kemalism and official Sunnism and providing an outlet for explorations of identity in fiction (Tüfekçioğlu 2011; Göknar 2013). The impetus in such fiction is often less an attempt at restoration of Ottoman history than a critique of the present (Göknar 2006, 38).

But in other quarters, including in some mass culture, neo-Ottomanism often reduces the recovery of history to its glorification. One observer, referring to the 2012 blockbuster film *The Conquest, 1453* and art exhibits, called this Ottomania (Çağaptay and Çağaptay 2012). Consumerism and political agendas feed the resurgence of the past through multifarious means and often contradictory aims: on the one hand, commodifying and sanitizing history to assert religious and ethnic power; and on the other, uncovering and challenging official narratives of past events and their legacies and implications for the present. Although this Ottoman past is not as extensively commodified and disseminated as the official Spanish one, in which a medieval Spain with questionable links to the present is promoted (see Chapter 3), neo-Ottomanism's representation of tolerance as cultural heritage also built a brand and an image for Turkey when its government curried favor with the Western powers and became a more popular tourist destination than it had ever been.

Although neo-Ottomanism is instrumentalized by state interests in the obvious ways its critics point to, another basis of the ideological work it does is to overturn stereotyped East-West imagery of the historical "terrible Turk" as a rival to European powers and the civilizationally backward "Muslim" of contemporary Western discourse. As Amy Mills sums up helpfully:

> The Ottoman past, both in Turkey and in the West, has long served as the very image of intolerance in the orientalist imagination that associates the Ottoman Empire with notions of Islamic or barbarian Turkish imperial rule. . . . In contemporary re-imaginations of the Ottoman legacy, we see a response to these Western geographic binary imaginaries emanating from a sense of disappointment with recent encounters with American and European foreign policy; the historic polarized image of the Ottoman past is turned on its head, as the Ottoman past is imagined to be a past of tolerance and inclusivity. (Mills 2011, 194)

Drawing on Wendy Brown's work on tolerance, Mills explains that the appeal to tolerance as a "civilizational discourse" is a Western strategy. Certainly, Turkish cultural discourses join the global multiculturalism and cosmopolitanism discourse that began in the late 1970s and valorize historical coexistence rather than national(ist) exclusions, just as Spain's promotion of medieval *convivencia* has helped erase the Black Legend image in part through the state promotion of medieval *convivencia*. Whether from a Turkish liberal cosmopolitan approach that favors pluralities or an Islamist perspective of tolerance as endemic to Islam from its early days, neo-Ottomanism performs the multiple functions of critiquing the Kemalist republic, dismantling Western stereotypes, and promoting pride in "national" heritage.

The events of 1992 underscore the role of Sephardi Jews in the emergent neo-Ottomanist discourse of the time, which has taken different forms since. The commemorative year of 1992 was observed in Turkey mostly as a celebration of arrival and refuge rather than as a memorialization of expulsion, revealing various cultural and political dynamics and interplay between official and alternative discourses of tolerance, gratitude, refuge, and return. Quincentennial activities in Iberia and the Americas garnered worldwide attention, but less known is the complexly woven set of remembrances that took place in Turkey. These were key to the construction of Turkish and Sephardi identities.

In 1992, Spanish, Jewish, Ottoman, and Turkish histories officially crossed roads once again in the celebration of a 500-year-old Sephardi presence in Turkish lands. The Quincentennial Foundation was established in advance of the quincentenary year and was composed of Muslim and Jewish members, including former Turkish statesmen and businessmen. The 1992 events were grand, involved the highest state officials, from the prime minister on down, and required extensive discursive monitoring to eliminate a more nuanced and fully realized history, with its discontents, especially of the republican period after 1923.

The 1992 commemorations in Turkey witnessed the unsurprising but frustrating mobilization of Sephardi history for Turkish national interests, including, as with Spain, proving their worthiness for European "partnership" (though it was, in Turkey's case, ultimately futile), countering Armenian claims, and cleansing human rights records (R. Bali 2000). As Rıfat Bali has shown (2012, 280–330), community leaders and their associates in the Turkish Jewish diasporas in Israel, Europe, and North America who were involved in the Turkish-based Quincentennial Foundation ensured that all forms of remembrance of 1492 and Ottoman Sephardi history thereafter were shaped and edited to proffer the most positive image of a modern, secular, and tolerant Ottoman Empire and Turkey. The expression of gratitude for tolerance, a constant among Jewish community leadership throughout the centuries (Rosen 2002; J. P. Cohen 2014,), was key.[2] The quincentennial observations in both Spain and Turkey offered dense moments in the construction of sanitized pasts: a harmonious medieval Iberia and a hospitable, multicultural Ottoman Empire. This pattern of narrative co-optation by states is common and distorts the remarkably long, complex, and rich extent and character of *actual* coexistence and survival of Jewish communities in Ottoman and Turkish lands while European Jewry was subjected at different periods to banishment and genocide.

Converts Lost and Found

Past converts and conversion were largely invisible in the commemorative and celebratory discourses of expulsion, refuge, and continuity both in Spain and Turkey, where normative faith communities and states were dominant. Conversos do appear more frequently in the relevant Jewish discourses, albeit often in limited ways as martyrs and heroes. There are also bizarre instances when converso continuity is invoked. For example, the president of the Spanish National Quincentenary Commission spoke in Israel in 1987 about looking forward in 1992 to celebrating Columbus's arrival in the Americas, an event that coincided, he explained, with the end of "a fruitful and very rich encounter among three brilliant cultures." He claimed also that in Spain "the seeds of Jewish culture were preserved through the crypto-Jewish converts in illustrious families and through distinguished figures of letters and politics" (Yañez 1987). Needless to say, these conversos were precisely the "seeds" that were maligned, persecuted, and then largely made to disappear rather than being "preserved."

The conversos' reappearance in such whitewashing state speech invokes the old genetic and blood discourse as seeds, this time to presumably celebratory ends. Rarely in evidence are the social, political, religious, and psychic complications of the converso or crypto-Jew whose descendants continued to inhabit Iberia or the Jewish converts to Christianity who landed in the Ottoman Empire. Of course, the Sabbatean converts to Islam, and much less their intersections with New Christians, are almost never part of any official Jewish or Turkish discourses, except in negative evocations. It is the work of scholars and novelists to explore the complexity of the known and imagined possible condition of conversos.

The Empire's Returned Jews

The Ottoman Empire had a particular relationship with Jewish conversos and their descendants who had reverted to Judaism in the safety of the empire. A few conversos were instrumental in the ascendancy of the Ottomans against their main Mediterranean rivals, Venice and Spain. The history of the Ottoman Sephardi community is frequently told as a settlement taking place in 1492 after the expulsion of normative unconverted Jews, but even before that annus horribilis, conversos and not just normative Sephardis had sought refuge and prosperity with the Ottomans. In his classic *History of the Marranos*, Cecil Roth suggests that the conquest of Constantinople by the Turks gave hope to the conversos from earlier waves of forced conversion in Spain that Christian rule would soon be eclipsed (1932, 151). Converso families from Valencia and elsewhere arrived in 1464 in Valona, Albania, an Ottoman city, where they returned to Judaism. Together with the refugees of 1492 who were settled in Valona by the Ottomans to trade with Venice, they later made up a third of the population of the city by the first decades of the sixteenth century (Roth 1932, 151; Veinstein 1987).

Jewish conversos came to the Ottoman Empire from Iberia, Amsterdam, and parts of what is now Italy more than a century after the Alhambra Decree. Their reasons for this migration go beyond religious freedom and trade opportunities; expulsion and persecution in Europe played a large role. In Europe, conversos, like Jews, were perceived to be associates of "the Turks." For example, in a converso trading city like Antwerp, the Portuguese *nação* (nation) was suspected of Judaizing. The community was subjected to rumors about their marked preference for "Turks" over Old Christians, trade with Ottomans, and perceived intention to migrate to Muslim lands, which aroused ire and led to their eventual expulsion (Cooperman 1998, 300–301).

Formerly New Christian Jews held important positions in trade, finance, and diplomacy in the Ottoman Empire and for a time distinguished themselves from the earlier exiles. Most of the later arrivals with roots in Portugal and Spain settled in Izmir, Salonica, Safed, and other cities, returning to Judaism, which they practiced in their own congregations. Those referred to as *francos*, hailing mostly from Livorno and settling in port cities of the Ottoman Empire to conduct trade, had also been New Christians who joined the normative Jewish world, but they retained their distinction for an extended period in some places (especially in Tunis). Some of them became "trans-imperial subjects," to use Natalie Rothman's term (2011), shuttling between Venice and the Ottoman Empire as well as among religions, cultures, and languages.

No former Judeoconversos or other Jews ever commanded as much known influence as the legendary Dona (Beatriz de Luna) Gracia Mendes Nasi and her nephew, Joseph Nasi. After the death of her husband, New Christian Gracia herself became a banker to kings and lived in various European cities after a time in Venice. She finally settled in Istanbul, renounced her Christian identity openly, and took up Judaism. Also known as La Sinyora, Mendes Nasi lobbied Ottoman Palace officials on behalf of fellow New Christians who remained in Christian lands, providing help to new arrivals. She endeavored to establish a homeland for the persecuted in Tiberias, where she sponsored a yeshiva. La Sinyora also led a famous attempt at an Ottoman trade boycott in response to the pope's persecution of conversos in the Adriatic port city of Ancona.

Gracia Mendes Nasi has become a Sephardi icon as a power broker and defender of Jews and conversos and is the subject of contemporary fiction, including a Turkish-language play and a novel by Turkish Jewish authors Beki L. Bahar and Aaron Nommaz. Her nephew, the aforementioned former converso Joseph Nasi, continued her legacy in trade and diplomacy, negotiating with Europeans to further Ottoman interests. He became a key player in helping Selim I conquer the island of Cyprus. As a result of the victory, Nasi was declared the Duke of Naxos. Because of his prominence, scholars believe that he is the inspiration for Marlowe's Barabas in *The Jew of Malta* (Brandt 2012, 6). Nasi was not alone: Salomon ibn Yaish (Abenyaish), another former converso in the Portuguese court (as Alvaro Mendez), also earned a dukedom of Mytiline (Midilli) for his diplomacy, especially between England and the Ottomans. Because of Gracia Mendes Nasi's effort, albeit unsuccessful, to secure a haven in Tiberias for Iberian exiles, her nephew's role in this war has been presented in widely read recent anti-Semitic conspiracy writing as the hidden (and enduring) alliance between the Spanish Jews and the Ottoman leadership to fulfill proto-Zionist ambitions for a Jewish home in the Mediterranean islands in exchange for Jewish resources (Küçük 2003, 140).[3]

Formerly Christian Jews and their descendants were also among those who followed Sabbatai Sevi, the self-declared seventeenth-century messiah with a tremendous following in the Mediterranean and all over Europe. When Sevi converted to Islam under threat by the regime of Sultan Mehmet IV, some of the formerly Christianized conversos also chose Islam along with their messiah in 1666, a link that Shafak and Ternar make in their novels. It is not often discussed that Sabbateans' ancestors include not only normative Jews expelled from Spain but also Iberians who had converted to Christianity in Spain or (more frequently) Portugal, reverted to Judaism after leaving the peninsula, became Muslim after 1666, and were a part of closed communities with syncretic practices until the past few decades.

From Amsterdam to Istanbul, Portuguese returned Jews had embraced Sabbatai Sevi as the messiah. In Izmir they published messianic texts, including Menasseh ben Israel's *La esperança de Israel* (Hope of Israel) in Spanish (Barnai 1993). In discussing Sevi's conversion to Islam, Yosef Yerushalmi observes that "marranos could understand, perhaps better than other Jews," that "conversion might simply be a mask for an inner existence of a radically different order" (1981, 304). Turning from Jew to Christian, back to Jew, and then to Muslim—this made sense in the divided, bounded realms that Iberian exiles traversed and transgressed across the Christian and Ottoman Mediterranean.

Far from being vintage social and religious curiosities, the dizzying conversions and reconversions that connect Iberia to the Ottomans are the stuff of both contemporary popular and literary historical novels on the one hand and, on the other, conspiracy writing in Turkey, the popular genre that blurs the boundaries between fiction and nonfiction without self-reflexivity. Conspiracies can be attributed to any minoritized or dissident group in Turkey, whether Muslim, Christian, or Jewish; in some ways, to be a member of a minoritized group is to live with a public secret (Taussig 1999) that is easily re-presented as a conspiracy.

Sabbateans were one of most consistent targets of both conspiracy accusations and racism, especially through the 1990s and early 2000s. The syncretic and unique beliefs and rituals of the community, which was divided into three separate groups early on, and the long-standing maintenance of Judeo-Spanish (Ladino) and Jewish names and much else have been kept secret; in public, however, profession of orthodox Sunni Islam and the assumption of traditional Muslim names and identity continued through the centuries. But information circulated on some of the singular, heterodox, and metareligious (Şişman 2015, 237) beliefs and practices, endogamous marriages, and secret rituals, albeit often in distorted fashion. Sabbateans' endorsement of Western-style modernization projects from the nineteenth century on and their involvement in constitutional and then republican revolutions around the same period have been fodder for inflated and erroneous claims about the secret power of this long-suspect community of Sevi's followers and their descendants (M. D. Baer 2009; Şişman 2015). The terms by which Sabbateans are known are derogatory: *Dönme* is derived from the verb *dönmek*, "to turn," with the pejorative implication of "turncoat." Although the label is also used to refer to transgender people, in conspiratorial thought *dönme* refers mainly to Sabbateans, also called Salonicans (*Selanikli*), because most lived in Salonica until the 1923 Greece-Turkey population exchange, when, as Muslims, they were compelled to leave.

The title of a study by Turkish historian Rıfat Bali, *A Scapegoat for All Seasons* (2008), is plainly indicative of the perception of the Sabbateans. Conspiracy theories about the community emerged in several different periods in the twentieth century (Nefes 2014; Şişman 2015). In the 1990s and 2000s Sabbatean figures of the past and those of Sabbatean origin in the present were at the center of conspiracy theories in the popular nationalist media. This was also roughly when the liberal media were turning their attention to cosmopolitan minorities and their disappearance. The *dönme* have been positioned as a secret caste, a group of hidden heirs to tremendous spheres of power and influence in Turkey with a history of collaborating with foreign entities against Turkish interests. In overlapping anti-Salonican and anti-Semitic conspiracy discourses, the *dönme* and the Jews are often held equivalent because of the Sabbateans' Jewish origins, even though Jewish Orthodoxy considers Sabbateanism heretical and Sabbateans not Jewish.

Important scholarly works have appeared about Sabbatai Sevi and his followers and descendants, beginning with Gershom Scholem's monumental 2016 study that traces the roots of the movement variously to kabbalistic mysticism, Christian messianism (cf. Barnai 1993), and Muslim mystical traditions. But few studies focus on the many contemporary descendants and their fate in Turkey. This is not just because few believers are left or because many descendants have become invisible in mainstream Sunni Turkish culture, despite the racialized efforts to out them. It is also because, whatever their beliefs and lifestyles, they hide themselves, having long been targeted. Conspiracy literature and media discourse, in their widespread dissemination of rumors and quasi-fictional "histories," can drown out nonpartisan scholarship and literature. There is little fiction published in Turkey about Sabbateans,[4] though there are suggestions of its incipient moment in Shafak's novel. Ternar, writing outside Turkey, connects the world of the conversos with the Sabbateans much more explicitly.

One problem with writing about Sabbateans is that to be interested in or to defend such communities or cultures can also lead to accusations of minority (including *dönme*) identity, secrecy, and conspiracy, or worse. For example, in her short essay "Conspiracy Theories" (2005), Shafak reports that she was rumored to be a hidden Jew after the publication of *Mirrors of the City*, which only added to other speculations and accusations about her identity and allegiances.

Conversos in Turkish Literature

Although the noise about converts and hidden identities created by left- or right-wing conspiracist nationalist Turkish writing and politics has been loud, with those about Sabbateans strangely shrill and threatening, different voices, however less audible, have also contributed to the contemporary imagination about histories of Sephardis and conversos. The figure of Dona Gracia Mendes Nasi, who inspired works in other languages, including French author Catherine Clément's *La Señora* (1993) and Naomi Ragen's *The Ghost of Hannah Mendes* (1998), published in the United States, has appeared in Solmaz Kâmuran's popular *Kirâze* (2000) and in some brief scenes of the internationally popular Turkish historical melodrama serial *Muhteşem Yüzyıl* (The Magnificent Century). *Kirâze*, the best-known Turkish fiction about Ottoman Jews, chronicles the life of Esther Handali, known as Ester Kira, a daughter of Spanish exiles who became a *kira* or *kyra*, the term for an influential Jewish female supplier of luxury goods and other intermediary services to the harem who served rulers' mothers in the sixteenth century. Notwithstanding the eponymous title drawing on Ester's nickname, Kâmuran's popular novel is not just about Ester; it also treats in broad strokes a century-long history after the expulsion and sympathizes with the plight of Jewish refugees from Spain, though Ester's personality, unlike those of the many other Jewish characters, conforms to stereotypes of ruthless and conniving Jewish intermediaries.

Kirâze's short chapters, organized around historical battles, executions, and strategic meetings as well as the personal destinies of Ester's family members, take place in dozens of locations, from Medina del Campo and Rhodes to Fez, Mohàcs, London, and the Vatican, to name just a few. The power mongering and excesses of the rival Ottoman, Spanish, British, and Venetian Empires and of the Papacy, the Tudors, the Medicis, the Borgias and so on are also exposed, but the novel partakes in the contemporary wonder at the multiculturalism of sixteenth-century Istanbul, home to "a thousand and one colors and flavors," like "a lively and harmonious Byzantine mosaic" (Kâmuran 2000, 189). The novel thus participates, without ignoring the discontents of empire, in the neo-Ottomanism of its publication period by positioning Ottoman modes of *convivencia* in terms of a contemporary multiculturalism. Iconic converso figures also make appearances in *Kirâze*. For example, Gracia Mendes Nasi's plans for a homeland for Jewish refugees in Tiberias are represented in scenes in both Istanbul and Tiberias.

Another recent historical novel, Metin Arditi's French-language *Le Turquetto* (2011), complements what I see as Kâmuran's neo-Ottoman approach to the early modern period and Jews, which is characterized by an affirmative vision of the empire's multiculturalism but is sometimes depicted as stereotypes of minorities. Arditi is of Turkish Jewish background and lives in Geneva; he writes in French. In an interview with a Turkish newspaper, Arditi recounts his upbringing in Istanbul as a multilingual Jew with a Catholic nanny as a continuum of the rich multicultural heritage, adding that he sees himself as an Ottoman (S. Bali 2011). In his novel the Sephardi Ottoman protagonist, a painter, takes the reverse route: He travels from his birthplace in Ottoman lands to Christian realms to practice his art. But because he cannot reveal his religious identity in Europe, he becomes a crypto-Jew. Although he succeeds tremendously in his artistic ambition, he reveals his hand in a painting with secret Jewish content, which results in his having to seek refuge in Istanbul.

Contributing to the contemporary neo-Ottomanist perspective through Sephardi history locally is Beki L. Bahar's *Donna Grasya Nasi*, the award-winning 1993 play based on Gracia Mendes Nasi's life. The playwright is a prominent Turkish Jewish author. The dramatic piece depicts Mendes Nasi and her nephew, Joseph Nasi, as subjects with undivided loyalties to both their generous new hosts and the persecuted European Jews. The play avoids nefarious or secret plots, and Mendes Nasi is presented in quasi-feminist terms as a formidable visionary woman. Bahar, who made a significant place for herself in Turkish Jewish letters before she died in 2011, prefaces *Donna*

Grasya Nasi by explaining that hers is a contribution to the 1992 commemoration, imbued with gratitude, of the refuge and salvation of the Jews and marranos (Bahar 1993, vi).

Opening the play is Cemal Reşit Rey's symphonic poem *Fatih* (Mehmet the Conqueror), a 1953 tribute by the renowned Turkish composer for the 500th anniversary of the 1453 conquest of Constantinople, which both glorifies Mehmet and positions him as a fair warrior, unlike his depictions in European culture. The conquest is represented on Bahar's stage in the same terms as in Rey's musical piece: A post-conquest announcement by the Turks, represented by an offstage crier, guarantees freedom of religion to Muslims, Jews, and Christians. This is juxtaposed to the next bit of news, heard again from offstage, about the turning point forty years later in the same century: the Spanish Edict of Expulsion. Bahar's contrasting of the two official pronouncements theatrically accomplishes the goals of the quincentennial and reaffirms the nostalgic approach to Ottoman *convivencia*. Her well-known poem "Ezan, Çan, Hazan" (*Adhan*, Bell, *Hazan*), also composed for the quincentennial, distills this spirit of coexistence through the eponymous aural signs of the three religions present in Istanbul that rose to the ears of the 1492 refugees as sounds of freedom.

In the play the tribulations of Grasya, her sister Brianda, and the family as a whole come to an end in the Ottoman Empire, where, true to her actual biography, Mendes Nasi also tries to save other conversos by using her influence. The character, internally divided as a Christian Jew at the beginning of the play, quickly becomes a fully identified Jew, albeit without many signs of piety or devotion. Bahar contributes to the 1992 celebrations by putting a formidable converso Jewish woman character, born and raised a Christian, at the center of the quincentennial, although the celebrations overall deemphasized or ignored the background and trajectory of the returned conversos and Christianized Jews in the Ottoman Sephardi world.

More than two decades after Bahar's effort, 2016 saw the publication of the first Turkish-language novel dedicated to Gracia Mendes Nasi: Aaron Nommaz's *Kanuni'nin Yahudi Bankeri Dona Gracia* (Dona Gracia, Kanuni Suleiman's Jewish Banker). Nommaz is a Turkish businessman, engineer, and honorary consul of Portugal in Istanbul with Portuguese Jewish roots in Izmir. In *Kanuni'nin Yahudi Bankeri Dona Gracia*, Nommaz's first work of fiction, La Sinyora emerges as an Ottoman and Jewish patriot. The novels of Bahar and Nommaz, whose second work of fiction is about Joseph Nasi, vindicate conversos for the normative Jewish community by emphasizing their Jewishness rather than duality or ambiguity and by underlining their contributions to their Ottoman saviors. Their vision is in direct contrast to the conspiracy theorists' demonization of the converso Jewish hand in building the empire, corrupting the dominion by compelling the elites to adopt "Jewish agendas." These influential returned conversos of the Ottoman Empire, then, far from being forgotten historical figures, continue to appear in contemporary fictional and purportedly nonfictional conspiratorial imaginaries of the Ottoman and Jewish past, variously depicted as abject, grateful, formidable, assimilated, or conspiring subjects.

Shafak and Ternar's novels about conversos, Sabbateans, and crypto-Jews present critiques of Christian and Jewish practices of conversion and do not challenge the neo-Ottomanist discourses of tolerance. Yet the works go beyond simply advancing neo-Ottomanism or approaching converts only as martyrs. Rather, as we will see, they suggest the impossibility of fixed identities on which such affirmations of tolerance and coexistence are based. Moreover, acts of conversion and their aftermath provided writers interested in early Ottoman Sephardi history and its aftermath with alternatives to the official stories about normative Jews and their benevolent hosts. Fictionalized converso experiences allowed the presentation of a more complex picture not simply of historical events but especially of their perceptions.

Dangerous Multiplicities and Convergences

Shafak's particular choices to tell the story of Spanish and Ottoman Jews are uncommon in Turkish literature, though they are based on particular tendencies in both Turkish and world writing, including the privileging of cultural connectivities and convergences. Before we explore the way Shafak's works accord with the globalized novel thematically and structurally, let us dwell for a moment on Shafak's rehabilitative use of language in *Mirrors of the City*, which also partakes of ideas about connectivity, albeit with a specific Turkish inflection.

Earlier generations of authors in republican Turkey had abided by the state-imposed language reforms, begun in the 1920s to create a New Turkish that sought to purify the language of Arabic and Persian vocabulary, which at that time was associated with the Ottomans and denoted religious, antisecular, non-Western, and non-Turkic identification. The national language corresponding to the new national identity as Turkish (rather than Ottoman) was created by substituting such "foreign" vocabulary with newly invented words or Turkish ones excavated from ancient texts or the speech of Anatolians collected in the early days of the republic in linguistic salvage efforts. New Turkish, then, was also in part "old Turkish," found in the texts of the Selçuk or Oğuz tribes, for example, predating the formation of the Ottoman language.

Some authors, especially those born in the early years of the republic, were attached to this project. They used the newly revived vocabulary and invented some others to replace the linguistic ancien régime, the heterogeneous Ottoman with its thousands of Arabic and Persian words and expressions. New Turkish affirmed the legitimacy of the national project in some aspects but was often deployed to subversive philosophical and literary ends to overturn narrative and linguistic conventions. Although the use of New Turkish lent itself to fascinating experiments, its underlying politics of purification and monolingualism to bolster a reformulated "Turkish" identity excluded regional and ethnic varieties and all kinds of minor tongues not viewed as Turkish (belonging to a Turkish *volk*). It also marginalized and buried the many other languages of the old empire.

For the likes of Shafak, then, the revival of Ottoman language in the 1990s is a sign of heterogeneity and mixture, which authors "return" to republican Turkish language and culture. As the author herself has explained, her use of "old words and new words" and "Sufi terms" led to the description of her work as neo-Ottoman, therefore "traditionalist," but she explains this "expanding" of language as "cosmopolitan" (quoted in Furlanetto 2015, 163).

The deployment of Ottoman words to tell the story of Spanish Jews of the sixteenth and seventeenth centuries is not necessarily, then, in the name of a historical realism that replicates the period's idiom; nor is it a fanciful archaizing. Shafak, like Solmaz Kâmuran and other authors who have written on this period, foregrounds the syncretic qualities of Ottoman life and knowledge suppressed in the republican period. So it is fitting that linguistic recoveries give body to returns of neglected historical matter such as of the Ottoman conversos. The recuperation of Ottoman and Arabic vocabulary has long ceased being subversive, but at play is Shafak's interest in experimentation and liberal-cosmopolitan literary politics, which benefit from local and global literary trends and tendencies. Cannily, her anachronistic vocabulary, both "native" and foreign, both recognizable and unknown, tells the parallel story of the uncanny consciousness of conversos, conceived in Shafak's work and in other works we have discussed as repositories of a productive doubleness. Shafak's celebration of Ottoman cosmopolitanism (Furlanetto 2015) overlaps with and diverges from official neo-Ottomanisms in her representation of converso history in Spain and the Ottoman Empire and conforms to the impulses of the global novel.

The desire for a temporal and spatial convergence that Istanbul, the eponymous city of mirrors, represents is also an impulse of the contemporary world novel. The globalized novel works with the principles of "circulation, sedimentation, and linkages" (Cooppan 2013, 616) that create overlapping transnational spatialities and temporalities. Because it seeks to reflect but also *make* such a world, *Mirrors of the City* also reminds us of one of the most famous literary expressions of the desire for seeing and presenting the world as a whole: Jorge Luis Borges's "The Aleph." In the Argentine author's famous short story, the Aleph is primarily spatial, a *hic-stans*, and is the name for the point in someone's basement through which all points can be seen simultaneously.

> The Aleph was probably two or three centimeters in diameter, but universal space was contained inside it, with no diminution in size. Each thing (the glass surface of a mirror, let us say) was infinite things, because I could clearly see it from every point in the cosmos. I saw the populous sea, saw the dawn and dusk, saw the multitudes of the Americas, saw a silvery spider-web at the center of a black pyramid, saw a broken labyrinth (it was London), saw endless eyes, all very close studying themselves in me as though in a mirror, saw all the mirrors on the planet (and none of them reflecting me), saw in a rear courtyard on Calle Soler the same tiles I'd seen twenty years before in the entryway of a house in Fray Bentos, saw dusters of grapes, snow, tobacco. (Borges 1998, 283–84)

In Shafak's ideal city, places *and* times merge, drawing also on mirrors.

> Miguel'in aynalar şehri de yakını ve uzağı, görüneni ve görünmeyeni, yerleri ve gökleri gösterecekti. Şehrin aynalarında, geçmişin geleceği nasıl baştan

çıkarttığını, geleceğin nasıl tava gelip geçmişin icinde kendinden geçtiğini ve bugünün geçmişin rahminde nasıl günbegün, anbean büyüyüp şekil aldığını seyredecekti. Aynalar şehrinde, doğup büyüdüğü ve belki de bir daha asla ayak basamayacağı bu toprakları doya doya görebilecekti. Aynaların sayesinde gurbetin içindeki sılayı, sılanın içindeki kainati ve kainatin içinde de kendi suretini temaşa edebilecekti. (Shafak 1999, 157)

As he begins his journey toward Istanbul, Miguel's city of mirrors would show the near and the far, the visible and the invisible, the lands and the skies. In the mirrors of the city, he would watch how the past seduces the future, how the future gets tricked and loses itself inside the past, and how the present grows and takes shape in the womb of the past. In the city of mirrors, he would see to his heart's content these lands in which he was born and had grown up and might never step foot on again. Thanks to the mirrors, he would contemplate the home within exile, the universe within the home and his own shape in the universe.

In what follows, Miguel says that the city in which all times and places converge is a utopian one that would embrace him "without wrenching him away from his woeful past" ("onu hazin geçmişinden koparmadan"; 158). That city is Istanbul, which allows Miguel to preserve his past. The Ottoman capital is a harbor not only because Miguel can recuperate safely an identity that had to be hidden but also because it is one that offers convergent temporalities and spatialities, allowing for the places and times of memory to flow through and intermingle within it. Istanbul, then, is an ideal cosmopolitan city of convergences whose inhabitants do not have to shed prior identities—a vision befitting the neo-Ottomanism that Shafak borrows from extensively (Furlanetto 2015). But in *Mirrors of the City*, Istanbul is not necessarily a utopian space, as we will see.

In the intense compulsion toward convergences in Shafak's work and the contemporary novel we sometimes find a kind of omnivorousness. *Mirrors of the City*, like her other early works, is overstuffed with metaphysical images and dilemmas, aphorisms, and historical and mystical references, connecting events, ideas, and cultures that are separated by centuries and oceans. The concepts of convergence, unity, and the cosmic are evoked in several ways. For example, there are intermittent references to "the circle," prevalent in the thought of Ibn Arabi, which stands for divine oneness and infinity. The name Borges chose for his short story, the Aleph, is indicative of his interest in mysticism and refers to the first letter of the Hebrew and Arabic alphabets, which in the Lurianic Kabbalah tradition is also the letter that makes possible all the other letters. Not incidentally, Elif Shafak's first name, a common one in her generation in Turkey, is the Turkish for the Arabic *aleph*, which the author associates also with Borges (Shafak, n.d., 79). When asked what word she would like to add to the dictionary, Shafak chose *aleph*, because she was inspired by Borges and also because the word is relevant to Christian, Jewish, and Muslim mystical traditions (79).

Mariano Siskind argues that "The Aleph" and another well-known story by the Argentine author, "Tlön, Uqbar, Urbis Tertius," present a cosmopolitan discourse of "standing in front of the whole world," one beyond limitations and (divisive) differences (Siskind 2007, 77). I would add that the world novel often emulates a version of an Aleph-like universe even though it cannot provide the simultaneity of visuality the Aleph affords. The world novel's overlapping multiplicities in spatiality, temporality, and perspective are in part attempts to display and also forge a world-as-the-Aleph. Shafak's ideal city of mirrors, a version of the Aleph, is the counterpoint to the Iberia she depicts, where boundaries proliferate murderously and people are severed from time, space, and memory. Although Istanbul does not necessarily turn out to be ideal for her characters, it makes it possible for convergences of all kinds to take place. A world novel like Shafak's attempts to depict and foster convergence at the same time as it fragments worlds through literary devices of changing points of view, varying human and nonhuman voices, and antilinear storytelling. Its compulsion is to connect and expose destructive boundaries that impede connection and, sometimes, to offer idealized models of coexistence.

But multiplicity does not necessarily originate in connectivity and is infelicitous under the wrong conditions. This is made obvious from the outset of *Mirrors of the City*, many of whose characters struggle with personal identity dilemmas because of secret converso pasts. The novel as a whole is built on uncertainties, with its characters at the mercy of external events and their own insecure and even unhinged identities. The dangers of contradictory multiplicities are embodied by Alonso de Herrera, the Inquisition judge with converso roots who is possessed by a voice that directs him like a puppet. The Pereira brothers are distraught after their father's revelation about their secret Jewish origins. Miguel, the particularly tormented brother given to strange fits, exhibits many of the symptoms of the crypto-Jewish body (see Chapter 1). In despair, he asks, "Tanımadığım daha kaç kişi var içimde yaşayan?" ("How many more people I don't know live inside me?"; Shafak 1999, 224). Being one's own enemy plagues Miguel throughout, even after he returns to Judaism. In some ways, he is the afflicted, abject crypto-Jew, a figure we have seen in Obejas's novel and that has long existed in European and Jewish imaginaries.

The ghostly and uncanny figure of the "Wandering Jew," later related to Bram Stoker's vampire (Davison 2004), is not unrelated to the crypto-Jew, a connection that Ternar indeed makes, as we will see. But *Mirrors of the City* and much of contemporary literary work about crypto-Jews follow instead the sentimental tradition of Grace Aguilar and George Eliot (see Chapter 1), which elicits sympathy for victimized conversos. Going beyond this conventional representation, Shafak places them in supernatural milieus to highlight the internal chaos that is the consequence of the repression. But differently from earlier texts, Shafak's novel does not rest on an inside-outside dichotomy often ascribed to converts, in which the public and private identities or faiths are clearly identified and separate. Rather, here the "inside" is nebulous; the secret (of being of Jewish descent), even when revealed, is still "unknown." As with Obejas's *Days of Awe*, secrecy endures even after revelation and safe return to Judaism.

One of the most significant discussions Miguel has with Rabbi Yakup in Istanbul concerns the Torah's use of the plural form in describing the Creator. The rabbi shares the Iberian kabbalistic interpretation on this endlessly debated question, adding that perhaps God also disliked loneliness. Shafak's return to historical struggles and questions regarding plurality and coexistence is undergirded with such myriad references to multiplicities and her vision of entangled temporalities and spatialities that constitute the world.

Jewish-Muslim Intersections in Shafak

Although Spanish conversos appear in other contemporary fiction primarily in the Christian-Jewish context and binaries, in Shafak's text it is the Muslim and Iberian converso fates that are intertwined. The two groups are represented as both victims and resistant subjects. *Mirrors of the City* has many pairs of Muslim (or Morisco) and crypto-Jewish characters who become inseparable in a Christian world, mainly in inquisitorial Spain. Isabel Pereira, the conversa, was saved as a child by Yaşlı, the Muslim/Morisco victim of the Plasencia del Monte massacres who is also a seer. The most significant of the Muslim-Jewish relationships in the books, the one between Isabel and Yaşlı is construed as the link between two fellow victims of the inquisitorial world. Yaşlı ("the old one" in Turkish) earned her name when she was a child, after her hair turned gray overnight while she was hiding during the massacres against Moriscos in her birthplace of Plasencia del Monte. Shafak recreates this event with some anachronism but also with many historically faithful details of crypto-Muslims and Moriscos after they had long been Mudejars (Muslims in Christian lands).

In other pairings, the best friend of Rabbi Yakup, who helps exiled Sephardi conversos return to the religion and the community in Istanbul, is the sheikh Süleyman Sedef Efendi. The sheikh's teachings also draw Miguel-become-Isak, who eventually runs away with his daughter, presumably to follow Sabbatai Sevi. In Istanbul the main support of Andres, the son born of Miguel and Isabel's adulterous passion, is the Muslim Zişan Kadın, whose piety comforts the young man. As for Isabel, when she leaves Spain for Istanbul, she becomes close to the all-powerful Kösem Sultan, whom she helps in furthering the regent's ambition to provide an heir to her son Ibrahim by preparing an elixir she had learned to make from her protector, Yaşlı. In Istanbul Isabel continuously looks for Yaşlı, because she is aware that some of the Moriscos who had been expelled from Spain following Philip III's decree of 1609 ended up settling in the Galata neighborhood in the seventeenth century, also a historical fact.

Although the focus of *Mirrors of the City* is on the Jewish family, unlike most other novels set in this period that are primarily about the fate of people of Sephardi origins, the Judeo-Muslim world and the intermingling of Jews' and Muslims' fates is also emphasized. The characters' relationships and shared suppression and the resort to secrecy under Christianity connect them. In addition, Jewish and Muslim traditions are fused in many episodes. For example, while still in Spain, Miguel has a symbolic dream about his journey into the underworld that includes both Joseph beseeching God to forgive his cruel brothers who have thrown him in a well and the angels Harut and Marut from the Qur'an.

With regard to Jewish-Muslim pairings and rescues in the novel, the neo-Ottoman or Turkish multicultural discourse is not the only one to be taken into consideration. As a global novelist bearing all the vagaries of that term, Shafak participates in social, political, and literary currents not only in Turkey but also beyond it. Jewish-Muslim coexistence in literature is not featured in only reductive, black-and-white terms of tolerance or oppression, as it is in some texts. Ottoman and other Judeo-Muslim culture and relations as a productive nexus with a complex history also appear in widely circulating literature with a cosmopolitan impulse. Works by Salman Rushdie, Tariq Ali, Amin Maalouf, Geraldine Brooks, and Joann Sfar, to cite only a few well-known examples, are propelled by a similar inclination that not only valorizes a past but also *makes* a world that destabilizes the discourses of perennial Jewish-Muslim hostility conjured by current geopolitics (Kandiyoti 2017). The staging of Jewish-Muslim cooperation and cooperation away from or under the yoke of the Christian world also interrupts "Judeo-Christian" and civilizational discourses that pit the West against the Judeo-Muslim world. The novel's representation of Ottoman multicultural coexistence, then, is a refraction of several ideological discourses that have their sources within and outside Turkey, without conforming to a particular one but collating several, as Shafak does in much of her writing.

Does the novel of Iberian Jewish history partake in the contemporary neo-Ottomanist construction of the empire as an idealized ground of multi-culturalism? In locating the utopian city of mirrors in Istanbul, a city where one does not have to shed past times and places, and in foregrounding Judeo-Muslim solidarities, Shafak gestures in that direction. On the other hand, *Mirrors of the City* does not resolve historical or metaphysical questions, nor does it position refuge in the Ottoman Empire as a felicitous ending for the tormented converso descendants. The Pereira family is broken and scattered; the final chapter's voice is that of the young Andres, who plans to see out his days in Istanbul by staying home to guard his secrets, hiding from the bustling city that frightens him. He says that he will stay, but he will betray the blood he carries in his veins (Shafak 1999, 278) and not recuperate Judaism by joining the normative community like other conversos. Return to the faith is hardly the *summum bonum* of existence and identity that it is in, for example, Eliot's *Daniel Deronda*. As for Miguel/Isak, he ends up pursuing yet another new faith, the highly unorthodox messianism of Sevi, deemed an apostate by many Jews. The traumatic Spanish past is perduring, despite the refuge Ottomans have offered.

A story about broken lives, *Mirrors of the City* continuously stages convergences that go against a perception of history dominated by the separation of oppressions and the occlusion of their transactional aspects within larger hegemonic systems. Moreover, Shafak's joining of Jewish and Muslim history, mysticism, and messianism is another strategy used to make a world of entanglements rather than a way to only reveal occluded convergences. The eponymous mirrors play many roles here, as they do in Ottoman and mystical literature in which humans are mirrors reflecting God's divine attributes, including beauty and love. The Andalusian Sufi thinker Ibn Arabi's "Man is the polished mirror that reflects the universe" is one of many mystical references to the mirror symbol (see Sells 1994, 63–89) and perhaps the most appropriate one to Shafak's use in this context. The tortured visionary Miguel, modeled but not named after Abraham Cardoso, is on a quest for a utopian place, a city of mirrors, where the past and the present, the visible and invisible, home within exile and exile within the universe, coexist.

Our authors do not simply invest the conversos themselves with enchantment but present their worlds and their revived legacies today as beyond the real and experiential for their uncanniness, their terrors, and their miraculous survivals. In Shafak's case, like the use of Ottoman vocabulary long out of circulation, such alternatives to the aesthetics of Kemalism also complement the themes of converso-Jewish-Muslim intersections and solidarities, which have been disappeared like so much in converso history itself, and lend themselves to both "real" historical and supernatural representations.

Mirrors, Djinns, and Judeoconversos

The mystical frames in both Shafak and Ternar's fiction draw variously on the supernatural and the kabbalistic and on Sufi ideas, and the mysticism of the converso and Sabbatean characters sometimes borders on madness, in similar and different ways from Fajardo's character Santiago. These representations suggest that for contemporary authors the converso condition is tied to mysticism in a special way. Of course, as mentioned earlier, this reflects the authors' knowledge of this early modern association with mysticism and messianism from Amsterdam to Istanbul. In *The Mystic Fable*, Michel de Certeau attributes "the upsurge of mystics in the sixteenth and seventeenth centuries," most famously Teresa of Ávila and John of the Cross along with "extremely numerous" others who were of Jewish background, to the "effect of the Jewish difference in the usage of a Catholic idiom" (1992, 23). Shafak and Ternar's penchant for representing the convert's mystical and mysterious consciousness and outlook echoes the history of conversos in Spain as well as Sabbateanism's messianic vision and its development in Salonica with some kabbalistic and Sufi influences (M. D. Baer 2009; Şişman 2015). But the novels also partake in the popular mysticism of the present period in Turkey, Europe, and the Americas, with the widely cited, practiced, and visible Sufism and/or Kabbalah study in various societies of the past few decades.

Shafak's writing is informed by what Erdağ Göknar has referred to as a long-standing "secular Sufism" in the Turkish novel, in which "intertextual allusions to the literature and history of mystical Islam enable the re-enchantment of secularized texts" (Göknar 2013, 211), although Shafak's use of enchantment and the supernatural is polyvalent and informed by multiple sources. Like Carvajal and Fajardo, Shafak too, then, represents converso returns in terms of varying reenchantments. Well-known for her interest in mystical Islamic and other thought, Shafak's 2010 novel *Forty Rules of Love*, based on the story of Rumi and Shams, became a best-seller, much to the distaste of many who find the globalized popularization of Sufism a debasement. *Mirrors of the City* also draws on popularized knowledge about mysticism, but for the most part, the converso central protagonists appear at the conjuncture of (Inquisition-induced) horror, fear, visions, and madness at the edges of some forms of the mystical.

Uncanny Conversos

The use of the supernatural in *Mirrors of the City* accentuates the uncanny quality of returning to the repressed history of conversos. As we saw earlier, in Turkey a racializing obsession with Sabbateans as conspirators in the 1990s and 2000s placed historical conversions in the middle of the current agenda. This was followed by another resurrection in the 2000s: the return of Armenian converts to Islam in the first decades of the twentieth century through a reconversion to Armenian Orthodoxy or an acknowledgment of an

Armenian past in Muslim families (e.g., in Shafak's *The Bastard of Istanbul*). In highlighting histories of conversion and returns, such as that of conversos and Armenians, Shafak also partakes in both global discourses and experiences of returns (see the Introduction; Hirsch and Miller 2011). Shafak's extensive use of the fantastic—from objects that become animated (a scalpel, a drinking glass, wine) to fantastic creatures (e.g., the tail that impregnates Elena, the woman who informs on the Pereiras in order to appropriate their son Andres) and figures from the Koran (the angels Harut and Marut) and from Jewish mystical tradition (the Maggid who saves Miguel and appears to Andres), and much more—expand on the ongoing representations of the converso condition and its returns as uncanny (see Chapter 1).

The return of the extinct is magical, and survival itself is an enchantment. Of course, enchantment itself is mobilized as a return to modes of the nonrational that have been lost to modernity. Shafak does not simply associate the converso with the nonrational. Anthropomorphized objects and strange creatures with agency express the fantastical nature and impact of the inquisitorial world, whose own reliance on the irrational creates, through the threat of violence, *delirio* (Hernández 2002; Chapter 2) in its subjects, such as Miguel with his tormented visions. Further, the mixture of supernatural elements with historical detail (albeit sometimes used anachronistically) creates uncertainty and ambiguity, even for readers familiar with a general history of Sephardi and Muslim Spain and those communities' flight to the Ottoman Empire, dislodging history's certainties and emphasizing the unknown, a preoccupation of writing on conversos whether by U.S. Latinx or Shafak.

The supernatural also lends the novel a sense of gothic horror, at times sensational and exaggerated, that anti-Inquisition fiction has featured for centuries, especially in Protestant countries. In England, for example, the anti-Spanish Black Legend served Gothic novelists "as a template for Catholic horror" (Roberts Mulvey 2016, 31) without including Jews. The crypto-Jewish story is also frequently told through Gothic elements, with dark spaces and individuals that hold atrocious secrets and characters who suffer floridly or commit unspeakable cruelties and betrayals, inducing a generalized sense of horror.

Mirrors of the City features the neogothic space referred to in Spanish as *la Casa Santa* (the Holy House), which is an inquisitorial torture chamber where it is the mind and not the body that is tortured. In *la Casa Santa*, where Isabel is taken after being informed on by Elena, time flows backward and individuals' memories are targeted by a toxic herb that first restores all forgotten memories and then imbues them with regret and shame, corrupting even the best memories. Ultimately, all boundaries between the real and the imagined, right and wrong, are blurred. Truth becomes a rabid dog that destroys everything violently, and memories begin to self-destruct to prevent the enormous pain. The memories that were interrogated in *la Casa Santa* committed suicide one by one, reports the narrator. The return to forgotten memories and remnants of lived experiences are subject to torture, which underscores once again what is lost to history and knowledge under repressive regimes. As Graff Zivin has shown in her analysis of scenes of torture, truth is not what is sought, despite the claims to that effect that support this particular practice of violence (2014). In Shafak, it is memory and other embedded remains of the past that are annihilated in an unreal way.

The Inquisition, unlike in eighteenth-century anti-Catholic novels, is not the only source of the supernatural in *Mirrors of the City*. Less nefarious creatures and beings from both Muslim and Jewish traditions are prominent. Historical events are also part of this unreal landscape, including the feverish prophetic dreams of the minor character Ester, an Istanbul Jew, predicting the arrival of a messiah, which signals the coming Sabbatean movement. By returning the converso and the crypto-Jew to Turkish and world literary memory, Shafak deploys the supernatural to highlight the uncanniness involved in the *compulsion* to mark and recuperate Jewish or other ancient identities and remnants.

Rembrandt's Model

Ternar's novel *Rembrandt's Model* also starts with a mystical, supernatural scene involving cemeteries and a strange flight, maintaining the sense of mystery and existential questioning inevitable in the context of the converso quest for identity and Sabbatean secrecy. Sara is an outsider who becomes immersed in the converso-Sabbatean past when Ali, whom she meets by chance and accompanies to his home on an island, introduces her to his astonishing library. This secret space is mostly filled with antique books pertaining to Sephardi and converso history, including, implausibly but interestingly, the original of the only book illustrated by Rembrandt: *The Piedra Gloriosa de la Estatua de Nebuchadnesar* (The Glorious Stone, or the Statue of Nebuchadnezzar) (1655), written by Menasseh ben Israel. The Hebrew printer and influential rabbi-scholar of Portuguese converso origin with messianic leanings in Amsterdam was instrumental in Oliver Cromwell's readmission of Jews to England, from which they had been banned since their expulsion in 1290.

Sara is at first astounded by Ali's collection and particularly by this book, which he explains as having been bequeathed to his ancestor and namesake Ali Efendi, the customs broker, by his best friend, Salih Efendi. Mystified, Sara gets lost in other books, ranging from works related to the Lurianic Kabbalah to the Islamic mystical works of Rumi and Ibn Arabi, who, as we have seen, also influenced Shafak and many other authors of the 1990s. To resolve Sara's questions about the history of the book and Ali's ancestors, the subsequent chapters of *Rembrandt's Model* tell the story of Samuel, who was taken in as a child by Jesuits when his Jewish parents disappeared in the inquisitorial Spanish world, which then leads to the story of Ali Efendi.

Always in an existential search for belonging, like Shafak's Miguel, Samuel the converso Jesuit, a common combination of the period, decides on a visit to Amsterdam to leave the Jesuits and rekindle the faith of his ancestors by joining the Jewish community there, almost all of whose Sephardi members are former conversos who returned in the safety of seventeenth-century Netherlands. Like many contemporary novelists, Ternar includes details of this in a well-documented chapter on the history of Jewish Spanish exiles. She includes historical characters in particular scenes, such as Menasseh ben Israel in his printing shop urging Samuel to stay in Amsterdam and return to Judaism. Subsequently, Samuel becomes a well-respected teacher to wealthy Amsterdam Sephardis but is still discontented and in search of a belonging that this prosperous, materialistic community does not provide. When he is falsely accused of heresy and excommunicated because of a petty grudge, he becomes homeless, which is how he meets Rembrandt on the street and becomes a model for the artist's famous "Jewish paintings."

Samuel's solution to his misery in Amsterdam is to go to Istanbul to join his old friend Alonso, a former Morisco, and to meet the messiah Sabbatai Sevi, whom he and other impoverished Jews in Amsterdam and many others all over Europe have come to believe in. In his study of Sevi, Gershom

Scholem explains that the devotion to Sevi was not limited to "the rabble"; "marranos everywhere," including the trading elite, were "leading supporters of the movement," and in the

> great centers of the former marranos (Salonica, Leghorn, Amsterdam, and Hamburg to name only the most important), the Sabbatian gospel was eagerly received; it evidently struck a chord in the hearts of those who had themselves, or whose parents had, been through the misery of a life of hypocrisy and dissimulation in Spain and Portugal. There was not a little of the desire to atone for their Christian past in the messianic enthusiasm of the marranos. (Scholem 2016, 485)

Ternar, who likely has read Scholem, gives the reader a sense of precisely this widespread fervor among formerly Christian Jews, but she, like Shafak, includes a Morisco figure. She expands the frame of reference that fictional Judeoconversos are usually found in by including Muslim convert characters and history as imbricated with the Jewish ones by way of Spain and its diasporas. Samuel's departure to Ottoman lands links the novel's present to its past, because Rembrandt gives him as gifts both Menasseh's *Piedra Gloriosa* and an engraving for which Samuel had modeled, which is why the book and the engravings are found in Istanbul in Ali's house in contemporary times.

Ternar's last chapter is Sara's first-person narrative, written five years after meeting Ali as a letter to him, about her discontent as an anthropology doctoral student in Montreal and as the girlfriend of a reluctant Canadian Jew who embraces otherness in his own anthropological work but keeps Sara, a non-Jew, at a distance. The book ends when Sara finds Sabbateans in Montreal and writes to Ali, another descendant of Sabbateans, to invite him into her life.

Like Shafak, Ternar animates the secret world, particularly that of the Sabbateans, with flying future queens of the Jews, lizards that emerge when a book about dragons is opened (though this too is specific, as dragons were associated with Sevi by Nathan of Gaza, his most influential supporter), and Sara's own seeing of historical figures in Ali's backyard. These fantastical aspects are mostly reserved for the contemporary part of the story, which is, interestingly, the more gothic part, though in the seventeenth-century section, Samuel is aided by the angel Sealiah, who makes appearances at key moments to guide him.

Unlike in *Mirrors of the City*, the horrors of the Inquisition are only in the background in *Rembrandt's Model*. A sense of existential search and loss dominates Samuel's story and, to a certain extent, Sara's. Samuel bemoans the loss of Spain and tells stories of its beauties to his young charge. He weaves tales of bravery and beauty in the lost homeland, and, together with the awed children, born in Amsterdam as descendants of exiles, he fantasizes about returning to their land of origin.

Samuel's story is told in a realistic manner, with many historical details about the seventeenth-century Amsterdam Sephardi community and its indigent non-Sephardis. As in other historical fiction (e.g., Liss 2003), the community seems unforgiving and harsh. The Maamad, the ruling council of the Jewish community charged with reinforcing a lost Judaism to its formerly Christian members and with compelling them to not disturb their Dutch "hosts," is meant to be reminiscent of the Inquisition. The Maamad monitors the community's conformism and encourages Jew-on-Jew spying, which leads Ternar's Samuel, like other characters in Jewish Amsterdam historical fiction, to invoke the Inquisition phrase "The ground has ears."

Of course, Samuel's excommunication, based on perjury, is also reminiscent of formerly converso Amsterdam's most famous banned figure: Baruch Spinoza. The family Samuel works for, the DaCostas, is a reference to another "heretic," Uriel da Costa, who was also excommunicated in the seventeenth century. The rebellion of these figures from converso backgrounds has been attributed to the intensive overall "missionizing effort" in Amsterdam to re-Judaize the former New Christians, including through an elaborate didactic print culture that is quite different from the "patchy" tradition and Tanakh-based faith practiced in Spain (Benbassa and Rodrigue 2000, xviii). Although most returned less problematically, these tensions have appeared in both the historical record and in fiction. Rembrandt, whose fortunes and interest in Amsterdam Jews are also detailed, and Menasseh ben Israel are historical figures mingling with the imaginary ones, just as in Shafak's work and other contemporary world historical fiction.

By exploring Sabbatean history without maligning or mystifying it, Ternar presents us with a past as a cascade of conversions, the Sabbatean one embraced by her characters with more hope and vision than even the returns to Judaism (Samuel) and Islam (Alonso). The novel's brand of Sabbateanism is multiply sourced, with a minor yet key character, Ali Efendi, who is not a Jew or a Judeoconverso but a Morisco. Ternar reinserts the movement into the Turkish and Jewish imagination, the dominant versions of which have vehemently rejected or forgotten about it. Indeed, she privileges it, reserving her critique for (and reproducing some stereotypes of) the normative Jewish communities and individuals, who are presented, from Amsterdam to Canada and whether observant or secular, as rigid and exclusive. Ternar also includes scenes in a Jewish studies class in Montreal where the Orthodox Jewish students contest the nondemonizing approach toward Sabbateanism by the professor, whom Sara suspects of being a believer himself.

The novel ends with Samuel's conversion to Sabbateanism and his becoming Salih Efendi, though this is not a true resolution, given that his new faith had to go underground again when its followers publicly followed Sunnism in the Ottoman Empire and Turkey. Even in contemporary Montreal, Sara is not sure who is and is not Sabbatean; adherents are still hiding themselves and communicating through secret signals. Still, the story that Ali was trying to tell Sara in his enchanted Marmara island library reaches closure and completion.

The past and the present connect not only causally in Ternar's novel but also in terms of identity and representational dilemmas as a continuum. Very much like Samuel, Sara feels out of place and searches for answers and belonging in Montreal, hoping to find it in someone like Ali, who embodies a messianic past. Once again, existential and identity questions inform the historically informed novel, whether in its chapters about the past or the present. Importantly, in parting from Rembrandt, Samuel chooses as his favorite a picture of himself with his back turned, because "in Europe, I have been faceless" (Ternar 1998, 126). Samuel, the eponymous "Rembrandt's model," tells the artist, "In all your pictures of me, I always appear humbly uncertain of my purpose, whether I am gazing at the sky, at another face, or at an imaginary viewer who is staring at me. I am never determined in your pictures. I always appear puzzled; as if I have just realized that my human limitations are insurmountable" (Ternar 1998, 127). Adding a layer of complexity to the common formulation about the double or rent consciousness of the converso who is "never determined" and the ambiguous "crypto-Jewish body," Ternar inflects Samuel's status with the vocabulary of invisibility that characterizes the representation of contemporary refugees, migrants, and rejects of the Western world. Samuel's "uncertainty," "puzzlement," "facelessness," and humility overlap with nonelite, dissident converso fates and with the condition of migrants in Europe today.

Samuel's temporary but significant status as a pariah-like homeless person in the seventeenth-century European city is linked to the present in other ways as well. When he is excommunicated and has no one to turn to in Amsterdam, Samuel enacts the (Christian) figure of the wandering Jew found in English gothic literature, such as Matthew Lewis's *The Monk* (1796) or, as Ternar notes in her acknowledgments, Charles Maturin's classic *Melmoth the Wanderer* (1820). The gothic figure of the wandering Jew in British literature becomes more grotesque and horrifying by the nineteenth century. In the vampire the figures of the wandering Jew and the crypto-Jew, expressing anxieties about undetectable assimilated Jews in Christian cultures, are conjoined to suggest monstrous shape-shifting and dissimulation (Davison 2004). In deliberate irony it is not the Christian world that condemns Samuel to wander homeless and belong nowhere but the Jewish one that had initially welcomed him into its bosom. As the transgression-policing Jewish community's actions show, the return to origins is problematic, and for Ternar normative communities are far from redemptive.

The homelessness of Samuel, who is a remnant of the perennially ambiguous converso, despite his return to Judaism, is echoed in one of the chapters about Sara in contemporary Montreal. In an act that is supposedly boundary-defying, Sara's graduate-student boyfriend and his housemate enjoy hosting homeless men, whom they "study" as social scientists, but Sara recoils from the wretchedness of the unhomed and from this kind of anthropological hospitality. Wandering, homelessness, nonbelonging, and multisited, multiple belongings with their discontents—these are the markers of the contemporary world novel. But Ternar distinguishes here among the condition of being unhomed on the streets and the kind of existential nonbelonging that has been the subject of modernist and contemporary fiction, exemplified frequently by conversos and crypto-Jews and marked by interstitiality, in-betweenness, and buried layers of identity and history.

Ternar's critique of the ethics of approaching the unhomed as subjects of investigation and emblems of an unstable modernity raises parallel questions about representing the converso condition as a model of modernity's secularism, skepticism, and cosmopolitanism that we have seen in contemporary scholarship and thought (in Chapters 1 and 4 especially). Samuel's awareness of having served as a "faceless" archetype of "uncertainty" for Rembrandt encapsulates the paradox of common representations of the converso: the one who *preserves* something timeless, despite great changes and hardships, in the visual style with which Rembrandt depicted Amsterdam Jews (including former conversos), but who is simultaneously a figure of modernity's uncertainty and flux.

In Ternar we find again the Muslim-Jewish pairing we saw in Shafak, this time between Salvador the converso, who becomes Samuel in Amsterdam, and Alonso, his best friend at the Jesuit monastery, a Morisco who in Istanbul takes on the name Ali and becomes a Sabbatean. At the beginning of the novel the twentieth-century Ali refers to his seventeenth-century ancestor Ali's best friend Salih Efendi, who is the final incarnation of Samuel the Jesuit converso Jew, now a Sabbatean. Shafak's reference to Morisco exiles in Istanbul is taken a step further here to represent a Moorish former Jesuit as a Sabbatean with a Muslim name. The Morisco-Judeoconverso solidarity we have already seen in Shafak finalizes in yet another conversion, this time to Sabbateanism, furthering an awareness of the kinds of obscured cultural and religious entanglements in the present that have been our subject.

By including two distinct time periods, the seventeenth century and the twentieth century, in her narrative, Ternar not only draws parallels between them and presents a different facet of the analogical deployment of converso history but also raises awareness of remnants: The multiple returns enacted in the novel—Samuel's to Judaism, Alonso's to Islam, and finally their joint turn to Sabbateanism—have their parallels in the remnants that fascinate Sara: Samuel lives on in Rembrandt's work; Ali's library is a wondrous place of the remaining documented proofs of these returns and developments; as a descendant, Ali embodies several histories of entanglement; and, finally, despite their seeming demise, Sabbateans continue to exist, even in Montreal. The return narrative's impulse to assert survival and contest extinction affirms itself here, as it is implied in Shafak and many of our authors. The island home, a Sabbatean site of memory, houses an alternative archive, like Ternar's novel itself, which, despite the stereotypes, serves as a portal to imagining uncanny pasts, convergences, and remains of Iberian and post-Iberian conversions. Ali's enchanted collection speaks not only to the desire to locate the secret and lost archives of the *dönme* but also to the impossibility of this desire, expressed through its fantastic elements for the foreseeable future. Only in an otherworldly realm can Sara or the reader access this buried knowledge lost to repression or hidden from view.

The contemporary Turkish and world fiction texts through which I have explored the interest in conversos investigate the psychic and social dynamics of conversion at particular moments of Spanish-Ottoman and contemporary Turkish history. The authors not only highlight the costs of and shifts in boundaries of religious and national belonging but also change Turkish writing's own categories. The biographies and linguistic choices of Shafak and Ternar, like those of Bahar and Arditi, test the boundaries of Turkish writing as a monolingual enterprise practiced inside Turkey by Turkish authors (usually with a dominant ethnoreligious definition of Turkishness as a referent). As those with a multiplicity of Ottoman and Turkish belongings and languages writing in Turkey, Europe, and elsewhere have shown, the nation-state model of defining Turkish literature is problematic and exclusionary. Writing in Turkish within or outside the boundaries of the Republic is also insufficient to define the literature of Turkey. Working in English and Turkish and as minoritized subjects, immigrants, diasporans, or writers who subscribe to multiple or no particular affiliations and labels, the authors who are the subjects of this chapter fictionalize conversion and Sephardi experiences in Ottoman-Turkish and European settings, connecting the Jewish-Muslim, converso-Sabbatean, and Ottoman-Spanish contexts and thereby expanding and transforming the Turkish literary canon as well as the world novel.

There is a particular way that stories about historical conversions speak to the situation of writers such as Bahar, Shafak, and Ternar, who might be perceived as incomplete in their Turkishness because of their linguistic choices, names or spelling thereof, non-Sunni backgrounds, geographic locations, identification with unsanctioned groups or ideas, or positionality in the nation-state or global arrangements of literature. As Halevi-Wise suggests, post-1492 stories of conversions and displacements serve "as a pliable trope that portrays paradoxical images of identity," contra those that "demand unambiguous or uniform allegiances" (2012a, 28). In addition, conversions and secrecies attract writers who want to recover histories and identities that are obscured and reviled and who want to provide an alternative archive of the historical consciousness of the present. In this case, they avail themselves of the redemptive neo-Ottomanist historical imagination and its cosmopolitan desires, which can easily fold into nationalist visions. But their works can also travel beyond its geographical and triumphalist boundaries. The actual and imagined past and continuity of the converso and Sabbatean worlds in the Ottoman Empire, Turkey, and the Americas in these works, despite their sometimes overwrought imagery, language, and representation, should lead us to an awareness of remnants and a reconsideration of extinction and survival. Finally, in lieu of the ideological severing among normative Sephardi, Jewish converso, Morisco, Muslim, and Sabbatean histories, reconstructed most commonly for instrumental and often pernicious reasons, imaginative approaches can lead us instead to think further about their mutually constitutive boundaries and entanglements.

CODA

WHY CONVERSOS? Why now? With our texts, we have traveled across the continents and periods in search of answers to these questions. Crossing centuries and the interior of Peru, northern Mexico, Costa Rica, Guatemala City, Oriente Province and Havana, New Mexico, Chicago, Miami, Paris, Venice, Salonica, Istanbul, Jerusalem, Safed, Madrid, Toledo, Málaga, Arcos de la Frontera, Livorno, and Lisbon, our authors have offered historical, genealogical, religious, and cultural convergences at the heart of the converso story that are compelling for us here and now. Relating conversos' multiple worlds, frequently forged under duress, opens up the space to offer many other narratives about suffering, survival, and solidarities. That is why converso stories matter to those with an ethical imagination, one that acknowledges the devastating power of boundaries and their submerged, plausible transgressions. They remind us in particularly relevant ways in the context of ongoing enclosures of communities, nations, and religions that convergences among seemingly discrete worlds can arise not only in freedom but also under oppression.

There are other reasons that the "lost" afterlives of conversions have been "found." Extinction and, particularly, survival are magnetic topics: *How*, we want to know, have people and cultures survived unbeknownst to most, and what has become of them as a result? Upon finding out about little-known survivals, our sense of the past shifts and our historical consciousness is intensified. But returning the past to the present without extensive archives and material remains is a difficult process that often involves the imagination, at which point truth claims and authenticities start competing. In narratives about crypto-Jews, the production of the individual self as a remnant and as an embodied archive of an otherwise little-documented past involves vastly varying resources, ranging from oral culture's rumors and gossip to historical speculation and advanced genetic technology. Paramemories, recollections, and enactments of ancestral experiences in the body flow, as we have seen especially in the work of Carvajal and Fajardo, from this productive and problematic conception of the self as the carrier of an ancient secret narrative.

The claiming of ancient identities itself is a dizzyingly complex affair that involves a romance of origins, stories of blood, and devastating secrets. But these are not just Gothic tropes that fuel the imagination. They make us ask difficult questions about our relationship to resuscitated pasts. How do we define "ruptures" and "continuities" of belongings, and what legal and social stakes are involved? How do such returns and revivals, often undertaken through the discourse of redress, challenge or legitimate the injustices of the present? Our texts have explored the fine line between these possibilities. The *experience* of an identity can be pitted against its "mere" biological inheritance, such as in the disagreement between Santiago and Dana in Fajardo's *Mi nombre es Jamaica*. Although the assumption of a particular genealogy and what I have called historicized affiliative self-fashioning can be restorative of a wrongfully suppressed history, it can also be appropriative of past and current identities. Despite these problematics, inheritance and genealogies continue to define the boundaries of inclusion in many legal, religious, and social contexts in which we find ourselves. These tensions, as elaborated in *Mi nombre es Jamaica* and elsewhere, remind us that we have not gone beyond "genealogical thinking," despite the secular-modern disavowal of blood and the critique of biologized belonging. Acknowledging this and deploying inheritance in alternative ways is what I see as the critical genealogy of Edgar Morin and Victor Perera, in which converso ancestry and self-declaration as a descendant or remnant serve not to enshrine heritage but to question and deploy it for progressive ends.

CODA

Contemporary converso-descent stories arouse not only fascination and sympathy but also disbelief and ire. Yet the history and return of crypto-Jewishness is more "out" than ever: The number of texts, conferences, and awards is growing, and social media presence and interested organizations' politicized endorsements are increasing. Indeed, to the delight of some and the disapproval of others, normative Sephardi and converso-descendant identities are in the process of merging in cultural and political encounters and cultural productions. The literary writing about the way converso identities cause shifts in our historical and genealogical consciousness is rather different in spirit and scope than these communal and political activities, though they certainly coexist in the same universe, where the idea of the crypto-Jew can both trouble and resolidify existing boundaries of Christian, Jewish, and Muslim belonging. But the texts we have examined put pressure on our perception of these boundaries and their histories by making "a world" (Cheah 2008, 2016) of known and imagined convergences and solidarities through difference, "intervals, mediations, passages, and crossings between national borders" (Cheah 2008, 25), and even despite borders.

In addition to examining the refigurations of the converso past in various national and transnational contexts, *The Converso's Return* bridges Sephardism and Sephardis. The *ism* frequently refers to the investment in Sephardi or Jewish Iberian history by individuals, groups, and states that are not necessarily Sephardi-identified or versed in Sephardi languages or practices but are nevertheless interested in their impact. Cultural and literary production by and about normative Sephardis is often treated separately from investigations of Sephardism, presumably a nonidentitarian project. Some of the authors featured in this book are not Jewish by ancestry but have immersed themselves in converso pasts and identities through their own lens of nation and empire, which is one indication of the relevance of converso histories. Analyses of their works accompany the investigations of Sephardi and converso descendant-identified writers' perspectives that are nourished by Sephardi and crypto-Jewish identities and cultures. The idea of the converso, however debated and controversial, is located within, and not at the obscure margins of, Sephardi, Spanish, Turkish, French, and Latinx writing, whatever the backgrounds of the authors who engage it. At the same time, narratives about converso history pose challenges to all these categories.

The cultural and literary analyses presented here also gesture toward another opening: a nonhegemonic vision of Hispanism that includes languages other than those of Spain, whether the dominant Castilian or the several regional languages. This vision also emerges from a particular kind of connection to Sephardi studies involving both Iberian and Atlantic history, shorn of interested philo-Sephardisms. To be sure, forms of Hispanism connecting Spain to its Jewish and Muslim past and Sephardi diasporas have been with us for a long time, as we have seen, including even under fascism: The establishment in the 1930s of the Escuela de Estudios Árabes, which about a decade later was incorporated into the Instituto Arias Montano for Arabic and Hebrew/Jewish Studies, in Spain was an institutionalized version of such a vision, which even has earlier precedents (Friedman 2011a). The work of Spaniard Américo Castro, who insisted on the essential role of the Jewish and Muslim presence in Spanish culture, challenging the conservative and Catholic basis of other Hispanisms, was in certain ways carried on in New York by Mair José Benardete and Federico de Onís, Sephardi Turkish and Spanish immigrants, respectively, who advanced the preservation and study of Judeo-Spanish folk and literary culture in a Hispanic frame for several decades, beginning in the 1920s. However, these perspectives largely left intact the national (and sometimes nationalist) and imperial drives that have also informed Hispanisms from Europe to the Americas.

A critical Hispanism that addresses the overlaps and crossings as well as the boundaries, exclusions, asymmetries, and dispossessions in texts and discourses about Iberian history and post-Iberian exiles, converts, and conquests is also essential to the study of Iberian Sephardism and its diasporas. This approach cannot be associated exclusively with Spain, Portugal, Europeanness, and/or whiteness. In addition to the key African and indigenous formations, it includes convergences of the Jewish and Muslim Middle East and North Africa with the variegated Luso-Hispanic Atlantic world in the making of inclusive Sephardiness, whose provenance in Iberia is but one of its sources. The converso story is a particular thread in these entanglements. Ideally, of course, Iberia and its empires and diasporas as a whole need to be integrated with Hispanic and Sephardi studies. Although I did not address, for reasons of space and language, the particular converso returns of current Portuguese speakers in Brazil, future studies need to join together and transform the various Iberianist frames.

In the context of Sephardi studies, crypto-Jewish and converso stories highlight Sephardi experiences as unbound by a Jewish frame and as a product of multiple historical and ongoing intersections. One of the goals of this study was to further much-needed research in the contemporary literature and culture of Sephardis and Sephardism, to create more space for Sephardi studies within the area of world literature and vice versa, and to consider genealogical thinking and historical consciousness as related and complex problematics for critical work about culture and literature.

NOTES

Introduction: Lost and Found?

1. On Alexandria Ocasio-Cortez, see Stanley-Becker (2018); for an analysis of the reactions, see Daniel and Greenberg (2019). See Linda Chavez's first-person article on her roots (Chavez 2012). On Maduro, see "Venezuelan President: My Grandparents Were Jewish," *Jerusalem Post*, May 16, 2013, https://www.jpost.com/Jewish-World/Jewish-Features/Venezuelan-president-My-grandparents-were-Jewish-313312 (accessed May 16, 2013). On Laurie Cardoza-Moore, see Lieberman (2016); and Hoffman (2019). For studies on converso genes in the Americas, see Vélez et al. (2012) and Chacón-Duque et al. (2018).

2. As examples of countless published pieces on these contemporary revelations, see, for example, Kelly (2004), who reports that Father Sánchez "sensed that he was different" even as a child and that for another New Mexican the acknowledgment of Jewish heritage was "like coming home." See also Milgrom (2012), Schwartzman (2015), and Chacón-Duque et al. (2018). The cases of northern Portuguese *judeus* or marranos, as they are known in Portugal and on the Spanish island of Mallorca (the Chueta community), are different in that the label of "Jew" has long been attached to them, voluntarily or involuntarily (see, e.g., Leite 2017; Pignatelli 2019; Yovel 2009). Although the revelations are not so new, as I explain later in this chapter, the attention and the return to Judaism are. The Portuguese contexts are important as well in the background of the Latin American migrations (as I explain), but in the chapter and the book as a whole I focus largely on the Spanish-speaking contexts.

3. See, for example, Hartman (1997, 2007, 2008). Stephen Best (2012, 2018) has an extended critique of what he calls "the recovery imperative" and "melancholy historicism" in the articulation of nondistinction between the past and the present.

4. Although I agree with some aspects of Fredric Jameson's original critique of presentism, I am not embarking on an investigation of whether this particular body of literary works exhibits "genuine historicity" (Jameson 1991, 19).

5. There are those who build narratives of the hidden traumas of their parents on their own, such as the children of Jewish Holocaust survivors who discover only as adults their parents' experiences. But in such experiences (e.g., Creet 2008; Kirschner 2007), the shocking discovery leads the adult children to the familial and public archives and sites of the hidden past, through which they reconstruct the painful stories that their parents concealed from them. In the case of converso descendants who suspect or are told about a Jewish past in the family, there is often little documented evidence left to reconstruct beyond a few names and dates.

6. Carvajal the Younger ("el moso") was a Spanish-born New Christian of a crypto-Jewish family who joined his renowned conquistador uncle of the same name in Mexico, then New Spain. Hounded and murdered by the Inquisition, as were dozens of his family members, Carvajal left behind autobiographical writings.

7. Although many disavowed and even reviled their past as Christians, and some wrote passionately about the superiority of the Judaism that they were now free to embrace, their writing reveals the continuing amalgamation of their Iberian formation with traditional Judaism—for example, Christian rhetoric combined with Jewish concerns (see, e.g., Bodian 1994, 2007; Graizbord 2008).

8. For Benzion Netanyahu, Francisco Márquez Villanueva, Antonio Jose Saraiva, and other historians, what they called marranism was an invention of anti-Semitism (see Yerushalmi 1981, 21). Other historians disagreed just as vehemently, arguing for the survival of converso practices and identities in Iberia and the Americas (e.g., Y. Baer 1961; Novinsky 2001; Révah 1959–1960; Roth 1932). Yosef Yerushalmi and others have since tempered these claims by explaining the possible communal and social (rather than theological) motivations of those particular rabbis who refused membership to some conversos. Further, Yerushalmi showed that conversos in Portugal had been under consistent pressure, being reminded incessantly of their Jewish origins, and therefore had little reason to yearn for Jewish belonging once they were out of Iberia, when they could live well as Catholics. For I. S. Révah (1959–1960), those who practiced some crypto-Judaism and wished to return were "potential Jews" starting over with shards of suppressed knowledge and faith. But for other scholars, they carried Judaism in their hearts and in their blood (Y. Baer 1961).

9. Among academic backers of crypto-Jewish or converso continuity in New Mexico, almost all of whom are Ashkenazi Americans, the best known is Stanley Hordes, a onetime New Mexico state historian. Hordes explained that in casual conversations, local people separately and repeatedly referred to rumors within and outside their families about Jewish origins or about customs that they could not always explain (and seemed Jewish to Hordes). These observations led Hordes to publicize

and write extensively about the remains of crypto-Jewish practice and material culture in the Southwest. His work was fueled by the enthusiasm and conviction of some of the Hispanic-identified New Mexicans who were eager to know more and sometimes assumed their Jewish heritage as they became more and more convinced. Other academics, including Janet Liebman Jacobs (2002) and Seth Kunin (2009), have published books in which they defend the primacy of the testimonies as key to understanding crypto-Jewishness. Folklorist and anthropologist Judith Neulander devoted years to challenging such claims with the assertion that the Jewish practices of animal slaughter (in which blood is drained), mirror covering as a sign of mourning, pork aversion, and so on were attributable to the spread in the Southwest of Pentecostalism or Seventh Day Adventism, which includes some of these customs. As the authors of an extensive article in *The Atlantic* pointed out in the early 2000s, the Seventh Day Adventist link was an earlier finding of Raphael Patai, who studied the crypto-Jewish claims of the inhabitants of Venta Prieta, Mexico, and came to this conclusion (Ferry and Nathan 2000). What seemed to be of crypto-Jewish origin in fact was not, they argued. Neulander accused Hordes of asking leading questions of Hispanic interviewees and driving them to conclusions about their Jewishness. She also questioned Jacobs's methods of presenting her Latinx subjects' testimonies about crypto-Jewish practices at face value. Hordes (2008), Kunin (2009), and others have refuted the rejection and skepticism of Neulander and of other journalists (especially Ferry and Nathan). Kunin (2009) extensively critiqued Neulander's denunciations of assertions and certainties around crypto-Jewish practices and focused instead on self-presentation and plausibility of continuity. Other Jewish studies scholars have also expressed doubt, one remarking in a review of Hordes's book that "nagging inconsistencies include the intense identification with Spain, even as the overwhelming majority of New Christians, Judaizing or not, were of Portuguese origin" and adding that "the disdain for Catholicism," which is a form of proof for some, could also be attributed to Native American origins of Southwest Hispanos, Latinx, and Chicanas/os (Ben-Ur 2009, 179). Some crypto-Jewish-identifying descendants, such as Ricardo G. Santos of Texas, have also criticized those he called "wannabe cryptos," Hispanos of the Southwest who jump to conclusions based on a few disputable or wrongheaded familial practices (Santos 1999, 121–22). Tomás Atencio, a New Mexican sociologist and activist, noted widespread awareness of crypto-Jewishness in his region but also noted in his research in the 1990s that the "proof" of crypto-Jewish presence and continuity in New Mexico "may forever be lost behind the veil of history." Instead, Atencio pursued an interpretation of "manito" (New Mexican Indo-Hispanic) culture as "possibly" including crypto-Jewish "remnants," such as culinary and slaughter practices, Friday rituals, vocabulary related to the Inquisition, and tendencies toward secrecy, without asserting these as concrete evidence (Atencio 1996). And a few historians have disagreed that there was any proof beyond rumors (Ben-Ur 2009, 181).

10. The fate of some descendants of conversos (known as Chuetas) in Mallorca, Spain, during World War II, was a concrete case in point of the feared connection between *limpieza de sangre* and Nazism: The community is one of the few that was continuously identified within and without as being of converso origin, despite the absence of Jewish practice or knowledge in hundreds of years, a manifestation of the power of prejudice that often defies belief for outsiders. In 1942 a census of conversos was carried out in Mallorca under pressure from the German consulate and with the support of the Spanish Falangists (Rozenberg 2006, 27–28). The project to deport these "Jews" to a concentration camp in Formentera o Cabrera never materialized, but the episode is a brief reminder of the dangers of blood logics.

11. Susan Martha Kahn observes: "Despite Ostrer's assertion that this isn't old-fashioned race science but, rather, a voluntary, shared project of self-discovery, his insistence does not assuage deep concerns about the implications of reinforcing notions of biological difference between population groups. . . . It is interesting to note that Ostrer is not the first modern Jewish scientist to embrace the notion of Jewish biological distinctiveness (see Hart 2011)—he is simply the most prominent to do so using the new, posteugenic vernacular of population genetics" (Kahn 2013, 921).

12. In our oral history project on people of Sephardi descent seeking Spanish and/or Portuguese citizenship, Dr. Rina Benmayor and I have interviewed converso descendants who have applied for or have already received citizenship. Our joint publications include "Ancestry, Genealogy, and Restorative Citizenship: Oral Histories of Sephardi Descendants Reclaiming Spanish And Portuguese Nationality" (Benmayor and Kandiyoti 2020).

13. See Gravé-Lazi (2016) on the figure "tens of millions"; and Abu El Haj (2012) and Charmé (2012) on the older organizations and the politics around "newly found Jews" (Charmé) and "diaspora Zionism" (Abu el Haj). Also see the websites of the following newer organizations: Zera Foundation: Reconnecting Into the Jewish People (https://zera-israel.org/); and Reconectar (http://reconectar.co/). For precedents, see Semi (2002) and Popkin (1989) on the quest for lost tribes in the early years of the Jewish State. Further, as Livia Parnes observes, Samuel Schwarz, the engineer who cultivated and studied the northern Portuguese New Christian/crypto-Jews in the 1920s, was an avid Zionist and was eager for the return of these Portuguese to the Jewish people. He positioned their para-Jewish syncretic rituals and practices as proof of their Jewish "nationality," and not simply of their religion (Parnes 2015). Schwarz was eager for the return of the Portuguese to the Jewish people, and his salvage ethnographic work of song and prayer collection and documentation served to further the Jewish national cause at a time when this was being defined. See also Leite (2017, 57) on the mythification and racialization of the community by Schwarz.

Chapter 1: Doubles, Disguises, Splits

1. Rodrigo Amador de los Ríos, the author of three volumes on the Jews of Spain and Portugal published in the last quarter of the nineteenth century, wrote from a Catholic point of view. He even blamed Judeoconversos for being the neophyte zealots of the Inquisition who were the true and worst persecutors of the Jews and inciters of mobs (García Arenal 2013, 7). See Friedman (2011a) on de los Ríos.

2. Renowned Brazilian author Moacyr Scliar's parodic 1983 novel *The Strange Nation of Rafael Mendez* can be considered an exception. See Halevi-Wise (2012b).

3. As Gerschom Scholem explains about this "strange action" of Sabbatai Sevi, who was known to be prone to depression and "queerness," "the advent of the messiah under the sign of Pisces is mentioned in Isaac Abravanel's commentary on Daniel" (Scholem 2016, 161).

4. A few examples include Ahdaf Soueif's novel *Map of Love*, Michael Cunningham's *the hours*, David Mitchell's *Ghostwritten*, Muñoz Molina's *Sepharad*, Elif Shafak's *40 Rules of Love*, and the play *7 Streams of the River Ota* by Robert Lepage. Rebecca Walkowitz has offered the useful term "the anthological novel" to describe "the geographic sampling and collating we see in Sebald's *The Emigrants*, Phillips's *The Distant Shore*, [and] Desai's *Inheritance of Loss*" (Walkowitz 2009, 571).

Chapter 2: Latinx Sephardism and the Absent Archive

1. For personal statements expressing this kind of sentiment of "difference," see also, for example, Kessel (2000, ch. 1); Milgrom (2012); and Herrera (2012, n.d.).

2. On the dominant definition of "Jewish American literature," see Kandiyoti (2012).

3. On the irony of Alejandra's passing as a white Christian American on account of her lighter skin and "despite" her Latinx and Sephardi heritage, see Freedman (2008, 243). "Marrano as metaphor" is also the relevant title of a well-known edited volume about the deployment of the converso as an analogy to our contemporary condition more generally (see Marks 1996).

4. I am thinking, for example, of *The Ballad of Little Jo*, Maggie Greenwald's memorable film on a cross-dressing woman passing as a man in the nineteenth-century U.S. West, a "wild" space of gender and racial crossings.

5. I borrow the phrase "absence of a queer past" from Kel Karpinski's (2016) seminar paper on *Days of Awe*, written for "The Transamerican Historical Imagination" graduate seminar I ran in Fall 2016 at the Graduate Center, City University of New York. I thank Kel Karpinski and the other students for stimulating my further thinking about the novel.

6. See Rubinstein (2010) and Casteel (2012) for original analyses of Native American and Jewish intersections in U.S. literature. Casteel's investigation brings together Sephardism and marranism in the works of key Native American authors' treatment of 1492 and crypto-Jewish and Native experiences.

7. For some of these analyses and lengthier treatments of the novel, see Suárez (2014), Duneer (2015), Concannon (2013), and Otero (2012).

8. Freedman opens his chapter on crypto-Jews with a telling anecdote: At a meeting about hiring a junior professor in Jewish American studies, a senior colleague dismisses the author's suggestion to create a position in Sephardi studies of the Americas with the words "the Sephardim are of no importance, in the U.S. None. At best—they're a footnote" (2008, 209). This comment is typical, not exceptional, in non-Sephardi Jewish academic, media, and political contexts in the United States.

Chapter 3: Return to Sepharad

1. In addition to performance and food, music also plays a role in "authenticating" the Jewishness of Spain, though Judith Cohen (2004) reports that the Judeo-Spanish songs that are played in the festivals in Ribadavia and Hervás are framed as having survived from the medieval period and retained by the locals, possible remnants of Sephardi Jews, even though the songs do not date to a period earlier than the nineteenth century.

2. On the necessity of forgetting, see, for example, Weinrich (2004), Augé (2004), and Ricoeur (2004, 503, 513).

3. For more extensive treatments of philo-Sephardism and other Spanish-Jewish relations and interactions in modern Spain, see Linhard (2014), who provides a helpful overview of other scholars and trends in the twentieth century (especially the Introduction). See also Beckwith (2020), Friedman (2014), Flesler et al. (2015), Flesler and Pérez Melgosa (2020), Ojeda-Mata (2018), Rohr (2007), Rozenberg (2006), and Tardieu Touboul (2009).

4. For more on philo-Semitism in Spain, see, for example, Linhard (2014) and Flesler and Pérez Melgosa (2020). On the paradoxes of Franco's approach to Jews and Sephardis, see Ojeda-Mata (2018).

5. In our oral history project on Sephardi descendants seeking Spanish or Portuguese nationality, which includes many converso descendants from the Americas, Dr. Rina Benmayor and I explore some of these questions.

6. For scholarship on contemporary Spanish Muslims and on current Spanish discourses on Islam, see, for example, Rosón Lorente (2008), Hirschkind (2013), and Rogozen-Soltar (2017).

7. The argument returns in prominent scholars Benjamin Stora and Henri Rousso's call for the need of history in our "age of memory." "History is an approach that puts the past at a distance," Rousso emphasizes, whereas "memory is a faculty that brings the past into the present. It is characterized by an affective, emotional relation to the past that ignores the hierarchies of time and abolishes distance" (Rousso 2002, 16). For the historian Benjamin Stora, memory is communal, which "creates a constant sense of absence because of the non-encounter between memories" (1991, 252). Rothberg's

analysis (2009) of texts in which the Jewish Holocaust does not serve as a means of separation (Jews from others) but is the basis of comparative and "multidirectional" encounters among memories is a response to these and other critiques of memory.

8. Anidjar argues that the blood narrative is a Christian one. Although Jews were associated with blood (the killing of Christ, blood libel, accusations of stealing the host and of being blood merchants) (Anidjar 2014, 69), in fact Christianity was associated with blood, especially as of the twelfth century. Anidjar explains Christian blood as vulnerable property, the shared substance of the community of Christians (306). By 1391 it was Western Christendom as a whole, he contends, rather than some irrational Spaniards, that, in practices of and related to the Eucharist, had come to consider Christian blood as substantially distinct from Jewish blood, whereas Christian blood was deemed vulnerable to Jewish blood (306). For Anidjar, the *limpieza de sangre* and the Inquisition are nonexceptional and the "quasi hermetic division of race from religion" is inaccurate (64).

Chapter 4: Sephardis' Converso Pasts

1. I thank Matt Goldish for generously sharing his knowledge and views with me.
2. Like Morin, Bensaïd grew up without religious observance but in an environment that did not tolerate anti-Semitism. His father, who like his mother was from Oran, had been a prisoner at Drancy, and members of his family in France died in the concentration camps. His father, a "non-Jewish Jew," according to Bensaïd, was buried without Jewish rites, at his request, though he wore a Star of David during his lifetime.

Chapter 5: Ottoman-Spanish and Jewish-Muslim Entanglements

1. The "openings" toward marginalized minorities were a short-lived state initiative for recognition and inclusion.
2. Observers and scholars in Turkey (e.g., R. Bali 2000; Hür 2009; Eldem 2013) and outside (e.g., Brink-Danan 2011; Mills 2011; J. P. Cohen 2014) who study Ottoman or Turkish republican Jewry have emphatically criticized mythologizing discourses both of the contemporary Jewish community leadership and of the state. Although the persecution and minoritization of many groups in Turkey deserves much critique, it is also important to understand the particular and changing nature of nationalisms as the foundation of the problem, especially in the republican period, rather than an abiding, fixed anti-Semitism inherent in Turkey and its peoples.
3. Based on no evidence, it is proclaimed in such writing that, for example, in the conquest of Cyprus, Sultan Selim's proclivity to drink and appetite for the vineyard-rich island was merely a cover for his drive to find Jews a homeland where a Jewish king would be installed (Küçük 2003, 140).
4. A sympathetic exception is Uluç Özüyener's recent wide-ranging historical novel *Paslı Anahtar*, Istanbul: Büyükada Yayıncılık, 2018.

BIBLIOGRAPHY

Abraham, Nicolas, and Maria Torok. 1994. *The Shell and the Kernel: Renewals of Psychoanalysis*, vol. 1. Trans. Nicholas T. Rand. Chicago: University of Chicago Press.

Abu El-Haj, Nadia. 2012. *The Genealogical Science: The Search for Jewish Origins and the Politics of Epistemology*. Chicago: University of Chicago Press.

Aciman, André. 2000. "In a Double Exile." In his *False Papers: Essays on Exile and Memory*, 107–10. New York: Farrar, Strauss & Giroux.

———. 2011. "Temporizing." In his *Alibis: Essays on Elsewhere*, 61–74. New York: Farrar, Strauss & Giroux.

Acıman, Stella. 2006. *Bir Masaldı Geçen Yıllar* [The Past Was a Fairy Tale]. Istanbul: +1 Kitap.

Aidi, Hisham. 2006. "The Interference of al-Andalus: Spain, Islam, and the West." *Social Text* 24(2): 67–88.

Aizenberg, Edna. 2002. *Books and Bombs in Buenos Aires: Borges, Gerchunoff, and Argentine Jewish Writing*. Waltham, MA: Brandeis University Press.

Alberro, Solange. 2001. "Crypto-Jews and the Mexican Holy Office in the Seventeenth Century." In *The Jews and the Expansion of Europe to the West, 1450 to 1800*, ed. Paola Bernardini and Normal Fiering, 172–85. New York: Berghahn.

Alcalá, Kathleen. 1992. *Mrs. Vargas and the Dead Naturalist*. Corvallis, OR: Calyx Press.

———. 1996. *Spirits of the Ordinary: A Tale of Casas Grandes*. San Diego: Harcourt Brace.

———. 1998. *The Flower in the Skull*. San Francisco: Chronicle Books.

———. 2007. *The Desert Remembers My Name: On Family and Writing*. Tucson: University of Arizona Press.

Alonso, Ana Maria. 2004. "Conforming Disconformity: 'Mestizaje,' Hybridity, and the Aesthetics of Mexican Nationalism." *Cultural Anthropology* 19(4): 459–90.

Anderson, Perry. 2011. "From Progress to Catastrophe." *London Review of Books* 33(15): 24–28. https://www.lrb.co.uk/v33/n15/perry-anderson/from-progress-tocatastrophe (accessed October 16, 2018).

Anidjar, Gil. 2008. *Semites: Race, Religion, Literature*. Stanford, CA: Stanford University Press.

———. 2014. *Blood: A Critique of Christianity*. New York: Columbia University Press.

Apel, Nora. 2002. *Memory Effects: The Holocaust and the Art of Secondary Witnessing*. New Brunswick, NJ: Rutgers University Press.

Arditi, Metin. 2011. *Le Turquetto: Roman*. Paris: Actes Sud.

Arendt, Hannah. 1973. *The Origins of Totalitarianism*, Part 1. New York: Houghton Mifflin.

Aronson-Friedman, Amy I., and Gregory B. Kaplan, eds. 2012. *Marginal Voices: Studies in Converso Literature of Medieval and Golden Age Spain*. Leiden: Brill.

Ashery, Oreet. 2008. "Shabbtai Zvi: The Saint/s of Whitstable." http://oreetashery.net/work/the-saints-of-whitstable/ (accessed October 6, 2019).

Atencio, Tomás. 1996. "Crypto-Jewish Remnants in Manito Society and Culture." *Jewish Folklore and Ethnology Review* 18(1–2): 59–67.

Augé, Marc. 2004. *Oblivion*. Minneapolis: University of Minnesota Press.

Avni, Haim. 1982. *Spain, the Jews, and Franco*. Philadelphia: Jewish Publication Society.

Azoulay, Ariella. 2011. "Archive." Trans. Tal Haran. In *Political Concepts: A Critical Lexicon*. http://www.politicalconcepts.org/issue1/archive/ (accessed May 2, 2018).

Baer, Marc David. 2009. *The Dönme: Jewish Converts, Muslim Revolutionaries, and Secular Turks*. Stanford, CA: Stanford University Press.

Baer, Yitzhak. 1961. *A History of the Jews in Christian Spain*, 2 vols. Trans. Louis Schoffman. Philadelphia: Jewish Publication Society of America.

Bahar, Beki L. 1993. *Donna Grasya Nasi: İki Bölümlük Oyun* [Dona Gracia Nasi: Play in Two Acts]. Istanbul: Isis Press.

Bali, Rıfat N. 1999. "Bir Varmış Bir Yokmuş, Bir Zamanlar Bu Diyarda Azınlıklar Yaşarmış" [Once Upon a Time, There Were Minorities in This Land]. *Virgül* 25(1): 4–7.

———. 2000. *Cumhuriyet Yıllarında Türkiye Yahudileri: Bir Türkleştirme Serüveni (1923–1945)* [Turkish Jews in the Early Republic: An Adventure in Turkification, 1923–1945]. Istanbul: İletişim.

———. 2006. *Maziyi Eşelerken: Tarih, Basın ve Popüler Edebiyat* [Digging Around in the Past: History, the Media, and Popular Literature]. Istanbul: Dünya.

———. 2008. *A Scapegoat for All Seasons: The Dönmes or Crypto-Jews of Turkey*. Istanbul: Isis Press.

———. 2012. *Model Citizens of the State: The Jews of Turkey During the Multi-Party Period*. Trans. Paul F. Bessemer. Madison, NJ: Fairleigh Dickinson University Press.

Bali, Serhan. 2011. "Kendimi Hâlâ Bir Osmanlı Olarak Görürüm" [I Still See Myself as an Ottoman]. *Radikal*, January 11, 2011. http://www.radikal.com.tr/yazarlar/serhan-bali/kendimi-hl-bir-osmanli-olarak-gorurum-1068100/ (accessed February 20, 2016).

Barkan, Elazar. 2000. *The Guilt of Nations: Restitution and Negotiating Historical Injustices*. Baltimore: Johns Hopkins University Press.

Barkey, Karen. 2008. *Empire of Difference: The Ottomans in Comparative Perspective*. Cambridge, UK: Cambridge University Press.

Barnai, Jacob. 1993. "Christian Messianism and the Portuguese Marranos: The Emergence of Sabbateanism in Smyrna." *Jewish History* 7(2): 119–26.

Baron, Salo W. 1928. "Ghetto and Emancipation." *Menorah Journal* 14(6): 515–26.

———. 1952. *A Social and Religious History of the Jews: Late Middle Ages and the Era of European Expansion, 1200–1650*. New York: Columbia University Press.

Beckwith, Stacy. 2012. "Facing Sepharad, Facing Israel and Spain: Yehuda Burla and Antonio Gala's Janus Profiles of National Reconstitution." In *Sephardism: Spanish Jewish History and the Modern Literary Imagination*, ed. Yael Halevi-Wise, 169–88. Stanford, CA: Stanford University Press.

———. 2020 (in press). "With Sepharad as a Void: Recent Reckoning with the Holocaust in Spanish Fiction." In *Spain, the Second World War, and the Holocaust: History and Representation*, ed. Sara Brenneis and Gina Herrmann. Toronto: University of Toronto Press.

Benbassa, Esther. 2003. "Questioning Historical Narratives: The Case of Balkan Sephardi Jewry." *Simon Dubnow Institute Yearbook* 2: 15–22.

———. 2010. *Suffering as Identity: The Jewish Paradigm*. London: Verso.

Benbassa, Esther, and Aron Rodrigue. 2000. *Sephardi Jewry: A History of the Judeo-Spanish Community, 14th–20th Centuries*. Berkeley: University of California Press.

Ben-Dor Benite, Zvi. 2013. *The Ten Lost Tribes: A World History*. New York: Oxford University Press.

Benjamin, Walter. 1969. *Illuminations*. Ed. Hannah Arendt. Trans. Harry Zohn. New York: Schocken.

Benmayor, Rina, and Dalia Kandiyoti. 2020. "Ancestry, Genealogy, and Restorative Citizenship: Oral Histories of Sephardi Descendants Reclaiming Spanish And Portuguese Nationality." Submitted for publication.

Bennington, Geoffrey, and Jacques Derrida. 1993. *Derrida*. Chicago: University of Chicago Press.
Bensaïd, Daniel. 2001. *Résistances: Essai de taupologie générale*. Paris: Fayard.
———. 2013 [2004]. *An Impatient Life: A Political Memoir*. Trans. David Fernbach. London: Verso.
Bensaïd, Daniel, and Claude Corman. 2002. "Le marranisme, un internationalisme réinventé: Entretien sur les mouvements d'émancipation d'hier et d'aujourd'hui." *Passant* 38 (n.p.). http://danielbensaid.org/Le-marranisme-un-internationalisme-reinvente?lang=fr (accessed June 30, 2017).
Ben-Ur, Aviva. 2007. "A Bridge of Communication: Spaniards and Ottoman Sephardic Jews in New York City (1880–1950)." In *Recovering Hispanic Religious Thought and Practice of the United States*," ed. Nicholas Kanellos, 25–56. Newcastle, UK: Cambridge Scholars.
———. 2009. *Sephardic Jews in America: A Diasporic History*. New York: NYU Press.
———. 2016. "The 'Spanish Jewish Project': Reciprocity in an Age of Westernization." In *The Languages of Modern Jewish Cultures: Comparative Perspectives*, ed. Joshua Miller and Anita Novinsky, 174–203. Ann Arbor: University of Michigan Press.
Best, Stephen. 2012. "On Failing to Make the Past Present." *Modern Language Quarterly* 73(3): 453–74. https://doi.org/10.1215/00267929-1631478.
———. 2018. *None Like Us: Blackness, Belonging, Aesthetic Life*. Durham, NC: Duke University Press.
Biale, David. 1982. "Masochism and Philosemitism: The Strange Case of Leopold von Sacher-Masoch. *Journal of Contemporary History* 17(2): 305–23.
———. 2008. *Blood and Belief: The Circulation of a Symbol Between Jews and Christians*. Berkeley: University of California Press.
———. 2009. "Blood and Belief: An Introduction to a Jewish Symbol." In *Jewish Blood: Reality and Metaphor in History, Religion, and Culture*, ed. Mitchell B. Hart, 14–30. Abingdon: Routledge.
Bielick-Robson, Agata. 2014. *Jewish Cryptotheologies of Late Modernity: Philosophical Marranos*. Abingdon, UK: Routledge.
Birnbaum, Pierre. 2008. *Geography of Hope: Exile, the Enlightenment, Disassimilation*. Trans. Charlotte Mandell. Stanford, CA: Stanford University Press.
Bodian, Miriam. 1994. "Men of the Nation: The Shaping of Converso Identity in Early Modern Europe." *Past and Present* 143: 48–76.
———. 2007. *Dying in the Law of Moses: Crypto-Jewish Martyrdom in the Iberian World*. Bloomington: Indiana University Press.
———. 2017. "Américo Castro's Conversos and the Question of Subjectivity." *Culture and History Digital Journal* 6(2): e018. http://dx.doi.org/10.3989/Chdj.2017.018.

Böhm, Gabriela. 2007. *The Longing: The Forgotten Jews of South America*. New York: Filmmakers Library.

Bonnín, Pere. 1998. *Sangre Judía: españoles de ascendencia hebrea y antisemitismo cristiano*, vol. 10. Barcelona: Flor del Viento Ediciones.

Bordwell, David. 2006. *The Way Hollywood Tells It: Story and Style in Modern Movies*. Berkeley: University of California Press.

Borges, Jorge Luis. 1998. *Collected Fictions*. Trans. Andrew Hurley. New York: Penguin.

Boyarin, Jonathan. 2009. *The Unconverted Self: Jews, Indians, and the Identity of Christian Europe*. Chicago: Chicago University Press.

Brandt, Bruce. 2012. "Critical Backstory." In *The Jew of Malta: A Critical Reader*, ed. Robert A. Logan, 1–26. London: Bloomsbury.

Brink-Danan, Marcy. 2011. *Jewish Life in Twenty-First Century Turkey: The Other Side of Tolerance*. Bloomington: Indiana University Press.

Bush-Bailey, Gilli. 2013. "Re-Enactment." In *The Cambridge Companion to Theatre History*, ed. David Wiles and Christine Dymkowski, 281–98. Cambridge, UK: Cambridge University Press.

Çağaptay, Soner, and Suna Çağaptay. 2012. "Ottomania All the Rage in Turkey." *Today's Zaman*, April 1. http://www.washingtoninstitute.org/policy-analysis/view/ottomania-all-the-rage-in-turkey (accessed April 10, 2018).

Calderwood, Eric. 2019. "Moroccan Jews and the Spanish Colonial Imaginary, 1903–1951." *Journal of North African Studies* 24: 86–110.

Carroll, Michael P. 2002. "The Debate Over a Crypto-Jewish Presence in New Mexico: The Role of Ethnographic Allegory and Orientalism." *Sociology of Religion* 63(1): 1–19.

Carvajal, Doreen. 2012a. *The Forgetting River: A Modern Tale of Survival, Identity, and the Inquisition*. New York: Riverhead.

———. 2012b. "A Tepid 'Welcome Back' for Spanish Jews." *New York Times*, December 8, 2012. https://www.nytimes.com/2012/12/09/sunday-review/a-tepid-welcome-back-for-spanish-jews.html (accessed July 10, 2017).

Cassin, Barbara. 2016 [2013]. *Nostalgia: When Are We Ever at Home?* Trans. Pascale-Anne Brault. New York: Fordham University Press.

Casteel, Sarah. 2012. "Sephardism and Marranism in Native American Fiction of the Quincentenary." *Melus* 37(2): 59–81.

———. 2016. *Calypso Jews: Jewishness in the Caribbean Literary Imagination*. New York: Columbia University Press.

Chacón-Duque, Juan-Camilo, Kaustubh Adhikari, Macarena Fuentes-Guajardo, Javier Mendoza-Revilla, Victor Acuña-Alonzo, et al. 2018. "Latin Americans Show Wide-Spread Converso Ancestry and Imprint of Local Native Ancestry on Physical Appearance." *Nature Communications* 9 (December 19). https://www.nature.com/articles/s41467-018-07748-z (accessed December 19, 2018).

Chajes, J. H. 2003. "City of the Dead." In *Spirit Possession in Judaism: Cases and Contexts from the Middle Ages to the Present*, ed. Matt Goldish, 124–58. Detroit: Wayne State University Press.

———. 2005. "He Said She Said: Hearing the Voices of Pneumatic Early Modern Jewish Women." *Nashim: A Journal of Jewish Women's Studies* 10(fall): 99–125.

Charmé, Stuart L. 2012. "Newly Found Jews and the Politics of Recognition." *Journal of the American Academy of Religion* 80(3): 387–410.

Chavez, Linda. 2012. "Nourishing Our Roots." *Boston Herald*, May 20, 2012. https://www.bostonherald.com/2012/05/20/nourishing-our-roots/ (accessed July 3, 2018).

Cheah, Pheng. 2008. "What Is a World? On World Literature as World-Making Activity." *Daedalus* 137(3): 26–38.

———. 2014. "World Against Globe: Toward a Normative Conception of World Literature." *New Literary History* 45(3): 303–29.

———. 2016. *What Is a World? On Postcolonial Literature as World Literature*. Durham, NC: Duke University Press.

Cheng, Anne. 2001. *The Melancholy of Race: Psychoanalysis, Assimilation, and Hidden Grief*. Oxford, UK: Oxford University Press.

Chow, Rey. 2012. *Entanglements, or Transmedial Thinking About Capture*. Durham, NC: Duke University Press.

Cohen, Judith. 2004. "'E Com Razões de Ladino': Judeo-Spanish Song as Identity Marker, from Iberian Neo-Sephardic Activities to the Internet." In *Proceedings of the Twelfth British Conference on Judeo-Spanish Studies*, ed. Hilary Pomeroy and Michael Alpert, 159–67. Leiden: Brill.

Cohen, Julia Phillips. 2014. *Becoming Ottomans: Sephardi Jews and Imperial Citizenship in the Modern Era*. New York: Oxford University Press.

Cohen, Martin A. 1972. "Some Misconceptions About the Crypto-Jews in Colonial Mexico." *American Jewish Historical Quarterly* 61(4): 277–93.

———. 1973. *The Martyr: The Story of a Secret Jew and the Mexican Inquisition in the Sixteenth Century*. Philadelphia: Jewish Publication Society of America.

Çolak, Yılmaz. 2006. "Ottomanism vs. Kemalism: Collective Memory and Cultural Pluralism in 1990s Turkey." *Middle Eastern Studies* 42(4): 587–602.

Concannon, Kevin. 2013. "The Politics of Waiting: Transnational Identity and Exile in Achy Obejas' *Ruins*." *LISA e-journal* 11(2). https://journals.openedition.org/lisa/5307 (accessed January 10, 2018).

Cook, Carol. 2001. "Plain and Simple Faith." *Haaretz*, October 1. https://www.haaretz.com/1.5418235 (accessed February 10, 2019).

Cooperman, Bernard Dov. 1998. "Portuguese Conversos in Ancona: Jewish Political Activity in Early Modern Italy." In *Iberia and Beyond: Hispanic Jews Between Cultures—Proceedings of a Symposium to Mark the 500th Anniversary of the*

Expulsion of Spanish Jewry, ed. Bernard Dov Cooperman, 297–352. Newark: University of Delaware Press.

Cooppan, Vilashini. 2013. "Net Work: Area Studies, Comparison, and Connectivity." *PMLA* 128(3): 615–21.

Corman, Claude, and Paul Pérez. 2000. *Sur la piste des Marranes*. Bègles, France: Éditions du Passant.

———. 2005. "L'entaille du commencement." *Les Temps Marranes*, April 1. http://temps-marranes.fr/lentaille-du-commencement/ (accessed July 3, 2013).

Creet, Julia, dir. 2008. *Mum*. CFMDC Distribution.

Cvetkovich, Ann. 2015. *An Archive of Feelings: Trauma, Sexuality, and Lesbian Public Cultures*. Durham, NC: Duke University Press.

Daniel, Max Modiano, and Maxwell Ezra Greenberg. 2019. "Ocasio-Cortez's Jewish Heritage Isn't About You." *Jewish Currents*, January 18, 2019. https://jewishcurrents.org/aocs-jewish-heritage-isnt-about-you/ (accessed January 18, 2019).

Davison, Carol Margaret. 2004. *Anti-Semitism and British Gothic Literature*. New York: Palgrave Macmillan.

De Certeau, Michel. 1992. "Introduction." In his *The Mystic Fable*, vol. 1, *The Sixteenth and Seventeenth Centuries*, trans. Michael B. Smith, 1–30. Chicago: University of Chicago Press.

Delgadillo, Theresa. 2011. *Spiritual Mestizaje: Religion, Gender, Race, and Nation in Contemporary Chicana Narrative*. Durham, NC: Duke University Press.

Derrida, Jacques. 1993. *Aporias*. Trans. Thomas Dutoit. Stanford, CA: Stanford University Press.

———. 1996. *Archive Fever: A Freudian Impression*. Trans. Eric Prenowitz. Chicago: University of Chicago Press.

———. 1998. *Monolingualism of the Other or the Prosthesis of Origin*. Trans. Patrick Mensah. Stanford, CA: University of California Press.

———. 1999. "Marx and Sons." In *Ghostly Demarcations: A Symposium on Jacques Derrida's Spectres of Marx*, ed. Michael Sprinker, 213–69. London: Verso.

Deutscher, Isaac. 1968. "The Non-Jewish Jew." In his *The Non-Jewish Jew*, 25–41. London: Oxford University Press.

Díaz-Mas, Paloma. 2007. "Judíos y conversos en la narrativa española de los años 80 y 90." In *El legado de Sefarad: Los judíos sefardíes en la historia y la literatura de América Latina, España, Portugal y Alemania*, ed. Norbert Rehrmann, 167–80. Salamanca: Amarú.

———. 2009. "España en la literature sefardí: entre historia y ficción." *Romanica Gandensia* 37: 225–36.

Docker, John. 2001. *1492: The Poetics of Diaspora*. London: Continuum.

Duneer, Anita. 2015. "The Old Man and the City: Literary Naturalism and the Postcolonial." *Studies in Naturalism* 10(2): 150–71.

Dweck, Yaakov. 2016. "Introduction to the New Princeton Classics Edition." In *Sabbatai Sevi: The Mystical Messiah, 1626–1676*, by Gershom Scholem, xxix–lxv. Princeton, NJ: Princeton University Press.

Efron, John. 2016. *German Jewry and the Allure of the Sephardic*. Princeton, NJ: Princeton University Press.

Egorova, Yulia. 2015. "Redefining the Converted Jewish Self: Race, Religion, and Israel's Bene Menashe." *American Anthropologist* 117(3): 493–505.

Eldem, Edhem. 2013. "Istanbul as a Cosmopolitan City." In *Backgrounds and Perspectives: A Companion to Diaspora and Transnationalism*, ed. Ato Quayson and Girish Daswani, 212–30. Oxford, UK: Blackwell.

Elkin, Judith Laikin. 1980. *Jews of the Latin American Republics*. Chapel Hill: University of North Carolina Press.

———. 1996. "Colonial Origins of Contemporary Anti-Semitism in Latin America." In *The Jewish Diaspora in Latin America: New Studies on History and Literature*, ed. David Sheinin and Lois Baer Barr, 127–42, New York: Garland.

Endelman, Todd. 1996. "Benjamin Disraeli and the Myth of Sephardi Supremacy." *Jewish History* 10(2): 31–32.

Eng, David L., and Shinhee Han. 2000. "A Dialogue on Racial Melancholia." *Psychoanalytic Dialogues* 10(4): 667–700.

Fajardo, José Manuel. 2004. *El converso*. Barcelona: Ediciones B.

———. 2010. *Mi nombre es Jamaica*. Barcelona: Seix Barral.

———. 2018. "La venganza literaria de los conversos españoles." *Zenda*, August 11. https://www.zendalibros.com/la-venganza-literaria-de-los-conversos-espanoles/ (accessed August 12, 2018).

Farhi, Moris. 2004. *Young Turk*. London: Saqi Books.

Feiner, Shmuel. 1996. "*Sefarad* dans les représentations historiques de la *Haskala*: entre modernisme et conservatisme." In *Mémoires juives d'espagne et du Portugal*, ed. Esther Benbassa, 239–51. Paris: Publisud.

Feitler, Bruno, and Claude B. Stuczynski. 2018. "A Portuguese-Jewish Exception? A Historiographical Introduction." In *Portuguese Jews, New Christians, and "New Jews": A Tribute to Roberto Bachmann*, ed. Claude B. Stuczynski and Bruno Feitler, 1–28. Leiden: Brill.

Ferruta, Paola. 2013. "In the Grip of Marranism: The Other Within Europe's Multiple Modernities." In *The Meanings of Europe: Changes and Exchanges of a Contested Concept*, ed. Claudia Wiesner and Meike Schmidt-Gleim, 47–60. New York: Routledge.

Ferry, Barbara, and Debbie Nathan. 2000. "Mistaken Identity? The Case of New Mexico's Hidden Jews." *Atlantic Monthly*, December, 85–96. http://www.indiana.edu/koertge/Honors204/altmon.html (accessed January 20, 2011).

Flesler, Daniela. 2008. *The Return of the Moor: Spanish Responses to Contemporary Moroccan Immigration.* West Lafayette, IN: Purdue University Press.

Flesler, Daniela, Tabea Alexa Linhard, and Adrián Pérez Melgosa. 2015. "Introduction: Revisiting Jewish Spain in the Modern Era." In *Revisiting Jewish Spain in the Modern Era*, ed. Daniela Flesler, Tabea Alexa Linhard, and Adrián Pérez Melgosa, 1–12. London: Routledge.

Flesler, Daniela, and Adrián Pérez Melgosa. 2008. "Marketing Convivencia: Contemporary Tourist Appropriations of Spain's Jewish Past." In *Spain Is (Still) Different: Tourism and Discourse in Spanish Identity*, ed. Eugenia Afinoguénova and Jaume Martí-Olivella, 63–84. Lanham, MD: Lexington Books.

———. 2010. "Hervás, *Convivencia*, and the Heritagization of Spain's Jewish Past." *Journal of Romance Studies* 10(2): 53–76.

———. 2020. *The Memory Work of Jewish Spain.* Bloomington: Indiana University Press.

Forster, Ricardo. 2003. *Crítica y sospecha: Los claroscuros de la cultura moderna.* Barcelona: Paidos.

Foster, Hal. 2004. "An Archival Impulse." *October* 110 (fall): 3–22.

Foucault, Michel. 2013. "Nietzsche, History, Genealogy." In *The Foucault Reader*, ed. Paul Rabinow, 76–100. New York: Pantheon.

Franklin, Ruth. 2004. "Identity Theft: True Memory, False Memory, and the Holocaust." *New Republic*, May 31, 31–37.

Freedman, Jonathan. 2008. *Klezmer America: Jewishness, Ethnicity, Modernity.* New York: Columbia University Press.

———. 2010. "Conversos, Marranos, and Crypto-Latinos: The Jewish Question in the American Southwest (and What It Can Tell Us About Race and Ethnicity)." In *Boundaries of Jewish Identity*, ed. Susan A. Glenn and Naomi B. Sokoloff, 188–202. Seattle: University of Washington Press.

Freeman, Elizabeth. 2010. *Time Binds: Queer Temporalities, Queer Histories.* Durham, NC: Duke University Press.

Freud, Sigmund. 1958 [1919]. "The Uncanny." In his *On Creativity and the Unconscious*, trans. Alix Strachey, 122–61. New York: Harper & Row.

———. 1959 [1939]. *Moses and Monotheism.* New York: Vintage.

Friedman, Michal. 2011a. "Jewish History as 'Historia Patria': José Amador de los Ríos and the History of the Jews of Spain." *Jewish Social Studies* 18(1): 88–126.

———. 2011b. "Reconquering 'Sepharad': Hispanism and Proto-Fascism in Gimenez Caballero's Sephardist Crusade." In *Revisiting Jewish Spain in the Modern Era*, ed. Daniela Flesler, Tabea Alexa Linhard, and Adrián Pérez Melgosa, 50–75. London: Routledge.

———. 2014. "Reconstructing 'Jewish Spain': The Politics and Institutionalization of Jewish History in Spain, 1845–1940." *Hamsa: Journal of Judaic and Islamic*

Studies 1: 55–67. http://www.hamsa.cidehus.uevora.pt/hamsa_n1/publications_n1/5MichalFriedman.pdf (accessed June 4, 2019).

Funkenstein, Amos. 1989. "Collective Memory and Historical Consciousness." *History and Memory* 1(1): 5–26.

Furlanetto, Elizabeth. 2015. "'Imagine a Country Where We Are All Equal': Imperial Nostalgia in Turkey and Elif Shafak's Ottoman Utopia." In *Post-Empire Imaginaries? Anglophone Literature and the Demise of Empires*, ed. Barbara Buchenau and Virginia Richter, 159–81. Leiden: Rodopi.

Galante, Avram. 1932. *Turcs et juifs: Études historique, politique.* Istanbul: Haim Rozio.

García Arenal, Mercedes. 2013. "Creating Conversos: Genealogy and Identity as Historiographical Problems (After a Recent Book by Ángel Alcalá)." *Bulletin for Spanish and Portuguese Historical Studies* 38(1): 1–19.

"General Franco Gave List of Spanish Jews to Nazis." 2010. *The Guardian*, June 20. https://www.theguardian.com/world/2010/jun/20/franco-gave-list-spanish-jews-nazis (accessed March 3, 2015).

Gerber, Jane S. 2012. "Sephardic and Syrian Immigration to America Acculturation and Communal Preservation." *Sephardic Identity in the Americas: An Interdisciplinary Approach*, ed. Margalit Bejerano and Edna Aizenberg, 38–66. Syracuse: Syracuse University Press.

———. 2015. "Pride and Pedigree: The Development of the Myth of Sephardic Aristocratic Lineage." In *Reappraisals and New Studies of the Modern Jewish Experience: Essays in Honor of Robert M. Seltzer*, ed. Brian Smollett and Christian Wiese, 85–103. Leiden: Brill.

Gilman, Sander. 2006. *Multiculturalism and the Jews.* London: Routledge.

Gilroy, Paul. 2004. *After Empire: Melancholia or Convivial Culture?* Abingdon, UK: Routledge.

Gitlitz, David M. 2002. *Secrecy and Deceit: The Religion of the Crypto-Jews.* Albuquerque: University of New Mexico Press.

Glaser, Amelia M. 2015. "The Heirs of Tul'chyn: A Modernist Reappraisal of Historical Narrative." In *Stories of Khmelnytsky: Competing Literary Legacies of the 1648 Ukrainian Cossack Uprising*, ed. Amelia M. Glaser, 127–38. Stanford, CA: Stanford University Press.

Glenn, Susan A. 2002. "In the Blood? Consent, Descent, and the Ironies of Jewish Identity." *Jewish Social Studies* 8(2–3): 139–52.

Glick, Thomas. 1997. "On Converso and Marrano Ethnicity." In *Crisis and Creativity in the Sephardic World, 1391–1648*, ed. Benjamin R. Gampel, 59–76. New York: Columbia University Press.

Göknar, Erdağ. 2006. "Orhan Pamuk and the 'Ottoman' Theme." *World Literature Today* 80(6): 34–38.

———. 2013. *Orhan Pamuk, Secularism, and Blasphemy: The Politics of the Turkish Novel.* New York: Routledge.
Golden, Gloria, Andrea Alessandra Cabello, and Sohaib Raihan. 2005. *Remnants of Crypto-Jews Among Hispanic Americans.* Mountain View, CA: Floricanto Press.
Goldish, Matt. 2001. "Patterns in Converso Messianism." In *Jewish Messianism in the Early Modern World*, ed. Matt Goldish and R. H. Popkin, 41–63. Dordrecht: Kluwer.
———. 2004. *The Sabbatean Prophets.* Cambridge, MA: Harvard University Press.
———. 2008. *Jewish Questions: Responsa on Sephardic Life in the Early Modern Period.* Princeton, NJ: Princeton University Press.
Goldman, Dara. 2004. "Next Year in the Diaspora: The Uneasy Articulation of Transcultural Positionality in Achy Obejas's *Days of Awe.*" *Arizona Journal of Hispanic Cultural Studies* 8: 59–74.
Goldschmit, Marc. 2008. "Cosmopolitique du marrane absolu." In *Derrida à Alger: Un regard sur le monde*, ed. M. Chérif, 141–50. Arles: Actes Sud.
Goytisolo, Juan. 2002. "La historiografía española y la herencia de Sefarad." *Letras Libres* 43(July). https://www.letraslibres.com/mexico/la-historiografia-espanola-y-la-herencia-sefarad (accessed March 9, 2018).
———. 2014. "Tres glosas de la España Judeoconversa." *Letras Libres* 57(May). https://www.letraslibres.com/mexico/tres-glosas-la-espana-judeoconversa (accessed March 9, 2018).
Graff Zivin, Erin. 2008. *The Wandering Signifier: The Rhetoric of Jewishness in the Latin American Imaginary.* Durham, NC: Duke University Press.
———. 2014. *Figurative Inquisitions: Conversion, Torture, and Truth in the Luso-Hispanic Atlantic.* Evanston, IL: Northwestern University Press.
———. 2017a. "Deconstruction and Its Precursors: Levinas and Borges After Derrida." In *The Marrano Specter: Derrida and Hispanism*, ed. Erin Graff Zivin, 138–55. New York: Fordham University Press.
———, ed. 2017b. *The Marrano Specter: Derrida and Hispanism.* New York: Fordham University Press.
Graham, David J. 2014. "Contradictory Constructions of 'Jewish' in Britain's Political and Legal Systems." In *The Social Scientific Study of Jewry: Sources, Approaches, Debates*, ed. Uzi Rebhun, 141–59. Oxford, UK: Oxford University Press.
Graizbord, David. 2003. *Souls in Dispute: Converso Identities in Iberia and the Jewish Diaspora, 1580–1700.* Philadelphia: University of Pennsylvania Press.
———. 2008. "Ethnicity and Religion Among the 'Men of the Nation': Toward a Realistic Interpretation." *Jewish Social Studies* 15(1): 32–65.
Graizbord, David, and Claude B. Stuczynski. 2011. "Introduction." *Jewish History* 25(2): 121–27.
Gratton, Johnnie. 2005. "Postmemory, Prememory, Paramemory: The Writing of Patrick Modiano." *French Studies* 59(1): 1–7.

Gravé-Lazi, Lidar. 2016. "Reaching Out to Descendants of Conversos." *Jerusalem Post*, July 11. https://www.jpost.com/Israel-News/Reaching-out-to-descendants-of-conversos-460035 (accessed July 15, 2016).

Graziano, Frank. 1999. *The Millennial New World*. Oxford, UK: Oxford University Press.

Gürsel, Nedim. 1993. *Bozkırdaki Yabancı: Çağdaş Türk Edebiyatı Üzerine* [The Stranger in the Steppe: On Modern Turkish Literature]. Istanbul: Yapı Kredi.

Gutiérrez y Muhs, Gabriela. 2006. *Communal Feminisms: Chicanas, Chilenas, and Cultural Exile—Theorizing the Space of Exile, Class, and Identity*. Lanham. MD: Lexington.

Guttman, Amy. 2013. "Spanish Town to Host Its First Seder in More than 500 Years." *NPR Blog*, March 25. http://www.npr.org/blogs/thesalt/2013/03/22/175081553/spanish-town-to-host-its-first-seder-in-more-than-500-years (accessed February 13, 2016).

Halevi-Wise, Yael. 2012a. "Introduction: Through the Prism of Sepharad: Modern Nationalism, Literary History, and the Impact of the Sephardic Experience." In *Sephardism: Spanish Jewish History and the Modern Literary Imagination*, ed. Yael Halevi-Wise, 1–32. Stanford, CA: Stanford University Press.

———. 2012b. "The Life and Times of the Pícaro-Converso from Spain to Latin America." In *Sephardism: Spanish Jewish History and the Modern Literary Imagination*, ed. Yael Halevi-Wise, 143–66. Stanford, CA: Stanford University Press.

Halevy, Schulamith C. 1999. "Jewish Practices Among Contemporary Anusim." *An Interdisciplinary Journal of Jewish Studies* 18(1): 80–100. http://doi.org/10.1353/sho.1999.0067.

Hall, Stuart. 2003. "Creolité and the Process of Creolization." In *Creolité and Creolization: Documenta 11,_Platform 3*, ed. Okwui Enwezor, 27–41. Ostfildern-Ruit, Germany: Hatje Cantz.

Hammerschlag, Sarah. 2010. *The Figural Jew: Politics and Identity in Postwar French Thought*. Chicago: University of Chicago Press.

Hart, Mitchell. 2009. "Jewish Blood: An Introduction." In *Jewish Blood: Reality and Metaphor in History, Religion, and Culture*, ed. Mitchell B. Hart, 2–14. Abingdon, UK: Routledge.

———. 2011. "Jews and Race: An Introductory Essay." In *Jews and Race: Writings on Identity and Difference, 1880–1940*, ed. Mitchell B. Hart, xii–xxxix. Waltham, MA: Brandeis University Press.

Hartman, Saidiya. 1997. *Scenes of Subjection: Terror, Slavery, and Self-Making in Nineteenth-Century America*. Oxford, UK: Oxford University Press.

———. 2007. *Lose Your Mother: A Journey Along the Atlantic Slave Route*. New York: Farrar, Strauss & Giroux.

———. 2008. "Venus in Two Acts." *Small Axe: Caribbean Journal of Criticism* 12(2): 1–14. http://doi.org/10.1215/-12-2-1.

Hernández, Theresa Marie. 2002. *Delirio: The Fantastic, the Demonic, and the Réel.* Austin: University of Texas Press.

Herrera, Miriam M. 2012. "Fear of Snakes: The Dynamics of Fear and Hiding Among Crypto-Jews." *HaLapid: The Journal of the Society for Crypto-Jewish Studies* 22 (summer). http://scjs.us/articles.php (accessed June 3, 2015).

———. n.d. "Personal Stories of Crypto-Jews/Anusim." http://www.miriamherrera.com/crypto-jewishlinks#DESTINATION5 (accessed March 22, 2018).

Hip Hop Hoodios. 2005. *Agua Pa' la Gente.* Jazzhead Records, B0007NFL, compact disc.

Hirsch, Marianne. 1997. *Family Frames: Photography, Narrative, and Postmemory.* Cambridge, MA: Harvard University Press.

———. 2012. *The Generation of Postmemory: Writing and Visual Culture After the Holocaust.* New York: Columbia University Press.

Hirsch, Marianne, and Nancy K. Miller. 2011. "Introduction." In *Rites of Return: Diaspora Poetics and the Politics of Memory*, ed. Marianne Hirsch and Nancy K. Miller, 1–20. New York: Columbia University Press.

Hirschkind, Charles. 2013. "The Contemporary Afterlife of Moorish Spain." In *Islam and Public Controversy in Europe*, ed. Nilüfer Göle, 227–40. London: Routledge.

Hoffman, Maayan Jaffe. 2019. "Evangelical Leader Accuses AOC of 'Goebbels Style' Propaganda." *Jerusalem Post*, April 16. https://www.jpost.com/American-Politics/Evangelical-leader-accuses-AOC-accuses-of-Goebbels-style-propaganda-586970 (accessed June 1, 2019).

Hordes, Stanley M. 2008. *To the End of the Earth: A History of the Crypto-Jews of New Mexico.* New York: Columbia University Press.

Huggan, Graham. 2002. *The Postcolonial Exotic: Marketing the Margins.* London: Routledge.

Hür, Ayşe. 2009. "Münferit (!) antisemitizm vak'aları" [Isolated (!) Antisemitic Events]. *Taraf*, February 8.

Hutcheon, Linda. 1989. *Historiographic Metafiction: Parody and the Intertextuality of History.* Baltimore: Johns Hopkins University Press.

Huyssen, Andreas. 2003. *Present Pasts: Urban Palimpsests and the Politics of Memory.* Stanford, CA: Stanford University Press.

Iğsız, Aslı. 2015. "Palimpsests of Multiculturalism and 'Museumization of Culture': The Greek-Turkish Population Exchange Museum and Istanbul 2010 European Capital of Culture Project." *Comparative Studies of South Asia, Africa, and the Middle East* 35(2): 324–45.

———. 2018. *Humanism in Ruins: Entangled Legacies of the Greek-Turkish Population Exchange.* Stanford, CA: Stanford University Press.

Illas, Edgar. 2015. "On Universalist Particularism: The Catalans and the Jews." In *Revisiting Jewish Spain in the Modern Era*, ed. Daniela Flesler, Tabea Alexa Linhard, and Adrián Pérez Melgosa, 106–23. Abingdon, UK: Routledge.

Israel, Jonathan I. 2002. *Diasporas Within a Diaspora: Jews, Crypto-Jews, and the World of Maritime Empires, 1540–1740*. Leiden: Brill.

Jacobs, Janet L. 2002. *Hidden Heritage: The Legacy of the Crypto-Jews*. Los Angeles: University of California Press.

Jakobsen, Janet R. 2003. "Queers Are Like Jews, Aren't They? Analogy and Alliance Politics." In *Queer Theory and the Jewish Question*, ed. Daniel Boyarin, Daniel Itzkovitz, and Ann Pellegrini, 64–89. New York: Columbia University Press.

Jameson, Friedrich. 1991. *Postmodernism, or the Cultural Logic of Late Capitalism*. Durham, NC: Duke University Press.

Jessurun d'Oliveira, Hans Ullrich. 2015. "Iberian Nationality Legislation and Sephardic Jews." *European Constitutional Law Review* 11(1): 13–29.

Johnson, Erica. 2014. "The Neo-Archive: Dionne Brand's *A Map to the Door of No Return*." *Meridians: Feminism, Race, Trasnationalism* 12(1): 149–71.

Kahn, Susan Martha. 2013. "Who Are the Jews? New Formulations on an Age-Old Question." *Human Biology* 85 (2013): 919–24.

Kâmuran, Solmaz. 2000. *Kirâze*. Istanbul: Inkilap.

Kandiyoti, Dalia. 2012. "What Is the 'Jewish' in 'Jewish American' Literature?" *Studies in American Jewish Literature* 31(1): 48–60.

———. 2016a. "Sephardic-Spanish Encounters." Paper presented at the American Comparative Literature Association, Cambridge, Massachusetts, March 19.

———. 2016b. "Writing and Remembering Jewish Middle Eastern Pasts." In *Cambridge History of Jewish American Literature*, ed. Hana Wirth-Nesher, 320–42. Cambridge, UK: Cambridge University Press.

———. 2017. "Imagining Cosmopolitanism and Coexistence: Jews, Muslims, Language, and Enchantment in Joann Sfar's *The Rabbi's Cat*." *Prooftexts: A Journal of Jewish Literary History* 36(1–2): 53–82.

Kaplan, Yosef. 1997. "The Self-Definition of the Sephardic Jews of Western Europe and Their Relation to the Alien and the Stranger." In *Crisis and Creativity in the Sephardic World, 1391–1648*, ed. Benjamin R. Gampel, 121–45. New York: Columbia University Press.

Karakoyunlu, Yılmaz. 1990. *Salkım Hanım'ın Taneleri* [Salkım Hanım's Necklace]. Istanbul: Doğan Kitap.

Karpinski, Kel. 2016. "Looking for the Queer Past in *Days of Awe*." Unpublished seminar paper, Transamerican Historical Imagination, Graduate Center, City University of New York.

Katznelson, Ira, and Miri Rubin. 2014. "Introduction." In *Religious Conversion: History, Experience, and Meaning*, ed. Ira Katznelson and Miri Rubin, 1–30. New York: Columbia University Press.

Kaye/Kantrowitz, Melanie. 2007. *The Colors of Jews: Racial Politics and Radical Diasporism.* Bloomington: Indiana University Press.

Kedar, Benjamin Z. 1996. "Expulsion as an Issue of World History." *Journal of World History* 7(2): 165–80.

Kelly, David. 2004. "DNA Clears the Fog over Latino Links to Judaism in New Mexico." *Los Angeles Times*, December 5. http://articles.latimes.com/2004/dec/05/nation/na-heritage5 (accessed December 18, 2019).

Kessel, Barbara. 2000. *Suddenly Jewish: Jews Raised as Gentiles Discover Their Jewish Roots.* Lebanon, NH: University Press of New England.

Kidd, Kenneth. "'A' Is for Auschwitz: Psychoanalysis, Trauma Theory, and 'the Children's Literature of Atrocity.'" *Children's Literature* 33: 119–44.

Kirschner, Ann. 2007. *Sala's Gift: My Mother's Holocaust Story.* New York: Free Press.

Klor de Alva, Jorge. 1995. "The Postcolonization of the (Latin) American Experience: A Reconsideration of 'Colonialism,' 'Postcolonialism,' and 'Mestizaje.'" In *After Colonialism: Imperial Histories and Postcolonial Displacements*, ed. Gyan Prakash, 241–75. Princeton, NJ: Princeton University Press.

Kristeva, Julia. 1991. *Strangers to Ourselves.* Trans. Leon S. Roudiez. New York: Columbia University Press.

Küçük, Yalçın. 2003. *Şebeke: Network* [Network]. Istanbul: Ithaki.

Kunin, Seth Daniel. 2009. *Juggling Identities: Identity and Authenticity Among the Crypto-Jews.* New York: Columbia University Press.

Labanyi, Jo. 2002. "Introduction: Engaging with Ghosts; or, Theorizing Culture in Modern Spain." In *Constructing Identity in Contemporary Spain: Theoretical Debates and Cultural Practice*, ed. Jo Labanyi, 1–14. Oxford, UK: Oxford University Press.

LaCapra, Dominick. 1984. "Is Everyone a Mentalité Case? Transference and the 'Culture' Concept." *History and Theory* 23(3): 296–311.

———. 1998. *History and Memory After Auschwitz.* Ithaca, NY: Cornell University Press.

———. 2009. *History and Its Limits: Human, Animal, Violence.* Ithaca, NY: Cornell University Press.

Lanzmann, Claude. 1990. "Les non-lieux de la mémoire." In *Au sujet de* Shoah*: Le film de Claude Lanzmann*, ed. Claude Lanzmann, 280–92. Paris: Belin.

Le Guin, Ursula. 1992. Review of *Mrs. Vargas and the Dead Naturalist* by Kathleen Alcalá. https://www.calyxpress.org/shop/mrs-vargas-and-the-dead-naturalist/ (accessed March 20, 2019).

Leite, Naomi. 2017. *Unorthodox Kin: Portuguese Marranos and the Global Search for Belonging.* Berkeley: University of California Press.

Lewis, Bernard. 1993 [1968]. "The Pro-Islamic Jews." In his *Islam in History: Ideas, People, and Events in the Middle East*, 2nd ed., 137–51. Chicago: Open Court.

Lewis, Matthew Gregory. 1796. *The Monk: A Romance.* n.p.

Lieberman, Randall P. 2016. "Christian Supporter of Israel Visits South Florida." *South Florida Sun-Sentinel*, August 2. https://www.sun-sentinel.com/florida-jewish-journal/fl-jjps-pjtn-0803-20160802-story.html (accessed June 10, 2019).

Linhard, Tabea. 2014. *Jewish Spain: A Mediterranean Memory*. Stanford, CA: Stanford University Press.

Liss, David. 2003. *The Coffee Trader*. New York: Ballantine.

Livaneli, Zülfü. 2011. *Serenad* [Serenade]. Istanbul: Doğan Kitap.

López, Iraida H. 2015. *Impossible Returns: Narratives of the Cuban Diaspora*. Gainesville: University Press of Florida.

López, Kimberle S. 2002. *Latin American Novels of the Conquest: Reinventing the New World*. Columbia: University of Missouri Press.

Love, Heather. 2009. *Feeling Backward: Loss and the Politics of Queer History*. Cambridge, MA: Harvard University Press.

Lowe, Lisa. 2016. *The Intimacies of the Four Continents*. Durham, NC: Duke University Press.

Mariscal, George. 1998. "The Role of Spain in Contemporary Race Theory." *Arizona Journal of Hispanic Cultural Studies* 2: 7–22.

Marks, Elaine, ed. 1996. *Marrano as Metaphor: The Jewish Presence in French Writing*. New York: Columbia University Press.

Marlowe, Christopher. 1592. *The Jew of Malta*. n.p.

Martínez, Demetria. 2005. *Confessions of a Berlitz-Tape Chicana*. Tulsa: University of Oklahoma Press.

Maturin, Charles. 1820. *Melmoth the Wanderer*. Edinburgh: Archibald Constable.

Melammed, Renée Levine. 2004. *A Question of Identity: Iberian Conversos in Historical Perspective*. New York: Oxford University Press.

———. 2010. "Identities in Flux: Iberian Conversos at Home and Abroad." In *Late Medieval Jewish Identities: Iberia and Beyond*, ed. Carmen Caballero-Navas and Esperanza Alfonso, 43–53. New York: Palgrave Macmillan.

Menocal, María Rosa. 2002. *The Ornament of the World: How Muslims, Jews, and Christians Created a Culture of Tolerance in Medieval Spain*. Boston: Little, Brown.

Mignolo, Walter D. 2002. "The Geopolitics of Knowledge and the Colonial Difference." *South Atlantic Quarterly* 101(1): 56–96.

Milgrom, Genie. 2012. *My 15 Grandmothers: The Journey of My Soul from the Spanish Inquisition to the Present*. Charleston, SC: CreateSpace.

Millas, Herkül. 2005. *Türk ve Yunan Romanlarında "Öteki" ve Kimlik* ["The Other" and Identity in Turkish and Greek Novels]. Istanbul: İletişim.

Mills, Amy. 2011. "The Ottoman Legacy: Urban Geographies, National Imaginaries, and Global Discourses of Tolerance." *Comparative Studies of South Asia, Africa, and the Middle East* 31(1): 182–95.

Montoya, Richard. 2010. *Palestine, New Mexico*. New York: Samuel French.
Moreiras, Alberto. 2012. "Common Political Democracy: The Marrano Register." In *Impasses of the Post-Global: Theory in the Era of Climate Change*, vol. 2, ed. Henry Sussman, 175–93. London: Open Humanities Press. http://quod.lib.umich.edu/o/ohp/10803281.0001.001/1:10/—impasses-of-the-post-global-theory-in-the-era-of-climate?rgn=div1;view=fulltext (accessed June 10, 2015).
———. 2017. "Infrapolitical Derrida: The Ontic Determination of Politics beyond Empiricism." In *Derrida and Hispanism*, ed. Erin Graff Zivin, 116–37. New York: Fordham University Press.
Morin, Edgar. 1986. *La méthode*, tome 3, *La connaissance de la connaissance*. Paris: Seuil.
———. 1989. *Vidal et les siens*. Paris: Seuil.
———. 1992 [1977]. *Method: Toward a Study of Humankind*, vol. 1, *The Nature of Nature*. Trans. J. L. Rolan Bélanger. New York: Peter Lang.
———. 1994. *Mes démons*. Paris: Stock.
———. 2009 [1989]. *Vidal and His Family: From Salonica to Paris—The Story of a Sephardic Family in the Twentieth Century*. Trans. Deborah Cowell. Sussex, UK: Sussex Academic Press.
Muchnik, Natalia. 2011. "Being Against, Being With: Marrano Self-Identification in Inquisitorial Spain." *Jewish History* 25(2): 153–74.
———. 2014. "Judeoconversos and Moriscos in the Diaspora." In *The Expulsion of Moriscos from Spain: A Mediterranean Diaspora*, ed. Mercedes García-Arenal and Gerard A. Wiegers; trans. Consuelo López-Morillas and Martin Beagles, 413–40. Leiden: Brill.
Muhteşem Yüzyıl [The Magnificent Century]. 2011–2014. Written by Meral Okay and Yılmaz Şahin. Directed by Yağmur Taylan, Durul Taylan, Mert Baykal, and Yağız Alp Akaydın. Produced by Timur Savcı. Tims Productions.
Muñoz Molina, Antonio. 2003 [2001]. *Sepharad: A Novel of Novels*. Trans. Margaret Sayers Peden. New York: Harcourt.
Nash, Catherine. 2004. "Genetic Kinship." *Cultural Studies* 18(1): 1–33.
Nefes, Türkay Salim. 2014. "The Function of Secrecy in Anti-Semitic Conspiracy Theories: The Case of Dönmes in Turkey." In *Conspiracy Theories in the United States and the Middle East: A Comparative Approach*, ed. Michael Butter and Maurus Reinkowski, 139–56. Berlin: Walter de Gruyter.
Nelson, Alondra. 2008. "Bio Science: Genetic Genealogy Testing and the Pursuit of African Ancestry." *Social Studies of Science* 38(5): 759–83.
———. 2016. *The Social Life of DNA: Race, Reparations, and Reconciliation After the Genome*. Boston: Beacon Press.
Netanyahu, Benzion. 1995. *The Origins of the Inquisition in Fifteenth-Century Spain*. New York: Random House.

Neulander, Judith. 1994. "Crypto-Jews of the Southwest: An Imagined Community." *Jewish Folklore and Ethnology Review* 16(1): 64–68.

———. 1996. "The Crypto-Jewish Canon: Choosing to Be 'Chosen' in Millennial Tradition." *Jewish Folklore and Ethnology Review* 18(1–2): 19–58.

Nieto-Phillips, John. 2004. *The Language of Blood: The Making of Spanish-American Identity in New Mexico, 1880s–1930s*. Albuquerque: University of New Mexico Press.

Nirenberg, David. 2002. "Mass Conversion and Genealogical Mentalities: Jew and Christians in Fifteenth-Century Spain. *Past and Present* 174(February): 3–41.

Nommaz, Aaron. 2016. *Kanuni'nin Yahudi Bankeri Dona Gracia* [Kanuni Suleyman's Jewish Banker Dona Gracia]. Istanbul: Destek.

———. 2018. *Yahudi Casus Jozef Nasi* [Joseph Nasi, the Jewish Spy]. Istanbul: Destek.

Nora, Pierre. 1989. "Between Memory and History: Les Lieux de Mémoire." *Representations* 26(spring): 7–24.

Nordau, Max. 1897. "Address on the Situation of the Jews Throughout the World." In *The Jubilee of the First Zionist Congress, 1897–1947*, 56–62. Jerusalem: Executive of the Zionist Organisation. http://ufdc.ufl.edu/UF00072101/00001/58j (accessed December 5, 2019).

Novinsky, Anita. 2001. "Marranos and the Inquisition: On the Gold Route in Minas Gerais, Brazil." In *The Expansion of Europe to the West, 1450 to 1800*, ed. Paolo Bernardini and Norman Fiering, 215–42. New York: Berghahn.

Nyong'o, Tavia. 2018. *Afro-Fabulations: The Queer Drama of Black Life*. New York: NYU Press.

Obejas, Achy. 1998. *We Came All the Way from Cuba So You Could Dress Like This?* Pittsburgh: Cleis Press.

———. 2001. *Memory Mambo: A Novel*. Pittsburgh: Cleis Press.

———. 2002. *Days of Awe*. New York: Ballantine.

———. 2009. *Ruins*. New York: Akashic Books.

Ojeda-Mata, Maite. 2006. "Thinking About 'the Jew' in Modern Spain: Historiography, Nationalism, and Anti-Semitism." *Jewish History and Culture* 8(2): 53–72.

———. 2015. "'Spanish' but 'Jewish': Race and National Identity in Nineteenth and Twentieth Century Spain." *Jewish Culture and History* 16(1): 64–81.

———. 2018. *Legitimizing Identities: Modern Spain and the Sephardim*. Trans. Pamela Lalonde. Lanham, MD: Lexington Books.

Onar, Fisher Nora. 2009. "Echoes of a Universalism Lost: Rival Representations of the Ottomans in Today's Turkey." *Middle Eastern Studies* 45(2): 229–41.

Ostrer, Harry. 2012. *Legacy: A Genetic History of the Jewish People*. Oxford, UK: Oxford University Press.

Otero, Solimar. 2012. "The Ruins of Havana: Representations of Memory, Religion, and Gender." *Atlantic Studies* 9(2): 143–63.

Pamuk, Orhan. 1985. *White Castle*. Trans. Victoria Holbrook. New York: Braziller.

———. 1998. *My Name Is Red*. Trans. Erdağ Göknar. New York: Vintage Books.

Parfitt, Tudor, and Yulia Egorova. 2006. *Genetics, Mass Media, and Identity: A Case Study of the Genetic Research on the Lemba and Bene Israel*. London: Routledge.

Parnes, Livia. 2015. "Introduction et notes." In *La découverte des marranes: Les crypto-juifs au Portugal*, by Samuel Schwarz. Paris: Chandeigne.

Pasco, Allan H. 2004. "Literature as Historical Archive." *New Literary History* 35(3): 373–94.

Perelis, Ronnie. 2017. *Narratives from the Sephardi Atlantic: Blood and Faith*. Bloomington: Indiana University Press.

Perera, Victor. 1970. *The Conversion*. Boston: Little, Brown.

———. 1995. *The Cross and the Pear Tree: A Sephardic Journey*. Berkeley: University of California Press.

———. 2003. "One Writer's Quest for the Many Circles of the Ancestral Past." *Washington Post*, August 10. https://www.washingtonpost.com/archive/entertainment/books/2003/08/10/one-writers-quest-for-the-many-circles-of-an-ancestral-past/e53c3aab-3a21–47f2–b339–72690001be6c/?utm_term=.3853f7fccef6 (accessed February 3, 2019).

Pérez, Emma. 2003. "Queering the Borderlands: Excavating the Invisible and Unheard." *Frontiers: A Journal of Women Studies* 24(2–3): 122–31.

Perry, Ashley. 2016. "The Next Stage of Zionism." *Jerusalem Post*, May 8. http://www.jpost.com/Opinion/The-next-stage-of-Zionism-453459 (accessed January 2, 2020).

Pfefferman, Naomi. 2009. "Digging for Jewish Roots in 'Palestine, New Mexico.'" *Jewish Journal*, December 16. http://jewishjournal.com/culture/arts/75085/ (accessed June 1, 2019).

Pianko, Noam. 2015. *Jewish Peoplehood: An American Innovation*. New Brunswick, NJ: Rutgers University Press.

Pignatelli, Marina. 2019. *Cadernos de orações cripto-Judaicas e notas etnográficas de Judeus e Cristãos-Novos de Bragança*. Lisbon: Etnográfica Press.

Popkin, Richard H. 1989. "The Rise and Fall of the Jewish Indian Theory." In *Menasseh Ben Israel and His World*, ed. Yosef Kaplan, Richard H. Popkin, and Henry Méchoulan, 63–82. London: Brill.

Pulido, Ángel. 1993 [1905]. *Españoles sin patria y la raza Sefardí*. Granada: University of Granada Press.

Quijano, Aníbal. 2000. "Coloniality of Power, Eurocentrism, and Latin America." *Nepantla: Views from South* 1(3): 533–80.

Ragen, Naomi. 1998. *The Ghost of Hannah Mendes*. New York: Simon & Schuster.
Ragussis, Michael. 1994. "The Birth of a Nation in Victorian Culture: The Spanish Inquisition, the Converted Daughter, and the 'Secret Race.'" *Critical Inquiry* 20(3): 477–508.
———. 1995. *The Jewish Question and English National Identity*. Durham: Duke University Press.
Révah, I. S. 1959–1960. "Les Marranes." *Revue des études juives* 118: 29–77.
Ricard, Virginia. 2005. "Against Oblivion: Henry Roth's 'The Surveyor.'" *Journal of the Short Story in English* (44): 49–63. https://jsse.revues.org/428 (accessed April 22, 2018).
Ricoeur, Paul. 1988. *Time and Narrative*, vol. 3. Trans. Kathleen Blamey and David Pellauer. Chicago: University of Chicago Press.
———. 2004. *Memory, History, Forgetting*. Trans. Kathleen Blamey and David Pellauer. Chicago: University Press of Chicago.
Riley, Patrick. 2004. *Character and Conversion in Autobiography: Augustine, Montaigne, Descartes, Rousseau, and Sartre*. Charlottesville: University of Virginia Press.
Roberts Mulvey, Marie. 2016. *Dangerous Bodies: Historicising the Gothic Corporeal*. Manchester, UK: Manchester University Press.
Rogozen-Soltar, Mikaela H. 2017. *Spain Unmoored: Migration, Conversion, and the Politics of Islam*. Bloomington: Indiana University Press.
Rohr, Isabel. 2007. *The Spanish Right and the Jews: Antisemitism and Opportunism*. Sussex, UK: Sussex Academic Press.
Romero, Elena. 1982. *La creación literaria en lengua sefardí*. Madrid: Mapfre.
———. 1983. *Repertorio de noticias sobre el mundo teatral de los Sefardíes Orientales*. Madrid: Instituto Arias Montano.
Rosaldo, Renato. 1989. "Imperialist Nostalgia." *Representations* 26(spring): 107–22.
Rosen, Minna. 2002. *A History of the Jewish Community in Istanbul: The Formative Years, 1453–1566*. Leiden: Brill.
Rosón Lorente, Javier. 2008. "¿El retorno de Tariq? Comunidades etnorreligiosas en el Albayzín granadino." Doctoral dissertation, University of Granada, Spain.
Roth, Cecil. 1930. *L'Apôtre des marranes*. Paris: Univers israélite.
———. 1932. *A History of the Marranos*. Philadelphia: Jewish Publication Society of America.
———. 1955. "Were the Sephardim Hidalgos? History Disputes Their Claim to Aristocracy." *Commentary*, August 1. https://www.commentarymagazine.com/articles/were-the-sephardim-hidalgoshistory-disputes-their-claim-to-aristocracy/ (accessed April 17, 2019).
Rothberg, Michael. 2009. *Multidirectional Memory: Remembering the Holocaust in the Age of Decolonization*. Stanford, CA: Stanford University Press.

———. 2011. "From Gaza to Warsaw: Mapping Multidirectional Memory." *Criticism* 53(4): 523–48.
Rothman, Natalie. 2011. *Brokering Empire: Trans-Imperial Subjects Between Venice and Istanbul*. Ithaca, NY: Cornell University Press.
Roudinesco, Elisabeth. 2013 [2009]. *Revisiting the Jewish Question*. Trans. Andrew Brown. Cambridge, UK: Polity Press.
Rousso, Henri. 2002. *The Haunting Past: History, Memory, and Justice in Contemporary France*. Trans. Ralph Schoolcraft. Philadelphia: University of Pennsylvania Press.
Rozenberg, Danielle. 2006. *L'espagne contemporaine et la question juive: Les fils renoués de la mémoire*. Toulouse: Presses Universitaires du Mirail.
Rubinstein, Rachel. 2010. *Members of the Tribe: Native America in the Jewish Imagination*. Detroit: Wayne State University Press.
Rushdie, Salman. 1995. *The Moor's Last Sigh*. London: Random House.
Said, Edward. 1983. *The World, the Text, and the Critic*. Cambridge, MA: Harvard University Press.
Salabert, Juana. 2001. *Velódromo del invierno*. Barcelona: Seix Barral.
Saldaña-Portillo, Josefina. 2001. "Who's the Indian in Aztlán? Rewriting Mestizaje, Indianism, and the Chicano from the Lacandón." In *The Latin American Subaltern Studies Reader*, ed. Ileana Rodríguez, 402–23. Durham, NC: Duke University Press.
Sanchez, George Emilio. 2010. "Shalom." *Cousin Corrinne's Reminder* 2: n.p.
Sand, Shlomo. 2009. *The Invention of the Jewish People*. Trans. Yael Lotan. London: Verso.
Santos, Richard G. 1983. "Chicanos of Jewish Descent in Texas." *Western States Jewish Historical Quarterly* 15(4): 327–33.
———. 1999. "Silent Heritage: The Sephardim and the Colonization of the Spanish North American Frontier." *Shofar* 18(1): 112–26.
Schapkow, Carsten. 2015. *Role Model and Countermodel: The Golden Age of Iberian Jewry and the German Jewish Culture During the Era of Emancipation*. Lanham, MD: Lexington Books.
Scholem, Gershom. 2016. *Sabbatai Sevi: The Mystical Messiah, 1626–1676*. Princeton, NJ: Princeton University Press.
Schorsch, Ismar. 1989. "The Myth of Sephardic Supremacy." *The Leo Baeck Institute Year Book* 34(1): 47–66.
Schorsch, Jonathan. 2009. *Swimming the Christian Atlantic: Judeoconversos, Afroiberians, and Amerindians in the Seventeenth Century*, 2 vols. Leiden: Brill.
Schwartzman, Bryan. 2015. "A Graphic Tale of the Bronx's Toughest Jew." *Forward*, August 17. https://forward.com/culture/318999/the-graphic-tale-of-the-bronxs-toughest-jew/ (accessed August 1, 2018).

Scott, James C. 1985. *Weapons of the Weak: Everyday Forms of Peasant Resistance*. New Haven, CT: Yale University Press.

———. 1990. *Domination and the Arts of Resistance: Hidden Transcripts*. New Haven, CT: Yale University Press.

Seixas, Peter. 2004. "Introduction." In *Theorizing Historical Consciousness*, ed. Peter Seixas, 3–20. Toronto: University of Toronto Press.

Sells, Michael A. 1994. *Mystical Languages of Unsaying*. Chicago: University of Chicago Press.

Semi, Emanuela T. 2002. "Conversion and Judaisation: The 'Lost Tribes' Committees at the Birth of the Jewish State." In *Judaising Movements: Studies in the Margins of Judaism*, ed. Tudor Parfitt and Emanuela Trevisan Semi, 53–64. New York: Routledge.

Shafak, Elif. 1999. *Şehrin Aynaları* [Mirrors of the City]. Istanbul: Metis.

———. 2004. "Söyleşi: Burhan Eren" [Interview: Burhan Eren]. *Zaman*, September 26. http://www.elifsafak.us/roportajlar.asp?islem=roportaj&id=90 (accessed April 2, 2014).

———. 2005. "Komplo Teorileri" [Conspiracy Theories]. *Elifsafak*, December 6. http://www.elifsafak.us/yazilar.asp?islem=yazi&id=115 (accessed May 30, 2018).

———. n.d. "Elif Shafak." *The Istanbul Review* 1: 76–79. http://www.elifsafak.com.tr/files/urun_urunler/235/dosya/tir-issue1.pdf (accessed November 8, 2017).

Shapiro, Susan. 1997. "The Uncanny Jew: A Brief History of an Image." *Judaism* 46(1): 63–78.

Shatzmiller, Joseph. 1985. "Politics and Myths of Origins: The Case of the Medieval Jews." In *Les juifs à l'égard de l'histoire: Mélanges en l'honneur de Bernhard Blumenkranz*, ed. Gilbert Dahan, 49–61. Paris: Picard.

Sheppard-Brick, Laura. 2002. Interview of Achy Obejas. *The Jewish Reader*, July. http://www.yiddishbookcenter.org/story.php?n=10061 (accessed July 1, 2012).

Shohat, Ella. 2006. "Taboo Memories, Diasporic Visions: Columbus, Palestine, and Arab Jews." In *Taboo Memories, Diasporic Voices*, ed. Ella Shohat, 201–6. Durham, NC: Duke University Press.

Shohat, Ella, and Robert Stam. 2012. *Race in Translation: Culture Wars Around the Postcolonial Atlantic*. New York: New York University Press.

Shoulson, Jeffrey S. 2013. *Fictions of Conversion: Jews, Christians, and Cultures of Change in Early Modern England*. Philadelphia: University of Pennsylvania Press.

Silverblatt, Irene Marsha. 2004. *Modern Inquisitions: Peru and the Colonial Origins of the Civilized World*. Durham, NC: Duke University Press.

Silverman, Joseph H. 1976. "The Spanish Jews: Early References and Later Effects."

In *Américo Castro and the Meaning of Spanish Civilization*, ed. José Rubio Barcia, 137–66. Berkeley: University of California Press.

Siskind, Mariano. 2007. "El cosmopolitismo como problema politico: Borges y el desafío de la modernidad." *Variaciones Borges* 24: 75–92.

Şişman, Cengiz. 2015. *The Burden of Silence: Sabbatai Sevi and the Evolution of Ottoman-Turkish Dönmes*. Oxford, UK: Oxford University Press.

Skolnik, Jonathan. 2014. *Jewish Pasts, German Fictions: History, Memory, and Minority Culture in Germany, 1824–1925*. Stanford, CA: Stanford University Press.

Slavet, Eliza. 2009. *Racial Fever: Freud and the Jewish Question*. New York: Fordham University Press.

Society for Crypto-Judaic Studies. n.d. "The Atlantic Monthly Exposé." https://cryptojews.com/2018/07/the-atlantic-monthly-expose/ (accessed December 18, 2019).

Socolovsky, Maya. 2003. "Deconstructing a Secret History: Trace, Translation, and Crypto-Judaism in Achy Obejas's *Days of Awe*." *Contemporary Literature* 44(2): 225–49. http://doi.org/10.2307/1209096.

Sommer, Doris. 1991. *Foundational Fictions: The National Romances of Latin America*. Berkeley: University of California Press.

Sorkin, David. 1999. "The Port Jew: Notes Toward a Social Type." *Journal of Jewish Studies* 50(1): 87–97.

Stam, Robert. 1989. *Tropical Multiculturalism: A Comparative History of Race in Brazilian Cinema and Culture*. Durham, NC: Duke University Press.

Stanley-Becker, Isaac. 2018. "Alexandria Ocasio-Cortez Reveals Jewish Ancestry at Hanukkah Celebration." *Washington Post*, December 10.

Stewart, Charles. 2016. "Historicity and Anthropology." *Annual Review of Anthropology* 45: 79–94.

———. 2017. "Uncanny History: Temporal Topology in the Post-Ottoman World." *Social Analysis* 61(1): 129–42.

Stora, Benjamin. 1991. *Le gangrène et l'oubli: la mémoire de la guerre d'Algérie*. Paris: La Découverte.

Stratton, John. 2000. *Coming Out Jewish: Constructing Ambivalent Identities*. London: Routledge.

Studemund-Halévy, Michael, and Gaélle Collin. 2013. "The Wondrous Story of Diego de Aguilar." In *Sefarad an der Donau: Lengua y literatura de los Sefardíes en tierras de los Habsburgo*, ed. Michael Studemund-Halévy, Christian Liebl, and Ivana Vucina Simovic, 239–94. Barcelona: Tirocinio.

Suárez, Lucía M. 2014. "Ruin Memory: Havana Beyond the Revolution." *Canadian Journal of Latin American and Caribbean Studies / Revue canadienne des études latinoaméricaines et caraïbes* 39(1): 38–55.

Suleiman, Susan Rubin. 2003. "Facts, Writing, and Problems of Memory: The

Wilkomirski Case." In *Cultures of Forgery: Making Nations, Making Selves*, ed. Judith Ryan and Alfred Thomas, 187–98. New York: Routledge.

Tamarkin, Noah. 2014. "Genetic Diaspora: Producing Knowledge of Genes and Jews in Rural South Africa." *Cultural Anthropology* 29(3): 552–74. https://journal.culanth.org/index.php/ca/article/view/ca29.3.06/319 (accessed May 27, 2017).

Tardieu Touboul, Eva. 2009. *Sephardisme et hispanité: L'Espagne à la recherche de son passé (1920–1936)*. Paris: Presses Universitaires de la Sorbonne.

Taussig, Michael. 1999. *Defacement: Public Secrecy and the Labor of the Negative*. Stanford, CA: Stanford University Press.

Ternar, Yeshim. 1998. *Rembrandt's Model*. Montreal: Véhicule Press.

This Stage Magazine. February 7, 2012. "Association for Jewish Theatre Conference: Days 1 and 2." https://thisstage.la/2012/02/association-for-jewish-theatre-conference-days-1-and-2/ (accessed June 10, 2015).

Torpey, John. 2003. "Introduction." In *Politics and the Past: On Repairing Historical Injustices*, ed. John Torpey, 1–36. Lanham, MD: Rowan & Littlefield.

Torres-Saillant, Silvio. 2002. "The Indian in the Latino: Genealogies of Ethnicity." *Latino Studies* 10(4): 587–607. https://doi.org/10.1057/lst.2012.42.

Trigano, Shmuel. 2000. *Le Juif caché: Marranisme et modernité*. Paris: Pardès.

Tüfekçioğlu, Zeynep. 2011. "Sufism in Turkish Crime Fiction: The Mystery of Shams-i Tabrizi in Ahmet Ümit's *Bab-ı Esrar*." *European Journal of Turkish Studies* 13: n.p. http://ejts.revues.org/4532 (accessed November 16, 2017).

Valerio, Max. 2001. "The Atlantic Monthly Expose." *HaLapid* 8(1): 4–5, 8–10. https://cryptojews.com/wpcontent/uploads/2018/07/Volume_VIII_Winter_2001_Issue_1.pdf (accessed June 1, 2015).

Valle, Victor. 1988. "Radio Review: The Exodus of New Mexico's 'Hidden Jews.'" *Los Angeles Times*, July 15. http://articles.latimes.com/1988-07-15/entertainment/ca-6983_1_mexico-jews-radio (accessed March 30, 2019).

Van Alphen, Ernest. 2001. *Armando: Shaping Memory*. Rotterdam: NAi Publishers.

Van den Boer, Harm. 2000. "Exile in Sephardic Literature of Amsterdam. *Studia Rosenthaliana* 35(2): 187–99.

Veinstein, Gilles. 1987. "Une communauté ottomane: Les juifs d'Avlonya (Valona) dans la deuxieme moitié du XVIe siècle." In *Gli Ebrei e Venezia, secoli XIV–XVIII*, ed. Gaetano Cozzi Secoli, 781–828. Milan: Edizioni comunità.

Veit, Phillip. 1974. "Heine, the Marrano Pose." *Monatshefte* 66(2): 145–56.

Velez, C., P. F. Palamara, J. Guevara-Aguirre, L. Hao, T. Karafet, et al. 2012. "The Impact of Converso Jews on the Genomes of Modern Latin Americans." *Human Genetics* 131(2): 251–63. http://doi.org/10.1007/s00439-011-1072-z.

Vigil, Ariana E. 2014. *War Echoes: Gender and Militarization in U.S. Latina/o Cultural Production*. New Brunswick, NJ: Rutgers University Press.

Viswanathan, Gauri. 1998. *Outside the Fold: Conversion, Modernity, and Belief.* Princeton, NJ: Princeton University Press.

Vitkus, Daniel. 2003. *Turning Turk: English Theater and the Multicultural Mediterranean, 1570–1630.* New York: Palgrave.

Wachtel, Nathan. 1977. *Visions of the Vanquished: The Spanish Conquest of Peru Through Indian Eyes, 1530–1570.* Brighton, UK: Harvester Press.

———. 2001. "Marrano Religiosity in Hispanic America in the Seventeenth Century." In *The Jews and the Expansion of Europe to the West, 1450 to 1800*, ed. Paolo Bernardini and Norman Fiering, 149–71. New York: Berghahn.

———. 2013 [2001]. *The Faith of Remembrance: Marrano Labyrinths.* Trans. Nikki Halpern. Philadelphia: University of Pennsylvania Press. (Original: *La Foi du Souvenir: Labyrinthes Marranes.* Paris: Seuil, 2001.)

Walkowitz, Rebecca. 2009. "Comparison Literature." *New Literary History* 40(3): 567–82.

Weber, Max. 1946 [1919]. "Science as Vocation." In *From Max Weber: Essays in Sociology*, ed. H. H. Gerth and C. Wright Mills, 129–56. New York: Oxford University Press.

Weinrich, Harald. 2004. *Lethe: The Art and Critique of Forgetting.* Ithaca, NY: Cornell University Press.

Wheelwright, Jeff. 2012. *The Wandering Gene and the Indian Princess: Race, Religion, and DNA.* New York: Norton.

Wolfson, Elliot R. 2014. *Giving Beyond the Gift: Apophasis and Overcoming Theomania.* New York: Fordham University Press.

Yañez, Luís. 1987. "Sefarad 92: El redescubrimiento de la España Judía Grupo de Trabajo." Speech given at Hebrew University, National Sephardic Library and Archives, Center for Jewish History, Box 2, Folio 6.

Yerushalmi, Yosef. 1981 [1971]. *From Spanish Court to Italian Ghetto: Isaac Cardoso—A Study in Seventeenth-Century Marranism and Jewish Apologetics.* Seattle: University of Washington Press.

Yovel, Yirmiyahu. 1989. *Spinoza and Other Heretics: The Marrano of Reason.* Princeton, NJ: Princeton University Press.

———. 2009. *The Other Within: The Marranos—Split Identity and Emerging Modernity.* Princeton, NJ: Princeton University Press.

Zerubavel, Eviatar. 2003. *Time Maps: Collective Memory and the Social Shape of the Past.* Chicago: University of Chicago Press.

———. 2012. *Ancestors and Relatives: Genealogy, Identity, and Community.* New York: Oxford University Press.

Zorlu, Ilgaz. 2000. *Evet, Ben Selanikliyim: Türkiye Sabetaycılığı: Makaleler* [Yes, I am Salonican: Sabbeteanism in Turkey]. Istanbul: Zvi (Geyik).

INDEX

Abu El Haj, Nadia, 43, 44, 127, 173, 266n13
Aciman, André, 172–73
Acıman, Stella, *Bir Masaldı Geçen Yıllar* (The Past Was a Fairy Tale), 219
Aidi, Hisham, 145
Affect. *See* Crypto-Jewish body
Affiliation and filiation (Edward Said), 174–75, 179, 180, 182, 199, 203, 204, 207. *See also* Historicized affiliative self-fashioning
Affiliative self-fashioning (Nelson), 174. *See also* Historicized affiliative self-fashioning
African Americanist thought, and missing archives, 14. *See also* Hartman, Saidiya; Best, Stephen
Aguilar, Grace, 70; *The Vale of Cedars*, 70–71, 77, 242
Al-Andalus, 32, 71
Alberro, Solange, 23, 51
Alcalá, Kathleen: 6, 9, 46–47, 86, 90, 110, 123, 165, 205; *The Desert Remembers My Name*, 120; *The Flower in the Skull*, 110; and Sephardi identity, 120; *Spirits of the Ordinary*, 16, 46–47, 87, 90–93, 95, 100–102, 106, 107–10, 112–13, 116–17; *Mrs. Vargas and the Dead Naturalist*, 90
Almansor (Heine), 69
Americas. *See* Transamerican
Amsterdam, 24, 33, 38, 171, 180, 190, 192, 230, 232, 246, 251; in *Rembrandt's Model*, 248–54
Analogy and analogical thinking. *See* Comparison and analogy
Ancestry and descent, 7, 12, 18, 41, 42, 43, 44, 66–67, 91, 157–8, 172, 176–179, 192–95, 201. *See also* Affiliation and filiation; Blood: Jewish; Genealogy, critical; Genealogical imagination and discourses; Kinship; *Limpieza de sangre* (purity of blood)
Ancestry testing. *See* Genetic ancestry testing
Anidjar, Gil, 43, 158, 176, 179, 221, 269n8
Anti-Semitism, 35, 46, 51, 67, 68, 71, 75, 111, 144, 154, 172, 190, 231, 233, 264n8; in *The Conversion*, 184–87; in *Days of Awe*, 99
Appropriation of identity and history, 16,

78, 79; vs. experience in *Mi nombre es Jamaica* (My Name is Jamaica), 150–51, 153, 154–57. *See also* Jewish victimhood and suffering: appropriation of
Archives, 14, 20; body as, 78, 131–32, 139, 140, 160; and contemporary literature and art, 15–17, 87; faux, 78; making of, 16, 20; and "neo-archive" (Johnson), 16; oral and folk, 15; of the present, 16; validity of, 15. *See also* Missing/absent/lost archives
Arcos de la Frontera, Spain, 128, 130, 131, 132, 137, 139
Arditi, Metin, 235
Arendt, Hannah, 42
Assimilation: in *Days of Awe*, 94–95, 102, 103, 106; and modernity, 8, 62; and multicultural societies, 41, 58–59, 81, 94–95, 122, 204; as parallel with history of conversos and crypto-Jews, 8, 46, 47, 56–58, 59, 60, 62, 69, 70, 81, 93–94, 101, 102, 173; as secularization, 57, 58
Authenticity (and truth): of crypto-Jewish/converso descent and identity, 7, 9, 25, 38, 39, 41, 45, 69, 76, 86, 123, 125, 153, 258, 264–65n9 (*See also* Conversos and crypto-Jews: claims and controversies regarding continuity in the Americas); in *Days of Awe* (Obejas), 100, 101–3, 135; in *Mi nombre es Jamaica* (My Name is Jamaica), 141, 153–55; 161, 169; of revival of identities, 25; in *Ruins*, 119–20

Baer, Marc, 233, 246
Bahar, Beki L., 231, 235–36, 237, 255
Bali, Rıfat, 218, 228, 233, 269n2
Beckwith, Stacy, 75, 76, 268n3
Behar, Ruth, 188–99
Belmonte, Portugal community, 34, 36

Benardete, Meir José, 122, 189, 260
Benbassa, Esther, 150–51, 152, 156; and Aron Rodrigue, 251
Ben Israel, Menasseh, 24, 110, 193, 232; in *Rembrandt's Model*, 249, 250, 251
Benjamin, Walter, 14, 136, 169
Benmayor, Rina, 266n12, 268n5
Ben-Rosh, Abraham. *See* De Barros Basto, Artur Carlos (Abraham ben-Rosh)
Bensaïd, Daniel, 59, 61–62, 63, 64, 115, 166, 179–80, 198, 269n1
Ben-Ur, Aviva, 41, 120, 121, 122, 123, 168, 265n9
Best, Stephen, 116, 136, 263n3
Biale, David, 43, 69, 158
Black Legend, 71, 143, 227, 247
Blasco Ibañez, Vicente, 67, 77
Blood (discourse of), 47, 52, 68, 126, 128, 178, 179, 269; vs. critical genealogy, 172, 174, 179; in *Days of Awe*, 112; and European racial thought, 158; Jewish, 16, 66, 127, 141, 176, 177; and Jewish peoplehood, 41; and Latinx/Latin Americans, 39, 40, 91, 112, 114, 119; in *Mi nombre es Jamaica* (My Name is Jamaica*)*, 141, 155–59, 162, 163, 166, 167, 169; role in Jewish thought, 43, 158; in Spain and Portugal, 23, 37, 150, 155–56, 157. *See also* Ancestry and descent; Genealogical imagination and discourses; *Limpieza de sangre* (purity of blood)
Bnei Anusim. *See* Conversos, crypto-Jews, and descendants
Bodian, Miriam, 55, 67, 264n7
Body and affect. *See* Crypto-Jewish body in literature; Archives: body as
Böhm, Gabriela, *The Longing*, 37, 39
Bonnín, Pere, *Sangre judía*, 147
Borderlands. *See* U.S.-Mexico border and borderlands

Borges, Jorge Luis, "The Aleph," 239–41
Boundaries and separations, as related to convergences, 10–11, 84, 88, 115, 131, 210, 214, 256, 257, 259
Brenner, Frédric (*Les derniers marranes*), 36, 37
Brazilian Associates of Descendants of Jews of the Inquisition (ABRADJIN), 37
Butler, Octavia (*Kindred*), 29

Cansinos Assens, Rafael, 143, 168
Caribbean, conversos and crypto-Jews in the literature of, 73–74, 89, 166
Cardoso, Abraham Miguel, 79, 215
Cardoso, Isaac Fernando, 215
Cardoza-Moore, Laurie, 1–2, 263n1
Caro Baroca, Julio, 66
Carpentier, Alejo, 74–75
Carvajal, Doreen, 6, 128, 136; *The Forgetting River*, 15, 20, 47, 86, 124, 127–40
Casas Grandes (Paquimé), Mexico, in *Spirits of the Ordinary* (Alcalá), 101, 107, 108, 109, 113
Casteel, Sarah, 5, 32, 73–74, 83, 113, 164, 166, 267n6
Castro, Américo 54, 66, 67, 142, 143, 162, 177, 260
Cervantes, Miguel de Saavedra, 66, 180, 222; *Don Quixote*, 52, 148, 149, 150, 161, 166, 167
Chávez, Denise, 86
Chavez, Linda, 1–2, 263n1
Cheah, Pheng, 12–13, 82, 84, 171, 214, 259
Chicanx crypto-Jewish descendants. *See* Latinx/Chicanx/Hispanic and Latin American descendants of conversos and crypto-Jews
Chow, Rey, 11, 88
Chuetas, 35–36, 147, 263, 266n10; in Spanish literature, 67–68, 75, 77

Citizenship, for Sephardis in Spain and Portugal. *See* Nationality Laws for Sephardi Jews in Spain and Portugal
Comparison and analogy, 131, 163, 164; and convergence, 12; in *Days of Awe* and *Spirits of the Ordinary*, 93–104; in *The Forgetting River*, 131; of Gaza and Warsaw ghetto, 163; in *Mi nombre es Jamaica* (My Name is Jamaica), 162–64; of the queer and the Jew, 102–3; of Sephardi history in literature, 82–83; in world literature, 82–83
Conquest of the Americas, 30, 33, 110, 111, 144; as connected with Jewish and converso history in fiction, 87, 93, 113, 117, 119, 141, 143, 164, 185
Conspiracy theories: in the Americas, 110–11; about Catalans, 75; and former conversos, 231; about Jews and Muslims (including Turks), 48, 221–22; and "the Judeo-Masonic conspiracy," 144; and Sabbateans (*dönme*) in Turkey, 42, 216, 232–34, 237, 246, 269n3. *See also* Anti-semitism
Convergence: aesthetic of, 11, 84–85, 89, 91, 129; and Borges's "The Aleph," 239–241; and conversion, 83–84; and converso and crypto-Jewish history, 64; and Cuban syncretism, in *Days of Awe*, 105–6; definition of 8; 9; ethics of, 163, 174; and Jewish and Muslim conversos, 210; and Jews and Muslims (*see* Jews and Muslims); in *Mi nombre es Jamaica* (My Name is Jamaica), 141, 162–69; in Morin's work, 173–74, 199–200, 204–5, 206; narrative of, 10, 12, 88, 162; in Perera's work, 174, 194–96, 206; in *Spirits of the Ordinary* (Alcalá), 110; and Turkish writing and Shafak, 237–45; and world literature, 12–13, 82–83, 84, 213–14,

220. *See also* Boundaries and separations as related to convergence; Entanglements; Mestizaje

Conversion: as analogous to assimilation, 56, 60; and autobiography/memoir, 182–83; as a challenge, 5; contemporary, 151; and decolonial thought, 42; and deconversion/return to Judaism, 24, 25, 33–34, 36, 37, 38, 39, 45, 88, 146, 152, 155, 178, 194, 232; and inconvertibility, 42; Hannah Arendt on, 42; and historical fiction, 220–21; and Sabbateans *(dönmes)*, 229, 231–32. *See also* Conversos and crypto-Jews and descendants; Sabbateans

The Conversion (Perera), 181, 183–91, 195

Conversos, crypto-Jews, and descendants: agents of globalization as, 55; agency of, 55; in the Americas, history of 22–24; assimilated, secularized Jews as (*see* Assimilation: as parallel with history of conversos/crypto-Jews); attitudes of in the Early Modern period, 54; claims and controversies regarding continuity in the Americas, 23–24, 38–45; 86, 154, 264n8, 264–65n9; evasion and dissimulation of, 7, 61, 63, 16; in Francophone thought, 9, 58, 59–62, 197–98; Gothic features in literature of, 214, 247–48, 250, 253, 258; in Hispanist thought, 9, 58, 62–64; and historians and historiography on, 15–16, 50–56, 264n8, 264–65n9; history of, in Spain, 21–22; in twentieth-century Portugal, 34–37; indeterminacy of, 9, 62, 63, 64, 100, 115, 120, 252–54; internal division in and divided/double subjectivity of, 49, 50–52; 60, 64, 182–83, 198, 239, 252; in literature since the nineteenth-century 65–84; 234–37; and/vs. marranos, 9, 53, 63; and martyrdom or suffering, 9, 11, 49, 55, 70; and the "memory boom," 35; as metaphor and analogy, 8–9, 57, 58, 59–65, 73–74, 93–104, 138, 173, 254; modernity and cosmopolitanism of, 11, 51–52; 57–58, 126, 197, 198, 216; mysticism and messianism of, 79–80; 245–56; and Muslims and Moriscos, 243; and normative Sephardi Jews, 170–208, 258; and the Ottoman Empire, 229; performance as, in *The Conversion*, 184–90; race and racialization of, 39–41; as resistant figures, 61–64, 198, 213; resurgence of knowledge about, 2–5; returns to normative Judaism of, 2–3, 33–34, 38, 178, 251, 264n7; and Sabbateans *(dönmes)*, 3–4, 42, 231–32, 246; Sephardi identity of 120, 122; skepticism of, 63, 125, 131–40; stereotypes of, 10–11, 49, 71, 97, 111, 173; terminology about, viii; tropes and ideas about, 50–65; 197–98; and young adult fiction, 77–78; and women and cultural transmission, 93. *See also* Conquest of the Americas; Marranos; Survival; Spain; Portugal

Convivencia, 4, 30, 32, 65, 72, 125, 145, 227

Corman, Claude, 62

Cosmopolitanism, 198; and Turkey, 209, 211, 212, 214, 216, 217, 218. *See also* Conversos, crypto-Jews, and descendants: cosmopolitanism and modernity of; Turkey: multiculturalism in

The Cross and the Pear Tree (Perera), 15, 171, 181, 182, 183, 184, 186, 190–95

Crypto-Jews. *See* Conversos, crypto-Jews, and descendants

Crypto-Jewish body in literature, 18, 78–80, 96–97, 133, 139, 140, 160, 167, 242, 252. *See also* Paramemory

Crypto-Jewish space, 130

INDEX

Cuba and Cuban Revolution. *See Days of Awe*
Cuban American literature, 8, 100; and exile, 47, 89
Cultural commuting (Melammed), 46, 54, 55, 189
Culture Clash, 117, 118
Cvetkovich, Ann, 14, 116, 138

Da Costa, Uriel, 38, 180; in *Rembrandt's Model*, 251
Daniel Deronda (Eliot), 68, 242
Days of Awe (Obejas), 78, 87, 91–101, 103–7, 113, 115–16, 121–22, 242, 267n3, 267n5
De Aguilar, Diego, 70, 71–72
De Barros Basto, Artur Carlos (Abraham ben-Rosh), 34–35, 36
De Carvajal, Luis, the Younger (*el moso*), 23, 264n6
De Carvajal y de la Cueva, Luis, 70, 109, 114
De Certeau, Michel, 114–15, 246
Delgadillo, Theresa, 90, 107, 113
Delgado, João Pinto, 52
Delirio (Marie Theresa Hernández), 114–15, 126, 135, 165, 187, 216, 247
De los Ríos, Rodrigo Amador, 66, 267n1
De Onís, Federico, 168
Les Derniers marranes (The Last Marranos), 36, 37
Derrida, Jacques, and *marranes/marranisme*, 8, 14, 36, 45–46, 59–61, 129, 201, 203
Descent. *See* Ancestry and descent
Deutscher, Isaac, 62, 179, 180, 205
Díaz-Mas, Paloma, 71, 75
Dictatorships; as allegories/analogies for crypto-Jewish history, 73, 93; anti-Semitism of, 144; in Latin America and Iberia, 29, 35, 75, 144; memory of, 131, 144
Disenchantment, 127

Disraeli, Benjamin, 222
DNA testing. *See* Genetic ancestry testing
Docker, John, 32
Dönme. See Sabbateans
Don Quixote (Cervantes), 52, 148, 149, 150, 152, 161, 166, 167

Efron, John, 69
Empty archive (Heather Love), 15, 133
Eng, David L. and Shinhee Han, 79, 97
Entanglements: defined, 11; historical, 10, 16, 47, 48, 55, 59, 68, 74, 84, 88, 92, 100–101, 103, 106, 110, 115, 123, 137, 141, 172, 176, 204, 206, 214, 254, 256. *See also* Convergence
Expulsion, of Jews and Muslims from Spain, 29, 30, 32, 33, 72, 80, 83, 87, 143, 145, 176, 222, 223, 229, 230, 236. *See also* 1492; Quincentennial of expulsion and Ottoman arrival of Spanish Jews

Fajardo, José Manuel, 6, 9, 80, 81; *El Converso*, 140; *Mi nombre es Jamaica* (My Name is Jamaica) 15–17, 18, 47, 78, 79, 83, 110, 121, 124, 125, 126, 127, 134, 140–43, 146–69, 170, 179, 186, 207, 245, 246, 258
Fantastic literary elements. *See* Supernatural literary elements
Farhi, Moris, *Young Turk* (2004), 219
Flesler, Daniela, 81, 146; and Tabea Linhard and Adrián Pérez Melgosa, 19, 30, 75, 268n3; and Adrian Pérez Melgosa, 19, 30, 37 125, 268n3, 268n4
Forgetting, 128, 130–31, 133–35, 268n2
The Forgetting River: A Modern Tale of Survival and the Inquisition (Carvajal), 15, 47, 86, 124, 127–40, 170, 207, 246, 256
Forster, Ricardo, 8–9

Foucault, Michel, 8
1492: 21, 22, 30, 32–33, 72, 83, 87, 176, 267n6; and decolonial scholarship, 33; as Ottoman refuge, 30, 222, 224, 228, 229, 230, 236; and two/multiple 1492s, 33; and Latinx literature, 117–20. *See also* Convivencia; Indigenous peoples of the Americas; Quincentennial of expulsion and Ottoman arrival of Spanish Jews; Spain
France, conversos and crypto-Jews in contemporary thought of, 9; 58, 59–62, 197–98
Franco, Francisco (dictatorship period of) and Francoism, 66, 68, 75, 83, 144, 184, 186, 187, 268n4
Freedman, Jonathan, 41, 101, 102, 267n4, 268n8
Freeman, Elizabeth, 27–28, 186, 187, 195
Freud, Sigmund, 27, 180, 181; *Moses and Monotheism* 19, 43, 60; "The Uncanny," 80–81, 133, 246
Friedman, Michal, 122, 144, 260, 267n1, 268n3
Funkenstein, Amos, 17, 133, 211

Galante, Avram, 223
Genealogical imagination and discourses, 7, 12, 18, 20, 21, 38, 41, 43, 46, 47, 66, 68, 74, 91, 159, 176–79; combined with historical imagination, 45, 46; in Morin and Perera, 170–208; and Sephardi superiority, 176–79
Genealogy, critical, 10, 163, 170–208; explained, 172, 258; purpose of, 174, 176, 195; and Sephardism, 204–5, 206–7
Genealogy, selective, 7, 45, 47, 147, 179, 180, 193, 206, 207. *See also* Ancestry and descent; Affiliation and filiation; Blood; Kinship

Genetic ancestry testing, 3, 20, 37, 44, 45, 174; among African Americans, 45, 174; in Israel, 43; and Jewish peoplehood, 44, 266n11; motivations for, 44; and nationality application in Spain and Portugal, 44; and reenchantment, 127; and suppressed identities, 45, 174
Gerber, Jane, 121, 178
Ghana, 27, 29, 126, 134
Gilman, Sander, 95, 96, 102, 103, 164
Golden Age Spanish literature and conversos, 54, 142
Goldish, Matt, 33, 38, 79, 178, 215
Goldschmidt, Marc, 60
Goytisolo, Juan, 142, 145
Göknar, Erdağ, 220, 225, 226, 246
Graff Zivin, Erin, 4, 5, 8, 9, 58, 61, 64, 68, 72, 73, 173, 198, 248
Graizbord, David, 51, 54, 177, 264n7; and Claude Stuczynski, ix, 51

Halevi-Wise, Yael, 5, 29, 31, 65, 66, 72, 255, 267n2
Hammerschlag, Sarah, 60
Hart, Mitchell, 43, 158, 266n11
Hartman, Saidiya, 14, 15, 29, 126, 134, 135, 156, 263n3
Haskalah and Sephardism, 31, 69, 71; and conversos and crypto-Jews, 69–70
Havana, Cuba. *See Days of Awe*
Heine, Heinrich, 69
Hernández, Marie Theresa, 114–15, 126, 135, 165, 187, 216, 247
Hip-Hop Hoodios, 91
Hirsch, Marianne, 19–20, 151, 156; and Nancy Miller, 27, 136, 169, 247
Hispanics in the U.S. *See* Latinx/Chicanx/Hispanic
Hispanism, 67, 121–22, 260–61
Hispanist thought, and conversos and crypto-Jews, 9, 58, 62–64

Historians: and historical transference (LaCapra), 168; representation of in *Mi nombre es Jamaica* (My Name is Jamaica*)*, 15–16, 148, 161–63, 168; and views and ideas about conversos and crypto-Jews, 50–56, 263n8, 264–65n9

Historical consciousness and imagination, 12, 13–17, 14, 16, 17, 38, 89, 117, 123, 133, 141, 163, 167–68, 170, 179, 211, 207, 258–59; defined, 17; and historicity, 17

Historical fiction: 15–17, 72–73, 220, 221, 251; and conversion, 221; and historiographic metafiction (Hutcheon), 72; in Turkey, 213, 220–21, 226

Historicized affiliative self-fashioning, 175–76, 180, 181, 192, 203, 204, 206, 207, 258

Holocaust, and Holocaust memory, 5, 11, 25, 32, 73, 131, 147, 151, 158, 264n5, 268–97; link to Inquisition, 76, 77; and multicultural literature, 95; role in Sephardism, 31–32, 73, 83, 93, 147

Hope of Israel (ben Israel), 24, 232

Hordes, Stanley, 264–65n9

Huyssen, Andreas, 26, 31, 32

Ibn Arabi, in Shafak's work, 213, 241, 245, 249

Identity. *See* Appropriation of identity and history; Authenticity (and truth); Sephardi Jews: identity of; Conversos, crypto-Jews, and descendants: claims and controversies of

Indigeneity and Chicanx literature, 118

Indigenous peoples of the Americas: connection to Jews and conversos: 110–12, in *Days of Awe* (Obejas), 93, 112; in fiction, 113, 267n6; in *Mi nombre es Jamaica* (My Name is Jamaica), 165–67; in *Palestine, New Mexico*, 117–18; in Sanchez, 119; in *Spirits of the Ordinary* (Alcalá), 107–10, 267n1

Inquisition, Spanish, 5, 21–24, 177, 247, 269n8; as allegory, 73, 131, 144; link to Holocaust, 76; in New Spain, 23; in *The Conversion*, 185; in *The Cross and the Pear Tree*, 184, 185, 192, 193; in *Days of Awe*, 97, 98, 99; in *The Forgetting River*, 128, 133, 138; *Mi nombre es Jamaica* (My Name is Jamaica), 162; in *Şehrin Aynaları* (Mirrors of the City), 243, 247–48; in *Rembrandt's Model*, 251

Instituto Arias Montano, 144, 185

Israel/Palestine, 147, 163; and converso/crypto-Jewish descendants, 44–45, 123, 136, 173; and "lost tribes," 25, 35, 44; in *Mi nombre es Jamaica* (My Name is Jamaica), 141, 152–53, 163, 164–65; and Morin, 203

Istanbul, 79, 183, 190, 213, 214, 217, 218, 230, 232, 235; in *Rembrandt's Model*, 248, 249; in *Şehrin Aynaları* (Mirrors of the City), 239, 240, 241, 244, 245

Izmir, 71, 230, 232, 236, 232

Jakobsen, Janet R., 102–3

Jewish American, community and literature of, 28–29, 41, 45, 86, 121, 267n2; in *Days of Awe*, 93–94, 121

Jewishness: and biology vs. culture, 40–43; and blood logics, 40, 42–43; converso descendants' impact on, 41; and genetic ancestry testing, 40, 44

Jewish victimhood and suffering: appropriation of, 152–53, appropriation of, in *Mi nombre es Jamaica (*My Name is Jamaica), 141, 147, 148–50, 154–56, 160–61, 168; as identity, 148–51, 152–53; in *The Forgetting River* (Carvajal), 130–31; and Holocaust

memory, 151. *See also* Crypto-Jewish body in literature; Conversos, crypto-Jews, and descendants: martyrdom or suffering of
The Jew of Malta (Marlowe), 222, 231
Jews and Muslims, 191, 210, 213–14, 216, 221; in contemporary and postcolonial literature, 221, 244; in Haskalah thought, 31; in *Rembrandt's Model*, 254; in *Şehrin Aynaları* (Mirrors of the City), 242–45; and Spain, 21, 22, 48, 80, 145
Juan Carlos, King, 30, 145
Judeo-Spanish (Ladino), 31, 200, 232; in *Mi nombre es Jamaica* (My Name is Jamaica), 154; Spanish intellectuals and, 143, 144–45; writing about conversos and crypto-Jews in, 71–72

Kahn, Susan Martha, 44, 266n11
Kâmuran, Solmaz, 213, 235, 238
Kaplan, Yosef, 53
Karakoyunlu, Yılmaz, *Salkım Hanım'ın Taneleri* (Salkım Hanım's Necklace), 219
Kemalism, 224, 225, 226, 227, 245
Kindred, 29
King of the Schnorrers (Zangwill), 177
Kinship, 12, 43, 46, 91, 127, 157, 179. *See also* Affiliation and filiation; Ancestry and descent; Blood; Genealogical imagination
Kirâze (Solmaz Kâmuran), 234–35
Kulanu, 37, 45
Kunin, Seth, viii, 40, 264–65n9

Lacandon Maya, and Perera's work, 194, 195
Ladino. *See* Judeo-Spanish
Lanzmann, Claude, 130
Latinx/Chicanx/Hispanic and Latin American descendants of conversos and crypto-Jews, 1–2, 85–86, 91; claims and controversies about converso identities, 23–24, 38–45, 86, 154, 264n8, 264–65n9; intersections with Sephardi Jews in the U.S., 40, 45; literature about, 85–123, 141; racialization of 39–40
Latin American literature and conversos, 68, 72–73
Leite, Naomi, 35, 37, 263n2, 266n13
Les Temps marranes, 62
Lindenberg, Daniel, 59, 63
Linhard, Tabea, 5, 19, 32, 75, 76, 83, 143, 187, 268n4; and Daniela Flesler and Adrián Pérez Melgosa, 30, 75, 268n3
Livaneli, Zülfü, *Serenad* (Serenade), 219
Livorno (Leghorn) and Livornese Jews, 33, 55, 58, 181, 199, 202, 204, 230
LaCapra, Dominick, 17, 168
"La Sinyora" Mendes Nasi. *See* Mendes Nasi, Doña Gracia
Lethe, 128
Limpieza de sangre or *pureza de sangre* (purity of blood), 21, 41, 52, 66, 67, 100, 157–58, 177, 266n10, 268n8, 269n8. *See also* Blood (discourse of): Jewish
Lindenberg, Daniel, 59, 63
Lineage. *See* Ancestry and descent
Liss David, *The Coffee Trader*, 76, 251
Lose Your Mother (Hartman), 14, 29, 126, 134, 135, 156, 263n3
Lost tribes, 24–26, 35, 110, 111, 137, 139, 266n13; and Antonio Montezinos, 24; of Jews as indigenous people, 24, 111–12, 195. *See also* Remnants
Love, Heather, 15, 133
Lowe, Lisa, 13, 16, 210

Mallorca. *See Chuetas*
Manet, Eduardo, 79
Mariscal, George, 110
Marks, Elaine, 9, 58, 59, 62, 267n3

Marlowe, Christopher, 222, 231
Maroons, 73–74
Marranism/*Marranismo/Marranisme*, x, 172–73, 263n8, 267n6; and crypto-Jews, 9; as metaphor, 9, 59–65, 74, 172, 173, 181, 196, 197, 198, 201, 202–5, 207, 267n3. *See also* France; Hispanist thought; *Neo-marranisme*
Marranos, 53; definitions of, x, 9, 63, 173. *See* Conversos, crypto-Jews, and descendants
Martínez, Demetria, 86, 114
Matute, Ana María, 68, 75, 77
Melammed, Renée Levine, 36, 46, 54, 93, 189
Memoir: and conversion, 182; historical, 180–83; and intimacy, 181–82. See also *The Cross and the Pear Tree*; *The Forgetting River*; *Vidal and His Family*
Memory, 130, 131, 132, 138; false, 160–61, 164, 167, 168, 171, 206, 224, 248; and memorialization, 134–35, 140; vs. history 150–51, 268–9n7. *See also* Crypto-Jewish body; Forgetting; Jewish victimhood and suffering; Memory boom; Multidirectional memory; Paramemory; Postmemory
Memory boom (Huyssen), 26–27, 131, 145, 152
Mendes Nasi, Doña Gracia, 70, 230–31; in Turkish fiction, 236–37
Mes Démons (Morin), 181, 202
Mestizaje, 88, 113–14, 118
Mignolo, Walter, 33, 42, 156
Miller, Nancy, and Marianne Hirsch, 27, 136, 169, 247
Mi nombre es Jamaica (My Name is Jamaica) (Fajardo), 15–17, 18, 47, 78, 79, 83, 110, 121, 124, 125, 126, 127, 134, 140–43, 146–69, 170, 179, 186, 207, 245, 246, 258
Minskii (Minsky), Nikolai, 70
Missing/absent/lost archives, 6, 9, 12, 14–15, 115, 116, 126, 133, 160, 168, 175, 210, 254–55; in African Americanist thought, 14; and the body, 18, 131, 132, 139, 258; in *Days of Awe*, 88, 106, 115, 118, 123; in *The Forgetting River*, 127, 131–33, 139, 140; in Latinx literature, 110, 113, 123; in *Mi nombre es Jamaica* (My Name is Jamaica), 151–52, 160; of Muslim and Jewish converts, 210; in *Palestine, New Mexico*, 118; in Queer studies, 14–15, 88, 98, 115, 138; in *Rembrandt's Model*, 255, 256; in *Spirits of the Ordinary*, 88, 108, 115, 123. *See also* Archives
Modernity. *See* Conversos, crypto-Jews, and descendants: modernity and cosmopolitanism of
Montezinos, Antonio, 24, 73, 110, 195
Montoya, José, 118
Montoya, Richard, 86, 110, 205; *Palestine, New Mexico*, 117–18
Moorish architecture and style, 31
Moors. *See* Muslims in Spain; Moriscos and descendants
The Moor's Last Sigh (Rushdie), 188, 244
Moreiras, Alberto, 9, 61, 62–63, 198
Morin, Edgar, 6, 9, 47–48, 57–58, 59, 61, 63, 171–74, 179, 205–6; and French *marranisme*, 197–98, 203–5; *Mes Démons*, 202–3; *and polyenracinement*, 48, 172, 180, 183, 197, 198, 200, 205; *Vidal and His Family*, 180, 181, 182, 198–202
Moriscos and descendants, 22, 145; and Jewish conversos in literature, 12, 210, 214, 243, 249, 250, 252; and Nationality Laws in Spain, 137, 145. *See also* Muslims in Spain
Muchnik, Natalia, 52
Multiculturalism: and difference, 59; and perceptions of medieval Spain, 32–33, 143, 144 (*see also*

Philo-Sephardism; Convivencia); in Turkey, 210–11, 212–13, 218–19, 224–25, 244–45. *See also* Cosmopolitanism; Tolerance

Multidirectional memory and fiction (Rothberg), 11–12, 151, 269n7

Muñoz Molina, Antonio, *Sepharad*, 75, 83, 147, 188, 267n4

Muslims in Spain, 125, 128, 142, 145, 146, 157, 268n6; as "Moors," 80–81. *See also* Jews and Muslims, Moriscos

Nação (the nation), 22, 53–54, 230; as agents of globalization, 55. *See also* New Christians

Nasi, Joseph, 222, 231

Nationality Laws for Sephardi Descendants in Spain and Portugal (2015), 2, 36, 124, 125, 136, 137, 145, 146, 266n12, 268n5; and descent, 44; and genetic testing, 44

Native Americans. *See* Indigenous peoples; Opata people; Tarahumara people

Nazis and Nazism, 41, 83, 266n10; in *Days of Awe* (Obejas), 100

Nelson, Alondra, 45, 168, 174, 175

Neo-marranisme/neo-marranes (Morin), 58, 181, 197, 201, 202, 203, 204, 205

Neo-Ottomanism, 212–13, 216, 224, 225–27, 235, 240, 244, 256; and language, 237–39; 245

Neo-slave narratives, 131

Netanyahu, Benzion, 22, 264n8

Neulander, Judith, 264–65n9

New Christians, 21–22, 33, 34, 52–54, 111, 177; as agents of globalization, 55; as Jews, 53; integration into Jewish communities, 54, 178; and slaveholding, 54. *See also* Conversos, crypto-Jews, and descendants; *Nação*

New Mexico: conversos and crypto-Jews in, 23, 40, 77, 85, 120, 264–65n9; Spanish identification in, 39

New Turkish, 237–38

Nirenberg, David, 21, 142, 176, 177

Noah, Mordecai Manuel, 112

Nommaz, Aaron, 231, 236

Non-Jewish Jew (Deutscher), 62, 179, 180, 205

Non-sites of memory (non-lieux de mémoire, Lanzmann), 130

Nora, Pierre, 150

Nordau, Max, 57–58

Novinsky, Anita, 51, 264n8

Obejas, Achy, 6, 9, 46–47, 86, 89, 205, 242; *Days of Awe*, 78, 91–101, 103–7, 113, 115–16, 121–22, 242; *Ruins*, 119, 120, 123, 268n7

Ocasio-Cortez, Alexandria, 1, 2, 263n1

Ojeda-Mata, Maite, 75, 146, 147, 187, 268n3, 268n4

Opata people, in *Spirits of the Ordinary*, 90, 108, 109, 111

Ostrer, Harry, 40, 44, 266n11

Ottoman Empire, 22, 172, 207–8, 209–10, 221–22, 224; Jews in, 220, 221–23, 230; as refuge for Iberian Jews, 30, 222, 224, 228, 229, 230, 236; and Spain in fiction, 216. *See also* Cosmopolitanism: and Turkey; Neo-Ottomanism; Quincentennial of expulsion and Ottoman arrival of Spanish Jews

Palestine, New Mexico (Montoya), 117–18

Pamuk, Orhan, 212, 213, 220–21

Paramemory, 19–21, 47, 123, 133, 135, 139, 140, 160, 167, 193, 207, 258

Parody and satire: in *Palestine, New Mexico* (Montoya), 117–18; in "Shalom" (Sanchez), 119

Passing, racial, ethnic, and religious, 42, 56, 61, 74, 97, 99, 156, 216, 267n3, 267n4

Past, the, and relation to present, 131, 136, 162, 168–69, 183–86, 252, 263n3. *See also* Convergence; Remnants
Perera, Victor, 6, 9, 15, 47, 171–74, 181–95, 198, 201, 205
Pérez, Emma, 14, 87, 115
Pérez Galdos, Benito, 67
Pérez Melgosa, Adrián, and Daniela Flesler, 19, 30, 37, 75, 125, 268n3, 268n4; and Daniela Flesler and Tabea Linhard, 30, 268n3
Philo-Semitism, 30, 154, 161, 184, 268n4
Philo-Sephardism, 31, 69–70, 75; in Spain, 125–26, 142–47, 162, 260
Picaresque, Spanish, 66
Polyenracinement (polyrootedness) (Morin), 48, 172, 180, 183, 197, 198, 200, 205
Population exchanges, 26; Greece-Turkey, 26, 233
Portugal: and the Belmonte community, 34–36; converso/crypto-Jewish/ New Christian communities of, 21, 22, 23, 33–36, 53, 54, 55, 86, 122, 158, 192, 230–31, 250, 263n2 264n8, 266n13; in *The Cross and the Pear Tree*, 184, 185, 191, 192–93; postdictatorship apology in, 30; returns to Judaism and, 36–37, 38, 177, 230–31. *See also* Conversos, crypto-Jews, and descendants; De Barros Basto, Artur Carlos; *Nação*; Nationality Laws for Sephardi Descendants in Spain and Portugal; New Christians; Schwarz, Samuel
Possession: and Jewish mystics, 160–61; in *Mi nombre es Jamaica* (My Name is Jamaica) 160–61
Postmemory (Marianne Hirsch), 19–20, 151, 156
Production of remnants. *See* Remnants, production of

Public secret (Taussig), 81, 116, 117, 232
Pulido, Ángel, 143–44
Pureza de sangre (purity of blood). See *Limpieza de sangre* (purity of blood)

Queerness: in *Days of Awe*, 106–7; in *Spirits of the Ordinary*, 116
Quincentennial of expulsion and Ottoman arrival of Spanish Jews: and conversos, 229; literary and cultural production, 31; in Spain, 30, 145, 227, 228; in Turkey, 30, 220, 227–28

Race and racialization: and blood in Jewish thought, 158; and crypto-Jewishness, 39–41; and 1492, 21, 33, 39; and Jews in the U.S., 68–69, 93–95, 99; of Latinx / Chicanx/Hispanics in the U.S. and Jewishness, 40–42. *See also* Whiteness
Racial melancholy (Eng and Han), 79, 97, 115
Ragussis, Michael, 68, 71, 222
Recognition, Sephardi-Spanish, 185–89; and nostalgia, 186
Reconectar, 37, 266n13
Reenchantment/enchantment, 127, 133, 134, 160, 245, 246, 247
Rembrandt's Model (Ternar), 209, 216–17, 248–56
Remnants, 6–7, 43, 221, 256; production of, and self as, 7, 18, 20, 125, 126, 132, 160, 163, 169, 172, 190, 206, 207, 248
Returns: in contemporary culture, 26–28; in contemporary Jewish, U.S., Latin American, Iberian fiction, 28–29; and conversion, 26; and disappointment, 126; to history without documentation, 6; to homelands (in Africa, Ghana, Eastern Europe,

Ottoman Empire), 27, 156; and the memory boom, 26–27; in *Mi nombre es Jamaica* (My Name is Jamaica), 161; to normative Judaism of converso and crypto-Jewish descendants, 2–3, 24, 25, 33–34, 36, 37, 38, 39, 45, 88, 146, 152, 155, 178, 194, 232; and the past, 130, 237–38; and population exchanges, 26; as re-enactment, 125; as (re)enchantment, 247; right to, 136; Sephardism and, 29–33; to Spain, 124–70; in *The Conversion*, 183–88; in *The Cross and the Pear Tree*, 190–91, 206; in *The Forgetting River*, 130–35; and the uncanny 80–82, 133, 246. *See also* Historical Consciousness; Nationality Laws for Sephardi descendants; Past, the

Révah, I. S., 67, 264n8

Ricoeur, Paul, 6, 13, 160, 268n2

Riera, Carmé, 75

Rodrigue, Aron, and Esther Benbassa, 251

Roth, Cecil, 34, 230

Roth, Henry, 78–79

Rothberg, Michael, 11–12, 32, 150, 151, 163, 268–69n3

Roudinesco, Élisabeth, 198

Rubinstein, Rachel, 110, 112, 113, 267n6

Rushdie, Salman, 72, 188, 244

Sabbateanism, 203, 216, 215, 217

Sabbateans (*Dönmes*/Salonicans), 3–4, 38, 48, 51, 193, 229; modernity and liberalism of, 51; Portuguese converso ancestry among, 3–4, 42, 231–32; Portuguese converso ancestry among in literature, 248–54; scapegoating of and conspiracy about, 42, 216–17, 232–34; and terminology, x, 64; in Turkish fiction, 233, 244, 248–55

Şafak, Elif. *See* Shafak, Elif

Safed, 19, 155, 159–60, 230

Said, Edward, 174–75

Salonica, 199, 200, 208, 230

Salonicans. *See* Sabbateans

Saltillo, Mexico, 90

Sanchez, George, 119

Scholem, Gershom, 215, 233, 250–51, 267n3

Schorsch, Jonathan, ix, 54, 73, 166

Schwarz, Samuel, 34, 266n13

Scott, James, 4, 61, 63

Secrecy, 115–16; in *Days of Awe* (Obejas), 96–99; in *Mi nombre es Jamaica* (My Name is Jamaica), 167; and the *Nação*, 55; 94; in *Spirits of the Ordinary* (Alcalá), 116; in *Şehrin Aynaları* (Mirrors of the City), 242. *See also* Public Secret (Taussig)

Secularization, 51, 56–58, 62, 173, 180, 181, 203–4, 246. *See also* Assimilation

Şehrin Aynaları (Mirrors of the City) (Shafak), 78, 209, 211, 212–16, 237–48, 251

Seixas, Peter, 16

Sepharad: A Novel of Novels (Muñoz Molina), 76, 83, 147, 188

Sephardi history: as comparison, 82–83, 174; in *The Cross and the Pear Tree*, 180–83, 190–91; in literature, 5, 9, 12, 147; in *Mi nombre es Jamaica* (My Name is Jamaica), 141; in *Vidal and His Family*, 180–83, 199–201; and the world novel, 82–83, 213–14, 217. *See also* Conversos, crypto-Jews, and descendants; Convivencia; Multiculturalism: and perceptions of Medieval Spain; Philo-sephardism; Returns; Spain; Genealogy, critical

Sephardi Jews: and citizenship in Spain and Portugal, 2, 36, 124, 125, 136, 137, 145, 146, 266n12, 268n5; and conversos and crypto-Jews and descendants, 120–21, 153–57,

170–72, 193, 201–2; in *The Cross and the Pear Tree*, 190–95; and forced conversions of, 21–24; identity of, 120–21, 191–92, 206, 198–202 (*see also* Appropriation of identity and history); intersections with Latinx in the U.S., 45; in the Americas, 31, 268n8; in *Mi nombre es Jamaica* (My Name is Jamaica), 152, 153–57, 161–63; in the Ottoman Empire, 220, 221–23; poetry of, 161; and Spain, 31, 124, 126, 143, 144, 185–88; in Turkey, 224, 235–36; in *Vidal et les siens*, 198–202, 205–6; in Vienna, 71–72. *See also* Conversos, crypto-Jews, and descendants; Convivencia; 1492; Genealogical imagination and discourses: and Sephardi superiority; Returns; Sephardism; Quincentennial of expulsion and Ottoman arrival of Spanish Jews; Spain

Sephardism, 29–33, 65, 75, 259, 267n6; in *Days of Awe*, 121–22; in Latinx literature, 91, 110, 120–21; of Morin, 196, 200–204. *See also* Philo-Sephardism

Sevi, Sabbatai, 69, 79, 203, 209, 216, 231, 250–51

Shafak, Elif, 6, 78, 209, 211, 212, 213; *The Bastard of Istanbul*, 211, 213, 247; *Forty Rules of Love*, 211, 212, 246, 267n4; *Şehrin Aynaları* (Mirrors of the City), 78, 209, 210, 211, 212–16, 220, 231, 233, 237–48

Shame, 69; and secrecy in *Days of Awe*, 96–97, 99, 106, 115, 172

Shavei Israel, 37, 45

Shohat, Ella, 33, 87; and Robert Stam, 33, 42, 87

Silverblatt, Irene, 111

Siskind, Mario, 241

Şişman, Cengiz, 51, 232, 233, 246

Slavet, Eliza, 43

Soares, Mario, 30
Society for Crypto-Judaic Studies, 37, 40
Socolovsky, Maya, 98, 100
Solidarity, 12–13, 84, 150, 154; among Jews and Muslims in fiction, 210, 216, 242–44, 245, 254. *See also* Jews and Muslims
Spain: and *Chuetas* in, 35, 36, 147, 263, 266n10; citizenship in, 2, 36, 124, 125, 136, 137, 145, 146, 266n12, 268n5; colonialism in North Africa, 31, 142, 143; and colonization of northern Morocco, 31; conversos and crypto-Jews in, 80, 142, 169; and *convivencia*, 32; historical memory in, 29, 35, 144; Jewish tourism in, 19, 125, 133–34, 268n1; and Jews in the Franco era, 184, 186–87; the Law of Historical Memory in, 144; medieval, as model, 32; Moorish, 32; and Ottoman Empire, 216, 222, 228, 232; philo-Sephardism in, 75, 125–26, 142–47; representation of, in *Days of Awe*, 39, 100; *The Conversion*, 183–88; in *The Forgetting River*, 130–35; in returns to, 80–81, 188–90. *See also* Blood: Jewish; Conversos and crypto-Jews and descendants; Franco; Expulsion; Inquisition; Muslims in Spain; Quincentennial of expulsion and Ottoman arrival of Spanish Jews; Returns
Spanish Civil War, 80, 131, 184
Spanish Jews. *See* Sephardi Jews; Spain
Spanish literature, and conversos and crypto-Jews: Golden Age, 66–67, 142; and lineage, 66–67; since the nineteenth century 67–68
Spinoza, Baruch, 38, 70, 180, 181, 192, 203, 251; in *Rembrandt's Model*, 251
Spirits of the Ordinary: A Tale of Casas Grandes (Alcalá), 16, 46–47, 87,

90–93, 95, 100–102, 106, 107–10, 112–13, 116–17
Spiritual *mestizaje* (Delgadillo), 90, 109, 113
Stam, Robert, 74; and Ella Shohat, 33, 43, 87
Stavans, Ilan, *El Illuminado*, 76–77, 106
Stewart, Charles, 17, 136, 211
Stora, Benjamin, 268n7
Stuczynski, Claude, and Bruno Feitler, 34; and David Graizbord, ix, 52
Sufism in contemporary literature, 217, 246
Supernatural (fantastic) literary elements: in *Rembrandt's Model*, 217, 250; in *Şehrin Aynaları* (Mirrors of the City), 213–14, 242, 246, 247; in *Spirits of the Ordinary*, 90–91
Survival, 2, 4–5, 221, 247, 256, 257; of crypto-Jewishness, 40; and paramemories 17–20; and resistance, 4, 7, 17–18, 61. *See also* Remnants

Tarahumara people, in *Spirits of the Ordinary*, 91, 107, 111
Taupologie (Bensaïd), 61–62, 63
Taussig, Michael, 81, 116, 117, 232
Temporality and time, 30–31, 169, 172–73; queer, 27–28
Ternar, Yeshim, 6, 9, 48, 81; and *Rembrandt's Model*, 209, 216–17, 248–56
Time. *See* Temporality and time
Tolerance, 30, 38, 59, 125, 216, 224, 225, 227, 228, 237, 244
Transamerican: narratives, crypto-Jewishness in, 89–117; perspectives, 87, 92, 195
Transatlantic narrative, 117, 141
Transgenerational/transtemporal transmission of trauma and memory, 19, 20, 79, 126, 132, 133, 134, 139

Trás-os-Montes, Portugal, 34. *See also* Belmonte, Portugal community
Trigano, Shmuel, 59, 197
Turkey: conspiracy theories in, 232–34, 237; and conversos, 229–32, 234–37; 244–45; historical fiction in, 213, 220–21, 226; language and language reform in, 237–39, 245; literature of, 209–18, 220–21, 226, 234–37, 238–55; minorities in, 218; Jews in, 30, 219–20, 223, 224, 227–28, 269n8; multiculturalism in, 210–11, 212–13, 218–19, 224–25, 244–45; nationalism in, 223, 269n2; quincentennial in, 30, 228; and Sabbateans, *see* Sabbateans (*dönmes*); tolerance discourses in, 216, 224, 225, 227, 228, 237; and Turkishness in literature, 255–56. *See also* Neo-Ottomanism; Ottoman Empire
Turks, European images of, 48, 227; as conspirators with Jews, in European images, 221–22; and conversos, 230

Uncanny, the, 80–82, 133, 242, 246–47
U.S. literature, conversos in, 76–77, 85–123
U.S.-Mexico border and borderlands, 112, 114, 116; and conversos in fiction, 47, 91; and queerness in, 14; syncretism, 91, 101, 102. *See also Mestizaje*; *Spirits of the Ordinary*

Valle, Victor, 40
Venice, 33, 213, 215, 229, 230
Venta Prieta, Mexico, 35, 265n9
Vidal and His Family (*Vidal et les siens*) (Morin), 180–83, 198–205
Viswanathan, Gauri 5, 7, 84

Wachtel, Nathan, 23, 53, 55, 58, 166

Wandering Jew, figure of, 242, 253; and crypto-Jews, 253; and vampires, 253

Whiteness, 88; and converso and crypto-Jewish descendants, 39, 40, 41, 87, 88, 110; in *Days of Awe*, 94, 267n3; of Jews, in the U.S., 39–40, 55, 94, 97. *See also* Race and racialization

World novel/literature, contemporary, 11, 12, 76, 213–14, 217, 220, 239, 244, 267n4; comparison and analogy in, 82–83; features of, 82, 84, 239

Yerushalmi, Yosef, 36, 51, 52, 56, 177, 178, 215, 232, 264n8

Yovel, Yirmiyahu, 36, 51, 52, 53, 54, 55, 56, 58, 66, 100, 106, 126, 263n2

Zerubavel, Eviatar, 7, 45, 179, 207

Zorlu, Ilgaz *Evet, Ben Selanikliyim* (Yes, I Am a Salonican), 216

Stanford Studies in Jewish History and Culture
David Biale and Sarah Abrevaya Stein, Editors

This series features novel approaches to examining the Jewish past in the form of innovative work that brings the field into productive dialogue with the newest scholarly concepts and methods. Open to a range of disiplinary and interdisciplinary approaches, from history to cultural studies, this series publishes exceptional scholarship balanced by an accessible tone, illustrating histories of difference and addressing issues of current urgency. Books in this list push the boundaries of Jewish Studies and speak compellingly to a wide audience of scholars and students.

For a complete listing of titles in this series, visit the Stanford University Press website, www.sup.org.

Dina Danon, *The Jews of Ottoman Izmir: A Modern History*
2019

Omri Asscher, *Reading Israel, Reading America: The Politics of Translation Between Jews*
2020

Yael Zerubavel, *Desert in the Promised Land*
2018

Sunny S. Yudkoff, *Tubercular Capital: Illness and the Conditions of Modern Jewish Writing*
2018

Sarah Wobick-Segev, *Homes Away from Home: Jewish Belonging in Twentieth-Century Paris, Berlin, and St. Petersburg*
2018

The authorized representative in the EU for product safety and compliance is:
Mare Nostrum Group
B.V Doelen 72
4831 GR Breda
The Netherlands

www.ingramcontent.com/pod-product-compliance
Lightning Source LLC
Chambersburg PA
CBHW031900220426
43663CB00006B/705